AMERICAN REBELS

AMERICAN REBELS

—◆◆◆—

How the Hancock, Adams, and Quincy Families
Fanned the Flames of Revolution

Nina Sankovitch

St. Martin's Press
New York

First published in the United States by St. Martin's Press, an imprint of St. Martin's Publishing Group

AMERICAN REBELS. Copyright © 2020 by Nina Sankovitch. All rights reserved. Printed in the United States of America. For information, address St. Martin's Publishing Group, 120 Broadway, New York, NY 10271.

www.stmartins.com

Maps by Jeffrey L. Ward

The Library of Congress Cataloging-in-Publication Data is available on request.

ISBN 978-1-250-16328-8 (hardcover)
ISBN 978-1-250-16329-5 (ebook)

Our books may be purchased in bulk for promotional, educational, or business use. Please contact your local bookseller or the Macmillan Corporate and Premium Sales Department at 1-800-221-7945, extension 5442, or by email at MacmillanSpecialMarkets@macmillan.com.

First Edition: March 2020

1 3 5 7 9 10 8 6 4 2

For Natasha,
guide, companion, sister, star

Contents

PART THREE

Flame (1774–1776)   197

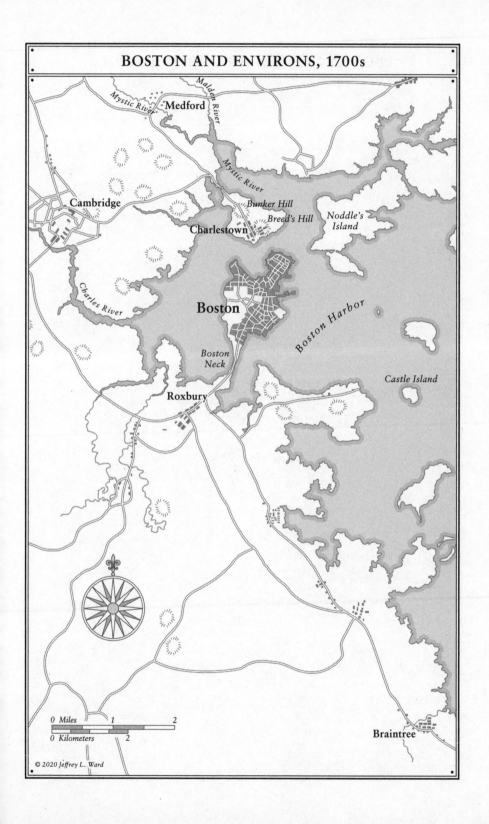

BOSTON AND ENVIRONS, 1700s

Malden River

Mystic River

Medford

Mystic River

Cambridge

Bunker Hill

Breed's Hill

Charlestown

Noddle's
Island

Charles River

Boston

Boston Harbor

Boston
Neck

Castle Island

Roxbury

0 Miles   1   2
0 Kilometers   2

Braintree

© 2020 Jeffrey L. Ward

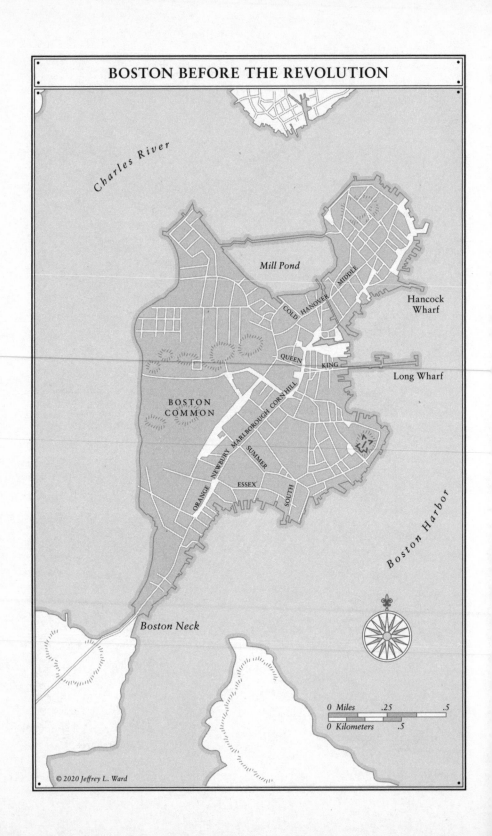

BOSTON BEFORE THE REVOLUTION

Charles River

Mill Pond

MIDDLE

COLD HANOVER

Hancock
Wharf

QUEEN

KING

Long Wharf

BOSTON
COMMON

CORN HILL

MARLBOROUGH

NEWBURY

ORANGE

SUMMER

ESSEX

SOUTH

Boston Harbor

Boston Neck

0 Miles .25 .5
0 Kilometers .5

© 2020 Jeffrey L. Ward

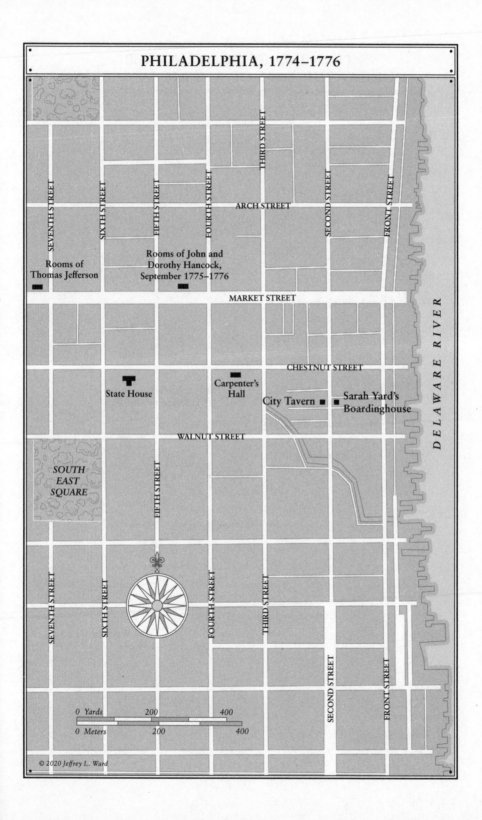

PHILADELPHIA, 1774–1776

SEVENTH STREET

SIXTH STREET

FIFTH STREET

FOURTH STREET

THIRD STREET

SECOND STREET

FRONT STREET

ARCH STREET

Rooms of
Thomas Jefferson

Rooms of John and
Dorothy Hancock,
September 1775–1776

MARKET STREET

CHESTNUT STREET

Carpenter's
Hall

State House

City Tavern ■ ■ Sarah Yard's
Boardinghouse

WALNUT STREET

SOUTH
EAST
SQUARE

FIFTH STREET

SEVENTH STREET

SIXTH STREET

FOURTH STREET

THIRD STREET

SECOND STREET

FRONT STREET

DELAWARE RIVER

| 0 Yards | 200 | 400 |
| 0 Meters | 200 | 400 |

© 2020 Jeffrey L. Ward

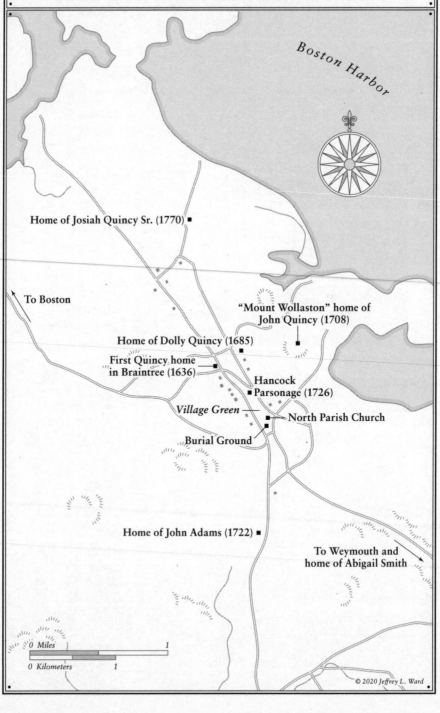

THE VILLAGE OF BRAINTREE
DURING THE TIME OF *AMERICAN REBELS*

Boston Harbor

Home of Josiah Quincy Sr. (1770) ▪

To Boston

"Mount Wollaston" home of
John Quincy (1708) ▪

Home of Dolly Quincy (1685) ▪

First Quincy home
in Braintree (1636) ▪

Hancock
▪ Parsonage (1726)

Village Green —

▪ North Parish Church

Burial Ground

Home of John Adams (1722) ▪

To Weymouth and
home of Abigail Smith

0 *Miles*   1

0 *Kilometers*   1

© 2020 Jeffrey L. Ward

The Families of Braintree

The Quincy Family

Edmund Quincy II (1628–1698) had thirteen children, including Daniel Quincy and Edmund Quincy III:

Daniel Quincy (1651–1690) + Anne Shepherd (1633–1708) = Colonel John Quincy

> Colonel John Quincy (1689–1767) + Elizabeth Norton Quincy (1696–1769) = they had three children, including Norton and Elizabeth

>> Norton Quincy (1716–1801) never married

>> Elizabeth Quincy (1721–1775) + Rev. William Smith (1706–1783) = Elizabeth, Mary, Abigail, William

>>> Mary Smith (1741–1811) + Richard Cranch (1726–1811) = Elizabeth, William, Joseph, Lucy

>>> Abigail Smith (1744–1818) + John Adams (see below) = Abigail (Nabby), John Quincy, Susanna (Suky), Charles, Thomas

Edmund Quincy III (1681–1737) + Dorothy Flynt Quincy (1678–1737) = they had four children, including Edmund Quincy IV and Josiah Quincy

> Edmund Quincy IV (1703–1788) + Elizabeth Wendell Quincy (1706–1746) = Edmund Quincy V, Henry, Abraham, Elizabeth, Katy, Esther, Sarah, Dorothy (Dolly)

>> Sarah Quincy (1736–1790) + William Greenleaf (1738–1793) = John Hancock Greenleaf

>> Elizabeth Quincy (1729–1770) + Rev. Samuel Sewall (1715–1771)

>> Esther Quincy (1738–1810) + Jonathan Sewall (1729–1796) = Jonathan, Stephen

>> Dolly Quincy (1747–1830) + John Hancock (see below) = Lydia, John George Washington

Josiah Quincy (1710–1784) married three times:

+ Hannah Sturgis Quincy (1712–1755) = Edmund, Samuel, Hannah, Josiah Quincy Jr.

+ Elizabeth Waldron Quincy (1722–1759) = Elizabeth

+ Anne Marsh (1723–1805) = Nancy, Frances

Edmund (Ned) Quincy (1733–1768) + Rebecca Lloyd: marriage planned, but Ned died

Samuel Quincy (1735–1789) + Hannah Hill (1734–1782) = Hannah, Sam Jr., Thomas

Hannah Quincy (1736–1826) + Bela Lincoln (1734–1773) = no children

Josiah Quincy Jr. (1744–1775) + Abigail Phillips (1745–1798) = Josiah III, Abigail

The Hancock Family

Bishop John Hancock (of Lexington, 1671–1752) + Elizabeth Clark (1674–1760) = they had seven children, including the Reverend John Hancock and Thomas Hancock

The Reverend John Hancock (1702–1744) + Mary Hawke (1711–1783) = John, Mary, Ebenezer

Thomas Hancock (1703–1764) + Lydia Henchman (1714–1776) = adopted John Hancock following death of his father, Reverend Hancock, in 1744

John Hancock (1737–1793) + Dolly Quincy (see above) = Lydia, John George Washington

The Adams Family

Joseph Adams (1654–1736) + Hannah Bass (1667–1705) = they had nine children, including John

Deacon John Adams (1691–1761) + Susanna Boylston (1708–1797) = they had four children, including John

John Adams (1735–1826) + Abigail Smith (see above) = Abigail (Nabby), John Quincy, Susanna (Suky), Charles, Thomas

PART ONE

Tinder

1744–1764

The most important part of everything is the beginning.

—Josiah Quincy Jr.

Prologue: A Village Mourns

Every moment of our existence has some connection . . .
to an eternal succession of future ages. . . .

—Edmund Quincy IV

In the spring of 1744, a congregation in the small village of Braintree, south of Boston in the Massachusetts Bay Colony, gathered to mourn the death of their minister, the Reverend John Hancock. Outside the church, the heavens opened up. Rain streamed down, drenching the wild bluebells that grew in the high meadows of Penn's Hill overlooking the sea, dripping from the apple trees planted in ordered lines behind the village's low houses, and running in widening rivulets between freshly plowed spring fields. Inside the church, its stone walls were streaked with black lines of damp and the windows steamed in the warmth rising off the gathered mourners.

Six years earlier, in 1738, Reverend Hancock gave the funeral sermon for Braintree villager Edmund Quincy III, who had died the year before while visiting England. There was no body to bury but much to mourn. In his sermon, Hancock lamented the many afflictions of the Quincy family, having endured a year of many family deaths, including the death of Edmund's wife, Dorothy Flynt Quincy. But not only had the family suffered from their losses, Reverend Hancock preached: the community as a whole had been wounded, for the strength of the whole derived from the contributions of each individual inhabitant.

What Reverend Hancock could not have known in 1738—and what no one in the church knew on the day of his funeral in 1744—was that from this village, Braintree, and this parish, the North Parish, would come the men and women who would shape the history of America. From the Quincy family, whose losses were so heavy in 1738; from the Adams family, whose patriarch served as deacon to the North Parish Church; and from Reverend

Hancock's own family would come the leaders of the next generation, the rebels who would foment a revolution.

The rebels were still children—or not yet even born—and their time to lead was still decades away. But their story—the shared story of John Hancock, Dolly Quincy, John Adams, Abigail Smith, and Josiah Quincy Jr.— began on that day in May 1744, when a community gathered to mourn their spiritual leader.

Reverend Hancock's son John was seven years old when his father died. On the day of the funeral, he sat in the same pew he had sat in every Sunday listening to his father preach. Beside him sat his mother, Mary Hawke Hancock, his sister, Mary, and his brother, Ebenezer.

"Braintree may this day be called Bochim, a place of Weepers," began the Reverend Ebenezer Gay.[1] Gay was minister of the Old Ship Church in Hingham but had come to Braintree to preach the funeral sermon of his good friend, John Hancock. Reverend Gay looked out over the crowded church, every pew taken up and more people standing with their heads bowed. All the community had come together to mourn the too-short life of a very good man.

Reverend Hancock had loved his North Parish ministry, a small but solid community of Congregationalists settled by the bay. He'd been raised inland, in the town of Lexington, the oldest son of the man he'd been named for, and in whose footsteps he had at first followed. His father was a minister so powerful that he was called the Bishop of Lexington, a minister so persuasive that a brand-new meetinghouse had been built for him when he commanded it, its spire visible from the countryside all around.[2] And yet when the younger Reverend Hancock was ready to preach, he left Lexington and came to Braintree, eager for the sea and for a different style of preaching.

Like the lighthouse that stood on Brewster Island in the bay, John Hancock saw his calling as that of a beacon of light through the dark. While his fearsome father had given fire-and-brimstone sermons filled with prohibitions and punishments, he built his ministry based on hope and comfort. His sermons offered the promise of eternal salvation through faith, and happiness on earth through hard work and the building of community. In his daily life, he showed gratitude for what God had given him and kindness toward the villagers who had come to rely on him.

The North Parish congregation was reminded now by Reverend Gay of just how caring their minister had been: "How Sweet to us hath been his Conversation! How sound his Advice! How kind his Assistance! How tender his Sympathy with us in our Troubles!"[3]

Reverend Gay asked the parishioners, "Is the Untimely Death of a Man of God to be Deeply Lamented?" After all, John Hancock had been only forty-one years old when he died from his short illness. "Who can forbear to mourn the untimely Death of the Man of God, whose funeral we are now attending? Is there a Person that does not from the bottom of his Heart sigh out the Lamentation over him, *Alas my Brother*? Or *O my Father, my Father!*"[4]

Young John Hancock had passed the grave dug for his father that morning. Walking with his mother and siblings to the meetinghouse from the parsonage where they lived, he had seen the open rectangle of black, framed by neat mounds of wet grass and brown earth. There was no shelter from rain in this graveyard, nor from the hard winds that came off the coast less than a mile away. By the time the funeral service ended, the graveside piles of earth and grass would be diminished, pummeled down by the elements. But the hole would remain, waiting to be filled.

Although there is no complete record of who attended the funeral, it is likely that Reverend Hancock's North Parish congregation turned out in full, despite the rain. Hancock knew them all personally, had baptized them, guided them, married them, and buried them for almost two decades. The minister recorded the dates of the ceremonies himself, as when he baptized his own son: "John Hancock, my son, January 16th, 1737."[5]

Certainly, Deacon John Adams would have attended the funeral of his minister, along with his two older sons, John and Peter. His wife, Susanna, however, might have stayed home with little Elihu, not even three years old. Deacon Adams' son John was a friend of young Hancock; he would later write that he had known John Hancock "from the cradle. . . . We were at the same school together, as soon as we were out of petticoats."[6]

Together with the other boys of the village, young Adams and young Hancock often escaped into the hills surrounding the village; they would find a flat slab of granite where they sat watching the ships passing in and out of Boston to the north and pitched rocks and acorns down the hill, aiming for but never hitting the glittering waters of the bay.

Members of the extended Quincy family would also have attended the funeral, filling out entire rows of pews. Edmund Quincy IV (the oldest son of Edmund Quincy III, who had been eulogized by Reverend Hancock in 1738), along with his wife, Elizabeth Wendell Quincy, would have attended, although how many of their eight children would have come along is unknown. Josiah Quincy, brother of Edmund Quincy IV, working now in Boston much of the time, would have tried to attend; he considered Reverend

Hancock a friend, and his two sons, Edmund and Samuel, were playmates of young John Hancock. Josiah's wife, Hannah Sturgis Quincy, would not have been in church but was most likely home with their youngest, a baby boy named Josiah after his father.

Norton Quincy, a cousin to brothers Edmund and Josiah, wrote in a letter about being in church that day. He would have come to the funeral with his parents, with whom he lived, John Quincy and Elizabeth Norton Quincy. Norton's sister Elizabeth was there with her husband, the Reverend William Smith. Elizabeth and William Smith lived in Weymouth, the next town over, where Reverend Smith served as pastor of the First Church.

Reverends Gay, Hancock, and Smith had shared their pulpits with one another, preaching from town to town. Their purpose, as Reverend Hancock put it, was "to shine in these dark Places of the Earth . . . to sing of the Mercy, the distinguishing Mercy of the Lord, in planting, watering, increasing, and defending them."[7]

Reverend Smith might have wondered why he hadn't been asked to give the funeral sermon, given his friendship with John Hancock and his wife's connections to Braintree, but in the end, he'd taken it all in stride. Elizabeth was pregnant that spring, and their daughter Abigail would be born in the summer. As the granddaughter of a Quincy, she would have social status; even with all his spiritual fervor, Reverend Smith was glad for the potential benefits such status would confer.

Braintree, like most villages settled by emigrants from England in the seventeenth century, was not separated, geographically or socially, along rigid class lines. All members of the community shared the village green and patronized the same shops and tradesmen; they bought their beer from the same brewery, and the younger boys all attended the same Dames School led by Mrs. Belcher; most of the older ones attended the local Latin grammar school. Three parish churches provided spiritual nourishment and everyone imbibed.

And yet subtle divisions were acknowledged. The villagers considered the Quincy family to be their local gentry, with their vast landholdings, fine houses with imported furniture, large libraries, and cellars stocked with Madeira and other wines from Europe; their sons would not attend the local Latin school but instead were students at the more prestigious—and rigorous—Boston Latin School.

The Hancock family was revered in the village for their association with the church and respected for their education: both Bishop Hancock and his son had attended Harvard.

The Adams family and others like them were the solid yeomen of the village, craftsmen and farmers who worked with their hands, prayed dutifully, and drank hard cider but never wines from faraway lands.

Despite these subtle class lines, the Hancock, Quincy, and Adams families all lived close by each other, with just a mile or two separating them. Edmund and Josiah Quincy lived in the houses that had been owned by their father, Edmund Quincy III. The oldest of the houses had been built in 1635, and Josiah lived there during the early years of his marriage to Hannah Sturgis; both Edmund and Samuel were born in the old house. Edmund Quincy IV lived in the newer house, built in 1685 and located close to a wide brook that teemed with eels. Surrounding the two brothers' homes was a large estate of outbuildings, well-tended fields, ornamental gardens, and orchards with "fine fruit trees."[8]

From the Quincy estate, it was a short walk to the village green of North Braintree and the parsonage of Reverend Hancock. The Hancock home was a "Handsome Country seat . . . containing besides a very commodious well-finished house, a good Barn, Out-Houses, fine Gardens and the best of orchards."[9] It was also dark and cold (John Hancock never forgot the frigid conditions of his father's parsonage during the long winter months) but its outlook was brightened in the spring by tall stands of lilac and clumps of yellow lilies.

A farther walk past the green and down the old Plymouth Road led to the Adams family farmhouse: from "both sides stretched away the wide fields of the farm . . . sprinkled with orchard trees and occasional pines and elms. The majestic sweep of the forest-covered slopes of Penn's Hill . . . and the more distant terraces of the Blue Hills bounded the vision."[10]

Up the hill that rose beyond the Adams property was the home of Norton Quincy and his parents, a tall and rambling house built high on Mount Wollaston, site of the original village settlement in 1625.

Living in such a close community, and regardless of class or status, the young people of the North Parish of Braintree felt connected to one another. They had been baptized together, schooled in the early years together, and raised together on the promises of their minister, the Reverend Hancock.

Now they, along with their parents and grandparents, mourned him. "It is the Death of a Prophet and of the Son of a Prophet, we are bewailing," preached Reverend Gay. "An able Minister of the New Testament taken away from us in the midst of his Days."[11] The stone-walled church of North Braintree echoed with sorrow.

Underneath the current of grief for the dead ran concern for the living. The parsonage would have to be vacated, another minister found, and a new place made for Mary Hancock and her children. It was assumed—and rightly so—that the old Reverend Hancock would invite his son's diminished family to live with him in Lexington. Work would be found for the wife and daughter, and the boys would be educated as best the local schools could do. Friends would be separated and new lives begun.

But even as the fortunes of these children of Braintree diverged, their futures would bring them together again. A shared promise connected them, fostered by the history, the land, and the people of Braintree. It was instilled in their blood and bones; distilled from their parents' lessons, the psalms they all knew by heart, and the books they read; nurtured by the fertile hills they roamed and the abundant wilderness that touched their tiny village; and strengthened by the cross-hatched, dependable order of the village itself, and the wide-open shoreline that could be seen from every promontory, with an expanse of blue leading all the way back to England.

The promise had been articulated in 1739 by Reverend Hancock, in a sermon in which he told his congregation that their "great Errand into this wilderness"—their "solemn covenant . . . of Liberty"—was grounded in the "good and early Foundation" laid by their forbears who first came to America from England.[12]

But it was not until his father's death in 1744 that events were set in motion which would propel young John Hancock and his village companions to hold that promise as sacred and inviolate. The covenant of liberty that they shared would be sharpened by ambition and envy, polished through friendships and love, and fought for in a revolution fomented by these children of Braintree.

These American rebels.

I

Founding a Village

Not such Another Place, for benefit or rest,
In all the universe can be possessed.

—Thomas Morton

The first Quincy to arrive in America was named Edmund, a name that would go on to be shared through generations of Quincys. Edmund Quincy and his wife, Judith, arrived in Boston in 1633, traveling from England with the prominent Puritan minister Joseph Cotton. Because of his association with Reverend Cotton, Edmund was able to purchase title to over four hundred acres of very good land, fertile and ready for farming, south of Boston.

John Winthrop, the governor of the Massachusetts Bay Colony, oversaw the purchase himself. The land had recently been confiscated—Governor Winthrop would have said "saved"—from a blasphemer and troublemaker named Thomas Morton, and Winthrop was eager to have God-fearing settlers purify the lands Morton had desecrated.

Morton had arrived in the Massachusetts Bay Colony eight years earlier, in 1625, traveling from England with Richard Wollaston, captain of the ship *Unity*. Wollaston's cargo was human, a large group of indentured servants whose contracts Wollaston hoped to sell to fishing companies operating out of Cape Ann and up the New England coast. Along with Morton and a fellow by the name of Fitcher,[1] after arriving in Boston Wollaston traveled south and set up a temporary camp on a low hill on the coast. The indigenous Massachusett tribe called the hill Passonagessit, meaning "little neck of land," for the way it jutted out into the bay. Under the leadership of sachem Chickatawbut the Massachusetts had cleared most of the trees on the hill, leaving a fertile and open hilltop attractive for farming.

Captain Wollaston, however, wasn't interested in farming. When he heard that there was a need for indentured workers at the plantations in Virginia, with prices paid even greater than those offered in New England, he decided to try his luck farther south. He returned to his ship, leaving only a small group of indentured men behind in the settlement on the hill. Morton and Fitcher would guard over the indentured men until Wollaston returned, and then they too would be sold off to work in fledgling colonial industries.

Waiting for Wollaston to return, Thomas Morton found himself becoming enchanted by the landscape around Passonagessit: "The more I looked, the more I liked it. . . . in all the knowne world it [cannot] be paralel'd, for so many goodly groves of trees, dainty fine round rising hillocks, delicate faire large plaines, sweete cristall fountains, and cleare running streames that twine in fine meanders through the meadows, making so sweete a murmering noise to hear."[2]

He became so enchanted that he decided to settle for good on these low hills south of Boston. But first, he had to start his own rebellion. Through skillful argument (he had trained as a lawyer at Clifford Inns, London) and a generous gift of more than a few barrels of beer (he had ample funds through family ties), Morton convinced the men left behind by Wollaston to rebel against their indentured status and start life over as free agents in the New World. Fitcher was run off the hill of Passonagessit and Morton became the new leader of the small band of men. He named his community Mare-Mount, meaning "a hill providing views upon the sea."[3]

Morton set up a robust trading post at Mare-Mount, inviting local Indians to trade goods, including highly lucrative furs, for guns and other supplies. As William Bradford, then governor of the Pilgrim colony at Plymouth, described it, Morton not only gave the Indians guns but he "taught them how to use them, to charge and discharge, and what proportion of powder to give the piece, according to the size and bigness of the same; and what shot to use for fowl and what for deer."[4]

From his own account, Morton got on quite well with the locals and wanted to live in harmony with them: "these I found most full of humanity, and more friendly" than the English Pilgrims.[5] He claimed that the purpose of the settlement at Mare-Mount was to create a community where the English settlers and the local Indians could live together, trade together, and prosper together. And the settlement did prosper, with brisk trade and plenty of furs acquired to send back to England.

But Governor Bradford and his band of Pilgrims saw a different purpose to Morton's settlement: they condemned it as a den of vice and iniquity. As Bradford wrote later, the settlers at Mare-Mount "fell to great licenciousnes, and led a dissolute life, powering out themselves into all profanesses. And

Morton became a lord of misrule . . . quaffing and drinking, both wine and strong waters in great excess."[6]

Outraged by reports of good times being had on the hilltop, the Pilgrims called Morton's settlement not Mare-Mount but Merrymount, a name intended to indict Morton and all his followers; "for the same Reason that the common People in England will not call Gentlemen's ornamented Grounds, *Gardens* but insist upon calling them *Pleasure Grounds*, i.e. to excite Envy and make them unpopular."[7]

While Morton's settlement continued to prosper, the Pilgrim trading posts floundered, and tensions between Morton and Bradford grew. The Pilgrims spread stories about Morton's arms deals with Indian populations (while ignoring the same weapons trading that went on by other settlers) and also shared largely embellished accounts of the debauched revelries enjoyed at Mare-Mount.

Morton himself bragged of his May Day festivities, during which a "goodly pine tree of 80 foote longe" was raised in the middle of the settlement and decorated with pairs of buck antlers nailed to the top in a particularly heathen flourish; tables of food were set out, barrels of drinks provided, and "drinking and dancing" ensued.[8] According to Morton, a good time was had by all.

But Governor Bradford put a sexual spin on the May Day merrymaking, alleging that Morton and his men invited "Indian women for their consorts, dancing and frisking together, like so many fairies, or furies rather, and [engaging in] worse practices."[9]

The fact that Morton was aligned with the Church of England and opposed to the Pilgrims at Plymouth was another reason for discord between the two settlements; Morton saw himself as "a man that endeavored to advance the dignity of the Church of England," while the Pilgrims were separatists who sought, as Morton put it, to "vilify" the Church of England.[10] Morton called the somberly dressed and dour Pilgrims "moles" and disdained their frugal and joyless lifestyle.[11]

Disturbed by the economic and religious threats posed by Morton (and the great fun he was having), in the early summer of 1628, the Pilgrim leaders sent Captain Miles Standish to "take Morton by force."[12] "Captain Shrimp" (as Morton called Standish, who was very short) and his company "fell upon [Morton] as if they would have eaten him: some of them were so violent that they would have a slice with scabbert."[13]

Standish arrested Morton and brought him back to Plymouth. Morton was exiled for a brief period to a deserted island off the coast and then trans-ported back to England in 1628.

Morton returned to Massachusetts a year later, intent on retaking his settlement on the hill. Finding a small but welcoming community still living there, as well as his glorious maypole still standing in the center of the vil-lage, he settled back into his Mare-Mount life. He resumed trading for furs but no longer dealt in arms or ammunition. He also invited the locals to live in his community, which they did, leading once again to rumors that Morton was engaging in sexual adventures proscribed by God.

Morton saw in his little community a model for living in the New World, a kind of utopia based on social integration with the native people, economic flexibility, and enjoyment of life with all its natural and manmade pleasures. But his "consorting" with Indians and having too good a time as a "Lord of misrule" rankled the Puritan authorities that were now coming to power in Massachusetts.[14]

In 1630 he was arrested again, this time under the orders of Governor Winthrop, Puritan leader of the Massachusetts Bay Colony. Morton was put on a ship to be sent back to England, the famous maypole was finally cut down, and the homes of Mare-Mount were burned to the ground. The fires were timed to coincide with Morton's departure by sea so that he could see the flames and smoke of his destroyed settlement from the ship.[15]

The hilltop at Mare-Mount was renamed Mount Wollaston and its lands were redistributed by Governor Winthrop, with the intent of returning the lands to placid, God-fearing settlers. Edmund Quincy was one of the lucky ones and, as a devout Congregationalist, received property on and around the low hill overlooking the bay. Fellow emigrants who received land grants on the hills of Passonagessit included the Coddingtons and the Hutchinsons, families with whom the Quincys quickly became friendly.

The peace and quiet sought by Governor Winthrop, by making land grants to emigrants of good reputation, was denied to him when the new settlers on the hill began to follow the radical teachings of one of their own. It was as if the hills themselves breathed rebellion into their inhabitants. Anne Hutchinson, married to William Hutchinson, arrived on the hill as an already strong and outspoken woman. While living in England she had questioned the practices of Puritan leaders there. But once she arrived in America, Hutchinson became even more critical of the ways in which Pu-ritan dogma was interpreted by both local ministers and colonial leaders, including Governor Winthrop.

When a minister named John Wheelwright, who was married to her husband's sister, arrived in Mount Wollaston, Anne helped him to become pastor of the local church. Strongly influenced by Anne Hutchinson and her spiritual convictions, Wheelwright began to preach in a way that brought him many followers, including the Coddingtons and the Quincys. But his preaching, and her convictions, also caught the attention of elder ministers in the colony.

Anne Hutchinson believed the covenant of grace, a tenet of Congregationalism that holds that certain people are destined for eternal salvation from birth, was proven only through direct communication with God, which she herself enjoyed on a regular basis. Hutchinson told her followers that the directives she received from God were more important in guiding how she lived her life than the dictates of local ministers, who tended to couch their commands in terms of the covenant of works, which held that doing good in the community was a way of proving one's worthiness and eventual salvation. Hutchinson rejected teachings based on the covenant of works; she saw outward acts of goodness as irrelevant, given that only internal communication with God assured salvation.

While the Congregationalist clergy did believe that grace was necessary for salvation, it was impossible for them to discard the covenant of works. How else could they impel their flocks to behave morally, to follow town and church rules, to perform the needed work to make the settlements flourish and grow?

Grace could only get the Puritans so far; they needed hard work to succeed. Adherence to strict rules of behavior set by the church was vital to the success of the communities in New England, and Anne Hutchinson's teachings about resistance to church rules—and her arguments against the usefulness of good works in achieving salvation—threatened the stability of those communities.

In 1637, the General Court of Massachusetts brought charges against Anne Hutchinson for the heresy of antinomianism, meaning operating "outside the law" of the church. (Charges of sedition for preaching against conventional doctrine in his sermons were brought against the Reverend John Wheelwright.) The court, led by Governor Winthrop, demanded that Hutchinson recant her criticisms of the clergy of Massachusetts. Hutchinson refused to back down and threatened the members of the General Court and the entire community for prosecuting her: "if you go on in this course you begin, you will bring a curse upon you and your posterity, and the mouth of the Lord hath spoken it."[16]

The court responded by banishing her from the colony; she was then excommunicated from the Puritan Congregational church. During her sentencing, she was "cast out" and delivered "up to Satan."[17] Reverend Wheelwright was also exiled; he left the colony for New Hampshire, where he founded the settlement of Exeter. Although he was an active supporter of Hutchinson and Wheelwright, William Coddington was not exiled; he chose to leave, however, following Anne Hutchinson and her family to Rhode Island. Once there, Coddington would play a prominent role in Rhode Island government, reaching the position of royal governor of the colony of Rhode Island in the 1670s.

After her husband died, in 1641, Anne Hutchinson left Rhode Island for New York, settling in a small community by Pelham Bay. In 1643, Anne and six of her children were massacred by local Native Americans. Her daughter, Susanna, was taken captive, and later ransomed back to Anne's son Edward, who was still living in Boston.

Edmund Quincy died early in 1637 before he and his family could be drawn into the battles surrounding Anne Hutchinson; thus, he unwittingly protected his family from possibly being charged with heresy themselves and losing their position—and lands—in Mount Wollaston. Nevertheless, his wife, Judith, and their two children were left "in the wilderness" (as the family lore went), and Judith was compelled to sell the lands on Mount Wollaston to Captain William John Tyng, one of Boston's wealthiest merchants.[18] She moved down into the sandy lands along the coast, into a house that would stay in the Quincy family for generations.

The lands sold to Tyng eventually came back to the Quincy family through marriage.[19] In the early 1700s, John Quincy (father of Norton Quincy and uncle to Edmund Quincy IV and Josiah Quincy) built a mansion on the hill where Thomas Morton had held his wild parties, not far from where Anne Hutchinson had lived with her family.

The selectmen of the village changed the name of their settlement from Mount Wollaston to Braintree in 1640, perhaps because of the controversies associated with the previous name. The name of Braintree was chosen from a well-favored town in England. But both the mansion built by John Quincy and the hilltop on which it stood would forever be known as Mount Wollaston.

Even with the change of name, the village of Braintree continued to foster a rebellious spirit in its citizens. The villagers of the eighteenth century would prove to be as fiercely independent in their political and religious convictions as both Morton and Hutchinson. But the Christianity they practiced would not have been sanctioned by the Congregationalism of their forefathers nor acceptable to the even more exacting Anne Hutchinson.

By the time Reverend John Hancock became minister of the Third Parish Church of Braintree in 1726, the families of the village, including the Adamses and the Quincys, no longer relied on predestination but instead demanded that each community member work hard to achieve satisfaction on earth and salvation in heaven.

They were still deeply religious and loyal to their local church, and they still followed many behavioral strictures of the Puritan church, including prohibitions against working on the Sabbath, playacting, dancing, or celebrating Christmas or Easter (and certainly no drunken celebrations around a huge maypole). What had changed was how they defined their own worth and their role in the world.

The people of Braintree believed not only in their individual abilities but also in their collective duty to determine their own fates and the shared future of their village. As Reverend Hancock preached, the "solemn covenant . . . of Liberty" was not obtained through faith alone but could only be realized through hard work performed by a community together.[20] And this sacred covenant would be protected against any and all usurpers who attempted to take their liberty away.

2

The Education of Boys

The Stream of Life sometimes glides smoothly on,
through flowry meadows and enamell'd planes.
At other times it drags a winding reluctant Course
through offensive Boggs and dismal gloomy Swamps.

—JOHN ADAMS

In July 1744, Thomas Hancock, younger brother to the recently deceased Reverend John Hancock, traveled from Boston to Lexington. Accompanied by his wife, Lydia, he traveled in a sturdy black coach edged in gilt and upholstered in thick maroon velvet. It was a fine coach but nothing like the one Thomas had ordered from England, due to arrive any month now. The new coach would be ivory-colored, with silver trim; the coat of arms that Thomas had fashioned himself—an emblem with three cocks, a dragon's tail, and a raised fist—would be painted in red and gold over its doors. Underneath the coat of arms, in gold script, the coach maker had been ordered to carefully paint the family motto that Thomas had invented: *Nul Plaisir Sans Peine*. No pleasure without pain.

Thomas and Lydia now traveled to Lexington to save their fatherless nephew John from a life of pain and bring him into a life of pleasure, in the form of wealth, education, and privileges that he had never imagined.

Thomas was the second-born son of the Bishop of Lexington. While his brother John went off to Harvard to become a minister, Thomas was told by his father to find a trade. At age thirteen, he left home and went to find work in Boston. He found a place as apprentice to a bookseller named Samuel Gerrish. Boston at that time was the biggest town in North America and the center of everything, including the publishing and selling of books. The people of the Massachusetts Bay Colony prided themselves on their high levels of literacy and their huge appetites for books of all kinds. Gerrish's shop, located on Cornhill Street, one of Boston's busiest, did a lively business.

Under an agreement signed between the Bishop of Lexington and Samuel Gerrish, Thomas served for seven years as Gerrish's apprentice, learning all the ins and outs of the bookbinding trade and working in return for no wages (he would be provided with food, drink, lodging, and laundry services). The contract further required that "Matrimony he shall not contract, Taverns and Alehouses he shall not frequent, at cards, dice, or any other unlawful games he shall not play."[1]

Having completed his seven years of learning, servitude, and good behavior, at the age of twenty-one Thomas set up his own shop selling books. He took out a notice in the Boston papers: "Thomas Hancock, at the sign of the Bible and Three Crowns, has for sale, *The Danger of People's Losing the Good Impressions made by the late awful Earthquake, A Sermon Preached a Month after it Happened*, by the Rev. Mr. Cooper, and all manner of other improving tracts."[2]

Within a few years, his inventory included "Bibles large and small, Testaments, Psalters, Psalm Books with tunes and without, Singing-Books, School-books. . . . Also Pressing Cartridge and Writing Paper, Books for Accounts or Records, Ink, Quills, Sealing-Wax, Inkhorns, Spectacles, Letter-cases . . . and all sorts of Cutlery ware at the lowest prices. . . . Books are also rebound."[3]

But Thomas' ventures soon expanded even further. He began to invest in enterprises run by established Boston merchants, inspired by the example set by an older bookseller by the name of Daniel Henchman. Henchman had a reputation for both boldness and independence—he had printed the Bible for distribution without the required approval of the king—and enjoyed a growing fortune built on his daring investments.

Thomas saw Henchman as not only a potential partner for ambitious ventures but also a possible father-in-law; he had met and admired Henchman's daughter, Lydia, and soon sought her hand in marriage. The couple were married in 1730. Thomas was twenty-seven and Lydia was sixteen. It was by all accounts a happy marriage for both Lydia and Thomas, and both son-in-law and father benefitted from their commercial connections.

Within just a few years, Thomas had moved well beyond books and was exporting rum to Newfoundland, oil to London, and fish to Spain. He'd invested in his own ships, commissioning the building of the *Thomas* and the *Lydia* for shipping goods from America to be sold in the West Indies and bringing goods from London to be sold in America. His stores and warehouses still sold books but also just about everything else anyone might want. The umbrella under which all his enterprises operated was called the House of Hancock.

By the year 1737 Thomas had become so wealthy that he was able to build a mansion for himself and Lydia on Beacon Hill. He bought land all around it to create an estate of rolling meadows, overflowing flowerbeds, and row upon row of fruit trees, including plum, peach, apricot, nectarine, pear, mulberry, gooseberry, and cherry. Most of the plants and trees were imported from England, but Thomas also sent out notices for sea captains to be on the lookout in any country they visited for "any small thing to beautify my garden."[4]

The furnishings for inside the house were also largely imported from England: not only the chairs, tables, and settees for the many rooms but also the glass for the mansion's fifty-four windows, the stone hearths, tiles for the fireplaces, customized wallpaper, and intricately carved and twisted balusters for the wide staircase in the vast entrance hall. The house itself was built of granite culled from quarries in Braintree. Granite stairs led from street to home, and above the front entranceway, a large stone balcony gave out on the Boston Common. Thomas said of his new estate, "the Kingdom of England don't afford so fine a Prospect as I have."[5]

As happy as Lydia and Thomas were together, and as wealthy as they were, they were unable to fulfill one of their most ardent wishes: to have a child. After Thomas' brother John died, it seemed the natural course of things to take on his oldest son as their protégé and adopted son. They would bring John Hancock to Boston to be educated, loved, and launched into the world as a representative of the House of Hancock.

It would not have taken long for young John to pack up his belongings in Lexington; little that he had there, where he lived off the frugal generosity of his grandfather, would be needed in Boston. For John's mother, Mary, the decision to let her son go to Boston was an easy one. Her own prospects were dim, living as she did with her father-in-law; she knew that if her son John got on well under the tutelage of Uncle Thomas, he would help out his two siblings in a way that the old bishop could not. She bid her son to do his best and write often, and promised there would be visits between the families. Thomas promised the same, and John took his leave of Lexington.

News of young Hancock's move to Boston quickly traveled to the village of Braintree. Already aware of the division separating him from the Quincy boys, John Adams, son of Deacon Adams, now had to accept that his childhood companion John Hancock was vaulting up into a higher social register—but through no action of his own. What was the use of hard work if a mere schoolboy could be lifted to wealth in one morning, while John Adams had only the prospect of farming and local government—the summit of his father's achievements—to look forward to?

Envy would plague John Adams throughout his life, both driving him forward and driving him mad: "The Scituation that I am in, and the Advantages that I enjoy, are thought to be the best for me by him who alone is a competent Judge of Fitness and Propriety. Shall I then complain? Oh Madness, Pride, Impiety."[6]

Henry Adams, great-great-grandfather to John, had come to the Massachusetts Bay Colony around 1632, from the village of Braintree in Essex, England. He settled his family in what was then called Mount Wollaston. Henry's son Joseph was the only one of his eight children to remain living in the small village; but Joseph's sons all remained in and around Braintree, and in 1691, his son John was born. Adams bought his own farm in 1720 (making him a freehold farmer, in that he owned his own lands) and then became a deacon at the North Parish Church. At the age of forty-three, he married for the first time. Susanna Boylston was fifteen years his junior and the daughter of a prominent Boston family.

Susanna Adams moved from Boston to Braintree to live with her new husband in his simple five-room farmhouse. He'd been happily ensconced there for years, but as their family grew—John born in 1735, Peter born in 1738, and Elihu born in 1741—and as Deacon Adams' responsibilities multiplied, the house grew tight with both bodies and tension.

Adams not only served as deacon of his church and as a town selectman but also worked all winter long as the local shoe cobbler, led the village militia, and managed a farm through his own work and the work of tenant farmers. People were always coming and going in the Adams house, with customers arriving for their shoes, selectmen convening for a meeting, parishioners seeking help, or militiamen showing up to plan out monthly exercises.

Deacon Adams felt impelled to care for all the people of his village, including the indigent. At times he brought destitute and homeless people into the farmhouse to live until they could get on their feet again. A hired girl lived in with the family, and "there was nearly always an Adams or Boylston cousin, aunt, uncle, grandparent, or friend staying the night."[7] There was never room enough for everyone in the home, or for everything going on there, or any space at all that allowed for just a little peace and quiet.

Susanna, raised in a fine house in Brookline, had led a more cosseted life as a girl than the one she took on as a woman. It was perhaps from his mother that John Adams Jr. inherited his peculiar and lasting quality of peevish superiority. Like Susanna, John often felt himself to be better than his peers, smarter and worthier; again, like his mother, he was particularly irked by the fact that his peers so often failed to recognize his incredible talents.

The role of farmer's wife in a small village never suited Susanna Adams and she sought to maintain what status she had by controlling the family finances. Arguments between husband and wife were frequent, especially "frets, squibs, scolds, rages, raves" over money. Young John spent many hours of his youth wandering the hills of Braintree on his own or with his friends, eager to be out of his chaotic and often acrimonious home. As he described it later, "Passion, Accident, Freak, [and ill] Humour" governed in the Adams household.[8]

And yet John had many happy childhood memories, spent "in making and sailing boats and Ships upon the Ponds and Brooks, in making and flying Kites, in driving hoops, playing marbles, playing Quoits, Wrestling, Swimming, Skaiting and above all in shooting."[9] When he was still just a boy of eight or nine, his schoolteacher, Joseph Cleverly, forbade John from bringing his gun with him to school. John left the firearm hidden away close by the school and picked it up after class, proceeding to shoot at crows and squirrels all the way home.

John later credited both his parents with teaching him important lessons for life, but he especially idolized his father: "In wisdom, piety, benevolence and charity . . . I have never known his superior."[10] When at age ten John professed his desire to leave school and become a farmer, his father, who harbored high hopes for his firstborn, said nothing to discourage his young son. Instead, he sent John to spend a day in muddy fields, where he was tasked with cutting thatch, a laborious and painful undertaking.

When his father asked him if he was now ready to pursue his studies, John answered that as raw as his fingers were, and as sore his back, school was simply a terrible chore for him. His father shook his head and sent John back to school the next day; John went but "was not so happy as among the Creek Thatch."[11]

According to John, the fault lay in his teacher: "Mr. Cleverly was through his whole Life the most indolent Man I ever knew. . . . His inattention to his Schollars was such as gave me a disgust to Schools, to books and to study."[12] When John at age fourteen again asked his father for permission to leave school and become a farmer, his father replied, "I have set my heart upon your Education." He asked John why he would not study harder and go to college. John answered simply: "Sir I don't like my Schoolmaster. He is so negligent and so cross that I never can learn anything under him."[13]

Father and son soon reached an agreement: if Adams could find a new school for John, the boy promised to "apply myself to my Studies as closely as my nature will admit, and go to Colledge."[14] And so, at age fourteen, John was sent as a day student to a local school for boarders run by Joseph Marsh.

The kindly and intelligent Marsh was finally able to inspire John Adams in his studies; his father "soon observed the relaxation of my Zeal" for guns, and "my daily increasing Attention to my books."[15] As a reward for his hard work, Marsh gave John a small book containing Cicero's orations. On the flyleaf, John wrote his name six times, as if to make sure of his possession of the treasured tome; he would keep it his whole life.

Later, he wrote to a friend that there was nothing like reciting Cicero to make one feel better: "It exercises my Lungs, raises my Spirits, opens my Pores, quickens the Circulations, and so contributes much to Health."[16]

John Hancock's education since being taken under the wing of Thomas and Lydia had been one of both privilege and expectations. The best of all was given to him—the finest clothes, a carriage for his own use, a magnificent bedroom, the huge manicured yard, and indeed the entire Boston Common at his door to play in. A private tutor was brought in to teach John, as his health was delicate (and would be all his life), and then at the age of eleven, he was enrolled in the Boston Latin School, run by the demanding taskmaster John Lovell. There he learned Latin, Greek, a bit of history and arithmetic, and the most important skill of all, handwriting. The last hour of every schoolday, a day which began at 7:00 a.m. and ended at 5:00 p.m., was spent in perfecting penmanship. This was his favorite hour at school; time spent at arithmetic came in a close second.

John used his great skill at writing to pen letters to his mother in Lexington, and to his sister and grandmother. When his grandmother fell ill, John offered to send a gift of "two oranges and six lemons."[17] Citrus was a treasure beyond measure in those days, and his offer underlined both his generosity (thanks to his uncle) and his kindness (which he would demonstrate all his life).

Thomas Hancock was well pleased with his nephew's growing talents. Good handwriting and agility at sums were both important to the career Thomas had in mind for John. More skills would be learned at Harvard, which John began to attend in the fall of 1750, and Thomas also began to bring his nephew with him to the offices of the House of Hancock and down to Clark's Wharf. (Early in the 1750s, Thomas renamed the wharf after himself, and it would from then on be known as Hancock's Wharf.) It was on the docks of Boston that John became enthralled with the work of his uncle, all the ships coming and going, with their wares from all over the world.

The business of House of Hancock had continued to expand, particularly in the field of government contracts. Much money was to be made in supplying everything the British army might need, from tents to building materials, food and drink, guns and ammunition, clothing and backpacks, horses and wagons. Thomas had taken the time to study the needs of the military, and now as he and John walked the docks, he explained to his nephew the ins and outs of outfitting an army.

The House of Hancock supplied the British in Canada as they built up their troops and forts; an even more lucrative contract for the firm had been providing goods and arms to the British forces in King George's War in Canada. When the French and Indian War began in 1754, supplying the British and Americans in their fight against the French would bring even more profit to the firm.

Under the tutelage of Joseph Marsh, it took John Adams less than a year to be fully prepared to sit for Harvard's entrance exams. In June 1751 notice of the exams was published in the local papers: they would be held in early July. John was all set to go when at the last minute, Marsh told John he couldn't accompany his student to Cambridge—John would have to face the examiners on his own. John was terrified; he set out on "a very melancholy journey" and, despite all his preparations, arrived in Cambridge certain that he would fail in the exams.

Presenting himself at Harvard Hall, he was brought into the examination room. He seated himself in a chair facing Edward Holyoke, president of Harvard, along with four other men, all tutors of the college. Henry Flynt, cousin to the Quincys, was one of the tutors. John took a deep breath and began the examination, first taking on a Latin translation (fortunately, he was allowed the use of a dictionary as an aid to his memory) and continuing from there. In the end, he acquitted himself well, "was declared admitted," and given a "Theme . . . to write on in the Vacation."[18]

Deacon Adams, overjoyed, happily sold off ten acres of his farm to pay the college tuition, and John began his classes in the fall of 1751. He was fifteen, the oldest freshman in his class. Both the Quincy boys and John

Hancock were already at Harvard, after being prepared at the elite Boston Latin School. Edmund Quincy was a senior, and Samuel Quincy and John Hancock were sophomores.

It was a time of reunion for the boys from Braintree. Samuel and Edmund Quincy, John Hancock, and John Adams renewed their childhood friendships. They socialized together, talking politics—Ned, as Edmund Quincy was called, was already a fiery proponent of the rights of colonists—and playing cards. But a sense of social distinctions lingered—or at least so John Adams imagined. Class rankings at Harvard at the time were based on social standing, and despite the boost Adams received for having the Boylston name on his mother's side, all the Quincy boys and John Hancock would consistently be ranked above him—and the fact of it, inked on paper for the world to see, rankled.

John Adams had worked hard for his place, but the economic fortunes of others seemed to count for more than his own meritorious efforts. He would just have to work harder, he decided. He knew those boys weren't better than him, and he would show the world it was so.

3

Worldly Goods, Heavenly Debates

We are on the waves sometimes to heaven,
and then sunk down to the bottom.

—JOHN ADAMS

In the early 1750s, the village of Braintree was once again rocked by religious scandal, similar to charges of heresy and sedition brought against Anne Hutchinson and her followers 114 years before. It all began when the North Parish Church found a new minister in 1745, to replace Reverend Hancock. They hired a recent graduate from Harvard, a young man by the name of Lemuel Briant. For close to a century Harvard had been turning out ministers, and the congregation of Braintree was certain that the revered college knew what it was doing by now.

But Harvard had been changing over the past few decades and Lemuel Briant was a product of those changes. By the early eighteenth century, the concept of determining one's own destiny—not leaving it to God alone to decide—had become acceptable and widespread. Educated New Englanders studied, or at least heard about, the works of John Locke, Isaac Newton, and Francis Bacon, and were convinced that human reason and private judgment had as much power over their lives as the church and its dogma.

Even Harvard, venerable stronghold of Congregationalism, had become a place that allowed debate over questions of theology and included the masters of the Enlightenment on its readings lists. Under President John Leverett, who stepped to the helm in 1708, Harvard changed from a college charged solely with training young men for the Congregational ministry to become an institution where students were educated for a variety of callings. Leverett made it a practice to call his graduates "Sons of Harvard," whereas previous presidents had always referred to them as "Sons of Prophets."[1]

The new liberalism worried many of the traditional Puritan preachers of Massachusetts. They became convinced that their congregations were turning away from the colony's original values of piety, simplicity, and frugality and turning toward sin and ultimate damnation. These preachers railed from their pulpits against society's changing values and protested what they saw as moral laxity in their congregations.

Following the teachings of George Whitefield, an evangelical minister from England, the conservative preachers of New England began a movement in the early 1740s that came to be known as the Great Awakening but at the time was called the New Lights ministry. The New Lights ministers wanted to bring their parishioners back to strict adherence to Calvinist Protestant doctrine and sought to do it through scaring them with lurid visions of hell.

As Jonathan Edwards preached in a sermon he gave in western Massachusetts in 1741, "*There* is the dreadful pit of the glowing flames of the wrath of God; there is hell's wide gaping mouth open; and you have nothing to stand upon, nor any thing to take hold of: there is nothing between you and hell but the air; 'tis only the power and meer pleasure of God that holds you up."[2]

Arriving in Braintree in 1745, Reverend Lemuel Briant took over the North Parish Church just as the influence of the New Lights ministers was reaching its peak in Massachusetts. Still a young man, just twenty-four, he took on the older, more conservative ministers of Massachusetts, immediately inserting himself—and the North Parish Church—into the controversy swirling around the New Lights.

Having been trained at Harvard under its newly broadened curriculum, Briant was a man who thought the best of other people and preferred to see hope, rather than doom, for all humankind. He liked to have a good time and believed everyone should find joy in their lives and spread the joy through good works. He discounted the threats of eternal suffering leveled by the New Lights ministers and instead focused his theology on the ability of human beings to think for themselves.

Preaching from his own pulpit in Braintree but also wherever else he was invited to speak, Briant charged the New Lights preachers with taking advantage of "the unthinking multitude" by claiming to be divinely gifted with the ability to interpret scripture for everybody else.[3] He accused the preachers of threatening their audiences with eternal damnation and turning them "into such fiery Bigots, as to be ready to die in the Defence of Stupidity and Nonsense."[4]

Briant found an example of such "Stupidity" in the so-called bonfire of the vanities, in which large fires, set by the New Lights ministers, were used to burn and destroy books they deemed dangerous, along with fancy clothes and household goods they condemned as frivolous. The fires were cheered on by frenzied crowds of converts, the hysteria running so high that in one instance the minister, James Davenport, took off his pants and threw them into the fire.

The New Lights' insistence on predestination—that one's fate, heaven or hell, was determined from birth—was especially troubling to Briant. Briant firmly believed in the individual's ability to decide for himself or herself what was right in the eyes of the Lord. Furthermore, Briant believed that the right choices would result in an individual's eventual salvation by a loving God (salvation by good works).

He questioned the doctrine of salvation by grace alone because it removed the role of personal responsibility, "so as to destroy all moral Agency, and set themselves down with this vain Thought, that nothing on their Part is necessary to Salvation, but if they are designed for it, they shall irresistably be driven into Heaven. . . . And if they are not, no Prayers, nor Endeavours will avail."[5]

Around the same time as the religious controversy in Braintree was heating up, news of a different kind rocked Boston. The *Bethel*, a small ship owned by the local mercantile firm of Quincy, Quincy, and Jackson (a partnership of Josiah Quincy, his brother Edmund Quincy IV, and their brother-in-law, Edward Jackson) had captured the *Jesus Maria and Joseph*, a Spanish galleon, as it traveled from Havana to Cádiz. England was at war with Spain (the War of the Austrian Succession), and news of the capture of an enemy ship was celebrated. Throughout the fall of 1748, newspapers were filled with accounts of the daring seizure on the high seas.

The chase occurred at night off the coast of Gibraltar. Under cover of darkness, Isaac Freeman, the captain of the *Bethel*, fooled the larger Spanish vessel into surrendering to his much smaller ship. Writing to Josiah Quincy later, Freeman described how as dawn broke over the seas and the size of the *Bethel* became apparent, the captured Spanish crew "were ready to hang themselves on sight of our six wooden guns, and [with] scarce enough men to hoist the topsails."[6] The Spanish ship was escorted all the way to Boston Harbor by the *Bethel* and its entire cargo off-loaded, now the property of Quincy, Quincy, and Jackson.

Chests of treasure, each one filled to the top with gold and silver pieces, were paraded through the streets of Boston by sailors armed with pistols and cutlasses, and cheered on by massive crowds; all of Boston was "wild with excitement."[7] In all, 161 chests were carried from the harbor to Josiah Quincy's home on Marlborough Street, there to be deposited in his cellar for safekeeping.

The captain of the captured ship was given two chests of money in recompense for his losses. Grateful for the unusually kind treatment he and his crew had received—more commonly, crew were imprisoned, ransomed, or impressed into naval service—the overjoyed Spaniard gave "a grand ball for his captors."[8]

Despite the lucrative seizure, the primary goal of the firm Quincy, Quincy, and Jackson was not privateering but rather the importing of goods from abroad to sell in the colonies. Given Josiah Quincy's outgoing ways—he was always the most talkative in the room—and his overall enthusiasm, he was the one charged with going to Europe to put the trading deals together. He did his job well and the firm prospered.

Josiah's search for goods and markets took him to Paris, Amsterdam, Cádiz, and Leghorn (as the English then called Livorno, Italy). Family history passed down the tale of Josiah impersonating a priest while in Italy, speaking only in Latin to men he met in coffeehouses and bars, and then having to run for his life when the locals caught on. When the *Bethel* captured the Spanish treasure ship in the summer of 1748, Josiah was abroad and had no idea of the treasures that awaited him. Arriving home on one of the spring ships, he went down to his cellars, took a good look around, and returned upstairs to celebrate with his family. All the long journeys spent away from home, separated from his wife, Hannah, and their four children could now be put behind him forever. He and his two partners had become among the wealthiest merchants in New England.

Edmund Quincy had already begun happily spending his newly won riches. He purchased a grand house in Boston on Summer Street, with a long garden that reached all the way back to the gardens of his brother Josiah's house on Marlborough Street. He then set about turning his Braintree home into a handsome country estate, building a waterfall in the creek that ran beside the house and making improvements to the formal garden. He added a long allée of lime trees along the gravel path that led to the house from the street, and he bought new furnishings for the interiors, including a harpsichord and more books for his already extensive library.

Edmund's wife, Elizabeth, continued to spend most of her time in the

Braintree home with her daughters, Katy, Esther, and Sarah, while Edmund traveled back and forth between town and country. When his youngest daughter, Dorothy, born in May 1747, was old enough to attend school, he brought her to Boston to attend a girls' academy there: "Daughter Dolly looks very Comfortable, and has gone to School, where she seems to be very high in her Mistresses' graces."[9] All of his daughters had been given an education—Edmund believed in teaching women to think for themselves—but now he had the money to offer the best education possible.

Dolly was the only child, of all Edmund and Elizabeth's nine children, to enjoy a childhood in this new world of expansive wealth. Although Edmund and Elizabeth were never poor, as a young wife and mother Elizabeth had had to run a small store out of their home to raise extra money for the family. Those days seemed to be over for good. Both Edmund and Elizabeth intended to enjoy their newfound wealth to the utmost, and to share the pleasures they could now afford with all the extended family, in Boston and in Braintree.

Because of the extensive time Josiah had spent abroad over the past ten years, he knew little about the spiritual controversy involving Reverend Briant and his pastorship in Braintree. But his cousin John Quincy, his brother Edmund, and Deacon Adams, all living in Braintree and active in the North Parish Church in the late 1740s and early 1750s, found themselves in the thick of it.

Although many Massachusetts ministers were sympathetic to Briant's characterization of the New Lights preachers as fanatical, Briant was widely criticized for daring to question settled dogma of Calvinist Protestantism and accused of skating dangerously close to heresy. In a sermon delivered from the South Parish Church of Braintree, Reverend John Porter from Scituate went so far as to accuse Briant of being among the "pretended Preachers of Righteousness," comparing him to "the Arians, Socians, Arminians, Antinomians, and even the Quakers."[10]

Like Anne Hutchinson before him, Lemuel Briant could rely on the faithful of Braintree to support him against accusations of heresy and shrug off the charges of antinomianism. But when Abigail Briant left her husband, claiming that he had mistreated her, the backing of his community began to falter. As Jonathan Mayhew, a Boston minister and friend to Lemuel Briant, reported in a letter, while there were those in the village who remained "generally well-satisfied with Him . . . [others] indeed give heed to the evil Reports which his wife spread concerning him."[11]

Stories began to circulate through the village in the summer of 1752 that Reverend Briant was not only a bad husband but he also failed as a minister because was too "jocular and liberal." As John Adams, now sixteen years old and a sophomore at Harvard, described it, "a Controversy was carried on between Mr. Bryant the Minister of our Parish and some of his People, partly on Account of his Principles which were called Arminian and partly on Account of his Conduct, which was too gay and light if not immoral."[12]

In December 1752, members of the North Parish Church called for a meeting to consider the behavior of their pastor; the council was held at the home of Deacon Adams. While a few of the attendees complained of Briant's "gross Errors of Arminianism" (alleging that Briant called into question accepted doctrines of original sin and the total depravity of humanity), arguments flew back and forth as to whether the young man had committed heresy. No resolution could be reached, and the council adjourned until January.

When they met again in the new year, once again convening in the home of Deacon Adams, one of the members of the church council accused Reverend Briant of mistreatment of his wife, along with "intemperance, gaming, neglect of family duties."[13] But again, no agreement could be reached as to the question of his heresy or how to deal with him.

John Adams was disturbed by the "Spirit of Dogmatism and Bigotry" that pervaded the debate over Briant.[14] Like his father, and like Reverend Briant, John believed "good deeds were more important than faith."[15] But many in the town, including John's uncle, Ebenezer Adams, ignored the many kindnesses and liberality of Reverend Briant and focused instead on Briant's attacks on accepted Protestant theology, his too-joyous demeanor, and his lack of humility.

Finally, in the spring of 1753, the North Parish Church appointed a new council to review the charges against Briant and decide once and for all what to do with him. This council was chaired by John Quincy, master of Mount Wollaston and cousin to Edmund and Josiah. Quincy and his committee did not take long to complete their assigned task. They cleared Briant of all charges of heresy and, furthermore, supported his continued ministry of the North Parish Church.

Most important, the Braintree Council proclaimed their commitment to a liberal theology that allowed differing interpretations of scripture, and that refused to demand "any particular Profession of a Minister's Faith at his Ordination." Even if a minister made "any such Profession, it could not destroy his Right of Private Judgment, nor be Obligatory upon him, any further than is Continued to appear to him agreeable to Reason and Scripture."[16]

In other words, men and women, gifted with reason and intelligence, had the right to assess for themselves the validity of church dogma and modify their behavior as they themselves saw fit and good.

This "right of private judgment" in spiritual matters would prove to be even more important to the colonists of Braintree when it came to political matters. If a church could lay down rules that, in the reasoned and reasonable opinion of a parishioner, might be best ignored, then a government that sought to bind its citizens in ways that the citizens found to be unjust could also be disobeyed. The colonists of this new world in which reason won out over dogma were coming to see that it was their right to interpret exactly what their obligations were to a government that, in their judgment, no longer deserved obedience or loyalty.

Reverend Briant, having fallen ill and now all alone in his parsonage (his wife having long gone), resigned from his pastoral duties at Braintree in October 1753. He was given a respectful send-off, organized by Edmund Quincy, in "thanks for his labors in the ministry among us." He died a year later in Boston at the age of thirty-three.[17]

After taking his share of the bounty earned with the capture of the *Jesus Maria and Joseph*, Josiah ended the business partnership with his brother and brother-in-law, and the firm of Quincy, Quincy, and Jackson closed its doors. Josiah wanted to settle down and become a country squire. First, he would find suitable furnishings for a new house, and then he would move back to his native village, set up some businesses there (glassmaking and cider-pressing for starters), and become involved in local politics.

Josiah took his time going through the Boston warehouses, picking out furniture to bring to the planned country estate in Braintree. Most of the fine pieces he chose had been imported from England—chairs and tables, even tiles for the fireplace. When he saw a grand Japanned chest, over seven feet tall on long, elegant legs, he knew he had to have it. The chest had been crafted in Boston and was decorated with deeply lacquered scenes depicting pastoral views of open skies, flying birds, and lazily grazing sheep; these were the country views he longed for.

Having inherited more than two hundred acres from his father, lands set high on a hill overlooking the bay and continuing down to the marshy coastline, Josiah considered building a new home for his family. But in the end, he chose to live on the green in the village, taking over the Hancock parsonage from the departing Reverend Briant. The handsome old home where John Hancock had spent his early years would never serve as a parsonage again.

4

The Education of Girls

If we mean to have Heroes,
Statesmen and philosophers,
We should have learned women.

—ABIGAIL QUINCY

Abigail Smith was just a baby the first time she came to Braintree, carried by her mother from Weymouth to meet her grandparents, Elizabeth and John Quincy. As she grew into a girl, Abigail came frequently on her own to the village. Walking the four miles to see her "merry and chatty" grandmother, she passed up hill and down in eager anticipation of the final ascent to the Quincy mansion overlooking the bay.[1] She stayed at Mount Wollaston for weeks at a time, spending her "early, wild, and giddy days" there, under the tutelage of her adoring and encouraging grandmother.[2]

As Abigail later wrote, she "chiefly lived during the early period of my life" with her grandmother, from whom she learned "many good Rules and Maxims."[3]

Her parents, Reverend William Smith and his wife, Elizabeth Quincy Smith, taught their children—one boy and three girls—to exercise decorum, principle, and prudence in their behavior. Mrs. Smith wrote to her son Billy, "As soon as you were capable of reasoning, you [were] treated like a reasonable creature—when anything was demanded of you, the reason was given."[4]

The children were expected to think beyond their own interests and desires in helping those in need, including the sick, the impoverished, and all those who had lost hope. Mrs. Smith was known throughout Weymouth for her acts of kindness that "at once promoted the publick Good, and that of Individuals, by the best kind of Charity."[5] To be of use in the community, to be respected in the community: these were the important attributes of a pastor and his family.

Reverend Smith had steered his congregation carefully through the turbulence brought on by the New Lights controversy. From the pulpit, he rejected the hysteria and the rigidity of the revivalist ministers, but he never refuted their sermons supporting the basic tenets of Congregational dogma.

Having observed the proceedings in Braintree against Reverend Briant, Reverend Smith's goal was to preserve peace in the Weymouth community and to also ensure his continued position there. His appreciative congregation listened as he preached forgiveness and grace and warned against gossip and idleness. Rationality and calm was the underlying spirit of everything Reverend Smith and his wife did in their community and in their home.

But while her parents taught lessons of charity, propriety, and reason, it was from her grandmother, Elizabeth Quincy—and her "happy method of mixing instruction and amusement together"[6]—that Abigail learned to embrace her natural rebelliousness and also to steady it with discipline and determination. Her parents might have complained about Abigail's "volatile giddy disposition," but her grandmother praised her spirit, for "wild colts make the best horses."[7] She understood that Abigail, like herself, saw nothing wrong in having a good time while also doing good work: life was not just to be endured but to be enjoyed.

These "excellent lessons which I received from my grandmother" were never forgotten: "I frequently think they made a more durable impression upon my mind, than those which I received from my own parents," Abigail would write later. Grandmother and granddaughter shared the same "lively, cheerful disposition," but what most impressed young Abigail, along with her grandmother's "unaffected piety," was her ability to be both good-natured and strong-willed; her grandmother was kind and cheerful but also exerted an "inflexible adherence to certain principles."[8] Abigail herself would be praised for both her generosity and her determination in the years to come.

During young Abigail's solo visits to Braintree, she also visited with her cousins, the sons and daughters of Edmund and Josiah Quincy. Of all her cousins, she admired Josiah's daughter, Hannah, most of all. Although Hannah was eight years older than Abigail, they were very much alike, both lively and bright and, like Abigail's grandmother, bold and forthright.

When Hannah's mother died in August 1755, at the end of a cool, damp summer, little Abigail was there to offer her older cousin whatever comfort she could. But Hannah's carefree days were over. At the age of nineteen, she had to become caregiver for her father and her twelve-year-old brother, Josiah Jr., who was often sickly, and also the caretaker of the parsonage on the green. Even when her father remarried in 1757, Hannah's duties continued, and in fact increased: with the arrival of her half-sibling,

Elizabeth, she now had a baby to care for, and also the girl's mother, who had fallen ill after the birth.

In the early spring of 1759, Josiah Quincy's home, the old parsonage, caught on fire. Although no one was hurt, Josiah Quincy was devastated by the loss of furnishings, books, and other treasures. John Adams, who had known Josiah his whole life, wrote in his diary, "That house and furniture clung and twined around his heart, and could not be torn away without tearing to the quick."[9] When just a few months later, Josiah's second wife, Elizabeth Waldron Quincy, died, despair descended upon Josiah and his household.

Josiah found a new home for his diminished family, and Hannah once more was left in charge of setting up the household and caring for all its inhabitants; her father, her younger brother Josiah, and the baby Elizabeth depended upon her. A few years later, this house too would burn down, and once again, the family would have to move. But in the meantime, Hannah would do her best to create a warm and attractive home for her father, her younger siblings, and the brothers who often came to Braintree to stay.

Ned, Hannah's oldest brother, was a merchant in Boston, and Samuel was now a lawyer, having apprenticed law with Benjamin Pratt, a one-legged, opinionated, but esteemed practitioner who taught his protégé well. Ned and Sam came to Braintree frequently and often brought along friends to enjoy a long weekend in the country. The gathered young people stayed up late, playing cards or backgammon, talking and laughing, and partaking of ample selections of wine or punch. Come Sunday, all drinking and playing were suspended; Sabbath was reserved for sermons, contemplation, and a large midday meal.

As a vivacious and smart young woman, Hannah held court among her brothers and their friends, along with her cousins Esther, Katy, and Sarah, daughters of Edmund Quincy (little Dolly, still a child, was not invited to these evening get-togethers). The young men and women paired off, stealing away to a side room, "and there laughed and screamed and kissed and hussled," then returning to the gathered company of friends, "glowing like furnaces."[10] When the weather was fine, the couples ventured outdoors, to a "sylvan spot" called "Cupid's Grove," where all sorts of romancing went on.[11]

Even John Hancock occasionally ventured out from Boston and its swirl of social events to join in the parties in Braintree. The House of Hancock had grown ever more prosperous with every passing year, and now John was in the thick of it, working side by side with his uncle. Still, he made time for his old playmates from childhood, especially fun-loving Sam and the still stodgy John Adams.

John Adams had first moved to Worcester following graduation from Harvard, working as a schoolteacher but then switching to law and studying under James Putnam, a Worcester lawyer. Through the law John hoped to finally rise to the social and economic position he felt he deserved: "What are the Motives, that ought to urge me to hard study? The Desire of Fame, Fortune and personal Pleasure."[12]

Ever ambitious, John had a habit of castigating himself for lost opportunities, and then rededicating himself to all work and no play. While he was still in Worcester studying law, he wrote to Sam Quincy, "I shudder . . . when the thought comes into my mind how many million hours I have squandered." He resolved to do better: "I every Day determine to begin a new Course of Life tomorrow."[13]

John moved back to Braintree in the fall of 1758, and in November, he and Samuel Quincy traveled to Boston together to be sworn in as lawyers. John was certain that his time had finally come to join with the ranks of the Quincys in both economic and social status: "to be plain, I am beginning Life anew. I have new Friendships to make, new Employments to follow, new Concerns, Prospects and Studies, opening before me."[14] He opened up his first law office in his father's home and began to seek out clients.

And yet there were distractions. John was "very fond of the society of females."[15] As eager as he was to succeed at the study of law, he wrote in his diary that "my mind is liable to be called off from Law, by a girl, a pipe, a poem, a love letter."[16]

Samuel Quincy welcomed John Adams into the evening get-togethers held at either the home of Josiah, his father, or of Edmund, his uncle. Sam had been well liked by his fellow students at Harvard, and now that he was starting out on a legal career, the lawyers and businessmen he met day-to-day liked him just as much. He was easygoing, witty, and kind.

As a child, Sam had suffered a terrible injury from a gunshot gone wrong and never picked up a gun again; he stayed away from sports, horseback riding, and other outdoor pursuits. Instead, he spent his free time, when he wasn't socializing with friends, reading volumes of classical poetry and writing his own verses on a variety of topics (including love, death, and Harvard), verses he freely and frequently shared with others.

Sam could talk for hours about anything, from the purpose of faith to a thorny legal issue, from the beauty of a summer evening to the terrors of an earthquake; he sprinkled all conversations with lines he'd memorized from poetry or ones he'd written himself, and often with more than a joke or two. He was happiest when talking late into the night or playing cards or listening to music, with a glass of punch at hand and in the company of as many lively men and women as he could bring together.

Sam's wide-ranging interests afforded him much pleasure but, in the eyes of John Adams, little achievement. What was the use of all this scribbling of verse, this chattering and laughing with friends, these hours spent at leisure, when there was work to be done? After returning home from an evening with the Quincys, Adams complained of all that time spent "playing cards, drinking punch and wine, smoking tobacco . . . while a hundred of the best books lie on the shelves. . . . What pleasure can a young man who is capable of thinking, take in playing cards?"[17] He wrote that "Cards, Fiddles, and Girls are the objects of Sam [Quincy]. Cards, Fiddles, and Girls. Kissing, Fiddling and gaming. A flute, a Girl, and a Pack of Cards."[18]

By the summer of 1759, Hannah Quincy knew the time had come to find a husband. She suspected that her father had begun looking for a new wife, and she didn't relish the idea of once again having to accustom herself to a stepmother or becoming nursemaid to more half-sibling babies. Although in public she claimed that "she would not be married by any means, these 4 or 5 years," she began to dream of having a home of her own—and for that she needed a husband. [19]

Anthony Wibird, the newly installed minister of the North Parish Church, was one candidate; he was intelligent and seemed kind, but he was also gawky and walked strangely, and his wig was always crooked upon his head. The friends of her brothers provided other likely suitors, and she toyed with each of them, not sure which young man was the best choice.

Bela Lincoln was tall, dark, and stern, a medical doctor with a good career ahead of him. As the son of an old friend of Hannah's father, he was a favorite of her family. Jonathan Sewall, a classmate of Sam's from Harvard, was poor but handsome and fun-loving; he was also a rising star in the legal world and had plenty of potential.

John Adams, with his chipmunk cheeks and beady eyes, was the sturdy and serious local boy Hannah had known for years; he was eager to spend any time he could with Hannah, and she basked in his attentions. And John, in turn, was infatuated with Hannah. Not only was she pretty and witty and gracious, but she was a Quincy, with all that name implied.

John craved the respect of others and worried that his own hard work wasn't enough to earn him what he wanted. He had been jealous of Sam's prestigious apprenticeship under Benjamin Pratt and was heartily insulted when, upon meeting Pratt, the old lawyer had dismissed him as unimportant, stating simply, "no Body in this County knows any Thing about you."[20] Now Sam Quincy had a position in Boston, where he enjoyed working "in the most busy office, in the Center of one of the best Libraries, and under the Instructions and Advice of One of the Ablest Masters in America," while he, John, worked out of a corner in his father's home.[21]

Nevertheless, despite both his disapproval and his envy, John grudgingly admired Sam for being an "easy, social, and benevolent companion, not without Genius, Elegance, and Taste."[22] He would later describe both Sam Quincy and Jonathan Sewall, whom he met through Sam, as two "of the most intimate Friends I ever had in my life."[23]

The young men stood beside one another during the at times frustrating practice of law and provided support during each other's romantic adventures. John Adams described his group as nourishing "the Wound [of love] in their Hearts . . . [consumed] with a hidden internal flame."[24]

Samuel, for all his flirtations, had begun seriously courting Hannah Hill, daughter of a wealthy Boston brewer, while Jonathan Sewall was falling for Esther Quincy. The two met on a boating party, and within just a few weeks, Sewall was sure she possessed every good quality, including "utmost pleasantness and good-Humour," "real Good Sense," "Delicacy of Manners and such becoming Modesty," as well having "as musical a Voice as Nature ever gave."[25]

While John Adams agreed with his friend Jonathan that Esther was "pert, sprightly, and gay,"[26] it was Hannah Quincy whom he adored: "that Face, those Eyes, that Shape, that familiar friendly look . . . I go to bed and lie ruminating . . . then fall asleep and dream . . . till morning Wakes me, and robs me of my Bliss."[27] And as cute as Esther might be, she "thinks and reads much less" than her cousin Hannah; to John, a woman who could both read and think was a treasure.[28]

Hannah teased John Adams but also invigorated him. She would offer hypotheticals to him—"Suppose you was in your Study, engaged in the Investigation of some Point of Law, or Philosophy, and your Wife should interrupt you accidentally and break the Thread of your Thoughts, so that you never could recover it?"—and then wait for his response, as if auditioning him for the role of husband.

John answered as best he could—"No man, but a crooked Richard, would blame his Wife, for such an accidental Interruption"—and waited for the next question.

"Should you like to spend your Evenings, at Home in reading and conversing with your Wife, rather than to spend them abroad in Taverns or with other Company?" Hannah demanded.

John answered, "Should prefer the Company of an agreable Wife, to any other Company for the most Part."

And finally, Hannah asked, "Suppose you had been abroad, and came home fatigued and perplexed, with Business, or came out of your Study, wearied and perplexed with Study, and your Wife should meet you with an unpleasant, or an inattentive face, how should you feel?"

"I would flee my Country, or she should."[29]

Deacon Adams warned John about his public pursuit of Hannah Quincy and the gossip that would result. John wrote in his diary, "the story has spread so wide that if I don't marry her, she will be said to have Jockied me. . . . A story will be spread, that she repelled me."[30] But Hannah would make a good partner, of that Adams was certain: "Good nature is H's universal character. She will be a fond, tender Wife and a fond indulgent mother."[31]

One evening in the summer of 1759, on a day when Bela Lincoln, another of Hannah's suitors, was away attending his patients in Hingham, John Adams almost proposed to Hannah. The two of them were alone in a quiet corner of the Quincy home, and the moment seemed to be right; as John wrote later, they were having the "conversation that would have terminated in a courtship . . . [and then] terminated in a Marriage."[32]

But just as he was about to speak, Esther Quincy and Jonathan Sewall burst through the door from the outside, where they had been walking together in the moonlit gardens. Their arms entwined, they announced their own happy engagement. John wrote later, "the Accident [interruption] separated us, and gave room to Lincoln's addresses. . . . and left me at liberty, if I will but mind my studies, of making a Character and a fortune."[33] Bela Lincoln asked Hannah to marry him just days after, and Hannah agreed.

John Adams wrote later (but never explained his statement) that marriage with Hannah would "have depressed me to absolute poverty and obscurity to the end of my life."[34] Perhaps he thought that operating under the shadow of her brothers, Ned, Sam, and the younger Josiah, he would have never emerged as his own man.

Having lost his Hannah, John once again resolved that he would make goals and stick to them; he vowed to dedicate himself to "the Prosecution of my studies. Now Let me form the great Habits of Thinking, Writing, Speaking. . . . Let Love and Vanity be extinguished and the great passions of Ambition, Patriotism, break out and burn."[35]

For all his new resolutions, however, another young woman intruded on John Adams' plans. John met Abigail Smith through his new friend, Richard Cranch, an acquaintance of Sam Quincy's who happened to be courting Abigail's older sister, Mary. Cranch had come to Massachusetts in 1746 at the age of twenty, well-schooled in the classics but ill-prepared to make a living. He was currently on his fourth business venture, this one in watchmaking, and failing just as miserably as he had failed in his previous attempts: making metal combs for wool carding; glassmaking; and creating candles from whale oil.

Despite his poor business acumen, Richard was one of the most intelligent men John had ever met, and one of the kindest. They would be lifelong friends.

Richard Cranch was a great favorite of Reverend William Smith of Weymouth and his children, and he thought highly of them in return. He'd fallen in love with Mary, but he also admired Mary's younger sister, Abigail, for her capacious wit, her intelligence, and her common sense. John Adams saw how much Richard liked the Smith daughters, and he had heard good things about Abigail through her older cousin, Hannah Quincy.

But John's first impressions of Abigail and Mary were not favorable: "Parson Smith's Girls have not . . . fondness, nor . . . Tenderness . . . [nor are they] candid."[36] Adams defined "candid" to be "a Disposition to palliate faults and Mistakes, to put the best Construction upon Words and Actions, and to forgive Injuries."[37] Being a man woefully concerned with being both understood and esteemed, the ability to make generous and forgiving assessments of character was a quality John sought in a potential mate.

As John spent more and more time with Richard and the Smith girls, however, he began to appreciate Abigail. She was still the feisty—John termed her "saucy"—girl favored by her grandmother, but John came to value her forthright and honest assessments.[38] She might not be "candid" under his definition, but she was honest, and a compliment from her meant more for being both sincere and, in John's eyes, well founded. Finally, a woman who understood him!

Not only was she smart but she was also cheerful, optimistic, and seemingly unflappable. Compared to his own moody and overwrought mother, and to Hannah, who had veered from suitor to suitor with her favors week to week, Abigail was the epitome of stability and grace.

"Ballast is what I want. I totter with every breeze," John wrote in his diary a year before meeting Abigail.[39] Continuing the boat metaphor, a few months later he added, "The only Thing I fear is, that all my Passions which . . . are the Gales of Life . . . will go down into an everlasting Calm. And what will [I do] if there is no Wind?"[40]

Abigail could provide the ballast for his boat, and the wind for his sails as well. John became smitten with her. Soon enough, Abigail would return the sentiment.

5

Changing Fortunes

Chimerical Happy World . . .

—EDMUND QUINCY V

Edmund Quincy declared bankruptcy in 1757. All the wealth he had gained by the capture of the Spanish treasure ship in 1748 was gone. The money had been spent through prodigious consumption and lost with what seemed to be a complete lack of business sense. Homes had been splendidly furnished, gardens made gorgeous, libraries filled with all sorts of books and manuscripts. But while money went out the door, none came back in.

After Quincy, Quincy, and Jackson closed its doors, the firm that Edmund ran with his two sons, Edmund V and Henry, never flourished. They bought items no one wanted, and the goods they supplied were often subpar. Jonathan Belcher, governor of New Jersey, complained that the supposedly "odorless" candles he bought from the Quincy firm had "as nauseous a Stink as any other Whale Oil"—and he no longer did any business with Edmund and his sons, nor did anyone who listened to Belcher's counsel.[1]

By the time Edmund declared bankruptcy, his house in Braintree had been mortgaged to Edward Jackson, his brother-in-law and former business partner. Jackson generously allowed Edmund and his family to continue living there, but when Jackson died, the house was put up for sale and the family had to move. Edmund still owned a house in Boston, but that property was on the market, to be sold to pay off debts, along with the family slaves and most of the household goods. An auction was scheduled and catalogs for the sale were drawn up. Edmund's libraries were so extensive that a separate auction catalog was created for all of the books he owned—and now needed to sell.

To all appearances, Edmund IV seemed largely unperturbed by the loss of his wealth. As John Adams wrote, "Quincy took his 'complete reduction'

quite calmly. That the event was impending [for some time] was one reason, and that Edmund was an unusually religious man, another."[2] Edmund
continued to rely on his faith in God: "nothing happens in these transient
moments but what is destined to prepare us for an everlasting life. What can
discourage a soul professed with this noble idea?"[3]

He simply went on with his life, making plans for future business endeavors, including the growing of grapes for wine, running a cider press, and
managing his own shop selling beer and liquors in the city. From his good
friend Ben Franklin, he received encouragement and advice. Ben had endured
his own money troubles, as well as pitfalls in the growing of grapes for wine,
and he wrote to Edmund, "I heartily wish you Success in your attempts to
make Wine from American Grapes."[4]

Edmund moved with his wife and daughters to modest lodgings in Boston. But they often returned to Braintree to stay with various members of the
Quincy clan. With Esther engaged to Jonathan Sewall, there were still three
unmarried daughters to marry off, and the Quincy parties were the most
likely avenues for finding suitable matches. Sarah Quincy became engaged
to William Greenleaf in the early 1760s; like her sister Esther, her engagement period was a long one, and the four Quincy girls—Katy, Esther, Sally,
and Dolly—("remarkable for their beauty") continued to be known as the
"lovely daughters" always ready for family parties and outings.[5]

The 1761 summer wedding of Samuel Quincy to Hannah Hill was just
such a party. Young women dressed up in white muslin embroidered with
flowers; the men paraded in brushed linen coats, their cravats brilliant in
the sunshine. John Adams wrote to Sam before the big event wishing him
great happiness with "joyful expectations of approaching wedlock"—and
he would have been invited to the celebration.[6] Abigail Smith, cousin to
Sam, would also have been in attendance, along with her sisters and Richard
Cranch, John Adams' close friend and her sister Mary's beau.

Although Josiah Quincy and his family wanted Sam's sister, Hannah, to
attend, their affection for Bela Lincoln, now her husband, had long faded.
Within just months of Hannah and Bela's wedding in May 1760, her family
realized that Lincoln was a beast. His treatment of her displayed both "Brutality and Rusticity"—in other words, he berated and bullied her, and most
likely physically abused her as well—but there was little they could do about
it.[7] Hannah had hoped for so much in marrying Lincoln but found herself
abused and degraded as his wife.

John Adams felt powerless to protect the woman he had once dreamed about. He wrote with vehemence in his diary, "A hoggish, ill bred, uncivil, haughty Coxcomb, as ever I saw. . . . His treatment of his wife amazed me. . . . Bela really acts the Part of the Tamer of the Shrew in Shakespeare." He lamented that Hannah's beauty and wit were fading, and she was "sunk into silence and shame, and Grief."[8]

The match of Sam Quincy and Hannah Hill was much happier, founded on mutual attraction and a shared appreciation for the finer things in life. When Sam arranged for Hannah's portrait to be painted by John Singleton Copley, the esteemed Boston portraitist, he worked with the artist to make sure his wife was presented "in the vanguard of taste," wearing "rich and sensuous" clothes that, while "exotic and alluring," aligned with Sam's views on appropriate female attire.[9] Although Sam liked to have a good time, he was no libertine and he preferred his women to dress modestly, while stylishly. As a poet he also appreciated symbolism, and while Hannah was sitting for the portrait, he brought her a sprig of larkspur to hold, symbol of "ardent attachment."[10]

Six years later, Sam Quincy had his portrait painted by Copley as well. He was dressed as a Crown lawyer, wearing the wig and black robe donned by all barristers admitted to the bar in England. While the uniform indicated his status, Quincy's affable expression and casual pose indicated that he was also "a man of urbanity, style, and charm."[11]

The two paintings hung side by side in Sam and Hannah's mansion on the fashionable South Street in Boston, alongside other paintings and treasures that Hannah's father had given them. Josiah Quincy gave the newly married couple a gift of property, four hundred acres in Lincoln, a farming village not far from Braintree; it was an appreciated source of extra income for the young couple with expensive tastes.

John Hancock was not present at the wedding of his old friend Sam Quincy. He was away in England, sent there by his uncle Thomas and aunt Lydia with two goals in mind. The first goal, a desire harbored by Aunt Lydia, was that her handsome and elegant nephew might achieve a final polish of British etiquette and fashion; the second goal, Uncle Thomas' wish, was to introduce John to the foreign agents and markets, both in England and on the continent, upon which the House of Hancock depended.

John went through a large cache of spending money in England, having himself a good time at the English court among the wealthy and the noble, and buying himself all the latest fashions for his evenings out. As he wrote to his uncle, trying to explain away the high expenses he was incurring, "I am not Remarkable for the Plainness of my Dress. . . . Upon proper occasions I dress as genteel as any one and cant say I am without Lace. . . . I find money some way or other goes very fast, but I think I can reflect it has been spent with satisfaction and to my own honor."[12]

In addition to outfitting himself to the degree desired by his aunt, and learning to swim in the Thames (a skill he hadn't mastered while living in America), John was also busy making the necessary rounds to the overseas agents of the House of Hancock. Going from office to office, in London, Bristol, and Manchester, and traveling to firms in Amsterdam and Hamburg, John met the men responsible for keeping goods and moneys flowing into the accounts of the House of Hancock.

By and large young Hancock impressed these men with his "agreeable" character: "he is a very worthy, well-disposed young gentleman" was the report back to Thomas.[13] John successfully secured lucrative contracts for his uncle's firm both in England and on the continent, including another contract with the Crown for supplying the needs of British troops in Nova Scotia.

During the year that John spent in England, he certainly enjoyed its pleasures and charms, but he did not succumb to them; he remained a Braintree village boy at heart. Unlike other colonial travelers to the mother country, John never felt envy for what the English had, nor did he attempt to ingratiate himself with the English gentry or try to portray himself as more than what he was, a young man from America.

Whereas Thomas had laid claim to a coat of arms, John wasn't interested in becoming noble or pretending to be. Being rich, well-dressed, and social was more than enough for him. When he fell ill and was cared for by a woman of the lower classes, John took her out for tea and meals; later he would be chided in the press for socializing below himself but John did not care. The woman was young, pretty, and kind—and again, that was enough for John.

He missed Massachusetts while he was away, writing to a cousin that he was eager to return to "the more substantial pleasures . . . in the enjoyment of my friends in America . . . whom I prefer to the showy and . . . superficial, flattering sincerity of many here." To his uncle Thomas, John swore that while "a man of fortune might live here as happy as possible . . . for me . . . the greatest estate in England would be but a poor temptation . . . to spend my days here."[14] The Braintree-born boy was ready to come home. He would never leave America again.

When John arrived back in Boston in the fall of 1762, he was met by a much-aged Thomas. His uncle suffered from gout, along with "a nervous disorder" and fatigue.[15] The firm's business was becoming more than he could handle—he was "Just Creeping about pretty poorly"—and the time had come to pass the mantle on to John.[16] He put his newly returned nephew in charge of many aspects of the House of Hancock, from managing the ledgers and account books to drawing up plans for future contracts and building new ships to meet those contracts.

John took on the work with diligence and energy. He offered Thomas the rest and respite he needed, and through his hard work, assured his uncle that he had taught his nephew well. In January 1763, Thomas made John— then twenty-six years old—a partner in his firm and changed the name to Thomas Hancock and Company.[17]

Thomas wasn't the only one impressed with young Hancock. John was invited to join the Masonic Lodge of St. Andrews in Boston, whose members included such prominent citizens as his old neighbor Josiah Quincy, the lawyer James Otis Jr., and Dr. Joseph Warren, a man a few years younger than John, who would become one of his closest friends.

Around this time, John was also invited to become a member of the Long Room Club, a secret society recently formed by Sam Adams, cousin to John Adams but from a previously wealthier side of the family. The purpose of the Long Room Club was to discuss colonial politics. Warren was a member, along with James Otis Jr., Dr. Benjamin Church, and the silversmith Paul Revere.

John Adams, an exacting observer of the work habits of others, took note of Hancock's diligence in business; he wrote that Hancock was "an example to all the young men of the town. Wholly devoted to business, he was regular and punctual at his store as the sun in his course."[18] But as devoted to the firm as John might be, he was also a man who liked to go out with his friends, drinking, talking, and playing at cards. He wanted men to like him, and he was as good at charming the merchants, shipbuilders, and sailors who came by the office during the day as he was at befriending the lawyers, politicians, journeymen, and craftsmen with whom he passed his evenings.

While Thomas was satisfied that John could manage the House of Hancock (as it was still called by many), Lydia became concerned that the social life of her nephew needed some direction, specifically in the nature of female companionship. There were rumors going around of John's involvement with a female tenant on Hancock's Wharf who was a purveyor of liquor, groceries, linen drapery—and possibly sexual favors. Whatever the truth of the rumors, it must have been a relief to Lydia when John took notice of the sister of one of his oldest friends.

John first saw Dorothy Quincy coming out of church one Sunday in the early summer of 1764. From that point on, he made it a point of frequently stopping by the Braintree home of Josiah Quincy Sr., where Dolly and her sisters were often visitors. Dolly was seventeen years old, Hancock was ten years older. Both were slim and of good height for their time; judging by their portraits later painted by Copley, with their high foreheads, dark eyes, and slender lips, the two might have been siblings.

From all accounts, the feelings between the good-looking pair were amiable from the start. But it would be more than a few years before a formal attachment was made.

King George III ascended the throne in October 1760. Toasts were made to his health throughout the British colonies, but John Adams' first mention of the new king already raised the specter of rebellion, in a message he sent to Abigail via her sister Mary. He had become close with all of Abigail's sisters but was especially warm with Mary, owing to her impending marriage to Richard Cranch, one of John's best friends.

In the message John warned "Mrs. Nabby" (as he teasingly called Abigail) against becoming "a most loyal subject to young George," for if Abigail were to show too much favor to George, "altho my Allegiance has been hitherto inviolate I shall endeavour, all in my Power to foment Rebellion."[19]

How true those words would be, he could not possibly know. But from that date on, love letters flowed between John and Abigail, with no intermediary required. He called her his "Miss Adorable," and she professed herself bound to him by "a three-fold chord," of humanity, friendship, and physical attraction.[20]

They began to spend as much time as they could together, John traveling back and forth to Weymouth, and Abigail coming to stay with her grandparents in Braintree. Their affection was deep and physical, with "two or three millions at least" of kisses exchanged by the fall of 1762.[21]

They flirted by mail, John demanding "as many Kisses and as many Hours of your company . . . as he [John] shall please,"[22] and Abigail replying in kind, as she began her letters with the endearment of "My Friend," a term of considerable intimacy in the eighteenth century, and ended with "Accept this hasty scrawl warm from my heart."[23]

Abigail's mother, proud of being from the Quincy family, had reservations about the suitability of John, son of a yeoman farmer. Abigail's father also opposed the match. He hated all lawyers, so much so that he refused to allow the horse of a lawyer to stable in his barn. When John came to visit the Smith family in Weymouth, he had to tie his horse up by the roadside. But the young couple persevered, hoping that in time the older Smiths would come to appreciate John as much as the younger ones did.

In the spring of 1761, the scourge of influenza that had been ravaging the colony passed through the village of Braintree. Both of John's parents fell ill. His father died in May; although his mother recovered, "being younger than my Father and possessed of a stronger constitution," she was still too sick at the time to attend her husband's funeral service. "It was a melancholy time in our house," John wrote later.[24] The home John had grown up in passed to his older brother, while John inherited the smaller house next door, along with forty acres of land.

Having become a property owner, John was now a member of the town of Braintree, entitled to vote at town meetings and partake in town politics. In his new status as landed citizen, he set about renovating the house he had inherited. He added a door where the kitchen window had been and converted the old kitchen into a sizable law office and library, while the kitchen was moved to a lean-to. The office was kept warm through the long, cold Braintree winters by the large hearth and bright all year long with its south-facing windows.

With a fine standing desk in one corner, an etching or two framed and hung above the fireplace, and shelves of books along the walls, John hoped his new office would impress clients. But first, he had to plot a course of action that would keep the office bustling.

Since he'd been admitted to the bar in 1758, cases had come his way but success had not. After losing his first lawsuit, a very public case of trespass with Josiah Quincy presiding as justice of the peace and Sam Quincy representing the defendant, John had despaired of his reputation: "It will be said, I undertook the Case but was unable to manage it . . . An opinion will spread among the People that I have not Cunning enough."[25]

John realized that his new status as town member offered him an opportunity to highlight his legal skills. He decided to align himself with the growing temperance movement in Braintree as a way of demonstrating his lawyerly abilities as well as—he hoped—solidifying his financial footing. The number of licensed inns in Braintree had proliferated in the 1750s, and the number of public drunks had likewise increased. John campaigned to limit the number of licenses to three and won the approval of the Braintree board of selectmen.

With his public profile raised, and in such a positive way (the measure had been largely supported by the townsfolk), the number of John's clients increased tenfold. Most of his clients were farmers, unable to pay big fees, but his legal career was well on its way. He would have to wait a number of years before he could marry Abigail, but the objections of her family would no longer be financial.

Jonathan Sewall was also finding his way as a lawyer. If he hoped to set a wedding date with Esther Quincy, he needed to become financially stable, especially now that Esther's father had lost his fortune and there was little that Esther could bring to the marriage. The path to that financial security came about through an unexpected alliance with Thomas Hutchinson, a wealthy lawyer with great ambitions for himself and the colony. Hutchinson would become a leading Loyalist and was already firmly aligned with Parliament and the Crown.

Hutchinson was named chief justice of the Massachusetts Supreme Court in 1760, taking the place of Jonathan's uncle, Stephen Sewall, who had died in the influenza epidemic. After his uncle's death, Jonathan discovered that the older man was bankrupt and had left many outstanding debts. Jonathan tried to have his uncle's debts paid by the provincial government, but his petitions for payment went nowhere, in large part due to the objections of James Otis Jr., a prominent Boston lawyer. Sewall swore enmity to Otis. Meanwhile, Otis had come to despise Hutchinson, because he believed his father should have been made chief justice, and not Hutchinson. Hutchinson in turn disdained Otis as a troublemaker. This triangle of dislike would play an important role in Jonathan Sewall's fortunes.

As a challenge to Hutchinson's new authority as chief justice, in 1761 James Otis Jr. brought a petition to the court, challenging the use of writs of assistance as a countermeasure against smuggling. The writs were a kind of general search warrant, easily issued and often violently enforced, that allowed royally appointed customs officials to search colonial property (ships and warehouses) and seize property deemed to be contraband.

Hutchinson, as chief justice, believed the writs were perfectly legal under English law, but Otis, arguing on behalf of the sixty-three merchants he represented, described the writs as "the worst instrument of arbitrary power, the most destructive of English liberty and the fundamental principles of law, that was ever found."[26] If the writs were allowed to stand, Otis predicted that the privilege of being safe in one's home would "be annihilated."[27]

Lawyers for the Crown's customs officials argued that use of the writs had been granted by Parliament and could not be taken away; colonial courts were well within their rights to issue such warrants and demand compliance with them, again under the authority granted to them by Parliament. Led by Chief Justice Hutchinson, the court ruled for the Crown officials and affirmed the legality of the writs of assistance across Massachusetts. Otis' petition was denied and the use of writs to search and seize goods of colonial merchants continued.

Protests broke out throughout Boston. For many, if not most, colonists, the sanctity of the home was protected under English law against marauding powers of Crown-approved officials. Hutchinson's decision was illegal, in their opinion. Hutchinson might have won the day in court, but as he watched the protests in the streets, he realized that objections to royal authority, not only in cases involving the search warrants but others as well, would continue if he did not step in to tamp down unrest in the colony. He sought out young lawyers who would defer to Parliament and were loyal to the Crown, in order to build up legal support for his own authority. Jonathan Sewall, being both a lawyer and a public enemy of Otis, was just the man to be courted over to Hutchinson's side.

After the conclusion of the writs of assistance case, during which Sewall had publicly supported the Crown, Hutchinson began sending prestigious and well-paying clients to Sewall. Sewall was an excellent lawyer, as his close friend John Adams attested to later: "Mr. Sewall had a soft, insinuating eloquence, which, gliding imperceptibly into the minds of a jury, gave him as much power over that tribunal as any lawyer ought ever to possess. . . . He was a gentleman and a scholar, had a fund of wit, humor, and satire, which he used with great discretion at the bar."[28]

But talented or not, it was only through the patronage of Hutchinson that Sewall had well-heeled clients knocking on his door—and Sewall knew it. Both his reputation and his client list grew, and for this he owed Hutchinson both deference and loyalty. It was all that Hutchinson had hoped for. Both men were happy: Sewall was earning a good income and could now marry Esther, and Hutchinson gained a strong legal mind in his corner to defend his actions as chief justice of Massachusetts.

In 1764, Jonathan Sewall and Esther Quincy were married. Edmund and his wife, Elizabeth, presided over a splendid party, largely paid for by their new son-in-law; all of Braintree society, and much of Boston's, came out to celebrate the nuptials. The couple moved into a fine house in Charlestown, and three years later, through the machinations of Hutchinson, Jonathan Sewall was named attorney general for the colony.

The writs of assistance case set the path that Jonathan Sewall would follow in the years to come, during which he supported all acts and measures taken by the British government in governing the colonies. But it also laid the paths of his friends, who would come to oppose the British government while fighting to uphold the rights of colonists.

John Adams had followed the writs case closely and went with Sam Quincy to watch as Otis made his arguments before the court. Both men heard the prophetic words spoken when Otis warned that arbitrary use of governmental power "in former periods of history cost one king of England his head and another his throne."[29]

It was only years later that John Adams understood the significance of the case decided that day in 1761: "Then and there the Child of Independence was born."[30] Lines were being drawn throughout the colony of Massachusetts and also among his friends.

The lines could be understood as questions: What did liberty mean? What did loyalty mean? On the one side, liberty was the right of the colonists to govern themselves, and duty lay only to the colony. On the other side, liberty meant living under the British constitution, and loyalty meant fealty to Parliament and the king. Jonathan Sewall was the first to take a side; the others would soon follow.

6

Colonial Enthusiasms

If this be enthusiasm, we live and die enthusiasts.

—JOSIAH QUINCY JR.

Josiah Quincy Jr. was the youngest man ever invited to become a member of the Long Room Club. Although the exact date of his first attendance at the secret meetings is unknown, he most likely started coming after he graduated from Harvard in the summer of 1763. He was nineteen years old and had just begun his legal apprenticeship with the esteemed Boston lawyer Oxenbridge Thacher, who had participated with James Otis Jr. on the writs of assistance case. The speech Josiah Quincy Jr. gave at his commencement, titled "Liberty," must have convinced Sam Adams to introduce the young man to Adams' conclave of political zealots.

Josiah was the youngest son of Josiah Quincy Sr. and his first wife, Hannah Sturgis. As a boy, Josiah had been frail and spent much of his youth tucked away to convalesce with a stack of books. While his body rested, his mind raced. He read every kind of book offered by his father's and uncle's extensive libraries, and then branched out when he entered college, going through Harvard's library like a hawk through a row of pigeons. Whereas his older brother Samuel, along with Sam's friend John Hancock, had been punished in college for excessive drinking and partying, the only discipline Josiah might have incurred would have been excessive library fines.

During the years that the Quincy brothers, John Adams, and John Hancock were at Harvard, "two-fisted tippling was at its peak . . . at no other period in the history of the Cambridge institution has so much liquor been consumed per capita."[1] Even John Adams, ambitious and studious, drank a tankard of hard cider every morning at breakfast. But for the youngest Quincy, it was books and not booze that consumed his hours while at school.

In his senior year, the year when students were permitted to take books out of the Harvard library, Josiah Jr. checked out a wide array of publications: the essays of the sixteenth-century philosopher Michel de Montaigne; the seventeenth-century political histories of Clarendon; the works of the English poet Cowley; Daniel Turner's *Syphilis: A Practical Dissertation on the Venereal Disease*; the aphorisms of the seventeenth-century Venetian physician Sanctorius; the verses of Stephen Duck, a contemporary self-taught English poet; the works of Aristotle; and the essays of the seventeenth-century English philosopher Ralph Cudworth (*A Treatise Concerning Eternal and Immutable Morality*), the Benedictine monk Bernard de Montfaucon (*Antiquity Explained, and Represented in Sculptures*), and the physician John Pechey (*General Treatise of the Causes and Signs of All Diseases*).[2]

Josiah read all the plays of Shakespeare and copied out entire passages into small pamphlets called "quartos," filling seventy pamphlets in all. He titled his pamphlets *Beauties of Shakespeare* and memorized dozens of lines from every play.[3] But his favorite books, and the ones from which he again copied line after line after line, were the books that explored the history of law and legal systems dating back to the Greeks and Romans and its present manifestations in English common law.

There was no question that Josiah Jr. would become a lawyer. After college, he began the study of law under the careful watch of Oxenbridge Thacher, who, like his young student, was broadly educated and well-read. To aid in his studies, Josiah created his first *Law Commonplace* book. On the cover of the book, he copied a quote from David Hume: "From law arises security; from security curiosity; and from curiosity knowledge."[4]

This first book was where Josiah kept notes that guided him in the years to come, including a record of his favorite legal maxims from Justinian, the sixth-century Roman emperor who compiled and unified Roman law; Sir Edward Coke, seventeenth-century champion of common law and liberty; and Sir Edmund Plowden, lawyer to Queen Elizabeth and brilliant legal theorist. Josiah also kept centuries-old maxims reflecting common sense and natural law, such as "To each, one's own house is the safest refuge" and "That which is useful is not spoiled by that which is useless."[5]

In *Law Commonplace*, Josiah copied out detailed notes about court cases that he observed during his apprenticeship with Thacher as well as ones that he read about in other people's accounts. In the margins of his notes on the cases, he scribbled his own legal analyses, especially of the interesting cases, along with explanations of different methods used for arriving at legal decisions.

In his notebook, he referenced all the cases he studied according to what type of law or legal question they dealt with, from domestic law to contract law to criminal proceedings. In many ways, his *Law Commonplace* books (more were to come) were the first textbooks for what would become Harvard Law School's famous Socratic method of teaching law: questioning and analyzing every legal decision made to understand how the correct—or incorrect—decision was reached.

Although most of the other members of the Long Room Club were more interested in politics than law, Josiah Jr. fit right in. His mentor Thacher, and Thacher's partner on many cases, James Otis Jr., engaged young Quincy in debates concerning the rights of the colonists against an overreaching government—and that topic was fascinating to the older members.

Seated around the low room of the club, above the print shop of Edes and Gill, publishers of the *Boston Gazette*, the other men listened while the lawyers, and Sam Adams too, made their arguments back and forth, laying out the rights and privileges of the American colonists: to be free from search and seizure, to be represented in Parliament, to be taxed fairly, to be heard in a court of law that was impartial.

Josiah insisted that the best protection for the colonists of Massachusetts came from the rule of law, which applied to citizens as well as to the Crown and Parliament. No government stood above the law, no political party or judge or monarch was exempt, argued Quincy. Laws protecting individual freedoms were inviolate, and indeed, following such laws endowed the government with the ability to operate harmoniously and productively. It was good for everyone, Josiah insisted.

Josiah traced his ideals for what the law could and should do back to ancient Rome, then followed them straight through to "the best asylum, that Glorious Medium, the British Constitution!"[6] The British Constitution was composed of all accepted law in England, including the Magna Carta, the 1689 Bill of Rights, Acts of Parliament, court cases, and legal conventions. Josiah was certain that there was no system for promoting private and public rights, and guaranteeing freedom for all.

When politicians failed to live up to their duties under the British Constitution, Josiah argued, it was the right—no, the duty!—of citizens to protest, and demand that the politicians reform their ways: "In defence of our civil and religious rights, we dare oppose the world."[7]

It soon became apparent to everyone attending the Long Room Club meetings that Josiah Quincy Jr. would be the successor in every way to Thacher, whose health was in serious decline following a smallpox inoculation received a few years earlier. In his conversations and writings, Josiah was out-Whigging the older man, previously the most Whiggish of colonial lawyers. Human reason, individual liberty, universal rights: these were the hallmarks of Whig thought and the backbone of both Josiah's and Thacher's legal and political convictions.

In 1764, Parliament passed the Sugar Act, billed as a bolster to the Molasses Act of 1733 (which had been largely evaded by the colonies through widespread smuggling). The Sugar Act was just one of many designed by Parliament to refill the coffers of the British treasury following the huge expenses exacted by the Seven Years' War, which finally ended in 1763. England gained new territories in the war (including New France in Canada, Spanish Florida, and numerous islands in the Caribbean), but the war had incurred high debts and there were rising costs associated with running the newly expanded empire. Citizens in England couldn't be taxed nearly enough to cover all the debts and costs. Taxing the colonies was the answer.

Thacher and Josiah Jr. were at the forefront of protests against what they called Parliament's illegal "taxation without representation." Article Twelve of the Magna Carta, they argued, provided that "no scutage or aid is to be levied in our realm except by common counsel of our realm."[8] If England sought aid through taxes, then the colonists demanded their right to common counsel, that is, representation of their rights in Parliament.

"We cannot conceive that [we] have forfeited [our rights] by . . . emigrating a thousand leagues, subduing immense forests, . . . protecting . . . British subjects . . . & thereby enlarging the British empire & commerce," Thacher wrote in a widely distributed pamphlet. He concluded with the essential point: "Now we have ever supposed this to be one essential right of British subjects, that they shall not be subjected to taxes which, in person or by representative, they have no voice in laying."[9] Josiah Jr. spread the pamphlet far and wide, advising the citizens of Massachusetts to take notice: their rights as citizens of Britain were being threatened.

When Thacher died early in 1765, Josiah inherited his legal practice. He hung a prominent but simple sign outside the door of his new law offices, becoming the first lawyer in Boston to proclaim his profession in that way.

He continued to serve Thacher's old clients but also brought in new clients of his own—all the while continuing to write about and fight for the rights of colonists under British law.

As Josiah worked to build up his practice, his health once again faltered, as it had so often when he was a boy. He consulted a doctor, who gave him the terrible diagnosis of consumption (tuberculosis); his brother Ned had been afflicted by the same disease for the past few years. The illness caused Josiah to grow evermore pale and gaunt: he looked years older than he was, and he became prone to fainting spells along with fits of coughing.

Even in his consumptive state, Josiah exuded energy and confidence. When he entered a room, looking about with his crossed eyes and his wild curls flung back, people paid attention. And when he spoke, people listened. His reasoning was clear, and his voice "was like the music of the spheres; soft and melodious, yet powerful, clear, and distinct. He had a tenor voice . . . and could be heard to the farthest verge of the most crowded assembly."[10] Josiah began to collect admirers, and his reputation for speaking truth to power grew.

Because of his political leanings, and because Thomas Hutchinson wanted to keep potential troublemakers out of political power in his colony, Quincy was never "admitted to the gown"; that is, he was never invited to wear the wig and robe of Crown-approved lawyers, as his brother Samuel had been. But Josiah didn't care. Even as a young lawyer, he had all the clients he needed. As he wrote later, "I proceeded . . . to manage all my own business . . . though unsanctified and uninspired by the pomp and magic of the long Robe."[11]

John Adams, who was less interested in politics than Josiah, concentrated on building his legal practice and courting Abigail. Despite his growing status in Braintree, Abigail's parents still did not approve of the young lawyer as a match for their daughter. Thinking to bring her parents round, Abigail began taking John to the home of her grandparents, John and Elizabeth Quincy, and their son, Norton Quincy. Abigail knew that if she could persuade her grandparents of John Adams' worth, her mother and father would be sure to follow.

John found the Mount Wollaston estate to be the most peaceful and beautiful place he had ever seen. He had always loved the landscape of

Braintree, but looking out over the sea from the Quincy mansion, he found true bliss: "Here is Solitude and Retirement. Still, calm, and serene, cool, tranquil, and peaceful." He walked from room to room, waxing on and on about the gorgeous views: "Out at one Window, you see Mount Wollaston, the first Seat of our Ancestors, and beyond that Stony field Hill covered over with Corn and fruits. At the other Window, an Orchard and beyond that the large Marsh called the broad Meadows."

It was as if all of the world was at his feet: "From the East Window of the opposite Chamber you see a fine Plain, covered with Corn and beyond that the whole Harbour and all the Islands. From the End Window of the East Chamber, you may see with a prospective Glass, every Ship, Sloop, Schooner, and Brigantine, that comes in, or goes out."[12]

The older Quincys were flattered by John's appreciation of their home and lands, and Norton Quincy enjoyed John's company; they all gave Abigail their blessing to marry John. Her relatives, Josiah Quincy and his sons, just down the hill, also made clear their approval of John. It was only a matter of time, Abigail and John reasoned, before Abigail's parents relented and the hoped-for marriage could finally come to pass.

On August 1, 1764, Thomas Hancock died. He'd suffered "a fit of apoplexy" (most likely a stroke) while walking into the council chamber of the Massachusetts Colony State House and died two hours later.[13] In his will, he left most of his wealth to his nephew, John; this included the shipping and merchant business and all its holdings as well as properties in Boston, along with tens of thousands of acres of land throughout Connecticut and Massachusetts. He left the mansion on Beacon Hill to his wife, Lydia, but she almost immediately gave the house and all its goods and lands to John, asking only that she be allowed to continue living there.

Without hesitation, John granted her request and promised to take the best care of her always. He loved his aunt as much as she loved him. John also vowed to his mother; sister, Mary; and brother, Ebenezer that their fortunes would be forever linked with his and they had little to worry about.

While Lydia may have hoped that now John and Dolly Quincy would finally become engaged, no such announcement came from the couple. They continued to see each other often, and John wrote notes to Dolly, which were delivered by messenger at all hours of the day, but no wedding plans were made or ever mentioned by either of them. Lydia kept careful watch, biding her time to make her plan of linking the Hancocks with the Quincys a reality.

Abigail Smith's parents finally gave her their approval of John Adams, and in October 1764, at her father's parsonage in Weymouth, they were married. Guests included a large contingent from Braintree, including the Adams family and all the members of the various branches of the Quincy family. Reverend Smith performed the wedding service, as he had for Mary when she married Richard Cranch in 1762, and as he would for his daughter Elizabeth when she married John Shaw in 1777.

For the wedding of his daughter Mary, Reverend Smith chose a reading from St. Luke, *Mary hath chosen that good part which shall not be taken from her.* When his daughter Elizabeth married John Shaw in 1777, Reverend Smith would once again go with St. Luke, choosing *There was a man sent from God, whose name was John.*

But when Abigail married John Adams, Reverend Smith's sermon was based on a reading from St. Matthew: *John came neither eating nor drinking, and they say he hath a devil.* Perhaps Abigail's parents had not completely come to terms with the marriage of their beloved daughter to lawyer John Adams; perhaps John would never be Reverend Smith's most favored son-in-law. But the Braintree Quincys liked the man and Abigail was happy with her choice.

Three years earlier, Abigail had written to Hannah Quincy Lincoln about searching for the love of her life but fearing that a good man was as hard to find as "justice, honesty, prudence, and many other virtues."[14] Now she had found her man, and in her estimation, he was filled with the virtues she revered.

It was around this time that twenty-year-old Benjamin Blyth of Salem drew pastel portraits of John and Abigail. These presumably were meant to be gifts for the newly married couple, to be displayed in the home they would now share in Braintree, much as the oil paintings of Sam Quincy and his wife, Hannah, commissioned from John Singleton Copley, were displayed in their town house on Summer Street in Boston.

Abigail Smith Adams, along with her portrait, settled easily into John's small farmhouse just down the hill from her grandparents and across the yard from John's mother, who lived in the larger farmhouse owned by John's brother. From her new home, Abigail could see the grasses of the coastline from one set of windows, and from the other windows, she looked out on the village she had loved as a child and would once again call home as a wife.

It was here in Braintree that lessons had been learned, not only by Abigail, schooled by her grandmother, but by Ned, Samuel, and Josiah Jr. and John Adams, who had absorbed lessons from their fathers, as well as from their early pastor, Reverend Hancock: to be grateful and to be caring; to build a community of hope and of opportunity. Lessons of hard work, optimism, and charity. In Deacon Adams' insistence that John go to college, there was also the lesson that in America there were no boundaries; there was only possibility.

Even Dolly Quincy, youngest of the Quincy clan, had the values of her community deeply instilled in her—by her father, a man who believed in the promises of God and the goodness of humanity, and by her cousins, men and women who believed that their colony was special and their rights sacrosanct.

As the year 1764 drew to a close, there were few in the colony of Massachusetts who could even contemplate the end of British rule in America. The conflicts that arose over issues of smuggling and taxation were largely due to the decades of laissez-faire that had been previously exercised by the mother country; each colony had been allowed to proceed as it wished, without heavy taxation or much interference at all, just so long as goods continued to be sent to England and trade among the empire's many holdings prospered. For most colonists, no matter how they felt about Parliament now trying to squeeze money out of the colonies, the king was still owed loyalty. Parliament could be straightened out and everyone would prosper once more.

Nevertheless, all the elements for a movement toward colonial independence from England were there. The years of neglect by Parliament had given colonists confidence in their ability to self-rule. More than one generation of New England men and women had been raised to think for themselves instead of just relying on king or church. While deeply faithful, colonists were also interested in the natural world, trusted science, and followed reason. And beyond the loyalty owed the king, these men and women felt duty bound to their communities, their families, and their colony. Fierce, certain, and strong, that sense of duty and responsibility would carry them far. All the way to revolution, if need be.

But first, flame had to be set to the tinder laid.

PART TWO

Spark

1765–1773

Let us catch the divine enthusiasm;
and feel, each for himself, the godlike pleasure
of diffusing happiness on all around us.

—JOHN HANCOCK

7

The Mobs of Boston

Happy People! Who enjoy this blessed Constitution.
Happy! thrice happy people! If ye preserve it inviolate . . .
—Josiah Quincy Jr.

The night of August 26, 1765, was clear but dark, the moon just a sliver of light in the sky over Boston. The air was warm and humid, the scent of the harbor strong as the tide drew out. Josiah Quincy Jr. was alone in the family home on Marlborough Street. His brother Ned was on Long Island in New York, spending time with the family of Rebecca Lloyd and doing all he could to secure her affections. Josiah Sr. was where he could almost always be found now: in Braintree, with two young children underfoot (born of Anne Marsh, his third wife) and plenty to do as justice of the peace for the town, and managing the glass- and chocolate-making factories he'd founded.

The bells of the Old South Meeting House had long pealed midnight, but Josiah Jr. was still awake. From his opened windows he could hear, coming across the rooftops and snaking through the narrow streets, sounds that carried in the heavy air: the swelling of voices into angry shouts, the pounding of feet, the loud ringing of wooden planks against metal. A mob had been raised, and now an invitation was being sent out, offered to all within hearing to join in.

Josiah knew, as all of Boston knew, that the mob tonight was led by Ebenezer Mackintosh and the Loyall Nine. Mackintosh was a shoemaker who had fought for England in the Seven Years' War, and his fellow founders of the Loyall Nine included Thomas Crafts, a painter; George Trott and Henry Bass, jewelers; Benjamin Edes, publisher of the *Boston Gazette*; John Smith and Steven Cleverly, braziers; John Avery and Thomas Chase, distillers; and Joseph Field, a ship captain.

What drove Mackintosh and the Loyall Nine, and what compelled the mob to follow where they led, was economic frustration, pure and simple. For the past few years Parliament had been tightening its control of Massachusetts. The British government felt that the New England colony had been following its own rules and its own laws and ignoring all efforts of the mother country to collect its due. Along with the Sugar Act of 1764, Parliament had imposed a long roster of import duties and put in place strong measures against smuggling. Even after the tax on sugar was repealed, the other measures remained.

To the colonists of Massachusetts, the way they had been running the colony suited them just fine. As they had prospered, so had the English, argued the colonists: for decades the English economy had benefitted from trade with New England. And when England needed help in fighting the Seven Years' War, the colonists had joined up and joined in. They sent their men by the hundreds to fight and did all they could to bolster supplies for the troops. There had been real profits in the supplying of goods, but there had also been real losses in the supplying of men—so many had died to keep the French at bay. How dare England now impose its financial costs on the colony, when so much treasure had already been paid with the lives of their own sons and husbands?

Josiah Quincy Jr., who was by nature and training impelled to look at the situation from both sides, understood why the British wanted to control smuggling and collect new taxes and more duties on even more goods. But the measures had been enacted by Parliament without the protections of representation and process guaranteed to the colonists. It was this failure to follow legal precedent that Josiah could not countenance. That England was ignoring the economic miseries of its colonies in imposing new taxes mattered less to Josiah than the fact that Parliament had trampled on the colonists' rights under British law.

John Hancock understood firsthand the economic miseries suffered by his fellow colonists. He was a merchant of goods after all, and the main source of income for all of New England was in supplying goods. For the past ten years, New England merchants had supplied three vibrant markets: the armies of England waging the Seven Years' War; England itself; and the English colonies of the West Indies.

Now those markets were gone or drying up. All the money that had been made in Massachusetts through the waging of war—supplying food, clothing, tenting, and weaponry to the British Army and colonial troops— was no longer coming in; while at the same time, the postwar depression in both England and the West Indies meant a spiraling downward in trade with those markets.

New England farmers, lumbermen, quarrymen, metalworkers, and fishermen suffered, as did everyone involved in the maritime and mercantile industries: merchants and trading agents, dockworkers and shipbuilders, sailors and warehouse laborers, rope makers and innkeepers and craftsmen of all types. Paul Revere, for one, almost went bankrupt when demand for his goods shrank down to the simplest of orders.

Stores and inns were shuttered, and major mercantile firms went under. Ships lay empty at the docks, and the docks themselves grew more silent by the day. As one enterprise fell, so others followed, each business dependent on the others. The *Boston Gazette* reported in early 1765, in a poem lamenting the demise of Nathaniel Wheelwright's trading company, how its "fiery Tail . . . swept lesser Stars Down from their sev'ral Orbits."[1]

As one of New England's wealthiest merchants, John Hancock was not yet suffering. The House of Hancock was still buoyant and solvent, largely due to the capital it floated on. But Hancock worried for his fellow colonists, and for himself: "It is very difficult to carry on business, and unless redress'd Trade must dwindle," he wrote to his agent, John Barnard, in England.[2]

In March 1765, news had arrived on the spring ships from England that a new tax was to be imposed on the colonists. Promulgated under the leadership of Prime Minister George Grenville, the Stamp Act would surpass all other taxes previously levied in both breadth and reach. The act decreed that any transaction requiring paper—any sale or trade, any professional or legal license, any court action, any contract of any kind, any newspaper or pamphlet, as well as such incidentals as playing cards—had to carry an official stamp. Each stamp would have its price, from low to very high.

The Stamp Act reached directly and deeply into the lives of every colonist and made them pay, again and again, for their daily activities.

Hancock, through his English trading agents, had received early warning of the impending act. He wrote back a warning in return: "I hear the Stamp Act is like to take place it is very cruel we were before much burthened we shall not now be able much longer to support trade, and in the end Great Britain must feel the ill effects of it."[3]

Hancock urged his British agents, whose fortunes were as much at risk as his own, to do what they could to ensure the act would not be enforced: "if the Stamp Act takes place we are a gone people—do help us all you can."[4] He himself felt the weight of responsibility for the economy of Boston, a duty instilled in part by his uncle Thomas and in greater part by the ambitions of his aunt, that John be a leader—not just a commercial leader but a community figurehead, revered and responsible.

The role of protector was one that John Hancock took seriously. He funded lavish public celebrations in Boston, provided firewood and foodstuffs to those in need, and helped widows and orphans. Even more important, he employed a vast number of colonists; John Adams reported that "not less than a thousand families were every day . . . dependent on Mr. Hancock for their daily bread."[5]

Hancock had been elected to serve as a selectman for Boston soon after news of the Stamp Act arrived. Along with his fellow selectmen, and his old friends from Braintree, Ned and Sam Quincy and their younger brother, Josiah (all now living in Boston), he worked on an official petition of protest against implementation of the Stamp Act, to be submitted to Parliament.

Hancock also continued to work against the act privately, particularly in letters to his agents and friends in England, urging them to lobby on behalf of the American cause: "I wish we could be help'd out of our present Burthens and Difficulties, our Trade is prodigiously Embarrassed, & must shortly be ruined. . . . I, however, hope we shall in some measure be Releiv'd, & Doubt not your good influences to forward it."[6]

Josiah Quincy Jr. lent his efforts to numerous legal challenges being formulated against imposition of the Stamp Act. As he would write later, the act was clearly "unconstitutional."[7] But when Sam Adams, his compatriot in the Long Room Club, invited him to meetings with the Loyall Nine convened at the Green Dragon Tavern, Josiah refused to attend. He knew that it was at such meetings that many mugs of ale and punch were shared, and lawbreaking plans of protest were hatched. Josiah preferred to work within the rule of law, rather than outside it.

But many colonists found more hope in the mob actions proposed by the Loyall Nine than in legal arguments and formal petitions. To the Loyall Nine and their followers, it seemed as if the ever-increasing burdens imposed by Parliament fell hardest on the working class of the colony. In the eyes of Mackintosh and his men, while the common people of the colony suffered, those colonists favored by the Crown flourished. Where else to focus the fomenting frustrations and growing anger but toward Crown officials, living high and mighty in their fine town houses? The elite would have to pay for their unfair privileges, and mobs would exact the payment.

Mobs were a feature of political protest that had come over to the colonies from England. Long used as the only weapon of the lower and artisan classes against the power of Parliament and the king, the results had been mixed in terms of effecting change. But as a venue for venting frustration, there seemed to be no better or more popular alternative, and recent mob-led protests in England provided vivid examples to the colonies: the 1763 uprisings in Devonshire to protest a cider tax; the Spitalfields riots of 1765 involving silk weavers angry over falling wages; and that same year, the violent gathering of over forty thousand weavers and glove makers upset over Parliament's increasing taxes and regulations.

Going back further, the Bushell riot in Glasgow in 1725 resulted in the destruction of the home of a member of Parliament, believed to be behind recent imposition of taxes; and in 1736, mobs in Edinburgh protested the prosecution of two smugglers. In both cases, the crowd was fired upon by British soldiers, and a number of protesters were killed. In 1725, the officer in charge in Glasgow was charged and convicted of murder but later pardoned by the Crown; in 1736, the same officer was once again charged, this time in Edinburgh. Not trusting the courts, the mob took matters into their own hands and, after dragging the officer from his quarters, executed him in a public hanging.

These anti-Parliament movements overseas were well publicized in the colonies and inspired the colonists to hold their own protests against unwanted taxes and intrusions. The colonists freely borrowed slogans from their English brethren, chanting "Liberty, Property, and No excise!"[8]

Thomas Hutchinson had already found himself the subject of mob threats. In the 1740s, he needed armed protection from crowds angry over his positions on currency and trade. In 1747, he served with Josiah Quincy Sr. on a town committee investigating mob action when people took to the streets to protest impressment—seizing men and forcing them into naval service. The committee described the troublemakers as "Foreign Seamen, Servants, Negroes and other Persons of mean and Vile Condition" who had "Committed great outrages and Disorders putting the Inhabitants of the Town in great Terror of their Lives."[9]

But the passage of the Stamp Act in 1765 ignited a collective fury both broader and deeper than any seen before. Fed by populist groups like the Loyall Nine, the anger and frustrations of the colonists were also spurred on by the press. The colonial newspapers were full of "Letters from a Gentleman" or "Poem Created in Honor Of," which were really diatribes, satirical in nature or straightforward in condemnation, condemning parliamentary policies governing Massachusetts.

The press was hugely influential because the vast majority of colonists could read—and did. They displayed a voracious appetite for printed reports of news, politics, gossip, and everything in between. As the *Boston Gazette* proudly declared in 1765, "The common people in the Colonies are in general so well-informed, that a man who cannot read or write, is looked on with as much pity and contempt as the ancient Romans would have view'd the Barbarians of old Britain."[10]

In the summer of 1765, some of the newspapers (the ones with Whig overtones) reported that Virginia had approved the resolutions written by the firebrand Patrick Henry and vowed to oppose any taxes imposed by Parliament, and further held "that any person" arguing for compliance "shall be deemed, an Enemy."[11] Bostonians against the Stamp Act roared in approval.

In fact, however, Virginia's House of Burgesses had rejected most of Henry's resolutions against the Stamp Act, including the one delineating enemies of the colony, and even Henry himself backed away from his proposed resolutions.

But the truth didn't matter as much as the message: the Stamp Act was to be opposed by any and all means. The men behind the Stamp Act—the uncaring, avaricious, and unjust elite class of politicians both at home and in England—had to be brought down, by word and by deed, and even by humor. The *Boston Gazette* printed a mock business proposal from an enterprising businessman that "all instruments be wrote on Bark, and so avoid the Stamp-Duties. . . . I am ready to Supply with good Writing Bark all those whose Consciences are bound by the late Act."[12] The *Boston Gazette* also reported that young women had joined the protest against the Stamp Act, and would refuse to marry, "as no Licenses for Marriage could be obtained" without an official stamp, and were "determined to join hands with none but such as will to the utmost endeavor to abolish the Custom of marrying with License."[13]

It was only a matter of time before humor and satire were left aside and the reactions to the Stamp Act became violent. Mobs were taking to the streets, and the focus of their ire were the wealthy and the well-connected.

John and Abigail Adams, living in their small farmhouse in Braintree, were not immune to the economic turmoils of their colony. As a lawyer, John's interests were bound up with those of his clients, and if his clients were low on funds, they would not be engaging a lawyer whose fees they would have to pay. As trade fell, legal work fell along with it, and the signs were all there for a further dampening of the economy, especially if the Stamp Tax was allowed to stand.

Try as he did to diligently build up his practice, John worried, and Abigail worried alongside him. She gave birth to their first child in July 1765, a girl they named Abigail and called Nabby. Much as Edmund Quincy's wife Elizabeth had done in the early years of their marriage, Abigail created a household budget, cut expenses, expanded the kitchen garden, and thought about opening a small shop, where she could sell household items.

From the windows of their home, John and Abigail could see the hills of Boston; although they couldn't hear the roar of the angry mobs, they had read about the crowds swarming through the streets at night, "like Devils let loose."[14] But as John wrote in a letter that was printed in the *Boston Gazette* on August 12, 1765, even more than the "blind, undistinguishing Rage of the Rabble," he and Abigail feared the tightening grip of the British government on its American colonies, epitomized now in the "rash, mad, and Dogmatical" Stamp Act.[15]

In Hingham, Bela Lincoln also seethed under the impending requirements of the Stamp Act. All the professions, lawyers and doctors included, would have to update their paperwork and licenses with the expensive new stamps, and Bela's medical practice and his farm were already being run at costs exceeding what Lincoln could bring in.

The year before, Bela had been one of a group commissioned by the General Court of Massachusetts to travel to London to present their petition of protest against the Sugar Act directly to Parliament. When the tax on sugar and molasses was repealed, Lincoln had felt hopeful that Parliament would ease back on their demands on the colonists of Massachusetts. But now an even more burdensome tax had been enacted, and all of Lincoln's efforts to help the colony seemed futile.

Esther Quincy Sewall wrote to her sister Dolly, who was living in Boston with her parents and sister Katy, and asked about the mood in town. In Charlestown, on the other side of the Charles River, where Esther lived with her husband, she felt safe within the confines of their home and society: most of their friends were part of the colony's administrative corps and had sworn fealty to the Crown when taking on their commissions. With Hutchinson's continued support, Jonathan's law practice only continued to grow.

But outside this bubble of comfort and security, Esther sensed a growing desperation in the streets of her waterside town and saw in the eyes of the market women a turn of resentment and anger. A tremor of anxiety ran under the lines of Esther's letter; Dolly knew her older sister had always been timid, but now she seemed frightened by the world around her.

While not fearful like her sister, Dolly nevertheless felt anxious about the rising tensions in Boston. Already her father's fledgling beverage business was suffering in the depressed economy, and rumors abounded of further troubles to come. Having secured a license in 1762 for the manufacture of cider, wine, and beer, Edmund had been building up a small storehouse, but sales were slow.

Business lagged even more as Edmund began to spend his days at the frequent conferences convened by Boston Town Meeting. A populist at heart, he was intent on contributing his voice to the growing demands of the citizens of Boston. Fearing the mob, he always made sure to return to his modest home by early evening from these meetings.

Once safely home, he shared all that had happened at the town meeting with Dolly and her sister Katy, sparing no detail in his recounting of the long debates. Politics interested the young women, particularly now that the interests of their sister Esther, married to a man with close ties to Crown officials, seemed at odds with the growing Whig sentiments of their father, their uncle Josiah Quincy, in Braintree, and their cousin Josiah Jr.

Politics, however, worried Dolly less than the state of the family business. Having already lived through one turn of fortune with her father, she feared another. The extended Quincy family would always support their own, Dolly knew, but in the back of her mind, another hope flared. John Hancock's attentions had continued; she was often invited to his mansion to attend the lavish dinners planned out by Lydia, with multiple courses made up of soups, meats, fish, fruits, pastries—and wine, plenty of wine. "I like pale Wine . . . I like rich Wine," John Hancock wrote to his agents in London, and they supplied him, sending in one shipment alone four hundred gallons of the best Madeira.[16]

Perhaps Dolly's future prosperity would be founded on more than just her father's spirits business. Lydia Hancock seemed intent on making it so, always encouraging her nephew in the young woman's direction and making sure Dolly felt welcome in their home. Dolly also enjoyed the time she spent in public with Hancock, basking in the prestige she received as his companion. Sound in both finances and politics, John Hancock just might be the right partner for her. Her mother, who spent most of her time in Braintree, thought so; her father, who kept his daughters close to his side in Boston thought so too. Dolly herself was coming closer and closer to the same conclusion.

The evening of August 26 started off with a large bonfire set to light in front of the home of the royal governor, Francis Bernard. Although Bernard complained often about the costs of raising and launching his ten children, in truth he was a wealthy man and a well-connected one; his wife was niece to William Barrington, who was the Second Viscount Barrington and the British secretary of war. Bernard was a smug man as well and deficient in understanding the people over whom he governed: he had predicted that his term as governor would be "quiet and easy."[17]

The bonfire burned hot, and the crowd grew. The dockworkers and small merchants shouted for Governor Bernard to come outside and respond to their complaints about taxes. But he did not appear. He remained hidden away behind the locked doors of his home, protected by a staging of armed soldiers.

Enraged, the group outside tore apart the fencing along the street, pulling the broken planks off and adding them to the fire, banging the staves against the metal stakes. This was the sound that Josiah Quincy Jr. heard through the open windows of his home. It was an invitation to join in the mob, and many answered the call.

Newcomers were welcomed. Barrels of punch and cider were brought in from neighboring taverns and drinks were offered up to any and all in attendance. Shouts of "Liberty and Property" rang out; this was "the Usual Notice of their intention to plunder and pull down a house," Bernard noted later.[18]

The angry crowd tumbled along the streets of Boston, gathering momentum as more and more people joined in. The swollen gathering of protesters broke apart to roam in smaller mobs around the city. One mob surrounded the home of Benjamin Hallowell, the comptroller of customs, but Hallowell convinced the group to accompany him to a tavern, where he purchased a barrel of punch for them.

While the gesture saved his house, the continued drinking only further inflamed the men, who went on to break into the house of William Story, an official from the High Court of Admiralty, which tried customs and smuggling cases. The mob tore his home apart from the inside out looking for official court documents, which were then burned in an impromptu bonfire.

Josiah Quincy Jr., listening from his home, feared that the house of Lieutenant Governor Thomas Hutchinson would be a likely target for the mob's anger. Doubts about Hutchinson's devotion to the colony had long been growing. Yes, it was true that in addition to his governmental duties, he had been writing a history of the colony, but such a project did not prove his allegiance to his fellow colonists. Ever since the writs of assistance case in 1761, Josiah Sr. and his sons Ned and Josiah Jr. had ceased to believe the lieutenant governor had their best interests at heart.

Rumors had spread over the past few weeks that Thomas Hutchinson supported the Stamp Act, and that he was behind the appointment of his brother-in-law, Andrew Oliver, as stamp master for the entire colony (this was later proved to be false). On August 14, a mob had gathered under a large elm tree at the corner of Essex and Orange streets, from which they dangled an effigy of Oliver. They then cut the effigy down and carried it through the streets in a mock funeral, finally beheading it in a grand display in front of Andrew Oliver's home. The mob pummeled the house with stones, forced their way in through a back door, and ransacked the wine cellar.

Now the time had come to attack the home of Hutchinson himself. The mob was at fever pitch, fed by liquor and frustration and anger. The different bands of marauders gathered together as one and marched to Hutchinson's mansion on Garden Court Street in the North End. The mansion had been built by Edward Hutchinson, Thomas' great-grandfather and the son of Anne Hutchinson of Braintree. Thomas had lived there with his wife for twenty years, and after she died in 1754, he remained in the home with his children. He never remarried.

Three generations of Hutchinsons had filled the three-story home with imported furniture and finely woven silk rugs, china from the Far East and silver forged in Boston, family heirlooms and portraits, and a library boasting hundreds of books. From the outside, its façade was elegant and imposing and it seemed impenetrable. But the night's events would prove otherwise.

As Hutchinson wrote later, he and his oldest daughter, Sarah, who had refused to leave the home without him, had just escaped through the back door when "the hellish crew fell upon my house with the rage of devils."[19]

The mob smashed through the front door with an ax, then every window and door was opened, thrown wide to allow dozens of men to stream in.

The marauders tore portraits and paintings from walls, stomped on chairs and overturned tables, threw china plates and cups to the floor, slashed through rugs, smashed windows and moldings, and tossed books from shelves, burning them in piles on the floor, along with official Crown documents rifled from desks. They carried off the silver as trophies of the evening but everything else was destroyed.

Hutchinson despaired when he found later that the mob "scattered or destroyed all the manuscripts and other papers I had been collecting for 30 years together besides a great number of Public papers in my custody."[20] He had in his possession papers from the very first settlements of Massachusetts. The mob cared nothing for history: the present was all that mattered, and the present demanded the destruction of everything in sight.

A group of men left the house and went out in search of Hutchinson himself, certain that he was hiding somewhere in the neighborhood. Hutchinson and Sarah ran through back gardens, going as fast as they could, and then hid in heavy bushes under the cover of darkness and waited for dawn to break.

Throughout the night, the mob continued their destruction: "Not contented with tearing off all the wainscot and hangings and splitting the doors to pieces they beat down the Partition walls . . . they cut down the cupola . . . and they began to take the slate and boards from the roof and were prevented only by the approaching daylight from a total demolition of the building. The garden fence was laid flat and all . . . trees &c broke down to the ground."[21]

By five o'clock in the morning, little of the house remained, save the foundation and portions of the walls. Hutchinson would later write to a friend, "Such ruins were never seen in America."[22]

Josiah Quincy Jr. was at breakfast when a messenger boy knocked at his front door. Josiah read the note quickly, standing in the hall. He raised his eyes to meet the pale face of the messenger and asked if the boy had seen the destroyed home.

The boy nodded.

Josiah turned back to the note. How could this be true? "One of the best finished houses in the province has nothing remaining but bare walls and floors. Gentlemen of the army, who have seen towns sacked by an enemy, declare they never saw such fury."[23]

And what of Hutchinson himself? The boy answered before turning to leave: rumor was that Hutchinson had fled with his daughter to join the rest of his family on Castle Island, stronghold of the British military in Boston Harbor. Josiah shut the door behind the boy and then returned to his library. How could peace ever be restored to Boston, he wondered; a city once ruled by law was now ruled by mobs.

8

Warmest Lovers of Liberty

It is commonly said that these Colonies were peopled by
*   Religion—*
But I should rather say that the Love of Liberty,
projected, conducted, and accomplished the settlement of
*   America.*

—John Adams

Josiah Quincy Jr. dressed hurriedly. It was the first day of the fall seating for the Superior Court of Massachusetts and he had clients to represent. As he pulled on his pressed jacket, he wondered if Thomas Hutchinson would take his place in court that morning. Hutchinson was usually the most well kempt of men and never looked more to advantage than when dressed for court, resplendent in black judicial robes embellished with thick golden bands and wearing a wig of white curls.

But Hutchinson's robes, bands, and wig had been burned to ashes last night, along with the rest of his clothes and all his furnishings, books, and papers—indeed, the entire house was gone. After such a devastation, would the chief justice be able to summon the strength to take his place at the center of the judges bench?

When Thomas Hutchinson passed through the door to enter the courtroom, the gathered lawyers and petitioners gasped. The first thing Josiah noticed was that Hutchinson was dressed in evening clothes; the second thing was that the man's fine silk breeches were soiled at the knees, as if he had been kneeling in mud. Above the breeches, his white shirt was rumpled and stained and his cravat lay limply at his neck, discolored with sweat. His meager hair had been clumsily pulled back, held with a simple ribbon. Josiah guessed the ribbon had been lent to him by one of his daughters.

It was Hutchinson's face that Josiah would remember always, "with tears starting from his eyes, and a countenance which strongly told the inward anguish of his soul."[1] The man looked exhausted, in heart and mind, his eyes hollow and rimmed with shadows, his mouth a thin line of suppressed emotion.

Everyone in the courtroom rose as Hutchinson took his place on the bench. They continued to stand as he turned to face them all, and then began to speak. Instead of proceeding to the cases that waited to be heard that day, Hutchinson told his fellow judges, along with the gathered lawyers, clients, and court watchers, what had happened to him and his family the night before. He explained that the clothes he wore on his back were the only ones he still owned: he was "destitute of everything, no other shirt; no other garment but what I have on."[2]

He went on to swear that the punishments exacted upon him and his family were unjust: "I call my Maker to witness, that I never . . . was aiding, assisting, or supporting . . . what is commonly called the Stamp Act." He finished by condemning all mob violence as warrantless, no matter the situation, but especially when "people, deluded, inflamed . . . [become] carried away with madness against an innocent man." He ended with the entreaty, "I pray that God give us better hearts!"[3]

Court was then adjourned for the day.

Josiah set out for his law offices on King Street but then turned around and began to walk the other way. He wanted to see Hutchinson's house for himself. What he saw left him stunned: "the destruction was really amazing," he would write later, and never forget.[4] It was a sight that would haunt him for both its warning and its premonition of just how far the fury of citizens could go when they were denied their rights and suffered economic hardships and uncertainties as a result.

When Josiah finally returned to his office, he was too agitated to work on the cases that awaited his attention. He paced back and forth across the narrow room that housed his working desk, pausing occasionally to look out the window. The street below was busy with life, people walking hurriedly, horses and wagons passing by. A normal day—but not at all normal, when such an evening had passed before.

Josiah sat down, reaching for his journal underneath a pile of law papers. He opened to an empty page and began to scrawl down all he remembered of Hutchinson's speech in court that morning, and then his own reactions to it and to the events leading up to the ransacking of Hutchinson's home. He wrote to restore order both within himself and out there, in the street outside his windows, in the colony for which he hoped so much.

Like the rioters of the night before, whom Josiah described as "too justly inflamed" and "the warmest lovers of liberty," Josiah was enraged by the "enslavers and oppressive taxmasters" in charge of the colony.[5] But unlike those who had caused "destructions, demolitions, and ruins," Josiah vowed to find recourse to "the slavery and distress of a despotic state" in "that best asylum, that glorious medium, the British Constitution. . . . Happy people who enjoy this blessed constitution!" He ended the journal entry with a quotation from an English play, in which the Roman senator Cato delivers a prayer to the deity of law:

> Remember, O my friends! the laws, the rights,
> The generous plan of power delivered down,
> From age to age, by your renowned forefathers,
> So dearly bought, the price of so much blood:
> Oh! Let it never perish in your hands,
> But piously transmit it to your children.
> Do thou, great Liberty! Inspire our souls,
> And make our lives in thy possession happy,
> Or our death glorious in thy just defence.[6]

For now, Josiah would keep his writings on liberty, justice, and the law confined to the courtroom and to the work he did for the Boston town committee. But soon, very soon, events would push him into the public sphere, and he would then share his thoughts with the world, all in hopes of shaping the opinions of the citizens he valued so much and saving the colony he loved.

Over the next few weeks, thousands of people across Massachusetts flocked to Boston to see the ruins of Hutchinson's house. When the novelty of the sight wore off, Hutchinson hired workers to rebuild the home much as it was. But he would never feel comfortable there again. Soon Hutchinson would look for a new house, leaving the terrible memories of the summer of 1765 behind.

Condemnation of the destruction of Hutchinson's home was widespread in Boston and across the province, but the motivation behind the attack was largely supported. As John Hancock wrote in a letter to England, "The injury that has been done . . . is what I abhor and detest as much as any man breathing and would go to great lengths in repairing his loss. But an opposition to the Stamp Act is commendable."[7]

Governor Bernard directed that Ebenezer Mackintosh, alleged leader of the attack on Hutchinson's home, be arrested and that other rioters be taken into custody as well. But Sam Adams, supported by a group of Boston merchants, forced Bernard to release Mackintosh; Adams' group threatened to take apart the customhouse where the man was being held, "stone by stone" if he was not set free. The others were sprung from jail late at night, with little obstruction from the jailer.[8]

Protests against the Stamp Act continued as the Loyall Nine, now broadened in membership and calling themselves Sons of Liberty, scheduled public events throughout the fall. Men designated to sell the stamps would be called out, one by one, and ordered to renounce their commissions. If they failed to do so, they would be subjected to the wrath of the mob. The Liberty Tree on Orange Street—where the effigy of Andrew Oliver had swung—was chosen as the site for the public humiliations. Stand by the tree—in the "Liberty Hall," as it was called—and renounce the title of stamp seller, the Sons of Liberty commanded, or be hanged by the condemnation of the mob.[9]

This Liberty Tree was just across the road from the rum distillery owned by Thomas Chase, one of the original Loyall Nine. Many meetings were held at the distillery, where, spurred on by both rum and speeches, incendiary acts were planned to protest parliamentary actions. The name of the tree became official when colonists nailed a copper plate engraved with the words TREE OF LIBERTY to its trunk and poems were written in honor of this "stately elm . . . whose lofty branches seem'd to touch the skies."[10]

Around the colony, and throughout America, other trees were claimed as liberty trees. In Harvard Yard, students of the college chose a stately elm for their "liberty tree" or "rebellion elm,"[11] and in New York City, perhaps with fewer trees to choose from, colonists erected a "liberty pole" on Golden Hill in 1766.[12] British soldiers were so angered by the symbolism of the pole that they chopped it down, but within months another pole was erected, which was once again cut down, and so the third pole erected was reenforced with iron bands.

John Adams joined in the protests against the Stamp Act by writing a series of anonymous letters that were printed in the *Boston Gazette* and together were titled "A Dissertation on the Canon and Feudal Law." Instead of attacking the act directly in his essay, John wrote about the history of the colony and the motivation of its earliest settlers: "It was not religion alone, as is commonly supposed [that settled America]; but it was a love of universal liberty. . . . Tyranny in every form, shape, and appearance was their disdain and abhorrence; no fear of punishment, nor even of death itself in exquisite tortures, had been sufficient to conquer that steady, manly, pertinacious spirit with which they had opposed . . . tyrants of . . . church and state."[13]

That same dedication to liberty existed still in the colony of Massachusetts, Adams argued, and "liberty must at all hazards be supported. We have a right to it, derived from our Maker. But if we had not, our fathers have earned and bought it for us, at the expense of their ease, their estates, their pleasure, and their blood."[14]

In what would prove to be prophetic posturing, Adams declared, "Rulers are no more than attorneys, agents, and trustees for the people; and if the cause, the interest and trust, is insidiously betrayed, or wantonly trifled away, the people have a right to revoke the authority that they themselves have deputed, and to constitute abler and better agents, attorneys, and trustees."[15]

While John had intended to keep the authorship of his series a secret for the time being, his fellow townsfolk in Braintree knew who had written the letters. In late September, John was asked to write up the town's instructions to its statewide representatives, using the arguments he had made in the press to explain and support Braintree's decision to officially oppose the Stamp Act.

John eagerly took on the assignment; he would work all night if he had to. With this document, he could become not only the voice of Braintree but the voice of all of Massachusetts. A committee had been formed to work with him, but John told the others, Norton Quincy included, that he could write up a draft on his own and then submit it for their approval.

John told Abigail proudly of the assignment he had been given. She agreed that it was both an honor and an opportunity; resigning herself to another evening on her own with the baby, she prepared a tray of tea and biscuits to keep John going through the night and took herself off to bed. In the morning, finding him still hard at work in his office, she brought him his customary tankard of hard cider and more biscuits. She sat beside John in his office, Nabby on her lap, while he talked to her of the ideas he had laid out so far.

Abigail offered her comments freely on what John had composed. John had come to expect her input on everything he did, and this work on behalf of the town meeting was no different. He listened to her reasoning, he turned to his law books, he sat by his window gazing out at the distant shoreline, sunlight wavering through the meadow grasses. Then he turned back to his work. By the end of the day, John had finished the instructions for the village of Braintree. The next day the drafting committee approved what John had written, and confirmation of the instructions by the selectmen of Braintree followed swiftly.

John made clear in the Braintree instructions that "the inhabitants of this province appear to be entitled to all the rights aforementioned, by an act of parliament [the colony's charter] . . . as well as upon principles of common justice; their ancestors having settled this country at their sole expense, and their posterity having approved themselves most loyal and faithful subjects of Great Britain."[16]

The Stamp Act, John wrote, violated the rights of the colonists: "We have Always understood it to be a grand and fundamental principle of the British Constitution that no Freeman should be Subjected to any Tax to which he has not given his own Consent in person or by proxy. . . . We take it clearly therefore to be inconsistant with the Spirit of the Common Law and of the Essential Fundamentall principles of the British Constitution that we should be Subjected to any Tax imposed by the British Parliament because we are not Represented in that assembly in any sense."[17]

The Braintree instructions were printed in the *Massachusetts Gazette* and the *Boston Gazette* in early October. Within days, forty towns across Massachusetts had adopted them as their own. The instructions to their statewide representatives were uniform and unambiguous: the people of Massachusetts refused to comply with the Stamp Act, as it had been illegally promulgated by Parliament. John and Abigail were proud, for John was now speaking for the whole colony, no longer anonymously but loudly and clearly as John Adams, Esq., of Braintree. "I am . . . under all obligations of interest and ambition, as well as honor, gratitude and duty, to exert the utmost of abilities in this important cause,"[18] John promised in his diary; and he delivered.

A new ship had been commissioned by John Hancock in the spring of 1765. When the ship took to the seas in the summer, it went by the name of *Liberty*. Along with its cargo, the ship carried a letter Hancock had written to John Barnard, his London agent, warning of the response of his colony if no relief came from enforcement of the Stamp Act: "it is a Cruel hardship upon us . . . we must be Ruined . . . the fatal effects of these Grievances you will feel very Sensibly."[19]

Hancock had read the tenor of his town accurately: the tide of discontent was rising and its waves would be felt across the sea. Hancock planned on being one of the leaders to swell the discontent and ride the resulting waves to public prominence. The youngest of Boston's five selectmen, he now became one of the loudest, and the one most willing to work with Sam Adams and his populist friends to bring about repeal of the Stamp Act, donating both his time and his money to support their efforts.

He joined with 250 other merchants of Boston in a boycott of trading with England. As he wrote in a letter to Barnard, again sent on the *Liberty*, he resolved to sell off all the stock presently in his warehouse and then shut down its doors and "never send one Ship more to sea nor have any kind of connection in Business under a stamp." Hancock threatened to "never import another shilling's worth of British goods"—and warned that all outstanding debts would be hard to secure, given that both venues for "remittances and courts of justice would alike vanish" under the Stamp Act.[20] "I will not be a slave," he declared a week later. "I have a right to the libertys and privileges of the English Constitution, and I as an Englishman will enjoy them."[21]

In the midst of the Stamp Act crisis, Hancock sought out John Singleton Copley to paint his portrait. Meeting at Copley's house, just down the hill from his own, Hancock laid out exactly how he wished to be painted. Certainly not as the wealthy prince of Beacon Hill, he explained. Such an image would jar with the political tempo of the turbulent year, when being a member of the elite meant a tainted link with the Crown, oppression, and tyranny.

Hancock might be known for "wearing lavender suits, driving in a bright yellow carriage, and exercising an extravagantly expensive taste for English goods," but in the portrait that Hancock commissioned, he asked that Copley present him in plain clothes, doing plain work; he was to be portrayed as a man of the people.[22]

Copley's finished portrait showed Hancock sitting on a simple wooden chair before a worktable, holding a quill pen with one hand while with the other, he folds back a page from the open ledger before him. He wears a dark blue coat over a simple white shirt; his wig is coiffed smooth, his face is serious. He is a man interrupted in a moment of work, waiting for the painter to finish so that he can get back to bolstering business and improving the economy for everyone.

Once painted, this version of John as the simple man of business was displayed prominently in the Hancock mansion for all to see, and pen-and-ink copies of it were distributed.

By early September 1765, boxes of official stamps began to arrive in the colony—called by Hancock "the most disagreeable commodity . . . that were ever imported into this country."[23] But there was nowhere for them to go but into storage on Castle Island: one by one, the Crown-appointed stamp distributors had quit their posts under pressure exerted by the Sons of Liberty.

On November 1, the date by which all listed items were to carry stamps, there was no change in how business was conducted in Boston, or anywhere else in Massachusetts. The stamps continued to languish on Castle Island, still in their boxes, with no one to sell them. Officers of the customhouse gave clearances for cargo coming into Boston and going out; they certified that no stamps were to be found and therefore compliance with the Stamp Act was impossible.

To celebrate Boston's repudiation of the Stamp Act, Hancock held a dinner at the Green Dragon Tavern on November 5, inviting members of the different political groups of Boston's North and South ends. For years November 5 had been celebrated as Guy Fawkes Day, with riotous celebrations, bonfires, and the burning of effigies of the Catholic pope, but Hancock hoped to transform the usual anti-Catholic hostilities into a movement of solidarity against Britain's policies in Massachusetts. The pope was no longer the enemy, Hancock argued: Parliament and its agents in the colony were.

Hancock had much to celebrate that evening. The boycott would actually help his business, as he had become overloaded with goods as well as with debts (money owed to his English suppliers). Now he could unload the stock in his warehouses, selling off goods as pre-boycott bounty, and at the same time place his failure to pay his debts at the feet of his English partners; after all, it was their fault the Stamp Act was passed, and it was up to them to make sure it was repealed. Hancock appeared as the patriot he wished to be and yet lost little from his "sacrifice" to the cause. In that spirit, he hosted the entire evening of food and drinks, and toasted his compatriots, old and new, one after another.

Even the Crown officials in New England had written petitions to Parliament to repeal the Stamp Act. Although these men could never condone intimidation or violence to achieve repeal of the act, the requests that came from Governor Francis Bernard, Thomas Hutchinson, and others begged for relief.

"There never was a poor people in so distracted a state as we are at this time. No officer of the crown is safe who shews the least disapprobation of the furious spirit prevailing against the stamp duty. I have felt the affects of popular rage more than has been known in America," wrote Hutchinson in a plea sent to Parliament in the fall of 1765.[24]

The Crown officials, in appealing to Parliament, made no references to violated rights, nor did they make allegations of tyranny or oppression; instead, they asked for repeal as a favor to loyal subjects. The unspoken message was clear: save us from the tyranny of these unruly mobs.

Reverend Smith in Weymouth, in his last sermon for the year 1765, preached from his pulpit, "render therefore to Caesar, the Things that are Caesar's and unto God the Things that are God's." As John Adams explained in his diary, "The Tenor of it was to recommend Honour, Reward, and Obedience to good Rulers; and a Spirited Opposition to bad ones."[25]

Adams wholeheartedly rejoiced in his father-in-law's "good deal of animated Declamation upon Liberty and the Times." Unlike many of the other ministers in and around Boston, who had been promoting "Passive Obedience—as the best Way to procure Redress," John Adams and Reverend Smith, and Abigail as well, were all of the same mind: "We have tryed Prayers and Tears, and humble Begging and timid tame submission as long as trying is good—and instead of Redress we have only increased our Burdens and aggravated our Condemnation."[26]

None of the three could support the tactics of the Boston Sons of Liberty—not yet—but nor would they stand by and passively accept the oppressions of their rights by a Parliament thousands of miles away.

In the new year, the boycott of British goods continued; so many merchants had agreed to nonimportation that ledgers on both sides of the Atlantic, once filled to bursting with notations and scribbles, check marks and sums, were reduced to single columns and null profits. Hancock had warned his agents months before—"the heavy Taxes laid on the Colonies will be a great Damp to trade . . . we shall have little or no Demand for Supplies from England, this ought to be Consider'd, and hope we shall be Reliev'd, we are worth Saving in this part of the World"[27]—and his threat had come true.

John Hancock heard from his British friends, and his agents in both London and Bristol: the slowdown in trade was hurting British suppliers, merchants, and traders in Britain. The pain extended to the British islands of the West Indies: "our sugar islands will be deprived of their usual supplies of provisions," wrote one leading merchant, and plantations on the islands would be "disabled from sending home their produce or even subsisting their slaves."[28]

In addition, and perhaps worst of all for the merchants of Britain, there would be "little or no chance" of collecting debts owed to them from the American colonists, a situation that could "prove fatal" to their business; those who survived would have to put "a total stop of all purchase of manufactures for a country whence no returns can be expected . . . it naturally and unavoidably follows that an exceedingly great number of manufacturers are soon to be without employ and of course without bread."[29] Lord Rockingham (who had replaced Grenville as prime minister of England) and Parliament were pressed hard by influential lobbies to repeal the Stamp Act and save the British economy.

On May 16, 1766, the *Harrison*, one of John Hancock's trading ships, pulled into Boston Harbor with the official news: the Stamp Act had been repealed by Parliament in March. The town burst into wild celebration. Bells pealed, guns were discharged into the sky, debtors' bills paid so that the jails would be emptied and the streets filled with happy revelers. The Liberty Tree was decorated with flags, and more flags flew from windows and balconies and fence railings. Josiah Jr. had instructed that his home just down the road from the Liberty Tree be festooned with red, white, and blue bunting, and a flag hung from the windows of Edmund Quincy's modest lodgings to the east.

Dolly and Katy walked the streets arm in arm, marveling at the joy expressed across the neighborhoods of Boston, from the narrow houses in tight lanes along the docks to the larger town houses along the Common and then spreading out to the North End. Governor Bernard opened his house to the selectmen of Boston and offered drinks all around in celebration, and even the lowliest deck swabbers secured tricolored ribbons to fly from the windows of the rooms they rented by Hancock Wharf. The relief felt by the colonists of Massachusetts was palpable: "Joy smil'd in every Countenance, Benevolence, Gratitude and Content seemed the Companions of all."[30]

The Sons of Liberty, funded in part by Hancock, staged the largest fireworks ever set off in America, and Hancock followed up their pyrotechnics with a show of his own set off from the yard in front of his mansion. He ordered that tables be set up along the Common with pipes of Madeira, barrels of cider, and foodstuffs, and also hosted a dinner for twenty-nine at the Bunch of Grapes tavern, where he invited one after another guest to give a toast.

Newly elected to the Massachusetts General Court, the highest political seat in the colony, Hancock was not only celebrating the end of the Stamp Act but the beginning of his political career. John Adams recorded the importance of Hancock's election as the moment when the town of Boston—and indeed the entire colony—"made that young man's fortune their own."[31]

Throughout the meal hosted at the Bunch of Grapes, Hancock made sure that everyone's glasses were kept full, providing all the wine necessary to drink to His Majesty's health. The gathered crowd was happy to praise King George, and even Parliament, for bringing relief to the colonies. As Hancock reported to his agent in London, "Our rejoicing has been conducted in a very decent, reputable manner; and I hope now peace and harmony will prevail."[32]

But Parliament was not done with the colonies. The Stamp Act had been repealed with full notice given, in the accompanying Declaratory Act, of "the absolute right of Parliament to bind the colonies in all cases whatsoever."[33] In the months to come, not only would taxes and duties once again be levied on the colonies, but this time, Parliament would ensure the physical means to enforce their implementation. Troops were on their way.

9

A Watchful Spirit

The spirit of liberty is and ought to be
a jealous, a watchful spirit.

—JOHN ADAMS

"What care I for News Paper Politicks?" John Adams wrote in a letter to his good friend and brother-in-law, Richard Cranch, in January 1767. "Since last May, my Heart has been at Ease . . . and the Governor and all his Friends and Enemies together cant trouble it."[1] While repeal of the Stamp Act had barely been celebrated in Braintree—the villagers are "insensible to the Common Joy!"—for John, the news had induced both elation and relief.[2] Now he could get back to work as a lawyer, putting politics, boycotts, and protests behind him. He needed to build up his legal practice and get his family back on sound financial footing.

John began riding the law circuit, going from court to court throughout Massachusetts and taking on new clients for all sorts of cases. His work took him away from home for days at a time, but traveling the circuit was the only way to build his reputation and the family fortunes. Abigail missed him terribly—"it seems lonesome here," she wrote to her sister; in another letter, she lamented that her husband was "such an Itinerant . . . that I have but little of his company."[3]

It was not only John's company that Abigail missed; in 1766, her sister Mary had moved to far-off Salem with her family. "O my Dear Sister I mourn every day more and more the great distance between us. I [wish] I could come as often again as I used to . . . I long to see you all," Abigail wrote in a letter; she then added that she wished their children might play together: "what would I give to . . . see them put their little arms round one an others necks, and hug each other, it would really be a very pleasing Sight, to me."[4]

By the start of 1767, Abigail was pregnant again, with her second child; a welcomed addition to the Adams family and another cousin for the

Cranches. But would the baby ever see his faraway cousins? And would John be home long enough to enjoy the new child? He was forever away on the court circuit, traveling for law cases.

John did make time in his busy court schedule to answer a series of letters that had been published in the Tory-leaning *Boston Evening Post*. The letters had been written by his old friend Jonathan Sewall. Writing under the pen name "Philanthrop," Sewall defended Parliament's colonial policies and argued that the strength and purity of the British Constitution was such that Parliament would never be able to "impose chains and shackles on the people, nor even attempt it."[5]

John's countering essays to Sewall's letters were published in the Whig *Boston Gazette* in early 1767 under the pen name "Governor Winthrop" (claiming direct connection to Massachusetts' first leader). John warned that "Liberty, instead of resting within the . . . constitution of government . . . has always been surrounded with dangers, exposed to perils." Paraphrasing from Tacitus, a favorite philosopher of his, John Adams wrote, "the first advances of tyranny are steep and perilous, but, when once you are entered, parties and instruments are ready to espouse you."

Stand always vigilant, Adams warned his fellow colonists, or we shall suffer, with "no hope of a remedy without recourse to nature, violence, and war."[6]

Late in the night of February 3, 1767, a fire broke out in the bakehouse building of one of John Hancock's tenants near Mill Creek in Boston. The fire quickly spread, razing more than twenty buildings by the time it succumbed to the efforts of firefighters. Fifty families lost their homes, and Hancock lost several buildings in addition to the bakehouse. When the General Court failed to provide funds adequate, in Hancock's opinion, to assist those who had lost not only their homes but everything they owned, he contributed his own funds, hundreds of guineas, to help them out.

The prince on the hill had deep pockets, and an open heart, and the people of Boston loved him for it. He would be elected to the House of Representatives in May by a large margin, reelected as town selectman, and also named fire warden for Boston.

John Quincy of Mount Wollaston, Abigail Adams' beloved grandfather, fell ill in the spring of 1767. By early summer, as the end of Abigail's pregnancy drew near, it became clear to all the family that he was dying. Although she dearly wanted to see her grandfather before he died, Abigail was warned away by both her husband and her uncle, Norton Quincy, for fear of potential risks to her or her unborn child. Abigail instead wrote her grandfather long notes of devotion, which she had delivered to Mount Wollaston, along with posies of lavender and buttercup culled from her garden. Abigail's mother, Elizabeth Quincy Smith, arrived from Weymouth and settled in the Adams farmhouse, traveling back and forth between the homes of her dying father and her pregnant daughter and serving as nursemaid in both.

On July 11, 1767, Abigail's first son was born. Abigail and John sent a message up the hill the following morning: their baby boy would be named John Quincy Adams. The next day, Abigail's grandfather died. Norton Quincy, the new master of Mount Wollaston, walked slowly down to his niece's home to deliver the news and see for himself this child who would bear his father's name.

After months of rumors, in August 1767 news arrived in Massachusetts that Parliament had passed a new series of measures to be enacted in the colonies. Called the Townshend Acts (named for the chief treasurer of Great Britain, Charles Townshend, nicknamed "Champagne Charley" for his spendthrift ways),[7] the new measures far exceeded the hated provisions of the Stamp Act. Duties were imposed on a large number of goods coming into the colony, including necessities like lead, glass, tea, paint, and paper. In addition, strong legal procedures were set in place to ensure those duties were paid immediately at the port of entry.

The measures enacted to combat smuggling were especially harsh. Any importers attempting to smuggle goods listed in the acts would have their vessels seized, as well as be subjected to fines, arrest, trial without a jury, and sentences of imprisonment. In order to enforce the measures listed, more British troops were to be brought to Boston and stationed within the town.

Abigail Adams heard the news of the Townshend Acts while John was again away on the law circuit. He was traveling with Samuel Quincy and Josiah Quincy Jr., the men sharing meals and beds as they made the rounds of New England courts. Abigail had no doubt that the new acts would have an impact on her life. John would get further drawn into politics, like a bee to honey—or like a moth to flame—and she would see even less of her husband.

Abigail wrote to John that she wished he would just come home; "Sunday seems a more Lonesome Day to me than any other when you are absent. . . . I hope soon to receive the Dearest of Friends and the tenderest of Husbands, with that unabated affection which has for Years past, and will whilst the vital Spark lasts, burns in [my] Bosom."[8]

Their son, little Johnny Adams, was growing quickly and had become "fat as a porpouse"[9]—much to his mother's relief, who believed plump children could better fight off the illnesses that left so many parents bereft. As babies and then toddlers, sturdy Johnny and chubby Nabby took after their father, "so very fat," while Abigail herself was "lean as a rale."[10]

She was most likely skinny from working so hard, as it was her duty to keep the farm going while John rode the law circuits; even when he was home, he was so busy with local politics that much of the burden of managing the household and the farm fell on Abigail. She was proud of the work that she did for her family; her desire to have John at home with her had more to do with the company he provided than the help he gave her. Now she feared that her husband would seek a wider arena than Braintree for his "politicking"—and that she would have even less of his attention and company than she had presently.

Resistance to the Townshend Acts was largely nonviolent for the first year after news of its enactment reached the colonies. Even Sam Adams advised his previously rowdy followers that there be "NO MOBS—NO CONFUSIONS—NO TUMULTS. . . . We know WHO have abus'd us . . . but let not a hair of their scalps be touched: The time is coming, when they shall lick the dust and melt away."[11]

Instead, resistance focused on causing as much economic harm to England as possible. By the fall of 1767, John Hancock, together with Edmund Quincy and other Boston merchants, began working on long-term plans for boycotting English goods, including tea, lace, and cloth, and implementing programs for colony-based production of goods.

Planning for the Boston boycott was shared with other towns and villages in Massachusetts, as well as with other colonies. The hope was that support for nonimportation would spread widely and the resulting economic strain inflicted on British trade would force a repeal of the Townshend Acts in England, in the same way that economic pressures had ended the burdens of the Stamp Act.

Tradesmen, manufacturers, and distillers willingly joined in the nonimportation plans. Thomas Hill, father of Sam Quincy's wife, Hannah, along with her grandfather, Henry Hill, were longtime advocates of the rights of colonists; they had joined in the Stamp Act economic embargoes and would do so again to protest the Townshend Acts. Thomas offered his services to the selectmen in enforcing nonimportation and fostering local production of goods; his expertise as a distiller and a businessman served the committee well, along with his dedication to the rights of the colonists.

What Thomas Hill thought of his son-in-law, Sam Quincy, who had thus far managed to support the rights of colonists without denying the powers of the Crown, Thomas Hill kept to himself; his daughter Hannah loved the man, and that was good enough for him. Sam was a Quincy, and that counted for something; he was also a Mason, and a member of the St. Andrew's Lodge, along with John Hancock, Paul Revere, Joseph Warren, and James Otis Jr., with whom he attended meetings at the Green Dragon Tavern. Thomas Hill admired all those men, and so, he reasoned, Sam Quincy must also have some good in him.

In Braintree, John Adams made sure the local selectmen followed the lead of Boston in drawing up their own plan for a boycott of British goods, and for improving production of local goods to replace British imports. He then did what he could to circulate the Braintree plan widely throughout the colony, with notices in the papers and letters sent from the selectmen of Braintree to committees from other towns. Communication was the key to ensuring widespread support of the boycott, and the boycott would succeed only if it were widespread.

Sam Adams encouraged Josiah Quincy Jr. to write publicly against the Townshend Acts. He had heard the young man speak with flourish and bravado, and he was sure Quincy could write in the same persuasive manner, thereby garnering more support for the economic boycott; even better, Josiah could bring in the diversity of supporters that Sam Adams was looking for.

While the Sons of Liberty could always count on their longtime followers of working men, Sam Adams wanted to expand membership in the group with the more prosperous classes of Boston. Josiah Quincy Jr., well-off himself, as well as erudite and intellectual, could bring those classes of men—and those who opposed Crown policies but were frightened by mob actions—into the fold.

Ned Quincy joined Sam Adams in encouraging his younger brother to follow in the footsteps of Oxenbridge Thacher, with whom Josiah had apprenticed, and become a great pamphleteer, that is, an essayist on political topics of the day. Eleven years separated the oldest and youngest sons of Josiah and Hannah Quincy, but the two were close, joined not only because of their Whig leanings but also because of their shared state of health: both were consumptives, their disease having been diagnosed at an early age.

Consumption was a harrowing condition; symptoms included weight loss, night sweats, daytime fevers, long periods of fatigue, and intermittent bouts of coughing up phlegm and blood. Ned and Josiah Jr. could go for weeks without any manifestations of the disease but then suddenly fall ill; during those times they remained at home, secluded and resting, hoping for new strength and another remission.

Desperate for relief from their condition but unwilling to undergo the painful treatments of bleeding and purging (vomiting brought on by emetics), the brothers sought the advice and care of Dr. Joseph Warren. Dr. Warren was a young man, just three years older than Josiah Jr. Having trained with the esteemed physician James Lloyd (uncle of Ned's beloved Rebecca Lloyd), he already enjoyed an excellent reputation as a doctor. Warren was warm and kind, generous to a fault; he was also a committed Whig. Whatever Dr. Warren could do for Ned and Josiah, he would do, he promised them.

Rest definitely helped, Dr. Warren told the brothers, but there were other things they could do as well. He advised Josiah and Ned to take in plenty of fresh air night and day and to avoid late nights out at crowded taverns or coffeehouses. They should try to eat frequent meals to stave off the "wasting away" associated with the disease and spend their evenings quietly but with ample refreshments taken. The two brothers thus spent many evenings at home together—often in the company of their new friend, Dr. Warren—partaking of cheese, bread, and ale and calmly talking politics.

By the end of the year, essays written by Josiah Quincy Jr. under the byline "Hyperion" began to appear in the *Boston Gazette*. In his essays, Josiah spoke directly to those men of law and business whom Thomas Hutchinson and Francis Bernard were trying to bring over to the side of the Crown, and whom Sam Adams was vying to recruit to the Sons of Liberty. He warned men of influence against falling prey to British flattery and bribes and advised them to remain resolute in defending the liberty of the colony: "Be not deceived my countrymen. Believe not those venal hirelings when they would cajole you by their subtleties into submission. . . . When they strive to flatter you by the terms of 'moderation and prudence,' tell them, that calmness and deliberation are to guide the judgment; courage and intrepidity command the action."[12]

The law was on the side of the colonists, Josiah insisted, and "the Genius of Liberty" still counted for something.[13] Using dramatic imagery—"A rank adulterer riots in thy incestuous bed, a brutal ravisher deflowers thy only daughter, a barbarous villain now lifts the murderous hand and stabs thy tender infant to the heart"—Josiah sought to equate the illegal measures taken by Britain to control the colonies with every colonist's worst nightmare of assault.[14] He then urged "my much-respected countrymen" to reject "the threats and vaunting of your sworn foes" and defend the liberty of the colony against all usurpers.[15]

The stir caused by the writings of Hyperion were immediate, causing consternation to Hutchinson and joy to Sam Adams. As Sam Quincy would describe it, in toasting his brother at a Sons of Liberty celebration, "We admire You . . . for your spirited introductions & not only because you have adopted The Sentiments of Liberty and Freedom with manhood, but because it is done at a Time when most wanted. . . . [You are a man] of Spirit and Abilities, equal to the Government."[16]

Sam Quincy especially appreciated his younger brother's devotion to pamphleteering as a way to bring about change; both brothers were wary of mobs and mob actions as a way to counter parliamentary actions. But while Sam Quincy still trusted Hutchinson and the other Crown officials to lead the colony, Josiah suspected that the interests of the people of Massachusetts clashed with the interests of those who governed them and that the rights of colonists were not being protected by government officials, either at home or in England.

In his essays, Josiah argued that the colonists must commit themselves to fight for their liberty: "In defence of our civil and religious rights, we dare oppose the world . . . if this be enthusiasm, we live and die enthusiasts. Blandishments will not fascinate us, nor will threats . . . intimidate. For under God, we are determined, that wheresoever, whensoever, and howsoever, we shall be called to make our exit, we shall die freemen."[17]

Consumptive that he was, Josiah knew his own death would come sooner rather than later—and while he still lived, there was only one fight worth making: the one to keep the colonies at liberty to command their own futures. Only after securing liberty for his fellow men, vowed Quincy, and "with the plaudits of his conscience," would he be ready to die. "A crown of joy and immortality shall be his reward," he wrote. "The history of his life his children will venerate. The virtues of their sire shall excite their emulation."[18]

Josiah might well be on his way to "a crown of joy and immortality," but as both his brothers advised him, he would first need to have "children" to "venerate" him—and children required a wife. Sam Quincy had his Hannah, and just this past spring, Rebecca Lloyd and Ned Quincy had become engaged. Josiah was already acquainted with Abigail Phillips, daughter of a wealthy Boston merchant, "an early attachment" having been formed between the two.[19] The Quincy brothers did what they could to foster the attachment and cozy the natural affinity along. They arranged evening carriage rides for the couple, where they could sit side by side under warm blankets, chatting away while the skies overhead turned from blue to navy to black, lit only by faraway stars and a rising moon. When the snow came, the carriage was exchanged for a sleigh and the drives continued.

Fresh air was what Dr. Warren had ordered, and the Quincy brothers took the prescription a step further: fresh air for the lungs and intimate conversations to strengthen the heart. Josiah Jr. must get healthy and stay healthy: the colony, and the family, needed him.

While Samuel Quincy deplored the harsh measures set forth in the Townshend Acts, he had no problem with the local representatives of the Crown, and in fact curried favor with both Bernard and Hutchinson. He was rewarded for his support when in November 1767 he was named solicitor general for the colony; Jonathan Sewall had resigned the post to become the colony's attorney general. The appointment offered a good salary and sound future—but required Sam to ally himself even more publicly with Crown officials. It was not hard for Sam to do; like his brother, he believed in the rule of law, but unlike Josiah Jr., Sam felt as much loyalty to the empire itself as to the laws of the empire.

Upon taking the position of solicitor general, Sam was required to take an oath of office, which included swearing loyalty to the royal government. He did so in good faith, and through the trials to come, he would remain bound to that oath. Even when finding himself on opposite sides to his brother and friends, he remained loyal to his oath of fealty to the government of England.

Sam and his wife, Hannah, were delighted with his new appointment.

The couple enjoyed the status the title of solicitor general conferred, as well as the steady income it provided. By this time, they had three children: Hannah, born in 1762; Sam Jr., in 1764; and Thomas, in 1766. Their large home on South Street was always lively with a steady stream of visitors coming by, children at play, and servants hard at work to provide the care and comfort friends and family were due.

Visitors to the home on Summer Street included Sam's brothers, Ned and Josiah Jr.; Hannah's brother Henry and his wife, Anna; and old friends such as the merchants John Rowe and Samuel Curwen, and fellow lawyer Robert Treat Paine. But more and more, it was a legion of British administrators and merchants who came to call, together with their fashionable wives: "the social privileges which surrounded British officials were held to have an attraction for Mrs. Quincy that she was able to communicate to her husband."[20]

Sam would later acknowledge that their true friends were New Englanders born and bred, fellow countrymen with whom they were "so long encircled with the dearest connections"—and that he had failed to understand the impact his appointment as solicitor general would have on those "dearest connections,"[21] as well as on his place in the extended Quincy family.

On December 21, 1767, John Dickinson of Philadelphia published the first of a series of letters in the Pennsylvania press. His "Letters from a Farmer in Pennsylvania to the Inhabitants of the British Colonies" set forth in plain language the argument that the elected assembly of each colony was the only authority that could impose taxes on its citizens; any tax imposed by Parliament constituted taxation without representation, violating basic principles of the British Constitution.

The "Letters from a Farmer" were reprinted in newspapers throughout the colonies, including all the Boston papers, and applauded far and wide. The selectmen of Boston were so impressed with how "the rights of American subjects are clearly stated and fully vindicated" that they passed a unanimous resolution to send official thanks to the "ingenious Author" for his work on behalf of all the colonies.[22]

Josiah Quincy Jr. marveled at the way in which Dickinson had managed to unify opposition to the Townshend Acts across the colonies, which were separated by vast physical expanses as well as cultural and religious differences. Information was not easily shared between colonial governments and travel between colonies was difficult. But if the disparate regions could overcome obstacles of distance and differences, and join together, Josiah knew they would constitute a formidable force that could bring about dramatic change in how they were governed.

Unjust policies fomented protests across the land; joining those protests together in a show of unity would force Great Britain to change the policies that caused the protests. "Thus, Goliath is killed by his own sword," Josiah would argue in the future; but he was already formulating plans to create a union of colonies that would force Britain to take notice and relent.[23]

As the year 1767 drew to a close, John Adams began to think that his energies and ambitions, not only for himself but for his colony, would be better served in a larger arena. Acting within the confines of Braintree chafed at his hopes of going further and doing more. He informed the selectmen of Braintree of his intention to move his family and legal practice to Boston and resigned as a member of the town committee.

"Am I grasping at Money, or Scheming for Power?" he wrote in his diary. "Am I planning the Illustration of my Family or the Welfare of my Country? These are great Questions."[24] He hoped that the year ahead would provide answers.

Abigail was unsure about the move to Boston. Unlike her mother-in-law, Susanna, Abigail had taken to the life of managing a farm and home; while she could sometimes become overwhelmed by her many responsibilities, she also gloried in doing her best at whatever task lay before her—and being acknowledged for her prowess and hard work.

Well-known in Braintree for her charity, her industry, and her good humor, she had become a natural leader in the small community. She advised local women on spinning their own linen, cotton, and wool, especially important now that British cloth was under boycott. In return, she sought from them recipes for teas made from chamomile leaves and loosestrife, hopeful that she could grow the plants and flowers she needed to brew her own. If she were to move to Boston, she worried that the tenant farmer left in her stead wouldn't be able to tend her garden to her exacting standards.

But Abigail finally agreed to the move. Whether in Boston or in Braintree, she would be a busy mother, and soon to be busier still, with another child on the way. At least in Boston, she might see more of her husband. He would be working from an office in their home, building his legal practice with Boston-based clients, and spending less time on the court circuit. And Abigail would be able to visit with her cousins, the daughters of Edmund Quincy who lived in Boston.

Like Abigail and her sisters, the Quincy cousins in Boston joined with other New England women in protesting the Townshend Acts; they wore homespun clothing, put away their English tea, and resigned themselves to frugality. As reported in the *Massachusetts Gazette*, the women of Massachusetts "have not worn ribbons for many years past . . . have made spinning their only employment, and drink nothing at their meetings but New England Rum."[25]

Men of New England also chose to drink rum, eschewing imported tea to protest parliamentary taxes: "a very patriotic gentleman . . . has written over his chimney piece the following words, *No Tea but as Much New England Rum as You Please*."[26]

Dolly Quincy, used to wearing nice English dresses of calico and chintz decorated with frippery, closeted her favorite garments with little enthusiasm. Even as other towns in Massachusetts, and then other colonies in America, joined the boycott of British goods, Dolly was a reluctant participant. When attending a dinner party at the Hancock mansion, she couldn't fail but notice that the dresses worn by many of the other women were of the finest materials and decorated with touches of lace and ribbon. The wives of wealthy colonial merchants and high-ranking Crown officers seemed unconcerned that they were flaunting the latest in British fashion.

But with her father, Edmund, serving on the Boston Committee for Non-Importation, Dolly had to dress the part of dutiful colonist. John Hancock, who liked nice clothes as much as Dolly did, understood her reluctance to dress down. Nevertheless, he willingly moderated his style to somber colors and simple waistcoats; following his example, Dolly did the best she could at revamping her older dresses into a more modest look. Her lovely ribbons and laces she threw into a drawer, to be salvaged later, when the boycott was over.

At the end of the year, John Hancock joined fellow members of the Massachusetts House of Representatives, including Sam Adams and Thomas Cushing, in sending a petition to the king of England. The petition asked the king to condemn the Townshend Acts as a violation of their "sacred right" to be taxed only by the acts of representatives elected by them and to repeal all its measures.[27] Governor Bernard labeled the petition treasonous, and in the end, the king would refuse to receive it.

The colonists, nevertheless, were sure that God and the law were on their side, and that their liberty would be protected by both. As Josiah

Quincy wrote in one of his Hyperion essays, "if our God be for us, who shall be against us? Though our enemies should be as the vermin of the field, or as the insects of the air, yet will I not be dismayed; for the breath of his mouth shall scatter them abroad, the power of his strength shall confound and overwhelm them with mighty destruction."[28]

The test would come soon.

10

The Arrival of Troops

The pulse of the people beats high,
and it may well be imagined,
that in our present state,
all ranks among us are much agitated.

—JOSIAH QUINCY JR.

On May 17, 1768, John Hancock watched from his harborside offices as the British warship *Romney* sailed into Boston Harbor. With fifty guns trained on the town, the *Romney* bore the clear message that the colonists must willingly submit to Parliament's latest demands in the form of the Townshend Acts or they would be forced to comply by the guns and troops of His Majesty, the king of England.

But the colonists led by Hancock, Adams, and the other Sons of Liberty had no intention of complying with the Townshend Acts, no matter the form of intimidation employed by the king and Parliament. Already in February, John Hancock and his fellow selectmen, along with Josiah Quincy Jr. and his brother Ned, had circulated a letter composed by the Massachusetts legislators condemning the Townshend Acts. The letter was distributed up and down the continental coastline, and sent to all other legislatures of the American colonies for approval.

In the letter, the New Englanders first asserted their strong allegiance to the Crown and then stated that Parliament, through its passage of the Townshend Acts, had unfairly taxed the colonists without their consent, given that they had no representative voice in Parliament: "his Majesty's American subjects . . . have an equitable claim to the full enjoyment of the fundamental rules of the British constitution; [and] . . . it is an essential, unalterable right in nature, engrafted into the British constitution, as a fundamental law, and ever held sacred and irrevocable . . . that what a man has honestly acquired is absolutely his own, which he may freely give, but cannot be taken from him without his consent."[1]

Governor Bernard condemned the circulated letter as treasonous and demanded that it be rescinded. Of the one hundred twenty members of the Massachusetts House, ninety-two refused to rescind circulation of the letter. "Ninety-two" became a rallying cry against the Townshend Acts across the land. Paul Revere crafted a silver bowl dedicated to "the Glorious Ninety-two," and presents for Massachusetts legislators flowed in from other colonies, including a gift of ninety-two drinking glasses sent from South Carolina.[2] In New Hampshire, the citizens of the town of Petersham carefully removed all but ninety-two branches from an elm tree, dedicating the tree to Liberty.[3]

Enraged by its refusal to rescind the letter, Governor Bernard dissolved the General Assembly of Massachusetts and prohibited its members from meeting. Josiah took to his pen to attack Bernard, in letters published in the *Gazette*. The right to peaceably assemble and to legislate, Quincy argued, were enshrined in the colonial charter, British constitutional law, and natural law. Governor Bernard had no authority to take such rights away.

Colonial resistance to the Townshend Acts, and Britain's determination to enforce them, had been tested with the arrival of John Hancock's ship *Lydia* to Boston Harbor in early April. The *Lydia* was laden with cargo, much of it taxable under the Townshend Acts. But Hancock had no intention of allowing customs officials to board the vessel in order to verify what sort of cargo the *Lydia* was carrying and what duties might be owed under the act. He publicly vowed that "he would not suffer any of [the Crown] officers to go even on board any of his London ships."[4]

James Otis Jr., who had been serving as Hancock's legal adviser, counseled Hancock on how to legally restrict access to the vessel. As he explained to Hancock, even British customs officers had to comply with the law; in order to be able to search a ship, they had to present a correctly drafted and executed warrant. Hancock just had to wait for the right moment to challenge the warrants carried by the customs men.

On the evening of April 9, Hancock received word at his home that the *Lydia* had been boarded by a customs inspector. He hastily threw on his coat and hustled into a carriage, instructing his driver to get him down to Hancock's Wharf as quickly as possible. He sent messages to a number of the men he employed at the wharf, and to James Scott, the captain of the *Lydia*, as well. The messages dictated by Hancock were carried out as instructed. The Sons of Liberty were put on alert, and men began to gather in anticipation.

When Hancock arrived at the wharf, he found that Owen Richards, the tidewaiter employed by the customs office, had already descended into the hold of the ship. Hancock, accompanied by a number of his men, rushed below. They surrounded the lone official, and Hancock demanded to see his warrant for searching the ship. As luck would have it, Richards' papers carried no date and thus were invalid. Hancock was well within his rights to have Richards removed from his ship, and he directed his men to do so. Richards was taken by the arms and forcibly removed from the *Lydia*.

A crowd had gathered at the wharf, summoned by the Sons of Liberty. The mood was tense, the crowd unsettled and anxious. Hancock took control of the situation, asking only that Richards be allowed to go home in peace; he told the crowd that it was best to retire for the evening, and that he himself was eager to get back to his bed. Having taken interviews of witnesses, Thomas Hutchinson wrote later, "Mr. H. was escorted up the wharf, he having the approbation of the spectators. He was obliged to entreat them not to remonstrate throughout the town."[5]

It was a public relations coup for Hancock: he had both defied the customs officers and prevented a riot. When Jonathan Sewall, in his capacity as attorney general for the colony, admitted he could not prosecute Hancock for failure to comply with customs, stating publicly that Hancock had acted "within the boundaries of the law" in protecting his ship the *Lydia* from an unlawful search, the coup seemed complete. Who was running things in Boston, was the question in many people's minds—the minions of the British Crown or the merchant prince on Beacon Hill?

John Adams was impressed by James Otis Jr.'s counsel. At the same time, Adams hoped that he himself might become a lawyer for his old childhood friend. He had finally moved his family into Boston earlier in the year and was working hard at building up his client base from their new home on Brattle Street. The house, where he had his office, was conveniently located close to both the wharves and warehouses of Boston and the town house where the state legislature met.

The substantial three-floor brick house rented by the Adams family was a pleasant place, painted white and with a fine garden at the back lined with pear trees and roses. The front of the house faced directly onto Brattle Square and the wooden church across the way.

THE ARRIVAL OF TROOPS

Looking out from the windows, it seemed to Abigail Adams as if all of Boston passed by their home, all day long and into the evening; sixteen thousand inhabitants, loud and boisterous and busy, a far cry from the five hundred or so families in Braintree, almost all of whom Abigail had known by name. But despite the "Noisy, Busy Town"—or perhaps because of its liveliness and energy—Abigail was happy those first months in Boston.[6]

As she had hoped, now that they lived in Boston, John was often at home, with his law office set up on the ground floor of their house. The Adams family's social life, which had once centered on the Quincys of Braintree, with Uncle Norton up on the hill and Josiah Quincy down the road, now expanded to include not only more Quincys—Josiah Quincy Jr. often came by for a meal—but also their new good friend and family physician Joseph Warren (whom they met through Josiah and Ned Quincy), and their old friends Jonathan Sewall and his wife, Esther Quincy Sewall, who lived just over the Boston Neck, in Charlestown.

Despite the published letters of debate that passed between Philanthrop (pen name of Sewall) and Governor Winthrop (pen name of Adams), the two old friends enjoyed spending time together; as John wrote, "although we were at Antipodes in Politicks We had never abated in mutual Esteem or cooled in Warmth of our Friendship."[7] The two men genuinely liked each other, and Abigail and Esther, cousins and girlhood friends, were also pleased with each other's company. And yet when Jonathan Sewall came to Adams with a proposal to serve as advocate general in the High Court of Admiralty, upon the direct request of Governor Bernard, John wasted not a moment's breath in turning down the offer.

As he recalled later, Sewall "knew very well my political principles, the system I had adopted, and the connections and friendships I had formed in consequence of them. He also knew that the British government, including the king, his Ministers, and Parliament, apparently supported by a great majority of the nation, were persevering in a system wholly inconsistent with all my ideas of right, justice, and policy." He told Sewall, "therefore I could not place myself in a situation in which my duty and my inclination would be so much at variance."[8]

Sewall begged John to reconsider the offer, and even returned to the Adams home three weeks later to ask again, but John remained firm: "I told him my answer had been ready, because my mind was clear, and my determination decided and unalterable."[9] As it turned out, John's legal skills would soon be called upon by another friend with whom he had shared happy moments in his younger days, but this time, it was a man whose political principles he shared.

Throughout the spring of 1768, Josiah Quincy Jr. lived alone at the family home on Marlborough Street. His brother Ned had gone on a journey south, catching a ride with a trading ship on its way to Barbados. The purpose of the journey was to restore Ned's health in time for his upcoming wedding. Rebecca Lloyd, his fiancée, had joined with the family in encouraging him to take the trip: the sunshine, the warm sea breezes, the fresh fruits of the island—all would play a vital role in staving off the consumption. Goodbyes were said and plans made for letters to be sent back and forth with trading vessels. A month or so away, and then Ned would return. A summer wedding could be planned, and then Miss Rebecca Lloyd would join the Quincy family.

With Sam married, and Ned soon to follow, it was time for Josiah Jr. to move things along with Abigail Phillips. She had become a trusted companion, as eager as he was to read and discuss all sorts of serious books and pamphlets. Her father, William Phillips Jr., both a Whig and an intellectual (he, along with his father, was a major benefactor of the Phillips Academy in Andover) approved of Josiah Jr., and was eager for the match to be made. Josiah's family was all for the marriage, and had been for months.

Feeling fit and strong, his consumption having gone into remission, Josiah finally proposed to Abigail in early April 1768. Plans were made for another Quincy wedding, to take place after Ned and Rebecca were married.

But at the end of April, Josiah Jr. received the news that his brother Ned had died in a shipwreck off the coast of Bermuda. Josiah traveled out to Braintree to deliver the terrible news to his father. His brother Sam came the next day, and the family settled Ned's accounts. They sent Rebecca a sad memento of the never-to-be celebrated union between her and Ned: a plate that had been made for the couple, a large serving dish of the finest bone china decorated with their joined initials. Josiah Jr. and Abigail would postpone their own wedding until the period of mourning had passed.

Sam penned a poem in his sorrow, likening a man's life to "a summer's day / some only breakfast and away / Others to dinner stay and are Full Fed." The last lines of the poem were meant as a comfort to his father, and for all the family: "he that goes soonest, has the least to pay."[10]

The family's faith was strong: Ned would soon arrive in heaven, with few sins for which to atone, and from there, bless his family on earth below.

In early May 1768, John Hancock's ship the *Liberty* dropped anchor in the harbor. While Hancock had successfully thwarted inspection of the *Lydia* through legal means, keeping royal customs officers off the *Liberty* proved more problematic. The captain of the *Liberty*, James Marshall, had listed the ship's cargo as twenty-five pipes of wine brought from Madeira, Spain (a pipe carried about 126 gallons). But when the tidewaiter Thomas Kirk came aboard to verify the amount, Marshall refused to let him inspect the cargo hold; instead, he forced Kirk below deck and locked him in a cabin. That evening and well into the night, Kirk lay awake, listening to the unmistakable sounds of Marshall and a few other men off-loading cargo.

At sunrise, Kirk was released from his impromptu prison and shown a cargo hold containing twenty-five pipes of wine. James Marshall lay on deck, worn out from his night's work but still defiant; he took Kirk by the arm and warned him that if he breathed a word of his captivity or what he heard during the night, Marshall himself would hunt Kirk down and kill him. Kirk, thoroughly frightened, agreed to keep silent.

Captain Marshall soon died of the exhaustion brought on by unloading the illicit cargo. A few weeks passed, and Thomas Kirk, no longer fearing reprisal, approached Benjamin Hallowell, chief customs officer, with his version of what had happened aboard the *Liberty*.

By this time, the British warship *Romney* had arrived in port, and Hallowell requested the assistance of its commander, John Corner, in carrying out a seizure of the *Liberty* as allowed under the Townshend Acts (any vessel suspected of use in smuggling could be seized). On June 10, Hallowell made a big show of parading down to Hancock's Wharf surrounded by Crown officials. He painted a broad arrow on the side of the *Liberty*, to indicate that it was now government property. John Corner arrived by water in a barge, ready to cut the *Liberty*'s lines and tow it away.

News traveled fast along the streets lining the harbor. John Corner was a man already despised throughout Boston for his efforts to impress vulnerable men into the navy and for his characterization of Boston as "a blackguard town . . . ruled by mobs . . . by the eternal God, I will make their hearts ache."[11] But there was nothing the gathered crowd could do when

Corner and his crew cut the lines of the *Liberty* and began to lead it away from its berth at Hancock's Wharf: Corner's crew was armed and ready to fire upon them.

Incensed, the crowd focused their anger on Hallowell and his entourage, who were standing on the dock, and began to pelt them with stones, sticks, and bricks. A boat belonging to a Crown official was lifted out of the water, carried through the streets, and then set alight on Boston Common, within yards of the Hancock mansion.

John Adams took up his defense of Hancock in the *Liberty* case even before official charges were brought. He had been taken on as counsel to Hancock a few weeks earlier, his appointment secured through Sam Adams. Sam was certain that his cousin John would serve Hancock's interests better than those "cringing Tory lawyers" Hancock had used in the past (not counting, of course, the decidedly anti-Tory Otis, whose health issues now interfered with his representation of Hancock).[12]

In a letter to Dennys de Berdt, the London agent for the Massachusetts House of Representatives, John Adams explained that Hancock had nothing to do with the fracas involving the *Liberty* and the burning of the boat belonging to a Crown official; "The truth is, the barge was burnt on a common surrounded by gentlemen's seats . . . the mean insinuation that it was done under the influence of Mr. Hancock is so far from the least shadow of the truth . . . the tumult was finally dispersed principally by his exertions, animated by his known regard to peace and good order."[13]

News of the *Liberty*'s seizure quickly traveled across Massachusetts and through all the colonies. Outrage over British enforcement tactics flared, and support surged for a continentwide boycott against Britain. Already New York and Philadelphia had agreed to impose their own nonimportation agreements; and in May, the traders and merchants of Boston agreed to take a hard line against imports. The Boston merchant John Rowe recorded in his diary that he and the other merchants and traders of the town had agreed "not to write for any goods after the first of June, nor Import any after the first Day of October, untill the Act the Imposing Dutys on Glass Paper &c be Repealed."[14]

In Virginia, George Washington led the way for his colony's nonimportation agreements; in South Carolina, "the generality of the people of this province" agreed "Not to purchase or cause to be purchased any goods whatever imported from G.B. except hard ware; 2. To go heartily to work in manufacturing their own & Negroes cloathing; 3. To avoid as much as possible the purchase of new Negroes; 4. To give all possible encouragement to the importation of such goods (not prohibited) as are manufactured in others of his Majesty's colonies."[15]

The only colonies not joining in the boycott were New Hampshire and New Jersey, but ports in all the other colonies refused to trade with Britain.[16] Although nonimportation would hurt the colonial economies, the hope was that the merchants and manufacturers in England would be damaged even more. Economic pressure had killed the Stamp Act; Sam Adams, John Hancock, and Josiah Quincy Jr. all hoped that such pressure would again succeed against the plans of Parliament.

But this time round, Parliament was determined to see its acts implemented. If the presence of the *Romney* was not enough to signal its resolve, more warships would be sent, along with more British troops. As Governor Bernard explained in a letter he wrote to Parliament, "Troops are not wanted here to quell a Riot or a Tumult, but to rescue the Government out of the hands of a trained mob, & restore the Activity of the Civil Power, which is now entirely obstructed." He added, "this aught to have been done two years and a half ago. If it had, there would have been no opposition to Parliament now."[17]

By mid-September, four months after the arrival of the *Romney*, two more British regiments on fourteen warships had arrived in Boston, sailing into the harbor and then angling their broadsides toward Boston, guns ready to fire. In one day, ten thousand British troops disembarked, carried by smaller boats to the wharf, where they then organized into lines. Josiah Quincy Jr., alerted by messenger, came out to watch in increasing disbelief as "with muskets charged, bayonets fixed, drums beating, fifes playing, and a complete train of artillery, the troops took possession of the Common, the State House, the Court House, and Faneuil Hall."[18]

John Hancock and his aunt Lydia could see the soldiers from their home on Beacon Hill. Dolly Quincy, her sister Katy, and her parents stood at the other end of the Common, close enough to the parading troops that they could smell the mixture of sweat and mildew that rose off the men; it was as if the uniforms had been in a damp, dark cargo hold and no amount of light could take away the rot. But under the bright sun, the colorful uniforms glowed—red for the soldiers and yellow for the drummers. The black tricorn hats worn by the infantrymen and the miter-shaped bearskin hats on the grenadiers made the men appear taller than they really were. Smelly or not, there was no denying how impressive these British troops were.

The drums of the soldiers, the pounding of their boots, and the whistle of the fifes could be heard from John and Abigail's house on Brattle Square to the grand town houses east of the Common, where Sam and Hannah Quincy lived, to those homes on Beacon Street to the north, where Abigail Phillips and her father could be found. Even with the windows closed and curtains drawn tight across the frames, Abigail Phillips could hear the roll and rhythm of the marching feet, boots on stones, one after the other.

Governor Bernard tried to convince the colonists of Massachusetts that the British troops arriving in Boston were simply being brought in from outlying frontier posts as a cost-saving measure; maintaining them at the borders of British territory was very expensive, and moving them close to supply lines was a more efficient way of protecting the colony.

But within days, the troops' true purpose seemed evident to everyone working the wharves: every ship coming in and leaving the harbor was boarded by customs officials for inspections, with British soldiers at their side every step of the way.

While troops sent in February had been housed in "Barracks built at the Castle . . . that there might be no Occasion of Quartering Them," there was no longer room on Castle Island for all the incoming soldiers, and the men had to find—or build—housing in Boston itself.[19] Soldiers patrolling the streets of Boston, living alongside the colonists: Josiah Quincy Jr., John Hancock, and John Adams all agreed that no good could come of it. They would soon be proved right.

"Opinions differ respecting what ought, and what will be, the deportment of this people," Josiah wrote to a friend. "On the one hand, a swarm of court dependents, and a standing army in the bowels of a state, have been, in all ages and nations, thought, and found to be the bane of civil freedom. On the other, an open rupture with Great Britain . . . is a dreadful alternative."[20] Liberty from England was not yet the goal; instead, what the colonists sought was liberty from its oppressive taxes, and from the troops sent to live among them and used to enforce such taxes.

The selectmen of Boston did all they could to prevent British troops from commandeering public spaces for their living and working quarters. While there was little that could be done to keep the soldiers and their officers out of Faneuil Hall and Town Hall, Crown officials ran up against legal barriers when trying to requisition private buildings for use by the British Army. Josiah Quincy Jr. advised one of his clients who owned a warehouse to deny entrance to Crown officials by whatever means necessary.

The man bolted all the windows of his building, barricaded the doors, and then released a statement to the effect that "his council [*sic*] were of the ablest in the province, and he should adhere to their advice be the consequences what they would."[21] He remained holed up in his warehouse—visited only by his lawyer—until all danger of requisition of his property had passed.

A complaint was issued against the warehouse owner and a legal case brought seeking to force him to open his property for use by the British Army. Chief Justice Hutchinson ruled against the Crown's complaint and upheld Josiah Quincy Jr. in the advice he had given his client: the law protected the property owner and he could not be forced to house soldiers in his warehouse.

But everyone in Boston worried that the day would come when the sanctity of private property would no longer be enough to hold back the rapacity of the British. They worried that so many troops, quartered on a public square or in public buildings, could move quickly to take over their town; never had their liberty felt so threatened, with soldiers all around them. All in all, there were over four thousand British troops in Boston, one to every four inhabitants of the town.

The colonists feared that even more measures meant to oppress and intimidate them were on the way: "British taxations, suspensions of legislatures, and standing armies are but some of the clouds which overshadow the northern world," Josiah Quincy Jr. bemoaned in the *Boston Gazette*. "Heaven grant that a grand constellation of virtues may shine forth with redoubled lustre, and enlighten this gloomy hemisphere."[22]

No matter the scope of British enforcement measures, Quincy declared that there would be no submission to the will of Governor Bernard or Parliament. "We Americans have a righteous cause. We know it. The power of Great Britain may oppress, nay, for a time apparently subdue us," explained Josiah in a letter to a friend. Before "all the freeborn sons of the north will yield . . . to any tyrannic power on earth," there will be a fight.

And the fight would be fierce: calling himself and all who stood with him "political dreamers," Josiah warned that "political dreamers are the most obstinate, and incorrigible, of all."[23]

John Hancock was arrested in November 1768 on smuggling charges arising from the docking of the *Liberty*. He was charged with importing one hundred pipes of wine valued at £3,000 without paying the taxes due and threatened with fines and penalties equaling close to £100,000 (including the value of the *Liberty*, still held by the British). John Adams agreed to represent Hancock in the case, and the trial was set for January 1769. Jonathan Sewall would be the prosecutor, representing the Crown.

As Adams prepared for trial, the happy days spent in the white house on Brattle Square during John and Abigail's first months in Boston seemed like a distant memory. A shadow had fallen over the household. British officers drilled their troops on the square, right under their windows. The clatter of boots and the call of orders rang through the home, disturbing the children and bringing on headaches in Abigail.

As winter settled in, the days shortened and the temperatures fell so precipitously that Boston Harbor froze solid. The air outside was damp and heavy with smoke from so many household chimneys; food was expensive and supplies scarce; the children, cooped up inside, became fretful; and the clients who came to John's office were grim, wary of what the future might bring as Parliament's grip tightened around Boston.

The gloom in the Adams home was temporarily cast away by the birth, on December 28, 1768, of John and Abigail's third child. They named her Susanna after John's mother and called her by the affectionate nickname of Suky. She was a beautiful baby, with hazel eyes and a rosebud mouth, but she seemed small and frail compared to Abigail's previous babies.

Abigail worried about Suky; she was always fretting and crying, and refused to nurse. Nothing Dr. Warren suggested seemed to help, and Abigail's own mixtures of herbs and poultices did little to revive the baby's appetite or strength. In the end, the decision was made to send Suky to the quiet and healthier environs of Braintree, where John's mother could care for her. Abigail wished she could have gone with her youngest, taking the older children and her husband along. Boston, with its unceasing noise, its cold and fetid air, and its ever-present British troops, was no longer a place to her liking—no longer safe, but menacing.

The smuggling case against John Hancock began in early 1769 and dragged on and on for three months. Jonathan Sewall, representing the Crown, produced little evidence to show conclusively that Hancock knew how much wine had originally been transported on the *Liberty* or that he had played a part in illegally removing pipes of wine from the vessel. Dozens of witnesses were called—"the Crown seemed determined to examine the whole town as witnesses"—including "his amiable and venerable Aunt Lydia."[24]

John Adams, representing Hancock, felt worn down by the prosecution, its monotony and relentlessness: "a painfull Drudgery I had of his cause. There were few days through the whole Winter, when I was not summoned to attend the Court of Admiralty . . . I was thoroughly weary and disgusted with the Court, the Officers of the Crown, the Cause, and even with the tyrannical Bell that dongled me out of my House every Morning."[25]

Finally, at the end of March, Jonathan Sewall called the case to a close, stating simply for the record, "Our Sovereign Lord the King will prosecute no further hereon."[26] Although no fines or penalties had to be paid, the *Liberty* was never returned to John Hancock, and the ship became the property of the Royal Navy. In the summer of 1769, angry colonists managed to board it and set it afire. It never sailed again.

11

Portents of a Comet

The pulse of the people beats high,
and it may well be imagined that in our present state
all ranks among us are much agitated.

—JOSIAH QUINCY JR.

In the summer of 1769, John Adams had a choice to make: get himself to Taunton for the sitting of the local court where he hoped to secure new clients, or wait a day in Boston and attend the grand feast planned by Sam Adams, John Hancock, and the Sons of Liberty. The feast was to celebrate the departure of Governor Francis Bernard; the hated administrator had finally been called back to England.

A petition sent to the king of England by the Massachusetts House of Representatives in the spring had included a list of seventeen complaints against Governor Bernard and a request that he be removed from office. The colonists' seething dislike for Bernard had turned into fury when a number of his private letters to friends in England were published. The letters proved the colonists' claims that he was distorting the truth of circumstances in the colonies—that he was a "little dirty TALE-BEARER."[1]

The colonists complained in their petition that Governor Bernard "had given a false and highly injurious representation" of the situation in Boston, not only in private letters but in government communications to Parliament and the king: "He has treated our Representative body with contempt. . . . He has been a principal instrument in procuring a military force."[2]

When the petition was published in full in the press in early June, the public humiliation for Bernard "stung like an adder."[3] Furious and disappointed, Bernard sent his own private request to the king, asking to be relieved of the terrible burden of governing Massachusetts. He wanted to leave the cursed colony just as much as the colonists wanted him gone.

King George acquiesced to both requests and called Bernard back to England. Church bells rang out in jubilation as his ship left the harbor; Bernard could hear the bells, and then the cannons, fired from Hancock's Wharf to speed him on his way. The *Boston Gazette* reported, "Tuesday last embarked on his Majesty's ship the *Rippon*, sir Francis Bernard . . . who for nine years past, has been a Scourge to this Province, a Curse to North America, and a Plague to the whole Empire."[4]

The purpose of the grand party held one week after Bernard's departure was not only to celebrate his leaving but also to commemorate the 1765 protests against the Stamp Act, seen by many as the start of effective colonial resistance to parliamentary overreach. For Sam Adams, the festivities, which would be attended by hundreds of citizens from Boston and surrounding villages, were also a celebration of just how successful he had been at enlarging the membership of the Sons of Liberty.

The day's celebrations began at the Liberty Tree in Boston. Toasts were made and drinks were taken, and then the group, traveling in 139 carriages with John Hancock at the head, moved on to Dorchester, to the grounds of the appropriately named Liberty-Tree Tavern. John Adams met the travelers at the tavern, intent on joining the party and with no regrets for missing court in Taunton.

On the contrary, he feared that if he were not in attendance, "many might suspect, that I was not hearty in the Cause . . . whereas none of them are more sincere, and steadfast than I am."[5] He happily "Dined with 350 Sons of Liberty. . . . We had two Tables laid in the open Field by the Barn, with between 300 and 400 Plates, and an Awning of Sail Cloth overhead."[6]

John Adams sat alongside a crowd of family and friends, including Josiah Quincy Sr. and his son Samuel, who still counted himself as a supporter of the Sons of Liberty, even if he would not call himself one. Sitting close by was the grandfather of Sam's wife, Henry Hill, who most definitely called himself a Son of Liberty. Josiah Jr. was not present, most likely due to the recurrence of the symptoms of consumption that would continue to plague him into the fall.

Sam Adams and John Hancock sat next to Joseph Warren and James Otis Jr., with other Massachusetts bigwigs spread out on either side. Paul Revere sat with Benjamin Edes and John Gill, publishers of the *Boston Gazette*, and other fellow Masons, including Joseph Tyler, John Jeffries, and William Palfrey. Representatives from other colonies were also present at the feast, including Philemon Dickinson, brother of John Dickinson, from Pennsylvania, and Joseph Reed from New Jersey.[7]

Many drinking toasts were made that day, more than forty-five in all.

Drinking beer and cider and, later, rum, men raised their glasses and drank to "Liberty without Licentiousness to all Mankind," to "A perpetual Constitutional Union and Harmony between Great Britain and the Colonies," to "the Liberty of the Press."[8]

After the meal, Philemon Dickinson stood up to sing the famous song written by his brother John, titled "The Liberty Song." Written to the tune of an old British war song, the words were already well-known to the crowd, and even John Adams, a shy singer, joined in singing its refrain: "IN FREEDOM we're born, and in FREEDOM we'll live / Our purses are ready, / Steady, Friends, Steady, / Not as SLAVES but as FREEMEN, our Money we'll give."[9]

Despite the many toasts, John Adams claimed not to have seen "one person intoxicated" and instead felt himself with a group deliberately "cultivating the Sensations of Freedom." Such feasts are important, Adams decided, "for they tinge the Minds of the People, they impregnate them with the sentiments of Liberty. They render the People fond of their Leaders in the Cause, and averse and bitter against all opposers."[10]

Nothing could dampen the spirit or the resolve of the revelers, not the heavy humidity of the day nor the downpour of rain that inundated the field in the late afternoon. All present were joyous in their cause of liberty and steadfast in their collective commitment to it.

But there were those in Boston, and throughout Massachusetts, for whom commitment to the cause was turning into more of a burden than they had anticipated. The boycott of British goods, begun in January with much fanfare and support, was taking a financial toll on store owners and shipowners alike. The economics of limited trading hurt just too much; even as John Hancock counseled that "we must live upon our own produce and manufactures," there were simply not enough goods manufactured or grown locally to substitute for the enormous quantities previously supplied by Great Britain and its colonies around the world.[11]

At the end of August, an article in the *Boston Chronicle*, a newspaper with Loyalist leanings, reported that some merchants were trading British goods in defiance of the boycott to which they had allegedly sworn allegiance. John Hancock's name was on the list of illicit traders, along with twenty-nine others.

Hancock immediately issued a statement that he had not undertaken any business in violation of Boston's nonimportation agreement. He then repeatedly denied the charges to all and sundry and finally published a definitive denial in the press: "This is ONCE FOR ALL to certify to whom it may concern, That I have not in one single instance directly or indirectly deviated from said Agreement; and I now publicly defy all Mankind to the Contrary."[12]

To further prove his commitment to the cause, Hancock publicly criticized his London agents for sending a shipment of goods to Boston despite his directions to the contrary, and he announced that any goods sent from England to the colony for his consignment would be sent back immediately upon arrival. He offered his ships free of charge to any merchant wishing to send goods back to England; supply crates would be provided for those merchants who had already unpacked their wares.

Hancock had his revenge on the *Boston Chronicle*, when with great glee and satisfaction, he purchased the debts owed by the paper and foreclosed on its owners. Using John Adams as his attorney, he shut the paper down, selling off its presses, type cases, galley trays, and every other piece of printing equipment. Its chief Whig competitor, the *Boston Gazette*, was the most likely purchaser of the equipment the Tory paper would no longer need.

Josiah Quincy Jr., John Adams, and John Hancock all agreed that nonviolent methods were the only legal and viable methods of forcing Parliament to repeal the Townshend Acts and remove or reduce the number of troops in Boston—and that the best leverage they had was economic. While they persisted in publishing editorials and letters, bringing lawsuits to force compliance with legal precedent, and submitting petition after petition, they continued to push their fellow colonists to stick to the boycott and hurt the British economy, with the hopes that such pain would finally compel Parliament to repeal the measures imposed on the colonists.

John Adams was asked by his cousin Sam to take on the case of four sailors who had resisted impressment to serve aboard the British frigate *Rose*. In the course of events, an officer in the Royal Navy had been killed, and now the sailors were charged with murder. The case would be brought in the Court of Admiralty, under the new measures imposed by the Townshend Acts; that is, the case would be tried without a jury, leaving the determination of guilt or innocence solely to a Crown-appointed judge.

John set to work, searching "all authorities in civil law, the law of nature and nations, the common law, history, practice, and everything that could have any relation to the subject."[13] And he found exactly what he was looking for: "the only British statute that included the word or idea of impressment."[14] Under that statute, the practice of impressment was expressly prohibited in America. Chief Justice Hutchinson had to concede the point, and the sentence of the five-judge court was unanimous: the sailors were found to have acted in self-defense in fighting against their unjust impressment. All charges were dropped and the men were released.

The victory in the *Rose* case brought Adams fame in the colony, accolades from the Sons of Liberty, and an onslaught of young men eager to be his law tutors. John chose two young students and got back to work on cases that would pay fees—unlike the case of the sailors accused of murder, which his cousin Sam had persuaded him to take on for little monetary recompense.

Throughout the summer and fall of 1769, Suky, John and Abigail Adams' daughter, remained in Braintree under the care of her grandmother. In June 1769, John wrote to Abigail from Falmouth, Maine, where he was appearing in the circuit court: "How long I shall be obliged to stay here, I cant say. But you may depend I shall stay here no longer, than absolute Necessity requires. Nothing but the Hope of acquiring some little Matter for my dear Family, could carry me, thro these tedious Excursions."

Missing his family so much, he sent love "to my little Babes" and then asked for news of his youngest, adding, "Cant you contrive to go to Braintree to kiss my little Suky for me?"[15]

How Abigail wished that she could do just that, but traveling to the village was no easy task: the road was rough, and the journey, at more than ten miles, was long. First the path wound through Dorchester, then on into Milton, where the Neponset River had to be crossed by ferry; then the path picked up again, but there were more brooks and streams to get over, and rough terrain along the shoreline; then the final stretch down along the coast to arrive in Braintree. The Adams family had no grand carriage or chaise, but only a cart. By the fall of 1769, Abigail was again pregnant; traveling any distance at all became even more arduous.

Despite the difficulties, Abigail did all she could to stay in close contact with her mother-in-law, Susanna, and her little daughter Suky; she even considered bringing the girl back to Boston. The previous spring, she and John had moved from the house on Brattle Street to a place on Cold Lane by the Mill Pond. The house was neither as neat nor as comfortable as the white house had been, but at least there were no soldiers drilling outside from dawn to dusk, and the air seemed purer close to the pond, the sun brighter as it glinted off the water. But in the end, Suky remained where she was and

Abigail continued to rely on whatever messengers she could find to bring her news from Braintree.

Throughout the fall of 1769, the presence of British troops, armed to the teeth, created an oppressive atmosphere in Boston. John Adams persuaded the Massachusetts legislature to petition Parliament for removal of the cannon and troops. He particularly objected to the positioning of cannons "at the very door of the State House where Assembly is held"[16] and argued that "debate of our Assembly must be free . . . Common decency as well as the honor and dignity of a free legislature will require a removal of those cannon and guards, as well as that clamorous parade which has been daily round our court."[17]

But Parliament refused to answer the petition, and both troops and cannon remained in town; in the harbor, British warships stood at anchor, armed and ready.

When a trailing comet appeared in the sky over Boston in October, there were many who took it as a bad omen. Ever since a "flaming comet" trailed across the sky in the months leading up to the Battle of Hastings in 1066, Englishmen had called the "comet-star" a "tiding of bitter woe." King Harold had ignored the prophecy and was killed by an arrow through the eye.[18] Many American colonists still carried the fears of their ancestors when it came to heavenly apparitions. They feared now that Parliament would never back down, and that with British troops stationed throughout the town and in the harbor there would be a high price—even a deadly one—for daring to defy Parliament's decrees.

For months, Josiah Quincy Jr. and Abigail Phillips had been putting off the date of their wedding. The delay was not due to the death of Ned or Josiah's workload—although he was very busy with "the multiplicity of his professional avocations"—but because his consumption had flared up in the summer and worsened with the fall weather.[19] Josiah returned to the care of Dr. Joseph Warren and once again followed the good doctor's prescribed regime of rest, fresh air, and plenty of good food. Abigail threw herself into nursing her husband-to-be, overseeing his menus and accompanying him to Braintree, where the sea air, fresh fish, and ample supply of vegetables did much to speed his recovery.

Finally, on October 4, 1769, Josiah and Abigail were married, in a ceremony held in the Old South Meeting House in Boston, where Abigail's father was a deacon. The party, attended by all the Quincy clan—cousins, aunts, and uncles—was held at the Phillips mansion on Beacon Street. Abigail was radiant that day, her face smiling and bright, her dark hair drawn back and crowned with curls. Her dress was simple, befitting the times, but around her waist she might have fashioned a girdle of fall roses, a custom of the current austerity. Josiah, tall and spare beside her, appeared the picture of good health, his cheeks pink and his eyes bright with joy.

Abigail knew the true state of Josiah's health. He would never be free of his affliction and would most likely die young. She had nonetheless chosen him to be her husband. As the attractive daughter of a wealthy man, she had her pick of suitors, but having been raised on the hero-hailing classics of Homer, Milton, and Edmund Spenser, she wanted someone beyond the usual merchant or lawyer, and in Josiah she found her ideal, an almost mythic character of integrity and resolve.

The two agreed that in having children, not only would the name of Josiah Quincy be carried on, but their shared values of courage, duty, and faith would also be passed on to future generations. As Josiah Jr. wrote to his own father, "Through your watchful care of my education, and your kind munificence, I am out of temptation to the meaner vices, and in that state, which . . . is the happiest human nature can boast, an independency, save on God and myself, for a decent support through life, and the hope of quitting the stage with that best human standard of true worth, the general approbation of my countrymen."[20]

As a wedding gift, Josiah Sr. gave the couple a bombé chest created by the Needham cabinetmaker Kemble Widmer; the elegant chest of drawers, made of rounded wood and inlaid with intricate borders, cost a small fortune because of its unique shape and intricately decorated surfaces, but it was only the first of many gifts that he would give them. Josiah Jr. gave his new wife a set of eight elegant Chippendale chairs, crafted in Massachusetts out of mahogany; the chairs were upholstered in woven silk from stock imported long before the boycott.

Abigail presented Josiah with a collection of books that to him constituted a veritable treasure; he had new shelves built in the library on Marlborough Street, anticipating spending many happy hours reading. Josiah was not a passive reader; he scribbled liberally in the margins of his books, recording the thoughts sparked by the text. For him, reading was a joy of discovery and new experiences, adventures made possible and safe for one with such health problems as he had. In reading, he could scale mountains and run rivers without leaving the security of his padded chair.

But it wasn't only adventure he sought in reading; it was knowledge. The joy of knowledge, of making connections between the past—ancient Rome, Greece, the empires of Constantinople and the Holy Roman Empire—and the present in which he found himself. Beginning a fresh *Law Commonplace* as a married man, his new journal would become just as filled as his old one had been, with page after page of quotations that he saved for future use—not only legal maxims but also moral ones, taken from sermons, stories, and treatises old and new.

Once settled in with Abigail on Marlborough Street, Josiah turned his attention back to politics and to securing "the general approbation of my countrymen."[21] A comet trailing across the sky didn't scare him. As a man of reason, and with his faith in the law, along with his conviction in the justness of the cause of liberty, he would do all that he could to help his fellow colonists in the fight against oppression.

As he wrote in his journal, quoting Bacon, "'Crafty men condemn studies, simple men admire them, and wise men use them.' Read not to contradict and confute, nor to believe and take for granted, nor to find talk and discourse—but to *weigh* and *consider*."[22] Josiah would set himself to weighing and considering, and then to writing. Not only for his legal clients, but for the future of his colony.

On November 7, 1769, Elizabeth Wendell Quincy died in Braintree. Edmund Quincy planned a lavish funeral ceremony—"fit for a Venetian doge"—for his beloved wife.[23] Dozens of relatives and friends attended the funeral, including Josiah Jr. and Abigail, Josiah Sr. and his third wife, Anne; Sam and Hannah Quincy; Hannah and Bela Lincoln; Norton Quincy; and John Adams' mother, Susanna, along with the Reverend Smith of Weymouth and his wife, Elizabeth. Edmund and Elizabeth's children were there: Dolly, Ned, Henry, Elizabeth, Katy, Sarah, and Esther (along with her husband, Jonathan Sewall).

The funeral party was given assigned places in the processional parade that followed Elizabeth Quincy's coffin from Josiah Quincy Sr.'s home in Braintree to the burying ground across from the North Parish Church. Elizabeth was laid to rest close to Edmund's parents, in a space where Edmund expected he would soon join her.

Edmund and Elizabeth had been married for over forty-four years. Edmund found it hard to imagine life without her, but he submitted to the will of God: "True love inspires us with a perfect submission to divine will," he wrote in a letter to his youngest daughter. "Persuaded that all things are governed by infinite wisdom and goodness, we submit to whatever happens."[24]

With Dolly's mother gone, Lydia Hancock contrived to bring the young woman closer into the Hancock family. She had grown genuinely fond of Dolly, but she was also convinced that John's marriage to her would be the final step in her yearslong plan of establishing her nephew as the most respected and favored man in Boston. By tying the names of Hancock and Quincy together through an unbreakable vow, John's social standing would be without question. Quincy was a name long esteemed in the colony, and one that could be traced back, allegedly, to the Baron de Quincy, second earl of Winchester, who was at King John's side when he signed the Magna Carta. To be part of that family would make the subsequent Hancock dynasty undeniably grand.

And there was yet another motive to Aunt Lydia's matchmaking. Lydia knew rumors still swirled about her nephew's supposed lover, an older woman named Dorcas Griffiths, whom Hancock allegedly visited often in her rooms on Hancock's Wharf. Lydia wanted those rumors quashed. Having first conferred with Dolly's father and garnered his approval, Lydia convinced Dolly to spend even more time at the mansion on Beacon Hill.

Under Lydia's careful chaperoning, Dolly was invited to stay for days at a time, sharing a roof but not a bed with John Hancock, and acting as Aunt Lydia's companion on many social visits throughout Boston. The news of the intimacy between the couple spread quickly and Lydia's plan seemed secure, as the rumors began to shift; the latest gossip was that John Hancock and Dorothy Quincy would certainly be married, it was only a question of when. No one mentioned Dorcas Griffiths anymore; especially when the woman publicly allied herself with a British officer and turned Tory.

12

Pressing Forward

May you have fortitude to suffer, courage to encounter,
activity and perseverance to press forward.

—JOSIAH QUINCY JR.

"Suffering well, our fortune we subdue," wrote a *Boston Gazette* columnist in January 1770.[1] Although the identity of the columnist is unclear, the pen of Josiah Quincy Jr. can be seen both in the words of Virgil that he quoted and the sentiments conveyed. The piece was written to rally the people of Boston to suffer the British troops and taxes, not in silence but in open rebellion. In the weeks that followed, Josiah would publish a number of pieces all with the purpose of inspiring his fellow colonists to rise up against British oppression.

In a letter published in the *Gazette* in February, under the pen name "The Independent," Josiah warned his fellow colonists that "America is now the slave of Britain . . . every day more and more in danger of an increase in our burdens, and a fastening of our shackles," and urged, "I wish to see my countrymen break off—*forever!*—all social intercourse with those whose commerce contaminates, whose luxuries poison, whose avarice is insatiable, and whose unnatural oppression are not to be borne."[2]

While Josiah continued to promote rebellion through nonviolent means (through the boycott of any and all goods produced in Britain), many of his Long Room Club associates were losing patience with nonviolent measures, and sought to accelerate a more active—and violent—rebellion against British oppressors. Led by Sam Adams, these Sons of Liberty sought to focus colonial ire on specific individuals, including the British soldiers who patrolled the streets and the shop owners who sold British goods, as well as the citizens who purchased them.

Sam Adams spent every night that winter going from tavern to tavern, meeting place to meeting place, attempting, like Josiah Jr., to revive resistance to Britain. But unlike Josiah, Adams and the original members of the Loyall

Nine encouraged the harassment—and worse—of any and all individuals associated with British oppression.

During his nightly tours of drinking establishments, Adams was often accompanied by men dressed like Mohawk Indians. In both British and American political cartoons, American colonists were depicted as Native Americans, and Liberty was often portrayed as a young Native American woman. What better costume to wear when protesting the British than the clothes of America's original inhabitants? The symbolism of the Mohawks was especially strong, given their ferocity in fighting against the English during the French and Indian War.

While Adams roused spirits and fervor in the taverns, outside on the streets of Boston, large gangs of young boys implemented their own effective forms of protest. Once the first snow fell in December, the boys packed snowballs with ice and stones and then launched them at passing soldiers, while harassing them incessantly with jeers and catcalls. Now the boys enlarged the pool of victims to include not only British soldiers but also anyone buying or selling British goods.

Every week the *Boston Gazette* published names of merchants who "AUDACIOUSLY continue to counteract the UNITED SENTIMENTS of the BODY of Merchants thr'out NORTH-AMERICA by importing British Goods contrary to the Agreement."[3] On market days, Thursdays, which were also school holidays, boys freed from the classroom set out to harangue any home or establishment where importers—those who sold or traded in British goods—lived or worked. The gangs of schoolboys broke windows or splattered them with mud or feces, threw rocks and sticks at proprietors and patrons, and launched snowballs. They destroyed or defaced shop signs, then made new signs featuring the word "importer" in black ink and a large painted hand pointing directly at an offending store.[4]

John Adams found the use of children to bolster the boycott of British goods distasteful; Josiah Jr. agreed and renewed his condemnations of moblike activity. John Hancock remained silent on the issue, happy to let Sam Adams bear the brunt of criticism. Hancock understood that the gangs of boys were effective in raising both spirits and ire, and could only help the cause of resistance.

Josiah Quincy Jr. and John Adams had offices close to each other, now that John had taken a small space on King Street near the State House for his legal practice. Having traveled together on the court circuits of Massachusetts and Maine, John and Josiah began to work jointly on a few cases in a partnership they both enjoyed. John found an unexpected friend in the younger Josiah, especially now that his interactions with Jonathan Sewall had dwindled to none, social or otherwise.

Sewall had been named judge of Admiralty for all of Nova Scotia, with a large salary and little work required (he could assign lawyers in Canada to take on his duties). Serving still as attorney general of the colony, he now received a double salary; the added prestige of holding the title of judge was another perk of the appointment. The Whigs of Boston attacked Sewall for accepting what they saw as a bribe to remain a Loyalist, and even his father-in-law, Edmund Quincy IV, wrote that Sewall had been "caught in a snare of six hundred a year."[5]

Jonathan and his wife, Esther, would soon move into a new home, a large and grand house in Cambridge purchased from Richard Lechmere, a Loyalist. The house was on Brattle Street, home to many of the consorts and colleagues of Thomas Hutchinson; so many Loyalists lived on the street that it came to be known as "Tory Row."[6]

While Esther withdrew into the luxuries still available to those associated with the British officials, her youngest sister, Dolly, enjoyed the more subdued but still pleasant lifestyle she shared with Lydia Hancock and her handsome nephew. The women of Boston had recently and very publicly confirmed their support of the boycott, as reported in the *Boston Gazette*: "upwards of one hundred Ladies at the North Part of this town" signed an agreement to drink no tea "till the Revenue Acts are repealed."[7]

No tea drinking, no wearing of lace, no salt on her bread: Dolly, as the daughter of one activist for colonial rights and the companion of another, would comply with the prohibitions—but living much of the time with the Hancocks, she could comply in comfort.

For political purposes, the Hancock household had to keep up the appearance of a relatively simple lifestyle. But John's land and real property holdings would always keep him wealthy, and his home was abundant with luxuries not available to Dolly's father and sisters or to her cousin Abigail Adams. Nevertheless, sales of goods from Hancock's warehouses were on a downward spiral; not only did he have fewer goods to sell, but fewer people had the means to buy them, especially as prices rose on scarce items. His shipping fleet continued to carry whale oil exports on his own account and freight for other merchants, but he had to be careful that shipments from England did not contain boycotted items, and his profits from carrying both oil and goods for others fell.

No matter the impact on his bottom line, Hancock remained dedicated to the economic boycott. Defying the orders of Acting Governor Thomas Hutchinson (a role Hutchinson took on following Bernard's return to England), Hancock convened meetings with his fellow merchants at Faneuil Hall to strategize on how to protect their trade while also protesting the duties and taxes imposed by Parliament. He, along with many others who were complying with the nonimportation agreement, felt especially angry toward those merchants who continued to "meanly sacrifice the rights of their own country to their own avarice and private interest" by trading in British goods.[8]

When Sam Adams asked Hancock to join in a mass demonstration against Hutchinson and his sons, Thomas Jr. and Elisha, who were both wealthy importers of British goods, Hancock refused. He was fearful of another mob attack on Hutchinson, and although he was no fan of the man, he wished him no harm.

Perhaps more important, Hancock turned down the request because Josiah Quincy Jr. warned him that such a mass demonstration could be viewed as mob action against a British governor, which would be "an Act of high treason."[9] Parliament had already in the spring sought to use the ancient Treason Act, promulgated in the times of King Henry VIII, to bring charges against members of the colonial government in Massachusetts, and the threat of treason now hung over every action any colonist might undertake to protest parliamentary measures.

Josiah Jr. suggested to Hancock that the march against Hutchinson had in fact been fomented by Hutchinson and his spies to trick Hancock and other Sons of Liberty; it was a "trap in order to ensnare them . . . [and] to take every advantage of them."[10] Following Josiah Jr.'s counsel, Hancock stayed home and the protest went on without him.

More than two thousand merchants and laborers surrounded Thomas Hutchinson's home, demanding that his sons cease and desist from the selling of "contraband tea" and that all other British goods be returned immediately to England.[11] Hancock, settled in for the night in his mansion, received the news from a messenger sent by Sam Adams: the protest had been handled peacefully, without violence. No one had been hurt, no damage was inflicted on Hutchinson's home, and the crowd had dispersed when threatened with charges of treason.

Josiah Quincy Jr. was gratified to hear that no charges of treason would be brought against any of the organizers of the protest. Once more, he set himself to work writing invectives against the Townshend Acts, with the goal of keeping nonimportation going. Compliance with the economic boycott was still the crucial focus of nonviolent protest; it was the colonists' best—and perhaps only—weapon against parliamentary programs of taxation, troops, and control of the courts.

Due to the lag in communication between the colonies and Great Britain, the colonists did not know just how well their economic boycott was working to mobilize merchants in Great Britain against the Townshend Acts. Parliament, now led by Prime Minister Frederick North, was in fact weighing the options of a partial repeal of the acts. Townshend himself had long since died, and the merchants of Great Britain were eager to start trading with the colonies again. Nevertheless, Lord North wanted to make sure the colonists understood that Parliament's right to govern the colonies was absolute and that as a source of revenue raising, Parliament would never give up on taxing the colonists.

On February 4, 1770, little Suky Adams died in Braintree. John and Abigail traveled with heavy hearts to the village. A bonfire was lit to thaw the ice and snow in the spot chosen for her interment in the burial grounds across from the North Parish Church. She would be buried near the grave of her grandfather, Deacon John Adams. In the spring, a small stone would be laid on the spot, just beyond a stand of early budding forsythia, but the space for grieving had already been marked in Abigail's heart. John Adams wrote nothing of the death in his diary.

But just a few weeks later, John wrote about the death of another child, "lately kil'd by Richardson."[12] The child was Christopher Seider, the eleven-year-old son of German immigrants. He was shot dead by Ebenezer Richardson, a former informer for the Crown customs office, who had come to the defense of a shopkeeper and importer, Theophilius Lillie, when Lillie became the target of an unruly gang of boys.

As Thomas Hutchinson would later describe it, "The whole Street filled with People who would suffer no person to go to his [Lillie's] shop."[13] Richardson, who lived close by, attempted to drive the boys away but only succeeded in further enraging them. The boys began to pelt Richardson with sticks and to yell epithets at him, circling around him like foxes in a chicken yard.

Richardson, retreating to his home, shouted out to the boys to disperse. They replied they "were as free as he to stand in the king's highway" and began to throw fruit peelings, small rocks, sticks, and eggs at his home.[14] A brickbat was thrown through a window, breaking the glass; soon, more windows were struck and rocks began to fly. One rock hit Richardson's wife, and others came close to striking his two terrified daughters. Richardson barricaded himself inside the home, along with a friend, George Wilmot, who had appeared out of the crowd to help.

Richardson and Wilmot went to the top floor of the house and stood by the now glassless window overlooking the crowd below. Looking up, the gathered mob could see that the beleaguered men wielded muskets. Richardson knelt to an opening and laid his musket across the bare sill. The crowd went still. Richardson fired. Pea-sized pellets of lead sprayed through the crowd, hitting a sailor in the leg, the hand of a young man, and the body of eleven-year-old Christopher Seider.

When Seider died later that night, Richardson was charged with murder. Josiah Quincy Jr. was chosen to defend Richardson as his court-appointed lawyer. Opposing him would be his brother, Samuel Quincy, acting as solicitor general for the colony. (Jonathan Sewall should have tried the case but excused himself, leaving it to Sam Quincy to prosecute.) Using the legal maxims of "a man's house is his castle" and he "is not obligated to fly from his own house," Josiah, assisted in the case by John Adams, argued that the shooting of the boy was a form of self-defense.[15] Richardson would be found guilty nonetheless but was pardoned by the king later in the year.

Rex v. Richardson was not the only case Josiah would be assigned to defend that involved mobs, trespasses, self-defense, physical harm, and even death. But Richardson's fatal reprisal against an enraged crowd would be long-remembered as the first of the many bloody incidents caused by the presence of British troops in Boston. As John Adams put it in another case he took on with Josiah, "Soldiers quartered in a populous town will always occasion two mobs where they prevent one. They are wretched conservators of the peace."[16]

Sam Adams and his Sons of Liberty planned to make Christopher Seider's funeral a political statement against the British troops patrolling Boston. The turnout was tremendous, despite the "snow & Hail . . . Smart Thunder & Lightning"[17] that had besieged the city days before. Close to three thousand people gathered for the funeral, "the largest perhaps ever known in America."[18] The procession of mourners began at the Liberty Tree and then proceeded along Orange Street to Newbury, then up Winter to end up at the Old Granary Burying Ground on the east side of the Boston Common.

Led by two hundred schoolboys, Seider's coffin was carried by six of his friends. Behind the coffin marched thousands of Boston citizens, followed by thirty chariots and chaises carrying another hundred or so mourners. Acting Governor Hutchinson cynically noted that if the Sons of Liberty had the opportunity to resurrect Seider, they "would not have done it, but would have chosen the grand funeral."[19]

Alerted by his fellow selectman John Rowe that he had better attend the funeral as a sign of fellowship with the citizens of Boston, John Adams wrote in his diary, "My Eyes never beheld such a funeral. The Procession extended further than can be well imagined. . . . This Shewes, there are many more Lives to spend if wanted in the Service of their Country. It Shews, too that the Faction is not yet expiring—that the Ardor of the People is not to be quelled by the Slaughter of one Child."[20]

John's prediction that the "Ardor of the People" would not be quelled would prove true. The "slaughter of one child" wouldn't suppress the will of the colonists; nor would the deaths of five civilians one week later, struck down by British soldiers in what would come to be called a massacre.

13

Mayhem and Massacre

Let us here pause, and view the citizen and the soldier.

—Josiah Quincy Jr.

On the evening of March 5, 1770, John Adams was at the home of his friend Henderson Inches, a Boston merchant, attending a meeting of a club of which he was a member.[1] It was a Whig gathering, men meeting to discuss how best to address the constriction of colonial rights under Parliament's regime of oppression. But all discussions were suspended when suddenly, "We were allarmed with the ringing of Bells, and supposing it to be the Signal of fire, We snatched our Hats and Cloaks, broke up the Clubb, and went out to assist in quenching the fire or aiding our friends who might be in danger."

But there was no fire: "In the Street We were informed that the British Soldiers had fired on the Inhabitants, killed some and wounded others near the Town house."[2]

Soldiers firing on citizens? It was unthinkable, and the idea of it frightened John Adams. The Massachusetts Charter prohibited British forces from taking offensive measures against colonists without permission of the colonial authorities; and the tacit agreement between colonists and Crown officials was that a semblance of order would be maintained while the issue of troops in Boston was debated in Parliament. If soldiers really had fired on citizens, John knew the entire town could turn into a rolling conflagration of riots, and no good would come from that, for anyone.

Abigail was home alone and John worried for her; she was, as he described, "in circumstances," pregnant with their fourth child. He hurried home, passing first in front of Town Hall, where, with relief, John found all was quiet; he then "walked down Boylstons Alley into Brattle Square, where a Company or two of regular Soldiers were drawn up in Front of

Dr. Coopers old Church with their Musquets all shouldered and their Bayonetts all fixed."

His fears once again aroused, he "went directly home to Cold Lane. My Wife having heard that the Town was still and likely to continue so, had recovered from her first Apprehensions, and We had nothing but our Reflections to interrupt our Repose. These Reflections were to me, disquieting enough."³

By morning, John and Abigail Adams would hear the news: three civilians had been killed the night before and many more wounded, in what Bostonians would call a "Bloody Massacre" and the British officers would term an "Unhappy Disturbance."⁴ John Hancock had received the message at midnight. He'd been home for the evening, holed up with his clerks going over ledgers, when there was a knock on his front door. He brought the messenger into his parlor, and his clerks gathered round to listen to his report.

The messenger told them that the day before, a young boy, apprentice to a wigmaker, had taken it into his head to taunt a British soldier, proclaiming to all who passed that the soldier had failed to pay his bills to the wigmaker. Captain John Goldfinch gave the boy little notice and continued on down King Street to his barracks.

But Hugh White, acting as sentry at the customhouse on King Street, heard the boy's jeers. He came out from his post to wave the boy away, proclaiming that Goldfinch was a gentleman, and as such, he paid all his debts. The boy answered that there were no gentlemen in the regiment, and White struck out in anger, knocking the boy to the ground with his musket.

A crowd quickly gathered and began yelling insults at White—"Bloody lobsterback!" "Lousy rascal!" "Lobster son of a bitch!" White retreated to his sentry post beside the customhouse, loaded his musket, and began to wave it about, all the while crying out for help: "Turn out Main Guard!"⁵

Captain Thomas Preston, in charge of the main guard, arrived on the scene, with the sole intent of taking Hugh White under his protection and back to the barracks. But by this time, men had converged from every corner of the city, armed with wooden staves and clubs. Other citizens, unarmed but concerned, also came running, responding to the ringing of church bells, which usually signified a fire in the town.

Over four hundred men, women, and children crowded into the small square in front of the customhouse. Whistles rang out and shrieks sounded from the streets and alleyways: all was mayhem.

Preston and his guard drew close to White, and White joined them in their line. With Preston slightly out in front of the others, the British soldiers then attempted to turn around and march back to their barracks. But the colonists would not allow them to pass.

The crowd pressed in upon the soldiers from all sides; the soldiers, tense and trembling, pushed forward, tentatively thrusting with their bayonets. From behind, the soldiers could hear a man yelling at them to fire, that he would "stand by you whilst I have a drop of blood. Fire!"[6]

Someone in the crowd threw a club, launching it in the air toward the guard. The heavy wooden club hit Hugh Montgomery, one of the British soldiers, knocking him to the ground. Montgomery jumped up, red-faced with anger, and shouted, "Damn you, fire!"[7] With that, he pulled the trigger of his musket. In the next minutes, other soldiers opened fire and stabbed at the crowd with their bayonets.

At the end of this brief bout of fighting—no longer than five minutes— Crispus Attucks, a former slave, lay dead, along with Samuel Gray, a rope maker, and James Caldwell, a sailor. Samuel Maverick, a seventeen-year-old apprentice, died at first morning's light from an injury from a musket ball; Patrick Carr, an immigrant from Ireland, would die two weeks later.

John Hancock shook his head in disbelief; he had both expected and dreaded a clash between soldiers and civilians, but now that it had happened, he was horrified by the magnitude of the violence. He sent his clerks home and asked the messenger to wait as he wrote out a series of notes to be conveyed to his fellow selectmen.

Peace, above all, had to be maintained, he counseled them; then, the problem of troops in the streets of Boston had to be addressed, once and for all. It was time for Acting Governor Hutchinson to protect the citizens of Boston and demand that the troops be removed from the city.

Samuel Quincy, woken from his sleep in the early hours of the morning, was of the same opinion: peace first; troops next. Arrests would have to be made, and the British soldiers held accountable for their crimes. But how to address the larger issue, the presence of so many British soldiers on American streets, terrorizing Americans? Samuel put the question aside. For now, as solicitor general of the colony, the trials were his concern. The legal process had to be perceived as fair and just, both in Massachusetts and in England. The men accused of firing upon the crowd must be immediately apprehended and indicted; legal counsel for these British defendants would have to be secured; and the trials should be held as quickly as possible.

Thomas Hutchinson, called out to the scene just before midnight, stood on the balcony of the Town House and addressed the crowd below: "The law shall have its course" was the promise that he made when urging them all to go home. "I will live and die by the law."[8]

By the following morning, Preston and eight of the soldiers under his command were under arrest for murder. John Hancock, meeting that morning at City Hall with Hutchinson, Secretary of State Andrew Oliver, and the British commander, Colonel Dalrymple, sought next to address the issue of the troops. While he attended the meeting with the acting governor, a huge turnout of citizens had convened in Faneuil Hall to demand the removal of the troops from Boston. They cheered the arrests of Preston and his men but protested that all other troops, guilty by association, should be evicted from the city as soon as possible. The crowd swelled to such a number that the meeting had to be moved to the Old South Meeting House, where John Adams and his cousin Sam stood together, seeking to maintain both the order and the energy of the crowd.

Hutchinson and Dalrymple seemed unwilling to yield to the demands of the selectmen of Boston or its townspeople. It was only when Hancock used the threat of more violence—"upwards of 4000 men [are] ready to take Arms . . . and many of them of the first Property, Character, and Distinction in the Province"[9]—that Dalrymple and Hutchinson finally agreed it was time to get all the soldiers out of the city. Andrew Oliver later recalled that, had the troops not been removed, "they would probably be destroyed by the people—should it be called rebellion, should it incur the loss of our charter, or be the consequence what it would."[10] Plans were made to evacuate the troops within days, moved to Castle Island in the harbor or sent out of the colony altogether.

In the meantime, however, in order to keep the peace, members of the Suffolk County Bar Association organized a volunteer brigade composed of lawyers, merchants, store owners, and other stalwarts of the community. They were charged with guarding Captain Preston and the other prisoners and keeping order in the streets. As reported in the *Boston Gazette*, "A military watch has been kept every-night of the townhouse and prison, in which many of the most respectable gentlemen of the town have appeared as the common soldier, and night after night have given their attendance."[11]

John Adams told Abigail about how awkward he felt taking his turn as watchman, encumbered by musket, bayonet, broadsword, and cartridge box—and yet how necessary such watch-taking was to ensure against more outbreaks of violence in the town. Every man had his duty to do, and John would do his. But in the days to come, much more than standing watch would be asked of him; and he would do what was asked, again, in the interests of protecting his colony.

Josiah Quincy Jr. was in his offices on King Street when a messenger from the city jail arrived. Captain Preston had asked for him to come to the jail. Quincy, intrigued, agreed. When he entered the captain's cell, the two men were left alone. Quincy emerged a short time later. He first asked that Preston be moved to more comfortable accommodations; then he arranged for a series of messages to be sent, addressing them to several leading men in the community. When Quincy finally left the jail, he hurried to his law office to await the response to his messages.

It was early evening by the time Josiah met with John Adams and leaders of the Sons of Liberty, including Sam Adams, Joseph Warren, and William Molineux. Thomas Cushing, William Cooper, and Josiah's father-in-law, William Phillips, arrived just after dinner, and Hancock came later, held up by business.

Gathered in Josiah's library, the men listened as Josiah laid out for them the request made by Captain Preston that morning: that Josiah represent the captain, and those men accused along with him, on the charges of murder. Josiah explained that he told Preston, "I would afford him my assistance; but . . . I made the most explicit declaration to him of my real opinion on the contests . . . and that my heart and hand were indissolubly attached to the cause of my country."[12]

Nevertheless, Josiah believed that "these criminals, charged with murder, are not yet legally proved guilty, and therefore, however criminal, are entitled, by the laws of God and man, to all legal counsel and aid." He told the patriots gathered in his library, "my duty as a man oblige[s] me . . . [and] my duty as a lawyer strengthen[s] the obligation" to defend the British men against the charges of murder. Josiah asked John Adams to join him on the case, but both men first awaited the opinions of the gathered Sons of Liberty.

Agreement was quickly reached that it was in the interests of the colony that the trial of Preston and his men be seen as just and fair; accordingly, Josiah Quincy and John Adams were "advised and urged" to undertake the defense of the accused British captain and his soldiers.[13] The only way to show both the colonists and the Crown that Massachusetts was a law-abiding colony was to follow the law and let the legal case unfold.

In any event, Sam Adams assured his fellow patriots, no jury composed of the citizens of Boston would ever allow these men to go free. John Adams and Josiah Quincy exchanged a glance: it was their job to make sure that even a jury made up of the most tried-and-true Sons of Liberty would do just that.

Captain Preston shared Sam Adams' opinion about a Boston jury; privately, he lamented that he was sure to "be at the mercy of a partial jury, whose prejudice is kept up by a set of designing villains, that only draw their subsistence from the disturbance they cause . . . [I anticipate] a shameful end."[14]

But publicly, Preston proclaimed his trust in the system, and he willingly put his future in the hands of Josiah Quincy Jr. and John Adams. The addition of one more to the legal team—Robert Auchmuty, a vice admiralty court judge and a Tory lawyer—added a layer of insurance to his cause.

Paul Revere's engraving of seven soldiers aiming muskets at a crowd of frightened colonists was published in Boston by the end of the month. Entitled "The Bloody Massacre perpetrated in King Street, Boston on March 5th 1770 by a party of the 29th Regiment," it would be reprinted around the colonies and in England in the weeks to come, inciting anger in the other colonies and an outpouring of support and condolences to their Boston compatriots.

The British version of the night's events, published mere days after the killings, portrayed the colonists as the villains who started the trouble and instigated a justified defense by the soldiers: "The natural desire of defending themselves, and the sense of the duty incumbent upon them in that unhappy moment to repel force by force in order to defend [against] . . . at least an hundred people, armed with bludgeons, sticks, and cutlasses, will be sufficient to account for their firing on the assailants."[15]

On the very day that the Boston Massacre took place—March 5, 1770—Parliament voted to repeal the Townshend Acts. All taxes on British goods coming into American ports were removed, with the exception of tea. As Lord North explained, the right to tax Americans was absolute; but for now, only the one tax would be collected. As for measures providing for the troops in Boston and for the juryless trials administered in admiralty courts, both would remain in force.

Americans would not hear of the repeal of the acts until May, when the news arrived on the *Haley*, one of John Hancock's ships. For many, the news was received with relief. But for Josiah Quincy Jr., with troops still stationed on Castle Island and taxes still taken on tea, it was both too little and too late: blood had been spilled and lives had been lost.

Although he still had faith in his king, all faith in Parliament and in their officials in the colony was gone. As for Governor Hutchinson, Josiah felt only deep disdain for the man; he described Hutchinson as an example of the maxim "Power of itself makes men wanton, distrustfull, and cruel," calling Hutchinson a "Little Caesar—a miniature tyrant."[16]

The important thing now was to demonstrate to the king (and prove to a distrustful Parliament) that the colony was both law-abiding and just. The trials of Preston and the others involved in the Boston Massacre would have to be conducted with the utmost legality, formality, and transparency. The verdicts reached had to be unimpeachable and final. With John Adams at his side, Josiah was determined to prove to the world that "nothing should appear on this trial to impeach our justice, or stain our humanity."[17]

Josiah Sr. was beside himself with worry when he heard through friends in Braintree that his youngest son would be representing "those criminals charged with murder of their fellow citizens." In a letter to his son, he asked, "Good God! Is it possible? I will not believe it."[18] He ended the letter with a plea: "it has filled the bosom of your aged and infirm parent with anxiety and distress, lest it should not only prove true, but destructive of your reputation and interest; and I repeat, I will not believe it, unless it be confirmed by your own mouth, or under your own hand." He signed off the letter as "Your anxious and distressed parent."[19]

Josiah Jr. quickly sent a response, to settle his rattled father's mind and heart. He first dealt with the actions of his father's supposed friends in Braintree: "Before pouring their reproaches into the ear of the aged and infirm, if they had been friends, they would have surely spared a little reflection on the nature of an attorney's oath and duty . . . and some small portion of patience in viewing my past and future conduct."[20]

Then he assured his father, "I dare affirm that you and this whole people will one day REJOICE that I became an advocate for the aforesaid 'criminals'" and added, "I never harboured the expectation, nor any great desire, that all men should speak well of me. To inquire my duty, and to do it, is my aim. Being mortal, I am subject to error; and, conscious of this, I wish to be diffident. Being a rational creature, I judge for myself, according to the light afforded me. When a plan of conduct is formed with an honest deliberation, neither murmuring, slander, nor reproaches move me. . . . There are honest men in all sects,—I wish their approbation;—there are wicked bigots in all parties,—I abhor them."[21]

Josiah Jr. had little need to worry that his reputation would suffer for taking on the defense of the soldiers. While there were some men on the street who attacked both Quincy and Adams for representing the accused murderers—"incurring a Clamour and popular Suspicions and prejudices"— the Sons of Liberty and their followers understood the important role the two men played.[22]

For the men who knew him—and the men whose opinion he valued— Josiah's integrity was without stain. In May 1770, even after taking on the Boston Massacre case, he was trusted with writing up the instructions for Boston's representatives to the Massachusetts General Court. The instructions would guide the legislators in all their dealings with the colonywide legislative body, and Josiah made sure that his guidance was for increased resistance to parliamentary control over colonial matters. When he presented his draft of the instructions, the document was unanimously accepted by the town committee without any changes made and then published widely for all to see.

Once again relying on his beloved maxims, Josiah wrote his instructions citing "Obsta principiis"—*resist the tyrant*—and stated that any royal decrees and prerogatives that did not advance the good of the colony were not binding, but should be rejected before any dangerous precedent was set: "The further Nations recede and give way to gigantick Strides of any powerful Despot, the more rapidly the fiend will advance to spread wild desolation."

As an example, British troops patrolling Boston fulfilled no good purpose, Quincy argued, and indeed created a "despicable situation." Therefore, the stationing of troops in Boston, even if quartered on Castle Island, must be protested at all costs, and with "open, manly, bold and pertinacious exertions for our freedom."[23]

Given that "a deep-laid and desperate plan of imperial despotism has been laid, and partly executed for the extinction of all civil liberty," Josiah also set forth in his instructions a call for a "firm and lasting union" to be cultivated with the other colonies of America.[24]

Thomas Hutchinson condemned Josiah's written instructions as "ravings . . . of political frenzy." In letters to England, Hutchinson implied that Quincy was a "mad" man and a "mere Coxcomb."[25] He wrote that Quincy's instructions, taken as a whole, "indicated to Government in England the design of a general revolt."[26]

But it was not revolt or rebellion that Quincy had in mind—not yet. He, along with John Adams and John Hancock, still firmly believed in a fruitful partnership with England; they did not contemplate the prospect of independence. As articulated by Josiah Jr., the stumbling block to preserving the relationship between colony and king was that the true state of matters in the colonies had been misrepresented in England (and Josiah largely blamed Hutchinson for this misinformation).

The solution was twofold: first, to present a united front as a colony, in union with other colonies, in demanding restoration of colonial rights; and second, to prove to the king just how devoted and law-abiding (to just laws) his colonists were. When both king and Parliament recognized the loyalty, worthiness, and diligence of the colonies, their full rights under the British Constitution, the charters of the colonies, and natural law would be restored.

What better way to demonstrate to the Crown and all of England the worthiness of the colonists of Massachusetts than to conduct fair and open trials in the aftermath of the Boston Massacre? John Hancock, John Adams, and the Quincy brothers, Sam and Josiah, were all in agreement: the deaths of the five civilians would be avenged but not by a mob.

Thousands had turned out for the largely peaceful funerals of the slain citizens; mourners marched soberly through the streets, and "most of the shops in Town were shut, [and] all the Bells were ordered to toll a Solemn Peal."[27] Now thousands more, at home and abroad in England, would watch justice unfold as the trial of Captain Preston and his soldiers began.

14

On Trial

Law, no Passion can disturb.
Tis void of Desire
and Fear, Lust and Anger . . .
Tis deaf, inexorable, inflexible.

—JOHN ADAMS

The trial of "the Inhuman Murderers of the 5 of March" was scheduled to begin in the late spring of 1770. Thomas Hutchinson, in his role as chief justice of the colony, did what he could to put off the trial, hoping the passage of time would subdue the protests sure to attend any judicial proceedings on the matter. He argued that not enough judges were available to sit for the trial (a quorum of four was required for cases of this kind); when Justice Peter Oliver fell from his horse in late May, injuring himself so severely as to require bed rest, there were those in the colony who accused Hutchinson of orchestrating the accident. The likelihood of Hutchinson tricking Oliver's horse into rearing was slim, but the outcome was certain: the trial was delayed until the end of summer.

John Adams welcomed the delay. He would finally have the time he needed to catch his breath, settle back, and take stock. He sat down at his desk and opened his diary for the first time in months. "The only Way to compose myself and collect my Thoughts is to set down at my Table, place my Diary before me, and take my Pen into my Hand. This Apparatus takes off my Attention from other objects."[1] He wrote happily of taking "an Airing in the Chaise" with his cousin Sam and enjoying quiet evenings with his wife and children (baby Charles had been born at the end of May). He wrote of his pride in having worked hard, rising out of "Obscurity" and planning well "for futurity." In his new state of satisfaction, he noted in his diary, "it is no Damage to a young Man to learn the Art of Living, early."[2]

The art of living was seen as a balance of duties and pleasure: this was a goal for which Adams had long strived. On the one hand, Adams' legal work was suffering because of the nonimportation measures still strong in

Massachusetts; "the Lawyers loose as much by this Patriotic Measure as the Merchants, and Tradesmen," he lamented.[3] But while the work that paid the bills faltered, his political work increased. He'd been asked to take James Bowdoin's seat in the Massachusetts House of Representatives, after Bowdoin was elected to the Provincial Council.

Being named a representative was an honor for John, and proof that his role as defense lawyer for the British soldiers did not harm his reputation among liberty-loving colonists. At the same time, the political role would place a strain on an already burdened schedule; "My health was feeble: I was throwing away as bright prospects as any Man ever had before him: and had devoted myself to endless labour and Anxiety if not to infamy and to death, and that for nothing, except, what indeed was and ought to be all in all, a sense of duty."[4]

John sought the counsel of his wife, whom he trusted to be both truthful and supportive. He laid out to her "all my Apprehensions" about taking on such a prominent political role in Boston; after breaking down "into a flood of Tears" Abigail then gathered herself and told John that "she thought I had done as I ought, [and] she was very willing to share in all that was to come and place her trust in Providence."[5]

Whatever happened to John and Abigail, it would be borne by both together. John would tend to the trials of Captain Preston and the soldiers, along with other cases; to politics; and to his public image. Abigail would take care of the four children, manage the move to a new home in Boston (back to Brattle Square), and keep track of farm affairs in Braintree.

Abigail lamented that months had gone by since she had written to her sister Mary in Salem. While Mary's trials were of a different nature— never enough money and a brilliant husband who was a repeated failure at business—the two sisters had always sympathized with each other's burdens and bolstered each other through problems. But with so much to tend to in Boston and oversee in Braintree, Abigail had no spare minute to write to Mary. John might have time to tend to his diary and shore up his energy for the fall trial to come, but Abigail passed the summer in a fog of work and grief, still nursing her sorrows over her lost child, Suky. Just when she needed her sister's counsel and comfort most, she was simply too tired to reach out for it.

In February 1770, Dolly Quincy's oldest sister, Elizabeth, died of a sudden illness. Dolly's father, Edmund Quincy IV, felt the loss keenly. Elizabeth's death reminded him of the loss of his wife, for whom his daughter had been named. The two women had shared many qualities, including those of piety and generosity, and both had been dearly loved by their husbands. Elizabeth's husband, the Reverend Samuel Sewall, deacon of the Old South Meeting House, spoke of her in his eulogy as his "amiable, virtuous, and desirable consort" and swore he could not live without her; he died eleven months later.[6]

Edmund found what comfort he could in his own deep faith, and in his certainty of a happy afterlife where both wife and daughter waited for him: "This present life is but infancy of our being, a prelude to a better existence, a Novice-ship."[7] But with political tensions high in Boston, and business slow due to the ongoing boycott of British goods and the rising costs of everything, there was little to make him smile in the here and now. Dolly tried to cheer her father with walks taken together in the Common and stories about the many dinner parties she enjoyed at the home of Aunt Lydia and John Hancock.

The dinner parties, made up of Boston merchants mixed in with Sons of Liberty, along with their wives and sisters, cousins and aunts, made for lively evenings, and great gossip with which to entertain her father. Dolly described in detail the five-course meals served in the sixty-foot dining room, its long table fitted out with plates, silver, and crystal and a silver candelabra alight with dozens of candles. Men and women sat side by side, talking over the woes and hopes of the colony. Dolly brought her sister Katy along with her whenever she could, and often Dolly's cousin and close friend, Helena Bayard, was also invited to accompany the sisters.

Hannah Rowe attended with her husband, John, and Sally Inches, formerly Sally Jackson and onetime dalliance of John Hancock, came with her husband, Henderson. Abigail and John Adams were absent from the dinner parties; although John now served as Hancock's lawyer, neither Abigail nor John Adams enjoyed big dinner parties. Nor could they reciprocate in kind, so they preferred to stay away.

On those evenings when the men took themselves off to the local coffeehouse after dinner for political (or other) discussions, the women left in the mansion found good company in one another, playing cards and talking until late into the night. The political discussions of the women could be just as fierce as the men's debates, and their commitment to the rights of colonists just as diverse and layered. Back in February, Sally Inches had bought a bolt of white satin for her wedding gown from a British importer and only apologized for buying banned goods after she was found out.

Sally now joined Dolly, Katy, and Helen in diligently swearing off all British accoutrements to their wardrobes, along with all other British goods, and their discussions were rife with complaints against Crown administrators. Hannah Rowe, wife of a leading merchant and often present at the dinner parties, led the charge against Hutchinson; she had been vilifying Hutchinson and his administration ever since he (correctly) accused her husband of helping to instigate mob protests against the Stamp Act. Aunt Lydia presided over the women's drawing room with quiet discretion; both in public and in private she kept her own political views under wraps, preferring to let her nephew make the stand for the Hancock name.

When the Superior Court of Boston sat again at the end of August 1770, the trial of Preston and his men was put off once more, rescheduled to begin at the end of October. The decision was also made to hold two trials, one for Captain Preston and one for the men under his command. Preston, whose case would be based on the argument that he never ordered his men to shoot at the crowd, was content with having two trials. The soldiers, however, whose defense was based on the claim that they had only fired when ordered to do so, worried that while their captain, "he being a Gentelman should have more chance for to save his life," the soldiers—"we poor men that is Obliged to Obay his command"—would lose theirs.[8]

For Quincy and Adams, the countering positions their clients wanted to take—Preston arguing the soldiers had fired on their own volition and the soldiers arguing they were firing under command—would have been difficult to present if all the accused had been tried together. Now with a split in the trials, a vigorous defense utilizing both arguments could be made. But Josiah Jr. had a different—and a much more expansive—defense planned for both Preston and the soldiers. It was a defense for which John Adams was not prepared and one he would do all in his power to negate.

Jonathan Sewall, as attorney general for the colony, should have taken the lead in prosecuting Preston and his men. But after enduring the setbacks and failures of both the *Liberty* and the *Lydia* smuggling cases, Sewall had begged off serving as lead counsel for the Crown. As John Adams put it, Sewall preferred "disappearance" from the courtroom rather than suffering humiliation in it.[9] Thomas Hutchinson directed Samuel Quincy, who had indicted Captain Preston and his men, to now handle their prosecutions.

Hutchinson was perhaps indulging in some malicious glee: he would enjoy watching the two Quincy brothers face off, both of them holding positions neither found natural. Samuel, loyal to the king and Parliament, and by extension to His Majesty's troops, would now have to seek death sentences for Preston and his men; Josiah Quincy, firebrand orator against the troops in Boston, would have to defend them and save their lives.

Captain Preston's trial finally began on October 23. With such a long delay between the bloody evening of March 5 and the trial, Sam Adams worried that public outrage over what he called "the murders" had dimmed. There was a strong desire among the colonists to return to business as usual; tensions with the troops had subsided and support for the boycott of British goods was fading. Other American colonies had reopened trade with Britain, and only the merchants of Massachusetts still adhered, in word at least, to the nonimportation resolutions. Finally, on October 11, 1770, the merchants of Boston voted to end the boycott of British goods.

The Sons of Liberty did all they could to stir up public indignation before the trials began. A broadside was printed in early October and distributed widely, containing an eleven-stanza poem lamenting the delay of "SEVEN long Months" since "INNOCENCE itself became a Prey. . . . Was it my Eyes Deceived me? Did I Dream? / or did I Clearly see through every Scene, / Blood Trickling down . . . GOD hath said, the Murderer SHALL NOT LIVE."[10]

The broadside sold briskly and was successful in reigniting interest in the cases about to start in the courthouse on Queen Street. But no matter how much excitement the broadside caused in the street, it was the men of the jury seated at trial who would determine the outcome. Back and forth the Crown and the defense proposed and rejected jurors; in the end, in both trials, the juries were filled primarily by men loyal to the Crown, either for business or political reasons, along with provincials from outlying villages who had little experience with standing troops (and troop-related tensions) as compared to citizens of Boston.

Samuel Quincy was the first to speak at Captain Preston's trial. His opening statement was uninspired and rote, merely noting the crime for which Preston was charged: willful premeditated murder for ordering troops to fire on the inhabitants of Boston on the evening of March 5, 1770. Quincy followed up his lackadaisical opening statement with a long parade of witnesses, questioned by both Quincy and his co-counsel, Robert Treat Paine. The collective testimony of the witnesses was meant to prove that Preston had both prepared his men to fire and ordered them to fire.

But the testimony offered was contradictory and presented instead a picture of mayhem and chaos. Far from demonstrating that the shootings of March 5 had resulted from a premeditated plan of action formulated and carried out by Preston, the witnesses provided vivid observations of townspeople taunting and insulting the soldiers and attacking them with snowballs, sticks, and stones. No two witnesses could agree on having heard Preston give the order to fire, and in fact, much of the shouting of "Fire!" "Fire, damn you!" was heard coming from the gathered crowd, both in front of and behind the soldiers, and not from the line of soldiers as they attempted to retreat to the barracks.

When it was time for the defense to make its case, the secret plan of Josiah Quincy Jr. became clear to John Adams. Josiah had prepared all the witnesses, but it would be John who questioned them on the stand. When Adams asked John Gillespie, a defense witness, what he had observed on the evening of March 5, Gillespie testified to seeing "a gang of townspeople, armed with sticks and swords" parading through the streets "at least two hours before the firing."[11]

Adams returned to the defense table and looked over the witness notes prepared by his co-counsel. His heart quickened: Josiah Quincy Jr. intended to put the citizens of Boston on trial. Josiah's witnesses would present testimony demonstrating that the mobs of the town, intent on driving the British troops out of Boston, had instigated the violence of March 5 and put the lives of Captain Preston and his men in danger. In response, Preston and his men had no choice but to fight for their lives. The case then became one of self-defense, with the mobs of Boston the perpetrators of violence and the British troops defending against it.

Adams drew Quincy aside and told him, firmly but softly, that he would present no more evidence placing the blame on the citizens of Boston or indicating that "the expulsion of the troops from the town of Boston was a plan concerted among the inhabitants."[12] Furthermore, he warned Quincy, if the young lawyer tried any more maneuvers to put Boston itself on trial, Adams would walk away.

Adams was wary of portraying the protesting citizens of Boston as lawless, especially because he viewed the parliamentary actions that instigated the protests in the first place as unlawful. In addition, the defense proposed by Josiah Jr. was unnecessary. Sam Quincy and the prosecution had failed to prove their case against Preston. Repeatedly, the prosecution witnesses had testified to the utter chaos of the evening, and there was no proof that Preston had prepared for or ordered the shootings. His acquittal was guaranteed.

Josiah Quincy Jr. finally acquiesced to Adams and withdrew those questions that would have elucidated for the jury both the motivations and the goals of the Boston mobs that cold March day. But he was only biding his time. He never trusted a mob, and he would do whatever he could to take away the power of the Boston mobs and restore the rule of law and order in Boston: not the order imposed by the British troops, but the order guaranteed to the citizens of the colony under its charter and under "that glorious medium, the British constitution."[13]

After four days of testimony, closing arguments began. John Adams offered a vigorous and impassioned display of rhetoric and maxims, offering the jury the legal high ground on which to acquit Preston. He also delivered a careful and detailed demolition of the testimony offered by opposing witnesses, giving the jury the plain facts upon which to find Preston not guilty. Samuel Quincy presented no closing argument or statement, leaving Robert Treat Paine alone in his attempt to present the mob as a normal occurrence in Boston and the response of Preston as planned, methodical, and ultimately murderous. Rather than defending his own life or the lives of his soldiers, Paine argued, the British captain went on the offensive and killed inhabitants of Boston.

The jury returned their verdict in three hours. Captain Preston was found not guilty. Preston expressed no gratitude to his defense lawyers but "immediately disappeared."[14] John Adams consoled himself with having performed "one of the most gallant, generous, manly and disinterested Actions of my whole Life."[15] (Adams must also have found consolation in receiving payment of over £100, a worthy sum that bolstered the Adams household budget considerably.)

Josiah Quincy Jr., meanwhile, took the verdict as a victory against mob rule and began preparing for the next trial, to be held in late November. He would have almost three weeks to prepare, and he vowed to himself that he would be ready. Adams might have shut him down in Preston's trial, but in the trials of the eight men serving under Preston, Josiah Quincy Jr. would have his day in court.

The trial of the eight soldiers began on a cold and wet day at the end of November. Despite the damp and the chill, Josiah Quincy Jr. arrived at the courthouse feeling stronger than he had since his wedding a year before. He had worked hard to prepare for court, but he had also taken care of his health. Diligently adhering to doctor's orders over the past weeks, he went to sleep early and slept long, he ate only simple food but ample amounts of it, and he imbibed little alcohol. Accompanied by his wife, he had enjoyed fresh air taken in drives through the countryside to spend time in Braintree with his father, Josiah Sr.

Whether it was the weight he had gained, the sleep and rest he had enjoyed, or the assiduous research and writing he had undertaken, Josiah Jr. walked into the courtroom exhibiting a new robustness to match both his will and his determination; John Adams be damned, this case was all his.

The jury, judges, and audience gathered in the courtroom on Queen Street fell quickly under Josiah Quincy Jr.'s spell. "Permit me, gentlemen, to remind you of the importance of this trial, as it relates to the prisoners. It is for their lives!" he began. "If we consider the number of persons now on trial, joined with many other circumstances which might be mentioned, it is by far the most important this country ever saw. Remember the ties you are under to the prisoners, and even to yourselves. The eyes of all are upon you."[16]

As he spoke, all attention was in fact riveted on him, standing still and tall before the jury. His unruly hair was held back by a ribbon, no wig on his head or barrister robes on his back. Josiah Quincy Jr. commanded respect, even with his bare head, crossed eyes, and austere and plain clothes. It was his voice that did it: as one observer noted, "His voice was like the music of the spheres; soft and melodious, yet powerful, clear, and distinct. He had a tenor voice [that] could be heard to the farthest verge of the most crowded assembly, and often far beyond."[17]

He took a deep breath and continued: "An opinion has been entertained by many among us, that the life of a soldier was of very little value,—of much less value than others of the community."

He paused, and then continued, "The law, gentlemen, knows no such distinction: the life of a soldier is viewed, by the equal eye of the law, as estimable as the life of any other citizen."[18]

John Adams, seated at the defense table, waited tensely for Quincy to begin what Adams was sure would be a condemnation of the Boston mob. But Quincy surprised him, and most likely everyone else in the courtroom.

"Boston and its inhabitants have no more to do with this cause than you or any other members of the community. You are, therefore, by no means to blend two things so essentially different as the guilt or innocence of this town and the prisoners together. The inhabitants of Boston, by no rules of law, justice, or common sense, can be supposed answerable for the unjustifiable conduct of a few individuals, hastily assembled in the streets."[19]

But just as Adams had let out his sigh of relief, the tone of Quincy's presentation turned. Quoting the words of John Dickinson, the "farmer of Pennsylvania," who had advised the colonists to act with "prudence, justice, modesty, bravery, humanity, and magnanimity," Quincy then asked the jury to consider whether "it [was] justice or humanity to attack, insult, ridicule, and abuse a single sentinel on his post? Was it either modest, brave, or magnanimous to rush upon the points of fixed bayonets, and trifle, vapour, and provoke, at the very mouths of loaded muskets?"[20]

Quincy proceeded to answered his own questions. "Hot, rash, disorderly proceedings injure the reputation of a people, as to wisdom, valour, and virtue, without procuring the least benefit . . . [and no one] would sacrifice his judgment and his integrity, to vindicate such proceedings." Having warned the jury against taking the side of the mob, Quincy then reminded the jury of their duty to be "zealous inquirers after truth . . . willing to hear with impartiality, to examine and judge for yourselves" the testimony to be presented.[21]

"You are not sitting here as Statesmen or Politicians," he warned the jury. "You ought to be careful to give a Verdict, which will bear the Examination of the Times, when the Pulses which now beat shall beat no more."[22]

Josiah Quincy Jr. then began his questioning of the witnesses. For this trial, Adams and Quincy had agreed that Quincy would handle both the prosecution and the defense witnesses, and Adams would present the closing argument. In all, between the Crown and the defense, over fifty witnesses were called. Josiah Quincy Jr. led his witnesses along, probing their observations and questioning their assumptions, to create a compelling picture of the night in question. Chaos had reigned when citizens and troops, forced to live and work in close confines, reached their limits of tolerance; in the end, the tragic consequences were the result, as John Adams put it in his closing argument, of "soldiers quartered in a populous town."[23]

Who could say who had fired at whom in such mayhem? Guilt could only be assigned where there existed proof of a trigger pulled or of a bayonet thrust; Josiah depended on the disorder of the recollections to blur lines of responsibility. As John Adams would argue at the end, without a clear line of guilt, no verdict could be returned.

Before John began his closing argument, however, Josiah once again reminded the jury of the importance of remaining unbiased, especially in these turbulent times, he argued, when both the impassioned mob and the watching world waited for the verdicts. But another quality was just as vital:

mercy. The jury, as "ministers of justice" must ensure that in the cause of "law and justice, . . . mercy . . . be executed in all . . . judgments." He paraphrased Shakespeare in his final words to the jury: "The quality of mercy is not strained; It droppeth like the gentle rain from heaven. . . . It is twice blessed; It blesses him that gives, and him that takes."[24]

In John Adams' closing argument, he reminded the jury that in order to protect the innocent, proof had to be certain, without any doubt or question: "We are to look upon it as more beneficial, that many guilty persons should escape unpunished, than one innocent person should suffer. The reason is, because it's of more importance to community, that innocence should be protected, than it is, that guilt should be punished."[25]

With thunder on his brow, John leaned in close to the jury: "the people shouting, huzzaing, and making the mob whistle . . . a most hideous shriek, almost as terrible as an Indian yell." He wondered aloud if, had the tables been turned and the citizens of Boston were so harangued and taunted and jeered, the civilians "would not have . . . shot down as many as were necessary to intimidate and disperse the rest."[26]

Josiah sat up straight, surprised by the turn in Adams' argument. Could it be that now Adams was willing to put the citizens of Boston on trial? The defendants also surged forward in their seats but for a different reason. Was Adams admitting the guilt of his clients?

But having presented the horrors of the mob, Adams assigned blame for its outrages not on the ones who had composed the mob but on the administration whose policies had enflamed it: citizens will turn "to mutinies, seditions, tumults, and insurrections . . . in direct proportion to the despotisms of the government. . . . The virtue and wisdom of the administration, may generally be measured by the peace and order, that are seen among the people."[27]

Furthermore, Adams added, it was the influence and actions of outsiders— "a Carr from Ireland and an Attucks from Framingham" who had behaved with the most violence and agitation, thereby besmirching "the good people of the town" of Boston.[28]

To the relief of his clients, Adams then reviewed all the testimony and concluded by stating that if the soldiers had acted against citizens of Boston, they had done so in self-defense only: "Facts are stubborn things; . . . nor is the law less stable than the fact; if an assault was made to endanger their lives . . . the law reduces the offence of killing, down to manslaughter."[29]

The jury returned six verdicts of not guilty, and two of manslaughter.

The two soldiers convicted of manslaughter, Mathew Kilroy and Hugh Montgomery, would be branded by fire on the hand—the letter *M* emblazoned on their thumb—while the other six soldiers were immediately released: "They went their way thro' the Streets, with little, if any notice."[30]

John Adams left the courthouse feeling exhausted and unfathomably downcast. Certainly, the outcome of the two trials had been a victory for the accused men, for the law, and for the colony. As John would write later, "Judgment of Death against those Soldiers would have been as foul a Stain upon this Country as the Executions of the Quakers or Witches, anciently. As the Evidence was, the Verdict of the Jury was exactly right."[31] But John felt overworked and underappreciated; he especially disliked having his loyalty to the colony questioned and lamented "the cloud of Toryism that has lately . . . passed over me."[32]

Samuel Quincy, having lost both trials (the guilty verdicts in two of the nine cases hardly counted as a win) also left the courthouse feeling disgruntled and uncertain, and with the same questions plaguing him about both his integrity as a lawyer and his loyalty to the colony. Just the other day Samuel had seen a flyer by the courthouse proclaiming that in the Boston Massacre trials, "the Court [had] cheat[ed] with a Shew of Justice." The flyer then exhorted fellow colonists: "we [must] rise up at the great Gale of Nature & Free the World from Such domestic tyrants."[33]

Samuel felt double-damned: he had lost the cases and, with that, incurred the wrath of Bostonians; if he had won the cases, he would have incurred the wrath of the Crown administrators, and the king too, no doubt. Copying the flyer word-for-word in a letter to his friend and co-counsel Robert Treat Paine, he added a note at the top: "Tribunitial, / unsuccessful / unrecompensed / Fellow-Labourer / Pro Rege & Grege!"[34] Underpaid, unsuccessful, but doing all for *for king and country*: Samuel would struggle to stay true to both.

Josiah Quincy Jr. was the only one who left the courthouse that day feeling satisfied. He was certain of his duty going forward and confident for his colony. When he spoke of his duty to John Adams, he used language that was sweeping and sure: "When a whole people present a criminal at the bar of justice, the sword must not linger in the hand of the executioner."[35] Josiah was referring to the entire colonial administration as that "criminal at the bar of justice." As he would argue again and again in the months to come, the dedicated guardians of the colony had to be ready to wield the sword to protect their liberty.

The sword proposed by Josiah was a metaphor only. John Adams understood that his friend was not advocating violence but rather "vigilance against encroachments" of colonial rights.[36] John took the message to heart. Vigilance must be kept and ambition tamed. One for the colony and the other for the man. And all for the good of his family. Of that, John was certain.

By the end of the year, what everyone in Massachusetts had anticipated now came to fruition: King George of England appointed Thomas Hutchinson both "Captain General, and Governor in Chief, of Massachusetts."[37] Hutchinson would not give up his seat on the Superior Court but would also continue to act as chief justice of the colony. A mingling of roles and a consolidation of power.

Power enough to crush John Hancock, John Adams, and Josiah Quincy Jr.—or just the kind of power that would propel the three men further along toward rebellion? Even as the clouds over Massachusetts darkened, the answer to that question would become clear.

15

Retreat to Braintree

How easily people change,
and give up their friends and their interest.

—JOHN ADAMS

In the early months of 1771, Josiah Quincy Jr. spoke to a gathering of selectmen from Boston. The group had convened at the home of John Hancock. Tea was served—"from Holland I hope," noted John Adams in his diary—and a discussion was held over how best to commemorate the Boston Massacre of the year before.[1] Josiah urged that a full-scale commemoration be instituted as an annual event to mark "the melancholy tragedy" and that the day also be used to condemn British encroachment on colonists' rights.[2]

"Vigilance must be maintained," he warned. Parliament had not relinquished its power over the colonies: a tea tax was still in full effect, and the troops had only been withdrawn from the city of Boston, not from the colony of Massachusetts. Quincy then shared a quotation from Edmund Burke: "'Public life is a situation of power and energy; he trespasses against his duty who sleeps on his watch, as well as he that goes over to the enemy.'"[3]

"'Arms and laws do not flourish together'" was another quotation he'd copied into his *Commonplace* book, and he meant to drive the lesson home not only to the elite of the colony gathered together in Hancock's mansion but to all the colonists of Massachusetts. A vigorous commemoration of the bloody massacre, held annually, would get the message across of the "fatal effects of the policy of standing armies, and the . . . quartering regular troops in populous cities in time of peace."[4]

"'By a numerous standing army . . . you may, indeed, prevent mobs and riots among the people,'" he thundered, quoting again from his beloved maxims. "'But if this method be continued for any long time, you will make your ministers tyrants and your people slaves.'"[5]

Writing in the *Boston Gazette* under the name of "Mentor," Quincy urged all colonists of Massachusetts to support the holding of "a decent, manly, and instructive commemoration of the melancholy tragedy of the 5th of March, 1770." With the support of the people behind him, the Boston town committee acted quickly to approve the event.[6]

As part of the commemoration, Paul Revere got to work creating a series of tableaux, to be displayed in his shop windows, that would bring back to vivid life the horrors of the massacre. In the first window, Revere presented Christopher Seider, dying from his wounds and surrounded by weeping boys; accompanying text read, "Seider's pale Ghost fresh-bleeding stands / And Vengeance for his Death demands." In the second window, the night of March 5, 1770, was illustrated in all its bloody violence, with British soldiers firing upon a crowd of cringing citizens; overhead, a banner proclaimed "FOUL PLAY."[7] And in the third window, Revere's display presented a woman pointing to a band of large and fierce soldiers as they charged toward a cowering group of unarmed men, women, and children.

Katy and Dolly Quincy accompanied their father to see the exhibition, stopping at the final window to stand awhile. The pointing woman, meant to represent America, was dressed in a fine gown and black cape, with her long skirt swaying back as if she were striding deliberately through a storm; she was dressed both for prayer and for battle. Her body was lithe and strong, but her face betrayed an agony beyond bearing as she anticipated the mowing down of her fellow Americans by the brutal British troops.

As the *Boston Gazette* reported, Revere's "well-executed" display, viewed by "many thousands," left all who saw it "struck with solemn Silence, and their Countenances covered with a Melancholy gloom."[8] The images were powerful, and they were understood. To remember the tragedy was to recall its causes; and with British troops still present in the city, although largely housed on Castle Island, the rancor ran deep.

On the night of March 5, 1771, Dr. Thomas Young, son of Irish immigrants and a vocal critic of parliamentary overreach, delivered the first memorial oration of the Boston Massacre at Factory Hall, also known as Manufactory House. The old linen factory on Long Acre Street had been one of the buildings Governor Bernard sought to requisition for troops in 1768 but the colonists had fought so hard against the takeover that Bernard had been forced to back down. As the site of such a successful rebuttal to British overreach, Factory Hall was seen as the perfect location for Dr. Young's address. Following his oration, the hall from then on became known as Liberty Assembly Hall.[9]

Abigail Adams, circa 1766.
Artist: Benjamin Blyth, Pastel
on Paper, Collection of the
Massachusetts Historical Society

John Adams, circa 1766.
Artist: Benjamin Blyth, Pastel on
Paper, Collection of the Massachusetts
Historical Society

North Parish Meeting House. Sketch by Eliza Susan Quincy, from the Eliza S.
Quincy Memoir in the Quincy family papers, vol. 45, Massachusetts Historical
Society

Josiah Quincy Senior's House, sketch by Eliza Susan Quincy, from the Eliza S. Quincy Memoir in the Quincy family papers, vol. 45, Massachusetts Historical Society

Edmund Quincy's House. Sketch by Eliza Susan Quincy, from the Eliza S. Quincy Memoir in the Quincy family papers, vol. 45, Massachusetts Historical Society

View of Mount Wollaston, home of John Quincy. Sketch by Eliza Susan Quincy, from the Eliza S. Quincy Memoir in the Quincy family papers, vol. 45, Massachusetts Historical Society

Dorothy Quincy (Mrs. John Hancock), circa 1722. Artist: John Singleton Copley, American, 1738–1815, Oil on Canvas, Charles H. Bayley Picture and Painting Fund and Gift of Mrs. Anne B. Loring, Photograph © 2020 Museum of Fine Arts, Boston

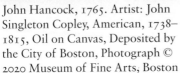

John Hancock, 1765. Artist: John Singleton Copley, American, 1738–1815, Oil on Canvas, Deposited by the City of Boston, Photograph © 2020 Museum of Fine Arts, Boston

Samuel Quincy, circa 1767. Artist: John Singleton Copley, American, 1738–1815, Oil on Canvas, Bequest of Miss Grace W. Treadwell, Photograph © 2020 Museum of Fine Arts, Boston

Mrs. Samuel Quincy
(Hannah Hill), circa 1761.
Artist: John Singleton
Copley, American 1738–
1815, Oil on Canvas,
Bequest of Miss Grace W.
Treadwell, Photograph
© 2020 Museum of Fine
Arts, Boston.

Thomas Hancock, circa 1758.
Artist: John Singleton Copley,
American, 1738–1815,
Oil on copper, National
Portrait Gallery, Smithsonian
Institution, Conserved with
funds from the Smithsonian
Women's Committee

Lydia Henchman Hancock, circa 1766. Artist: John Singleton Copley, Oil on copper, National Portrait Gallery, Smithsonian Institution; gift of Charles H. Wood

Josiah Quincy, Senior. Artist: John Singleton Copley, Dietrich American Foundation, photograph of painting by Gavin Ashworth

Boston Neck/Hancock Mansion, circa 1775, by Richard Williams. Reproduction Courtesy of the Norman B. Leventhal Map & Education Center at the Boston Public Library

Boston/British Troops on Parade, circa 1775, by Richard Williams. Reproduction Courtesy of the Norman B. Leventhal Map & Education Center at the Boston Public Library

A Plan of Boston and its Environs, 1775, by Richard Williams. Reproduction Courtesy of the Norman B. Leventhal Map & Education Center at the Boston Public Library

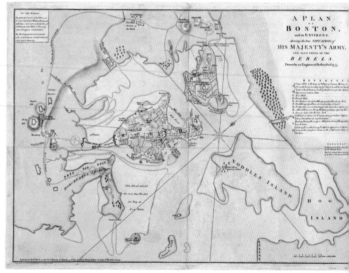

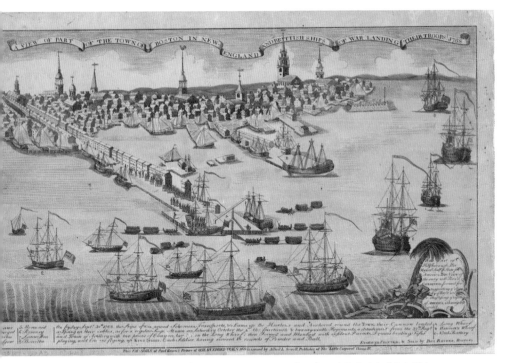

A View of Part of the Town of Boston in New England and Brittish [sic] Ships Landing Troops, 1768, by Paul Revere. Reproduction Courtesy of the Norman B. Leventhal Map & Education Center at the Boston Public Library

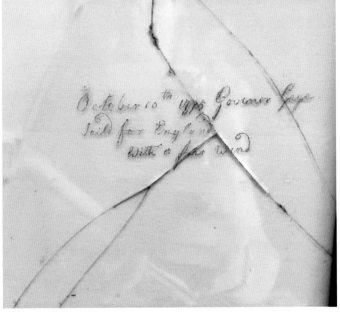

Josiah Quincy Senior's Etching on Glass, October 10, 1775. Photograph by the author, taken at the Josiah Quincy House, Quincy, MA, owned/maintained by Historic New England

Mourning Ring of Josiah Quincy Junior. Photograph by the author, from the Collections of the Massachusetts Historical Society

Josiah Quincy Senior House today. Photograph by the author

Edmund Quincy IV, date/artist unknown, photograph by the author, from the Dorothy Quincy Homestead, Quincy MA, owned/maintained by The National Society of the Colonial Dames of America, Massachusetts Society.

Thomas Hutchinson was enraged by the evening's commemorations, and by the citizens' insistence on calling the events of March 5, 1770, a massacre. (Even John Adams agreed with Hutchinson on that point, complaining that even after the acquittals of Preston and the soldiers, the people of Boston continued to speak of it "as a massacre, a bloody massacre, and the like."[10])

Hutchinson was becoming fed up with his fellow colonists, and especially with those who filled the newspapers with increasingly critical diatribes against himself and his administration. Articles condemning Hutchinson now appeared regularly in the *Boston Gazette* and other pro-colonist newspapers, including the *Massachusetts Spy*, which began publishing in 1770.

In an attempt to shut down unwanted press coverage, Hutchinson instituted legal proceedings against Isaiah Thomas, publisher of the *Massachusetts Spy*, for a piece written by Joseph Greenleaf, justice of the peace for Plymouth County and a member of the Sons of Liberty (and cousin of Sarah Quincy Greenleaf's husband, William). Hutchinson claimed that publication of Greenleaf's essay constituted seditious libel. The case was presented to the grand jury, but the jurors refused to indict Thomas, on the grounds that nothing in Greenleaf's piece could be proved false. Hutchinson's defeat was widely publicized, and jurors celebrated for their "great integrity and spirited behavior."[11]

Josiah Quincy Jr. watched Hutchinson's failure to suppress freedom of the colonial press with deep satisfaction, noting that "a free Press can never hurt an honest man."[12] Newly installed in law offices on Queen Street (adjacent to Benjamin Edes' and John Gill's *Boston Gazette* empire), Josiah felt more empowered than ever to write what he wished in the letters and essays he published not only in the *Boston Gazette* but also in other local papers. Although he had over two hundred legal cases on the dockets of the Boston courts, Josiah devoted hours to his political writing, and one of his favorite targets was Thomas Hutchinson, whom Quincy described as "the serpent, subtlest beast of all the field."[13]

If not for the reoccurrence of symptoms related to his consumption, Josiah might have called 1771 his best year ever. He was happily married and Abigail was pregnant with their first child. After the success of the Boston Massacre trials, there was ongoing demand for his legal work and, at the same time, the local papers clamored for more of his political tracts. But his health failed him again and again. Fevers and sweats plagued his nights, and violent coughing broke up the peace of his days.

He moved his office to Queen Street, which brought him closer to the offices of the *Boston Gazette*, but more important, brought him closer to home. Abigail was the chief draw, her care and her company the best boon to his health, along with the creature comforts of their house on Marlborough Street. With Abigail's help and the calm surroundings of his library (and the inspiration provided by the many tomes he had collected over the years), Josiah resolved to take better care of his health while also pursuing the legal work that grounded him and the political work that so invigorated him.

Edmund Quincy IV, father of Dolly, played his own role of resistance against what he called the "British occupation of Boston."[14] As a justice of the peace for the town, he always let colonists go free when they were brought before him on disorderly charges (and worse). The lawyer Benjamin Gridley, a Loyalist, claimed he had to resort to threats against Edmund to get him to finally put "one of the damned Sons of Liberty in Gaol!"[15]

After three years of living in Boston, John Adams had become increasingly disenchanted with town life. Although his political work continued, new legal cases were slow in coming and did little to inspire him. He'd lost a case against Jonathan Sewall, where Adams had represented the owners of a slave for whom Sewall was seeking freedom through an action called "replevin and trespass." These types of cases were called "freedom suits" and had been brought in increasing numbers in Massachusetts ever since the High Court in England, in a case called *Somerset v. Stewart*, declared slavery to be "odious" and held that no English law or statute allowed for it.[16]

Adams' loss in the case was expected; he wrote in a letter to a friend, "I never knew a Jury by a Verdict, to determine a Negro to be a slave. They always found them free."[17] Nevertheless, Adams would continue to take such cases when offered. Fighting for the continued enslavement of a fellow human didn't appear to bother him; a paying client was a paying client. In any event, he reasoned, slavery would die out as a "Measure of Economy" when slaves turned "lazy, idle, proud, vicious," thereby becoming "wholly useless to their Masters."[18]

Adams couldn't see the hypocrisy of arguing for the liberties of white colonists while defending the enslavement of black ones—but his wife could. Abigail would call John to task on it—but not yet.

With Josiah Jr. having moved away from the offices on King Street, Adams no longer enjoyed long afternoons spent debating with the younger man over how a case might be brought or complaining together over the demanding circuit court schedules. John missed the daily contact; his two law clerks were bright and ambitious, but neither could match Josiah for his understanding of the law or his pure love of it.

Abigail was always a good companion, and an honest sounding board for her husband's dreams and frustrations. But she too was feeling tired out by life in Boston. Raising four children, managing the household on Cold Lane, keeping up with farm matters in Braintree, and keeping the family budget was all taking its toll on her. She and John adored their children but the costs of raising them seemed to go higher and higher, as John's aspirations for the family grew and Abigail's own expectations for the children increased.

As John wrote to his friend and brother-in-law Richard Cranch, "In a little while Johnny must go to Colledge, and Nabby must have fine Cloaths, aye. . . . And very cleverly you and I shall feel when we recollect that we are hard at Work, over Watches and Lawsuits, and [our children] at the same Time Raking and fluttering away our Profits. Aye, and there must be dancing Schools and Boarding Schools and all that, or else, you know, we shall not give them polite Educations."[19]

The Cranches were themselves considering moving to Braintree. Richard's watchmaking business in Salem was failing miserably and Mary was eager to move back closer to her family. Braintree was just one town over from Weymouth, where Abigail and Mary's parents lived, and if Abigail and John were considering returning to Braintree, even better. Mary had a plan to run a boardinghouse and build the family wealth through her own labors.

Richard finally acquiesced with Mary's plans, and in the spring of 1771, they rented a large house in Braintree just a half mile away from the Adams family farmhouse. They began advertising for boarders and travelers; with no inn available in Braintree, there was sure to be business for their rooming house. Mary also vowed to try her hand at dairy work, and Richard bought up (with the financial assistance of Norton Quincy) some rocky acres of barely tillable land to try out farming.

John Adams reasoned that the time was right to move his own family back to the farmhouse in Braintree. Neither public committee work nor lawsuits seemed to bring him pleasure anymore; nor did they bring needed funds to the family treasury. Worst of all, neither his legal work nor his political work fed his ambitions to become a great man in the community; to the contrary, John felt that his community standing was suffering, even when he was acting on its behalf: "I have acted my sentiments [for my colony], with the Utmost Frankness, at Hazard of all, and the certain Loss of ten times more than it is in the Power of the People to give me, for the sake of the People, and now I reap nothing but Insult, Ridicule and Contempt for it, even from many of the People themselves."[20]

John was determined to "shake off a little of that Load of public and private Care which has for some Time oppressed me." He feared that if he did not leave Boston, he would soon "have shaken off this mortal Body."[21]

Within weeks of returning to the farm in Braintree, John felt better. He wrote in his diary, "Still, calm, happy Braintree. No journeys to make to Cambridge, no General Court to attend. I divide my time between law and husbandry. Farewell politics!"[22]

A few days later, again he wrote of his "Joy" and his "Pleasure, in revisiting my old Haunts, and recollecting my old Meditations among the Rocks and Trees, which was very intense indeed. The rushing Torrent, the purling Stream, the gurgling Rivulet, the dark Thickett, the rugged Ledges and Precipices, are all old Acquaintances of mine."[23] John Adams was glad to be home.

Abigail was also happy to be back in Braintree. She too welcomed the familiar sights, sounds, and smells of the village and their farm; no longer suffering the "Noisy Buisy Town," she settled happily into "my humble Cottage in Braintree. . . . Where Contemplation p[l]umes her rufled Wings / And the free Soul look's down to pitty Kings."[24] To have her sister Mary less than a mile away was an added benefit and the fulfillment of a long-held wish. Now their children could all play together, boys and girls scampering on the rocks along the beach or playing in the gardens behind the homes of the two sisters.

Mary was just as busy as Abigail, keeping both the boardinghouse and the dairy going and caring for the children, but nevertheless, Abigail and Mary could, after a separation of almost five years, once again see each other frequently—and they did. Abigail was also able to see her family in Weymouth more frequently now that she was back in Braintree; her mother often came to visit her elder daughters and their children, accompanied by Abigail's younger sister, Betsy. Betsy was a favorite aunt of young John Quincy Adams and a welcome presence to his father, John, who called Betsy "amiable" and "ingenious."[25]

It took no time at all for Abigail to reestablish herself as matriarch of the village. She encouraged other mothers in Braintree not only in their cottage industries of weaving and apothecary work but also in educating their children. She firmly believed that "much depends . . . upon the early Education of youth and the first principals which are instilled take the deepest root."[26]

Nevertheless, she often felt ill-equipped to meet the task: "With regard to the Education of my own children, I find myself soon out of my depth, and destitute and deficient in every part of Education."[27] She did what she could, and encouraged others to do the same, not only for their children but for themselves and for their country: "If we mean to have Heroes, Statesmen and Philosophers, we should have learned women"—and men.[28]

Josiah Quincy Sr. welcomed the Adams family back to Braintree. The village was growing by leaps and bounds, he told John, and business in local manufacturing was strong. Immigrants, mostly from Germany, worked in factories, such as Josiah's glassmaking and chocolate businesses on Shed's Neck (called Germantown for the number of Germans who lived and worked there). Immigrants also supplied needed labor as local farms prospered through a series of good harvests. Josiah assured John that in the new economy, he would find plenty of clients needing a lawyer.

The year before, in early 1770, the rented home of Josiah Quincy Sr. had burned to the ground (the second time this occurred; again, no one was hurt but furnishings and books were lost in the fire). Buoyed by his various business projects, including the purchase of properties throughout Massachusetts and beyond, Josiah Sr. decided the time had come to finally build a house of his own. The house would be built on property his father had left to him, acres of fields and pasture on a hill, with sloping meadows that led down to the water.

By the end of the year, Josiah's new house was finished. A magnificent Georgian mansion, it sat high above the surrounding fields and meadows, commanding a view of the sea and land all around. At the top of the house, a monitor had been built; Josiah loved nothing better than to sit in his warren and look out. He could see all the way to Boston Harbor and count the masts of the many ships passing through its waters. He could see the spire of the Old South Meeting House on Milk Street and, on a clear day, the treetops of Beacon Hill.

The rooms of the house were high-ceilinged, spacious, and airy and fitted out with finely sculpted moldings, European-patterned wallpaper, and multicolored fireplace tiles, all exhibiting the latest in fashion and elegance.

Josiah installed magnificent pieces of furniture into the house, including the large Japanned chest he had saved from two fires. The specter of fire haunted him, and he demanded extra vigilance on the part of all the servants to keep this home safe. He hoped it would be a lasting refuge for himself and his family for years to come.

John and Abigail were invited to visit the new home, along with Josiah's brother Edmund and his daughters Dolly and Katy. Josiah Jr. and Abigail came often, and even Samuel Quincy and his wife, Hannah, made the trip in a fine gilt carriage pulled by a pair of black horses. John Hancock and his aunt Lydia were also invited to Josiah's new home. Having known Reverend Hancock, and then lived in John's childhood home for a period of time, Josiah Sr. felt a bond with Hancock; and he was happy to see his niece Dolly involved with a leader of the colony who was known for his generosity and sense of duty.

In the late spring of 1771, Josiah's daughter Hannah Lincoln came on her own to see her father's new mansion. She had accompanied her husband, Bela Lincoln, to the hospital on George's Island in Boston Harbor, where she left him to take one of its famous rest cures. Lincoln was suffering from a disease of his digestive system and had grown gaunt, weak, and even more angry. Yet Hannah stood by him; her visit to her father was short, as she had promised Bela she would soon return to the island to oversee his recovery. But Lincoln's health continued to deteriorate, and Edmund Quincy wrote to his daughter Katy in July that "Poor Dr. Lincoln . . . is said to be in a very dangerous state."[29]

John Adams particularly enjoyed these evenings spent with old friends at the home of Josiah Sr. As had happened in the years when they had been in college together, their talks centered on politics: administration of the colony, the rights of colonists under the Massachusetts Charter, and the future of Massachusetts. John Hancock, John Adams, Josiah Quincy Jr.—each of the men had been developing his own ideas about how the colony should be governed. Now they found that their individual aspirations were shared, and the sharing only strengthened their resolve to relieve Massachusetts from what they all agreed was unwarranted parliamentary oppression.

The camaraderie of old friends was a much-needed balm to John Adams' soul. He had been feeling "quite left alone, in the World."[30] Now he found men who shared his distrust—and dislike—of Thomas Hutchinson. In Adams' opinion, Hutchinson was the man whose "Character and Conduct have been the Cause of laying a Foundation for perpetual Discontent and Uneasiness between Britain and the Colonies, of perpetual Struggles of one Party for Wealth and Power at the Expence of the Liberties of this Country."[31] Encouraged by his old Braintree friends, he felt renewed resolve to fight against Hutchinson: "Our sons, if they deserve it, will enjoy the happy fruits of their Fathers' Struggles."[32]

Josiah Jr. was just a boy when his brothers Sam and Ned, along with John Adams and John Hancock, gathered as college friends. But now he, like each of them, was a man working in the world, with direct knowledge of Parliament's efforts to control and guide the colonies in America—and like them, willing to fight to protect the liberty of the colonists from the over-reach of England. For Josiah, it was the legal institutions that would "rescue one right from the jaws of power, and restore one liberty to oppressed mankind," and he predicted, "how would grateful millions bless the institution!"[33]

For John Adams, it was hard work on the part of public servants that provided the only bulwark against administrative corruption and parliamentary oppression, no matter how thankless such work might be: "I have very cheerfully sacrificed my Interest, and my Health and Ease and Pleasure in the service of the People. I have stood by their friends longer than they would stand by them. I have stood by the People much longer than they would stand by themselves."[34]

And for John Hancock, it was the joined resolve of a community of dedicated citizens that held out the most hope for liberty from oppression; "I have always, from my earliest youth, rejoiced in the felicity of my fellow-men; and have ever considered it as the indispensable able duty of every member of society to promote, as far as in him lies, the prosperity of every individual, but more especially of the community to which he belongs."[35]

Only Samuel Quincy held back from the discussions shared by old friends. His silence was due to his roles as solicitor general and as justice of the peace in Boston, a new appointment; but he also kept quiet because of the secret source of his newly bolstered salary, which came from revenues gathered through the hated tea tax, the one tax still exacted from the colonists. While his brothers and friends devised new plans for getting rid of this final tax, Sam was profiting from it.

Thomas Hutchinson hoped to guarantee Sam's continued loyalty by masterminding his rising career, similar to what he had accomplished with Jonathan Sewall. To bring a Quincy into the Loyalist camp was a coup, and Hutchinson knew it. In 1771, Hutchinson had paid a handsome price for the Quincys' home on South Street; perhaps this was another clever ploy to draw Sam further into his debt. With the money from the purchase, Sam and Hannah were able to build a grand new home on Hanover Street, surpassing Josiah Sr.'s Braintree home in size, opulence, and luxury.

Samuel Quincy wasn't the only Braintree native courted by Thomas Hutchinson. Under express orders from Lord Hillsborough in England, Hutchinson sought at every turn to promote John Hancock and bring him into the Loyalist fold. With memories of the repealed Townshend Acts fading and trade once again picking up in Massachusetts, Hancock was looking to his businesses, stocking his warehouses, employing men to keep the House of Hancock humming. The politics of protest, Hutchinson believed, would be discarded by Hancock as he pursued his economic ambitions.

In December 1771, Hutchinson reported to General Gage in New York, without revealing the source of his knowledge, that Hancock had vowed to "never again" ally himself with the likes of Sam or John Adams.[36] In early 1772, he wrote to the former governor, Francis Bernard, now in London, that Hancock had completely broken with the Sons of Liberty: "Hancock has not been with their club for two months past. . . . His [defection] will be a great loss to them, as they support themselves with his money."[37]

Hutchinson perceived Hancock to now be an easy conquest, an ambitious merchant tired of the antics of the colonial troublemakers. All that was needed to bring Hancock firmly to the side of the Crown and Parliament was an appointment (or two) to high office. Once Hancock was offered and then accepted his new roles, the deal would be sealed and Hancock would be theirs. Hutchinson predicted that without Hancock's fortune and his magic touch with the citizens of Boston, Sam Adams and the Sons of Liberty would lose their footing in the colony. Then once again peace—as defined and imposed by Governor Hutchinson—would reign in Massachusetts.

16

Patriots Assemble

If to appear for my country is treason,
and to aim for her defiance is rebellion,
like my fathers, I will glory in the name of rebel and traitor,
as they did that of puritan and enthusiast.

—Josiah Quincy Jr.

On April 1, 1772, Hutchinson made the official announcement that John Hancock had been offered the commission of captain of the Cadet Corps (with the official rank of colonel) for the town of Boston, and that he had accepted the position. It was a position that would not only allow Hancock to achieve a military rank overnight, but it also played to his affinity for fine clothing and visual display. Within a week of receiving the commission, Hancock put an advertisement in the local paper offering employment to "Two fifers that understand playing. Those that are masters of music . . . are desired to apply to Col. John Hancock."[1] Although uniforms for the Cadets and their leader were supplied by the British authorities, Hancock took over their consignment. Hancock had always loved clothes and now he could satisfy his appetite for color and style while also flaunting his newfound role as commander. The uniforms he ordered were magnificent: tricorne hats trimmed in beaver fur and cocked just right, with a rosette to hold the fold; scarlet red jackets embellished with buff lapels and cuffs; and brilliant white gaiters that fastened over boots with black buttons.

But despite Hancock's very public celebration of his new role, his acceptance of the commission was not the coup Hutchinson had hoped for. Hancock was not switching loyalty; in fact, he considered the offer to lead the cadets to have come from the officers themselves, as it had been instigated by a unanimous vote of the men who served in the Cadet Corps.

As Sam Adams noted, "a reluctance at the idea of giving offense to an hundred gentlemen" led Hancock to accept the commission.[2] It was his sense of duty to his fellow citizens that pushed Hancock to accept the role offered by Hutchinson—and his loyalty, while ignored by Hutchinson, was noted by the Sons of Liberty.

The duty that Hancock felt toward his fellow colonists had long been understood by Sam Adams and the other Sons, and not only in the realm of politics. As trade eased with England after the Townshend Acts were rescinded and Hancock's warehouses began to fill with goods, owners of small village stores streamed into Boston to replenish their own stocks. With little money to offer and no track records in business, there were few merchants who would sell to these aspiring business owners. But John Hancock extended credit to those who expressed to him their sincere desire to work hard and shared with him their dreams of fortunes to be made.

Hancock didn't help only the small shop owners; he also sought, in his role as a merchant leader of Boston, to help other warehouse operators get their businesses up and running again. The important thing, Hancock reasoned, was to build a strong colonial business class, one that could speak in a united voice, when necessary, against the machinations of English politicians and suppliers. Trade was hard for everyone, with a surplus of goods flooding the market. The House of Hancock, even as it extended credit to others, found itself falling into debt with its suppliers in England. Hancock himself was never in danger of insolvency—with his vast real estate holdings in Boston and throughout New England and other investments, he was rich as Croesus—and he persevered, through good times and bad, in securing unity among colonial businessmen from the lowest shopkeepers to the largest importers.

In May 1771, when John Hancock was elected, with Sam Adams as his running mate, to once again lead the Boston representatives to the General Court, Hutchinson suddenly understood: Hancock was not his man and never had been. And when with great fanfare Hancock commissioned John Singleton Copley to paint a portrait of Sam Adams, and then hung it proudly in the drawing room of his mansion beside his own Copley portrait, Hutchinson knew he had lost Hancock for good. Hancock was no Royalist, no Loyalist, never had been and never would be.

The Copley portrait of Sam Adams clearly demonstrated where Hancock's loyalty lay and was an insult to Hutchinson on many levels. Adams stands at a table, the index finger of his left hand pointing to the Massachusetts Charter spread out before him. In his right hand, he holds the instructions created by the Boston Town Meeting on the day after the Boston Massacre, demanding that troops be removed from the town of Boston.

The demand had been made to Hutchinson, and Hutchinson had caved. Everyone who saw the portrait of Sam Adams knew immediately what it was meant to convey: Hutchinson was an attempted usurper of power; Sam Adams and the Sons of Liberty were protectors of the colony. The Roman columns, subtly presented in the background of the portrait, only emphasize the "association [of the Sons of Liberty] with republican virtue and rationality."[3]

Positioning the portrait of Sam Adams side by side with the "simple and unadorned" portrait of Hancock underscored the virtue and determination of both men and deliberately connected their leadership with the Puritan past of Boston. Hutchinson had considered Hancock, a rich merchant with a taste for luxury and beauty, to be a strange choice to lead the men on the street against the Royal administrators; after all, Hancock was more like an English lord than a North End dockworker in his tastes, education, and lifestyle.

But Hutchinson had forgotten where John Hancock came from. He was the son of a country minister who had taught his son the Puritan values of duty to community and sacrifice for the larger good. Reverend Hancock had sought in the small village of Braintree an opportunity for every soul in the community to know each other, to help each other, to communicate a desire for living a better life and join efforts across the community to reach a better life for all. Now his son John sought the same in the larger community of Boston.

Hancock not only helped both established and aspiring merchants of his colony; he also dedicated his funds and effort to improving life for all Bostonians. He had a bandstand built on the Boston Common and employed musicians to play there. He planted lime trees along the streets bordering the Common and laid out pathways for walking through the large public space. He gifted the town with a fire engine, and the selectman responded to the generosity by naming the vehicle in his honor—"the John Hancock"—and stationing it close to Hancock's Wharf.

Hancock contributed vast amount of funds to rebuild the Brattle Street Church, long in need of renovation, and allocated specific funds for the acquisition of a new pulpit, crafted from mahogany; a deacon's seat, also to be built from mahogany; a special table for communion; and a magnificent bell for the new belfry. When the pulpit could not be finished in time for the first sermon in the new church, Hancock made sure a pine substitute was made to be used in the meantime. He contributed money for another local church to purchase a new bell and for yet another to purchase a much-needed replacement Bible.

The destitute of Boston were most often on the receiving side of Hancock's generosity, with firewood provided in the cold months, paid work in the busy months of summer, and sustenance, both actual and spiritual, all year long. A specific bequest was made by Hancock to the Brattle Street Church to assist those "poor widows and others . . . who are reputable persons and unable to furnish themselves with seats" in the church.[4]

And when his younger brother, Ebenezer, turned to Hancock for help—not for the first time—having once again fallen into severe economic straits, John bailed him out of bankruptcy and set him up in a small shop in Boston. He then advised his brother, responsible now not only for himself but also for his pregnant wife, Elizabeth Lowell, to "Reflect on your former imprudencies and resolve to quit yourself like a man . . . always remember that by diligence and industry and good conduct a man will rub through this world with comfort . . . you are dependent on your own industry for your support, and that of your family . . . above all, be steadfast and unmoveable, always abounding in the work of the Lord."[5] Lessons of the father, to be shared among the sons.

In February 1772, Abigail Phillips Quincy gave birth to a baby boy. The child was named Josiah, after his father and grandfather, and both men were overjoyed with his arrival. By all appearances, he was a sturdy child, quickly growing plump and rosy-cheeked, much to his mother's joy and relief. The hoped-for heir, who would carry on the family values of community and faith, had been born as planned and was flourishing, as prayed for.

John Adams began traveling frequently into Boston as his legal work picked up; he even rented a small office in the city to address the "speedy revival of the suing Spirit,"[6] brought on by the renewal of trade with England. Just as Hancock had been courted by Hutchinson, Adams found he too was inundated with offers from local Crown officials to join their side. Adams wrote in his diary of how easy it would be to succumb, for such acquiescence would "make the Fortune of me and my Posterity forever."

Nevertheless, John remained firm in his resolve to resist the temptations posed: "I dread the Consequences . . . of such a Sacrifice of my Honour, my Conscience, my Friends, my Country, my God," predicting that the consequences would be "nothing less than Hell Fire, eternal Torment."[7] For the time being, he kept his head down, his nose to his desk of legal work, and his home—and heart—in Braintree.

John resumed the court circuit and once again began attending court in Plymouth, Barnstable, Taunton, Cambridge, and other towns throughout New England. The travel was a heavy burden, felt by both John and Abigail. They had taken their months together for granted and now sorely missed each other's company.

John wrote to Abigail in May, while out on the circuit, "I wish myself at Braintree. This wandering, itinerating Life grows more and more disagreable to me. I want to see my Wife and Children every Day, I want to see my Grass and Blossoms and Corn, &c. every Day. I want to see my Workmen, nay I almost want to go and see the Bosse Calfs's as often as Charles does."[8] And above all else, after his wife and children, he missed the comfort and peace of his library: "I want to see my books."[9]

Sometime in the year 1772, John Hancock commissioned Master Copley to paint a portrait of Dorothy Quincy. He instructed the artist to convey both Dolly's youth (although she was no longer considered a young woman at age twenty-five) and her virtue, which Copley did by dressing her in a modest gown, over which she wore a diaphanous apron embroidered with flowers. Copley also showed, through the intensity of her eyes, the seriousness of her expression, and the set of her chin, that Dolly was no simpering fool: under the direction of either John or Dolly or both, Copley was instructed to portray the woman as both intelligent and thoughtful.

The hallmark of the final portrait was not her beauty, for Dolly was not presented as a beauty or even as pretty; instead she appeared smart, strong-minded, and austere, a perfect role model for the Puritan-bred colonial woman. Hancock was well-pleased with the Copley portrait of Dolly, and displayed it in pride of place over the mantel in his dining room.

It was time now to introduce Dolly to more of the Hancock family. John and Dolly, accompanied by Aunt Lydia, traveled to Bridgewater, a small village to the south of Boston set deep in the rolling countryside. John's mother, Mary, lived there, and had for the past twenty years, after marrying Daniel Perkins, minister of the local parish church. Reverend Perkins and his wife welcomed the young couple and Lydia into their home. With their welcome, they gave their blessing to the union of John and Dolly.

In the fall, after they returned to Boston, John Hancock wrote to Jonathan Sewall about the "connection formed with the sister of your lady

[Sewall's wife, Esther]" and the need to keep between the two men "a perfect harmony and friendship" in view of that connection. And yet still no formal marriage proposal had been forthcoming from John to Dolly. Was it John who delayed the offer or Dolly who had made clear her reluctance to accept it?

Dolly was perhaps worried about John Hancock's health and his chronic struggle with gout. Already in 1768, he had complained of ill health—"I am very unwell," he wrote in a letter—but the symptoms of gout first appeared and then intensified throughout 1771.[10]

By 1772, his doctor, Joseph Warren, confirmed the diagnosis of gout. Swollen ankles, knees, and feet; skin the color of sea thrift, brilliant pink rings of pain. At times the pain was so intolerable that Hancock could not even leave his bed to attend town meetings and fulfill his role as moderator. Not even being carried in a sedan chair helped, as the slightest jostle of swollen limb against wooden frame caused the most exquisite pain, which brought him almost to fainting.

And yet Hancock remained committed to carrying out his political and social duties, rising from bed whenever possible and attending town meetings, get-togethers at the Bunch of Grapes, and always, always, the dinner parties planned by Lydia. The gout came and went—"I am so surprisingly recovered that I have plunged myself into the business of life again," he wrote to a friend after a bad spell ended—and by the end of July 1772, Hancock was well enough to take a boat trip with a group of male friends.[11] For two weeks, the men enjoyed leisurely sailing on the *Boston Packet*, a sleek vessel stocked with food and wine, and servants brought along to keep everyone comfortable.

As summer of 1772 turned to fall, it seemed as if the ambitions of John Adams had truly gone into hibernation; he desired nothing more than to sit with Abigail by the fireplace, a book on his lap and a lovely view out the window over his lands and the sea. He had a new baby boy now at home, Thomas, born on September 15, and his large family, from chubby little Tommy to sturdy Nabby, made him proud.

As his legal work increased, money worries had lessened. Politics faded from his mind. Years ago, he had promised his friend Richard Cranch (and his wife, Abigail) that he had left behind "Politicks . . . and the Governor and all his Friends and Enemies."[12] John now intended to make that promise stick.

But still, in the recesses of his brain, desire for something more lurked.

When a chance arose to purchase the building in Boston in which his town offices were housed, Adams found he had both the money and the willingness to do so. With such a building, he could move the family back to Boston and once again live and work from home, in the city where so many legal cases now clamored for representation. But should he move the family, pick up everything and return to the scene of so much stress and conflict?

Without consulting Abigail—a first for him, but perhaps he was worried that she would reject the idea—John decided to take the chance and buy the building in Boston. And yet he was still determined, as he wrote in his diary with vehemence, to stay out of politics in Boston: "I shall come with a fixed Resolution, to meddle not with public Affairs of Town or Province. I am determined, my own Life, and the Welfare of my whole Family, which is much dearer to me, are too great Sacrifices for me to make. . . . I will devote myself wholly to my private Business, my Office and my farm, and I hope to lay a Foundation for better Fortune to my Children, and an happier Life than has fallen to my Share."[13]

Without fanfare, John told Abigail to prepare to move to their new home; it was a fine building, he told her, located on Queen Street in Boston.

Samuel Quincy was also laying careful plans that involved both avoidance of politics and the securing of wealth. But unlike John Adams, Sam's wealth was tied to the Crown, and no matter how he tried to separate his own work as solicitor general from Governor Hutchinson's administration of the colony, the fact was, he was paid by the Crown and it was to the Crown that he owed his allegiance. And yet the manner in which Sam was perceived was not always clear-cut. Phillis Wheatley, a well-known black poet, wrote a poem in Sam's honor that was to be published in a collection of her works.

Wheatley was a black slave, owned by the Wheatley family of Boston, whom Sam served as family solicitor. She first achieved fame both in the colonies and in England for a poem she wrote in 1770, eulogizing the English minister and evangelist George Whitefield. An ardent colonist, though enslaved, Phillis wrote a series of poems elevating events and heroes of the colonial movement against British oppression; because Sam Quincy had prosecuted the perpetrators of the Boston Massacre, Wheatley saw him as a hero and titled her poem "To Samuel Quincy, a Panegyrick."[14]

Unfortunately, sufficient subscribers for the poetry volume could not be found and it was never published; the poem written in Sam's honor disappeared. But Wheatley was probably not alone in her view of Sam Quincy as a patriot. Loyalist or patriot—Sam still wondered if there was a way that he could be both.

In early fall of 1772, news arrived from England of yet another bill passed by Parliament with the intention of controlling colonial courts and legislatures. For months, there had been protests against Parliament's decision to pay the salary of Governor Hutchinson directly from the Crown; now this new bill required that the salaries of judges would also be drawn from the Crown budget, and not paid out of moneys controlled by the colonial legislatures.

Josiah Quincy Jr. quickly took to his pen to challenge the practice of paying colonial judges from the Crown's purse. As a father now, Josiah felt the weight of the legacy he had always wanted—a son who would be both proud of him and emboldened in his own life to strive for the betterment of all mankind—"I wish to see my country free and happy; that my children may partake as fair an inheritance as I have received."[15]

The urgency of creating the legacy intensified as Josiah's health deteriorated. Undaunted by the return of nighttime fevers and a purulent cough, Josiah used his illness as a spur, not only for himself but for others; he proclaimed himself publicly as being "advanced . . . in infirmity" and thus eager to "render the small residue of my days profitable to my species."[16]

Once again relying on the language of oppression and revolt, Quincy published a stirring diatribe in the *Boston Gazette* that stressed the necessity of impartial judges in a courtroom: "So sensible are all tyrants of the importance of such courts, that, to advance and establish their system of oppression, they never rest until they have completely corrupted, or bought, the judges of the land. . . . My countrymen, Great Britain, with legislative solemnity, has told you she can bind you and yours by her laws, when the parliament please. . . . Who appoints, who displaces our judges, we all know. But who pays them? The last vessels from England tell us—the judges and the subalterns have got salaries from Great Britain! Is it possible this last movement should not rouse us, and drive us, not to desperation, but to our duty?"[17]

In closing, he exhorted his fellow colonists: "The blind may see, the callous must feel, the spirited will act."[18]

And act they did. In October 1772, Sam Adams, urged on by Josiah Quincy Jr., called for the establishment of a "Committee of Correspondence . . . to state the Rights of the Colonists and of this Province" and to communicate those rights to the other colonies, as well as to "the World."[19]

The Committee of Correspondence formed; a group of twenty-one, they met to debate what course of action to follow in protesting Parliament's latest maneuvers. On November 20, 1772, the committee submitted a report to the town meeting. Sam Adams, along with James Otis Jr., Josiah Quincy, and Dr. Joseph Warren, had accomplished an unimaginable feat: in less than three weeks, they had brought their committee, with its participants of diverging views and backgrounds, to a place of agreement and certitude. Their report, which would be known as the *Boston Pamphlet*, laid the groundwork for that which Governor Hutchinson had long feared: rebellion.

"We the Freeholders and other Inhabitants of Boston," stated the report submitted by the committee, "apprehending there is abundant to be alarmed at the plan of Despotism . . . can no longer conceal our impatience under a constant, unremitted, uniform aim to enslave us, or confide in an Administration which threatens us with certain and inevitable destruction."[20]

The *Boston Pamphlet* set out in plain terms the rights of American colonists: "Among the natural Rights of all the Colonists are three. . . . First, a right to *Life*; Secondly to *Liberty*; thirdly to *Property*."[21] A long list of grievances was included, covering everything from tax revenues and tax collectors to control over the salaries of provincial government officers and the use (and abuse) of juryless admiralty courts.

In closing, the writers of the pamphlet (and surely Josiah was author here) invoked the law as both savior of the people and as an ideal worth fighting for: "Let us consider Brethren, we are struggling for our best Birth Rights and Inheritance. . . . Let us disappoint the Men, who are raising themselves on the Ruin of this Country. Let us convince every Invader of our Freedom, that we will be as free as the Constitution our Fathers recognized, will justify."[22]

John Hancock was not on the committee that prepared the *Boston Pamphlet*, in part because of bad health and in part because he was uncertain about the readiness of other towns and colonies to join Boston in its battle against Britain. Nevertheless, as moderator of the Boston Town Meeting, it was Hancock's duty to call for a vote on its approval. And once it was approved in a unanimous vote and then sent out for printing to be presented to the other colonies, it was Hancock's name, as moderator, that was prominently displayed on the first page in large bold type.

Now that his name was so intimately linked with the work of the committee, Hancock did not hesitate to publicize the *Boston Pamphlet* and advocate for cooperation across the colonies in protecting colonial rights and privileges. He urged towns to create their own committees of correspondence and write their own reports, as well as to sign on to the pamphlet. Colonists across Massachusetts, and America, responded by organizing their own local and regional committees to debate British policies and decide their political futures.

In England, Ben Franklin, having received a copy of the *Boston Pamphlet*, sent it out for reprinting and then went about London distributing it to pro-colonial advocates and their opponents alike. It was not lost on English readers of the pamphlet that its American authors had invoked the same reasoning used by the original founders of their colony for breaking with England in the first place: it was "that generous ardor for Civil and Religious liberty which in the face of every danger, and even death itself, induced our fathers to forsake the bosom of their Native Country, and begin a settlement in bare Creation."[23]

That same ardor for freedom would carry the colonists forward in their struggle to again assert their own sovereignty and right to liberty. While there were many in England who saw such passion as a danger to the status quo of empire, others recognized the resolve of the colonies as an opportunity for Parliament to ease off on the colonies and get things back to the way they used to be.

For the citizens of Braintree, the *Boston Pamphlet* was remarkably similar to the *Braintree Instructions* written in 1765 by John Adams, in which he had laid out in no uncertain terms the illegality of taxation of the colonists by Parliament. It was easy enough for the people of Braintree to now support the *Boston Pamphlet*, and to once again herald their native-born legal tactician.

John welcomed the praise but still persevered in his plan to stay out of politics. He wanted to keep to his plan of working hard, staying healthy, and cherishing his peace: "I must remember Temperance, Exercise and Peace of Mind. Above all Things I must avoid Politicks, Political Clubbs, Town Meetings, General Court. . . . I must ride frequently to Braintree to inspect my Farm, and when in Boston must spend my Evenings in my Office, or with my Family, and with as little Company as possible."[24]

For the time being, such a life would suffice for John Adams; and it would please Abigail as well (although she had objected to returning to Boston, unhappy to leave her sister Mary). But the plan John had laid out in September was already crumbling, bit by bit, and would soon be laid to waste not only by the rising ambitions of Adams but also by the persistent oppressions of Parliament and the hidden machinations of Hutchinson.

By the end of the year 1772, Josiah Quincy's health had deteriorated even further. The effort he put into creating the *Boston Pamphlet* took its toll, and his consumption returned in force and with violence: his coughing spells produced blood and led to throbbing headaches and sleepless nights, compounding his growing frailty. He suffered frequent fainting spells, and friends and family began to worry for his life. Dr. Warren, his partner on the committee to write the pamphlet and his always loyal friend and physician, advised Josiah to travel to softer climates for a long visit; a restful vacation in the southern colonies might just be what was needed to restore his strength and vitality.

But Josiah had a different goal in mind when he acceded to Dr. Warren's suggestion. He would willingly travel south but rest was not his primary intention. Instead, he would use the trip to begin a one-man campaign to first understand, and then corral, the political interests of the southern colonies, with the end goal of binding the interests of the South to the interests of the North.

Josiah knew there were colonists in the southern colonies as concerned as New Englanders about the state of affairs with Parliament. But the concerns of the Southerners were distinct from those of the Northerners: their economies were different; religion was treated in a different way; and the courts and the administrative offices in each colony were distinct, one from the other. "Were I to lament anything," Quincy wrote in his journal, "it would be the prevalent and extended ignorance of one colony with the concerns of another."[25]

His journey south would be a scouting trip, and a campaign to bring Southerners in line with Northerners. As he wrote in a letter to a friend, "Let us forgive each other's follies and unite while we may. . . . To think justly is not sufficient, but we must think alike, before we shall form a union; that truly formed, we are invincible."[26] And to be invincible was the goal, when facing the daunting powers of Britain.

17

Branching Out

A mutual exchange of sentiments will give us, as men,
knowledge of each other; that knowledge naturally creates
esteem,
and that esteem will, in the end, cement us as colonists.
—JOSIAH QUINCY JR.

On January 1, 1773, John Adams sat at his desk, at his new home on Queen Street in Boston, and took out his diary. "January the first, being Friday," he began. Then he continued, his quill pen scratching away on the manuscript paper, "I never was happier in my whole life than I have been since I returned to Boston. My resolutions to devote myself to the pleasures, the studies, the business and the duties of a private life are a source of ease and comfort to me."[1]

But like so many resolutions made in a new year, those of John Adams would not last the month. In just three days, he put pen to paper again but not to scribble private thoughts in his diary. John Adams, political pamphleteer, was back in business. Three of his pieces were published in the *Boston Gazette* in the month of January, and many more would come out over the next few months. Published under his own name, these very public—and very political—writings would bring him the fame he had craved as a younger man but would also divert him from a quiet private life—book on his lap, seat by the hearth, and Abigail nearby—for good.

John's writings began as an exploration of the law concerning the issues of judges' salaries and appointments and the importance of impartial justice; he argued that judges beholden to Crown or Parliament were simply not capable of carrying out their judicial duties. At the end of his first piece, after lengthy paragraphs in which he quoted two English legal experts, Sir Edward Coke and Sir Robert Raymond, and referred to dozens of English cases and proclamations, John added, "I have many more things to say upon this subject."[2] And indeed he did, as two more lengthy letters followed on the same subject within the month.

But he also branched off into the broader subject of how much control

Parliament could exercise over all the administrative positions of the Massachusetts colony. When at the end of January the Massachusetts House of Representatives asked John to revise its written response to Governor Hutchinson's recent speech to the General Court—in which Hutchinson asserted the absolute sovereignty of Parliament over the colonies—he quickly got to work.

Within a week, he rewrote the reply, creating a text fifteen pages long. In it, Adams argued that the original charter granted the colonists "all the Liberties and Immunities of free and natural Subjects . . . and a Legislative was accordingly constituted within the Colony; one Branch of which consists of Representatives chosen by the People, to *make all Laws, Statutes, Ordinances*, &c. for the well-ordering and governing the same."[3]

Although Governor Hutchinson repeatedly invoked "the Supreme Authority of Parliament" in setting the colonial legislative agenda, and Parliament "claimed a Power of making such Laws as they please to order and govern us," John argued that both the language and the intent of the Massachusetts Charter were both clear and binding: "it cannot be supposed to have been the Intention of the Parties in the Compact, that we should be reduced to a State of Vassallage, [therefore] the Conclusion is, that it was their Sense, that we were thus Independent."[4]

Leave the colonists to govern themselves under the charter, John advised: "Should the People of this Province be left to the free and full Exercise of all the Liberties and Immunities granted to them by Charter, there would be no Danger of an Independance [*sic*] on the Crown."[5]

It was not independence from England—the creation of a new country—that John Adams argued for; it was for colonists to be left to govern themselves, as citizens of England. He as yet had no thought of separating from Great Britain—nor had Josiah Quincy Jr. or Sr., nor Edmund Quincy, nor his daughter Dolly, nor John Hancock. These stalwart natives of Braintree might argue most forcefully for liberty, yet they still without hesitation pledged "Allegiance . . . to the King of Great-Britain, our rightful Sovereign."[6]

There was no thought of rebellion; in fact, as Josiah Quincy Jr. argued again and again, it was Parliament and its sycophants in the colonies who were "rebels" against the British Constitution. The colonists fighting for their rights were not only the true patriots and truly loyal to Great Britain; they were also the chosen ones of God. After all, Josiah wrote, "tyrants are rebels against the first laws of Heaven and society: to oppose their ravages is an instinct of nature, the inspiration of God in the heart of man. In the noble resistance which mankind make to exorbitant ambition and power, they always feel that divine afflatus [inspiration] which . . . causes them to consider the Lord . . . as their leader, and his angels as fellow soldiers."[7]

When Josiah Jr., John Adams, and John Hancock spoke of revolution, they spoke of it in terms of "that glorious aera [*sic*]" when, in 1688, James II was removed from the English throne and the rights and privileges of Englishmen were restored to them under the reign of William III.[8] As Josiah Jr. put it, in quoting the English legal genius Sir William Blackstone, the "flagrant abuse of any power, by the crown or its ministers, has always been productive of a struggle."[9]

A struggle, a revolution, a rebellion: for the patriots of Braintree, the words all signified justified agitation that was necessary to restore and protect the rights of colonists, both natural and man-given.

Governor Hutchinson, however, saw only treason in the colonists' protests and writings. To contest the will of Parliament and the king—whether disputing the right of Parliament to tax the colonists, or of the Crown to pay the salaries of judges and administrators, or of admiralty courts to hear cases without a jury—was rebellion against Crown and country. The *Boston Pamphlet* was, in Hutchinson's opinion, the culmination of the colonists' fomenting of rebellion: it was the "foulest, subtlest, and most venomous serpent ever issued from the egg of sedition."[10]

Josiah Jr. finalized his plan of departure from Boston, bound for Charleston; he would leave by early February 1773. Having lost his oldest boy, Ned, when he sought a travel cure for his consumption, Josiah Sr. worried that his youngest son's journey might be similarly ill-fated. Travel by sea was always with its risks, and in the winter months it was sure to be rough. The vessel would travel along the coastline for a good part of the journey, but by necessity it would venture out into the waters around Bermuda and then swing back toward the southern colonies.

Many a ship had gone down in those treacherous waters; the area was known as cursed. But his son Josiah was determined to go, and Abigail, his loyal wife, supported him in his choice. Josiah Sr. insisted that Abigail and the baby come out to Braintree to stay for the duration of Josiah's time away; the anxious grandfather hoped to find distraction in keeping the little boy entertained. He tried to convince his son to complete a final will, even sending the lawyer John Lowell to Josiah Jr.'s office on Queen Street, but the younger Josiah procrastinated and no final testament was taken.

Notices began flowing into Boston, addressed to the town meeting and sent from villages and towns throughout the colony, underscoring widespread approval for the *Boston Pamphlet* and offering promises that local committees of correspondence would be set up to keep vigilant watch over the workings of Parliament.

From Marlborough on the northern coast came the message "Death is more eligible than slavery." From Chatham on the Cape, "Our civil and religious principles are the sweetest and most essential part of our lives, without which the remainder is scarcely worth preserving." And from far out in the Berkshires: "As we are in a remote wilderness corner of the earth, we know little. But neither nature nor the God of nature requires us to crouch, Issaachar-like, between the two burdens of poverty and slavery."[11]

Hutchinson considered these incipient committees of correspondence to be agents of rebellion and treason, and claimed the documents produced by the committees were seditious, as they "would be sufficient to justify the colonies in revolting, and forming an independent state."[12] Together with his lieutenant governor, his brother-in-law Andrew Oliver, Hutchinson worked to suppress the committees, writing acid denunciations both of their purpose and of the characters of the men on the committees—"the worst of them one would not chose to meet in the dark and three or four at least of their correspondence committee are as black hearted fellows as any upon the Globe."[13]

But in a private letter to England, Hutchinson acknowledged that he was losing the battle against the committees. Their popularity was growing, and their ideas flourished: "a right to independence . . . is more and more asserted every day and the longer such an opinion is tolerated the deeper the root it takes in men's minds and becomes more difficult to eradicate but it must be done or we shall never return to good government and good order."[14]

On February 8, 1773, Josiah Quincy Jr. set sail on the *Bristol Packet* bound for Charleston. As the ship sailed down through Boston Harbor, Josiah could see his father's mansion on the hills of Braintree; he wrote in his journal, "I came in sight of my father's cottage," and it gave him such a sweet sentiment of both regret and renewal: "the sweetest harmony I ever caroled."[15] He began a new journal to record his travels south, dedicating it on the first page both to his wife, Abigail—"who has a right to a very large share of my thoughts and reflections, as well as to participate, as far as possible, of all my amusements and vicissitudes"—and to "a future witness to my self of my own sentiments and opinions."

He finished the dedication with the hope that "into whose hand this Journal either before or after my death may chance to fall, Excuse . . . those trifles and impertinencies I foresee it will contain."[16]

After a calm day of travel, which Josiah spent translating a passage of Virgil (brought on by the sight of his father's home on the hill: "We have left our country's borders and sweet fields"[17]), the weather—and Josiah's health—took a turn for the worse. "Exhausted to the last degree, I was too weak to rise, and in too exquisite pain to lie in bed."

When he attempted to go up on deck for fresh air, "My sickness came on with redoubled violence, and after several fainting turns, I was carried back to bed." Lying below deck was no better: "my pains came on so violent, and my cabin was so sultry and hot, to rise or perish seemed the only alternative."[18]

Josiah returned to the deck, assisted by two sailors of the watch. To his horror, the ocean was churning angrily all around him—"the waves seemed to curl with flames" and the sky overhead was "black and heavy." Josiah watched, mesmerized but terrified, as the "Seas rise in wrath and mountains combat heavens; clouds gage with clouds and lightenings dart their vengeful coruscations; thunders roll and oceans roar."

He retreated once again to his cabin, where he passed "Days of heat, cold, wind, and rain . . . I became pale wan and spiritless . . . every person on shipboard gave me over and concluded I should never reach land."[19]

The worst was still to come as the vessel sailed farther south, closer to "the latitude of the Bermudas, a latitude remarkable for storms and whirlwinds." A hurricane arrived with nightfall on February 21: "Rain, hail, snow and sleet descended with great violence and the wind and waves raged all night."

For days, storms pounded the vessel. Josiah, confined once again to his cabin, where he was flung from side to side by the force of the wind and the waves, could think only that he was "now in that latitude in which the remains of my Elder Brother lay deposited in the Ocean." Would he come to a similar end? He passed the nights in deep reflection, recalling to mind Hamlet's lamentation on the passage of time and futility of living—"Tomorrow, and tomorrow and tomorrow Creeps in this petty space [*sic*]."[20]

The captain of the ship, John Skimmer, would later recall, "I never saw so dismal a time in my life . . . [nor had any mariner on board] seen so terrible a time."[21] As the storm raged on, prayers began and final declarations were made. Destruction of the vessel was inevitable, and death imminent: "Every soul on board expected to perish."[22]

Josiah turned to his journal and wrote, "I regretted nothing more than that in past-times I had not been more of the true citizen of my country and the world;—more assiduous, more persevering, more bitter toward the implacable, more relentless against the scourges of my country, and the plagues of mankind."[23] Then he hunkered down in his bunk and began to pray.

Exhilarating news arrived in Boston from Virginia. The House of Burgesses—Virginia's legislative body—proposed that the American colonies create a network of intercolonial organizing in addition to the local committees of correspondence. The proposal matched the suggestion made by John Adams back in January when, in writing his reply to Thomas Hutchinson at the request of the Massachusetts House of Representatives, he had suggested a gathering of all the colonies to discuss and agree upon ideas "of very great Importance to all." He had used the word "Congress" to describe such a meeting.[24]

John Adams recognized that the fight of the Massachusetts colonists was the fight of all the colonies. He would no longer make arguments on behalf of Massachusetts alone but instead would fire salvos on the part of all Americans chafing under Parliament's far-reaching acts. Adams had joined with Josiah Quincy Jr. and John Hancock in branching out, and corralling forces far beyond their New England borders.

Approval for this coalescence of colonial protest and action roared into Boston, with notices, letters, and signed petitions of support. From Gorham, Maine, came this declaration: "The swords which we whet and brightened for our enemies [in the Seven Years' War] are not yet grown rusty"; and from Kittery: "We offer our lives as a sacrifice in the glorious cause of liberty."[25] Committees in Connecticut vowed to cut off trade with Britain and publicly shame any merchant or customer who chose to continue dealing in such goods.

John Adams understood this movement of colonial cooperation to be a wholly lawful campaign necessary to secure the rights of colonists: "Our own Happiness as well as his Majesty's Service, very much depends upon

Peace and Order; and we shall at all Times take such Measures as are consistent with our Constitution and the Rights of the People to promote and maintain them."[26]

The sanctity of good government was the focal point of their agitation, John Hancock insisted, vowing his highest allegiance to "righteous government . . . founded upon principles of reason and justice." And Josiah Quincy Jr., in a piece he published before leaving for Charleston, justified colonial resistance to illegal acts by Parliament as not only lawful but obligatory: "Is it possible [the acts of Parliament] should not rouse us, and drive us, not to desperation, but to our duty?"[27]

Among the patriots, the cause was property and liberty, not independence. Whether Loyalist or patriot, the colonists considered their rights to be English, even if their domicile was American. And in England, neither those who supported the colonists' rights nor those who opposed them gave a thought to a possible severance of the connection between England and its American colonies.

In March 1773, John Adams admitted to his wife, Abigail, what she already knew: he was back in the fray of politics. He'd spent the evening at Hancock's home on the hill, meeting with other agitators for colonial rights, and he realized he could not hold himself back from participating. As he wrote in his diary the next day, "I have never known a Period, in which the Seeds of great Events have been so plentifully sown as this Winter. A Providence is visible, in that Concurrence of Causes [which have] laid me under peculiar Obligations to undeceive the People, and changed my Resolution. I hope that some good will come out of it.—God knows."[28]

Perhaps it was seeing the portrait of his cousin Sam Adams hanging beside that of John Hancock in the Hancock drawing room that had pushed John Adams the final yard back into politics. He was an ambitious man, and it must have galled him to see Sam's face up there next to Hancock's when it was John Adams who had been the friend to young Hancock, his companion at college, and the patriot willing to represent the hated British soldiers after the massacre just to prove how law-abiding the colonists of Massachusetts really were. John's reputation suffered for that sacrifice made—"my conduct in it is remembered, and is alleged against me to prove I am an enemy to my country, and always have been"[29]—and what did he have to show for it?

Adams' envy of Hancock, mixed up with his admiration for the man and his desire to be recognized publicly, continued to both irritate and motivate him, as it had since the two were childhood friends. Never again would he back away, Adams vowed to himself, from the challenges of politics, public scrutiny, or public duty. He would play a commanding role in colonial politics and make his name—and one day his portrait would hang where everyone who was anyone could see it.

Abigail Phillips Quincy received a letter from Charleston at the end of March 1773. For weeks she had been worried about her husband; now she would know how he fared, if he still lived. She hesitated before opening the letter but then realized that her name on the envelope had been written in her husband's careful hand.

Josiah had arrived safely in Charleston on February 28. He wrote about the terrible voyage, and his fears: "I had not the least expectation of ever seeing you or my dear boy again; I was fully convinced we must perish." He quickly assured his wife of his health—"everything looks favourable at present that way"—and wrote about the ample "trade, riches, magnificence, and great state" in Charleston, adding there was "much gayety and dissipation."[30]

In his journal, Josiah wrote of his determination to bring about a union of the northern and southern colonies, and immediately upon his safe arrival in Charleston, he set himself to the task. A month of luncheons and dinner parties, sightseeing tours and teas with government officials, musical hall concerts and horseback riding ensued. Through it all, Josiah dedicated himself to getting to know the people of the South, their ways, manners, proclivities, and political inclinations.

Well-educated and well-mannered, soft-spoken and charming, of all the Sons of Liberty Josiah was best suited to the task of bringing the southern brothers into the fold of resistance against Britain. To the leaders of Charleston, who also happened to be the financial elite, this young Northerner seemed to be one of them: rich, savvy, cultured. He was well-dressed and well-shod and he powdered his hair just right. Josiah knew how to behave at the endless social gatherings hosted by southern gentility; he spoke easily with the men and understood the necessity of complimenting a woman upon her arrival into a room and escorting her into dinner.

He knew good wine—in one home, he complimented "the richest wine I ever tasted: Exceeds Mr. Hancock's . . . in flavour, softness, and strength"—and he recognized the virtue of a proper toast: "When passions rise may reason be the guide" was the toast of one young lady which he admiringly recorded.[31]

From his southernmost stop in Charleston, Josiah gradually traveled northward. He continued to write in his journals, commenting on the rich exterior displays of the southern men and women he met along the way—"a richness and elegance uncommon with us"—but at the same time questioning their internal strengths: "Nothing that I now saw raised my conceptions of the mental abilities of this people." And he later noted, "Cards, dice, the bottle and horses engross prodigious portions of time and attention."[32]

To Josiah, these Southerners were too absorbed by fun and games. He was scandalized by how their attendance at church on a Sunday was viewed as yet another occasion for socializing, not as the serious commitment to contemplation that churchgoing was in Congregationalist New England: "The Sabbath is a day of visiting and mirth with the Rich, and of license, pastime, and frolic for the negroes."[33]

Nevertheless, Josiah was heartened by meeting up with scores of active patriots, "hot and zealous in the Cause of America."[34] Once he finally encountered men he found to be of both sound mind and deep virtue, he felt that real friendships could be formed. After meeting Cornelius Harnett, described by Quincy as "the Samuel Adams of North Carolina," and a man of "philosophy and virtue," Josiah wrote, "From perfect strangers we became intimate—we formed an apparent affection and at parting both seem to be mutually and alike affected."[35]

Best of all, Josiah saw evidence of a sincere desire on the part of the southern patriots to unite with their northern counterparts: "The plan of Continental correspondence [is] highly relished, much wished for and resolved upon, as proper to be pursued."[36]

As he continued his travels northward, there would be places where he found less support for the continental union than he might have wished; "Boston aims at Nothing Less than sovereignty of the whole continent" accused one Southerner, and on another occasion, a Loyalist challenged "windbag" Josiah to a duel.[37] Josiah promptly fainted and the Southerner claimed Josiah's weakness was proof of the flaccidity of the northern patriots.

But overall, as the weeks passed and the lands gave way to more familiar territories of apple orchards and grazing cows (after the peach trees, cotton, and tobacco of farther south), Josiah was encouraged by the individual colonies' willingness to protest on behalf of their rights against Parliament and their interest in joining forces with colonies farther north.

For Josiah, the most disturbing aspect of his southern travels was the prevalence of slave labor. Josiah was disgusted by it. He not only found slavery contemptible, but he could not fathom how a slave owner could father slave children and then treat them so horribly: the "White man begets his likeness, and with much indifference . . . sees his progeny in bondage and misery, and makes not one effort to redeem his own blood."[38]

He saw the treatment of slaves as indications of southern hypocrisy: "There is much among this people of what the world would call hospitality and politeness, [but] it may be questioned what proportion there is of true humanity, Christian charity, and love."[39] With prescience, he noted that the issue of slavery would prove divisive and that its eradication, while necessary, would be difficult: "Slavery may truly be said to the peculiar curse of this land."[40]

Arriving in Maryland, Josiah was unimpressed by "Annapolis . . . a mighty poor, diminutive, little city . . . [it] makes a very contemptible appearance"—but as he traveled on, he found much to admire in both Pennsylvania—"this well regulated province"—and New Jersey—"'Tis indeed a fine country."[41]

Letters were sent back and forth to Josiah via family friends and connections, keeping him in touch with his wife and his father, his brother Samuel, and friends back in Boston. From his father, Josiah learned that his "sister Lincoln" had visited Braintree but was "greatly worn out with her constant attendance upon a gloomy, fretful, and sick" husband; "it is truly pitiable and the more so as it seems without Remedy."[42]

Josiah Sr. continued on with a litany of illnesses—"your two sisters [children born of Anne Marsh] have had the measles" and Anne herself "has had a most fatiguing Time of it." But thankfully, he wrote, he was healthy, and he looked forward to "your Wife's and my dear little grandson's coming . . . to tarry with us till she goes home to prepare for your reception."[43]

Josiah would soon be home, traveling up to New York City and from there taking a boat north to Rhode Island and onward to Massachusetts. The trip had been in many ways a success: important contacts had been made with southern patriots, including Charles Cotesworth Pinckney, Thomas Lynch, and Thomas Bee of South Carolina; William Hooper and Cornelius Harnett of North Carolina; and John Dickinson and Joseph Reed of Pennsylvania.

Most important, Josiah now had a deeper understanding of what Northerners shared with Southerners, and where they differed.

Josiah's health was much improved as well, his cough having faded away to a slight hoarseness now and again. He slept soundly at night, with no touch of fever, and his appetite had returned, fed in part by a succession of local treats, such as salt fish in broth, meat pies, peach jellies and preserves, "two sorts of nuts, almonds, raisins, 3 sorts of olives, apples," "sweet meats, oranges, Macarones, etc. etc."[44] Now he was bound for New York, where the chefs were reputed to be well trained and eager to show off.

Josiah enjoyed New York, taking a tour of the whole city with delight. In the evenings, he indulged in the many entertainments offered; he wrote in his journal, "if I had stayed in town a month should go to the Theatre every acting night. But as a citizen and friend to the morals and happiness of society I should strive hard against the . . . Establishment of a Playhouse."[45] Josiah was a New England Congregationalist to the core. There would be no playhouses allowed in Boston until late in the eighteenth century; actors might tread the boards in dissolute New York City but not in Puritan Boston, not as long as Josiah lived there.

And yet Josiah, judgmental Congregationalist that he was, also believed keenly in the freedom of religion. While traveling through the South, he experienced religious worship of all kinds, from Moravians to Quakers to Catholics to Presbyterians. Although he found little to admire in any of the practices (other than the music), at the same time he was adamantly in favor of its free exercise, as long as the power of God was acknowledged in its performance. After attending a Roman Catholic mass, he admitted, "In the words of the NEW England psalms—'In me the fire enkindled is.'"

He understood that his "sentiments and opinions may be presumed to be too much affected by former impression and byases [biases]."[46] He also understood that unity between the colonies could only be achieved if the differences between them were accepted, and if liberty and freedom were as liberally granted to one faction as to another.

Freedom: Josiah returned again and again in his journal to the question of slavery. He recognized its "barbarity" and predicted that "futurity will produce more and greater" problems arising from slavery. This was one issue on which he could not contemplate compromise: its continuation would inevitably result in "resentment, wrath, and rage."[47]

Josiah received news from his brother Samuel before departing New Jersey: "I had in my arms just a few minutes ago your Little Boy"—Josiah's heart leapt at the thought of seeing his son soon—and then Sam added, "Things public and private remain much as they were when you left us. The Spring Ships arrived yesterday and the day before but not a Word of News respecting America."[48]

In writing to his brother, Samuel ignored the weeks of gossip concerning a packet of letters sent via the spring ships from Benjamin Franklin in London to Thomas Cushing, Speaker of the Massachusetts House. The letters were rumored to contain damning information about Governor Hutchinson's treachery.

Through his connections with Hancock and Sam Adams, John Adams had had a glimpse of the missives and wrote in his diary on March 22, the "Seventeen Letters, written . . . by Hutchinson, Oliver, . . . will ruin this Country." The letters confirmed in Adams' mind that Hutchinson and his allies were "deliberate Villains, malicious, and vindictive, as well as ambitious and avaricious . . . profoundly secret, dark, and deep."[49]

Josiah would wonder later: how could his brother Samuel have ignored news of the letters in writing to his younger brother? The dynamite they contained would start an explosion, and the reverberations would shake the colony to its core.

18

Anxiety and Apprehensions

The Minds of the People were filled with Anxiety,
and they were justly alarmed with Apprehensions
of the total Extinction of their Liberties.

—JOHN ADAMS

In late May 1773, John Hancock stood up from his seat in the Massachusetts House of Representatives and walked to the center of the room. Josiah Quincy Jr. had returned from his southern journey just a few days earlier and was seated at the back, eager to catch up with local politics. John Adams was also present, having been recently reelected to the House, as was his cousin Sam Adams.

With the boycott of British goods behind him, Hancock could dress again as he wished (and not only when leading his Cadets). That day he was resplendent in a scarlet jacket over a dark gray silk vest, and black breeches atop blinding white stockings. Looking all about him, making sure he had everyone's attention, Hancock began to tell a story.

One afternoon as he was strolling by himself on the Boston Common, a man approached him—a man he'd never seen before. The man carried a large packet of letters, which he thrust at Hancock. The man told Hancock that some of the letters had the signature of Governor Hutchinson and others bore signatures of friends of Hutchinson. The man had no idea if the letters were fake or genuine, but he asked that Hancock oversee the formation of a committee to establish their authenticity, explaining that if those letters proved to be the real thing, the ensuing scandal for Hutchinson could be devastating.

Having finished his story, Hancock then reached beneath the desk behind him and pulled out a large packet of letters. The story told by Hancock was a complete fiction: the letters had come into his possession via Sam Adams, who had received them from Thomas Cushing, who had in turn received them from Ben Franklin, who had sent them from London. Franklin had asked that his role in the release of the letters be kept a secret, so Hancock and Sam Adams had come up with the story of the stranger on the Boston Common.

The letters, most of them written by Hutchinson to a friend in England, but also including letters written by Andrew Oliver, dated back to the late 1760s, and ranged over various issues of colonial administration. Over the next few weeks, details contained in the letters would leak out, and eventually the letters would be published in their entirety. As the fictional stranger on the Common had predicted, the scandal for Hutchinson was calamitous.

In one letter Hutchinson described the leaders of Boston as "Ignorant" and its citizens as cowards: "As the prospect of British revenge became more certain [with the arrival of troops in 1768] the people's courage abated in proportion." In a letter written in 1769, Hutchinson wrote: "There must be an abridgement of what are called English liberties. . . . I doubt whether it is possible to project a system of government in which a colony 3000 miles distant shall enjoy all the liberty of the parent state. . . . I wish the good of the colony when I wish to see some further restraint of liberty."[1]

In another letter dated around the same time, he asked for "standing troops . . . to support the authority of the government," and in still another he requested that Parliament approve as necessary the curtailing of "English liberties in colonial administration."[2]

Although the letters did not go far beyond statements Hutchinson had made publicly over the years, seen as a whole—and given the spin that Sam Adams applied to their publication in the *Boston Gazette*—public outrage was immediate. Hutchinson was now proven to be "the dangerous FOE of Liberty, of truth, and of Mankind."[3]

By summer, the outrage would turn violent, with effigies of Hutchinson and Oliver set afire and widespread protests in the streets.

John Adams was enraged by the letters, seeing in them the proof of Hutchinson's disloyalty to and betrayal of his own people: "Bone of our bone, born and educated among us! The sublety of this serpent, is equal to that of the old one."[4] The reference was to the serpent in the Garden of Eden, but now it would be the serpent itself cast out of Boston—or such was the fervent hope of the patriots.

The House charged Hutchinson and Oliver with "the great corruption of Morals, and all the Confusion, Misery and Bloodshed which have been the natural Effects" of their actions. Then the representatives passed a resolution, demanding that both men be removed from office.[5]

Hutchinson protested to the House that he had demonstrated neither "the Tendency [nor the] Design . . . to subvert the Constitution of the Government, but rather to preserve it entire."[6]

But by the end of June a petition signed by John Hancock and three other leaders of the House was sent to the king, asking for the removal of Hutchinson and Oliver from their posts. It was a largely symbolic move, most likely to be ignored, but the petition to remove Bernard had been successful, and the colonists were hopeful as well as vengeful.

John Adams, now fully back in the political arena, felt energized, powerful, ecstatic. When he had been elected to the House in May, his fellow representatives had nominated him to serve as a member of the Governor's Council, a legislative body whose members were nominated by colonists but had to be approved by the governor. Governor Hutchinson had vetoed Adams' appointment, and when a friend sought to console Adams for the veto, lamenting that not only was it a loss for the colonists but it would be a "check" on John's career, John had quickly responded: "I considered it not as a Check but as a Boost."[7] For who would want the approbation of Governor Hutchinson now?

Abigail took John's reentry into politics well, in part because of a new friendship she had formed with a woman who would serve as a mentor to Abigail. Sixteen years older than Abigail, Mercy Otis Warren was born and raised in Boston, where she had been tutored alongside her brothers in a politically active family. She now lived in Plymouth with her husband, James Warren (no relation to Dr. Joseph Warren).

James was a friend of John Adams and, like John, played a prominent role in both local and colonywide politics. Mercy, like Abigail, managed the family farm and raised the children. Mercy was also a published poet and a playwright. Her writings were pointedly political; her first play, titled *The Adulateur*, based on the events of the Boston Massacre, was an open indictment of Thomas Hutchinson and his policies.

In Abigail's first letter to Mercy, written after John and Abigail had been guests in the Warren home in Plymouth, she asked if the two could begin a correspondence: "I venture to stretch my opinions, and tho like the timorous Bird I fail in the attempt and tumble to the ground yet sure the Effort is laudable, nor will I suffer my pride . . . to debar me the pleasure, and improvement I promise myself from this correspondence."[8]

Mercy answered in the affirmative, and within a short space of time, she and Abigail became close epistolary friends. Not only did Mercy serve as a model politician's wife, but she also showed Abigail how to be a well-informed and politically engaged woman herself. John, already well-acquainted with Mercy through his friendship with her husband, was pleased with the closeness between the two women. Many letters would pass back and forth between all three of them over the coming months and years. Mercy was eager to forge closer ties to John Adams, whose future she foresaw as a good one, and she wished to tether her husband's career with John's. But she also sincerely liked both Abigail and John, and they admired her in return.

Abigail was growing in confidence, as her four children, curious and kind, grew under her tutelage into readers (by the age of nine, Nabby could—and did—read any book that Abigail offered her) and writers. As early as age six, John Quincy Adams was writing letters of substance to his cousins, such as the one in which he wrote, "i thank you for your last letter i have had it in my mind to write to you this long time but afairs of much less importance has prevented me . . . too much of my time in play there is a great Deal of room for me to grow."[9]

Having been given so much responsibility in caring for the farm and the children, as well as her community, Abigail was resolved to do it all "in the best manner I am capable of."[10] She already had firm ideas on a range of issues, including educating girls, ending slavery, and promoting self-reliance; her friendship with Mercy, an older woman who had forged her own place in colonial politics, would encourage Abigail to articulate her ideas more fully and act on her feelings with courage.

June 1773 was unusually hot. Although little rain fell, the air was heavy and damp. The dusty streets of Boston, combined with the humidity and heat, made for miserable conditions in town. Aunt Lydia took Dolly Quincy with her to Point Shirley on the north shore, where the Hancocks had a summer home. John joined the women when he could, and friends from surrounding houses were invited for cold suppers, tea parties, and carriage rides by the sea. Dolly had retrieved her ribbons and laces from the drawer where she had hidden them during the boycott of British goods, and once again she dressed in fine dresses of linen and silk, prettified with all the flimflammery she might desire.

And yet Dolly found that her tastes had changed. She no longer wanted lace-lined flounces or a trail of ribbons along her waist. Dolly would always dress well, as did John Hancock, but at her advanced age of twenty-six, and with her status as companion to the protector of Boston, she was no longer interested in trying to be the belle of the ball. Even as Aunt Lydia insisted on paying for her gowns, it was her father, a patriot and a religious stalwart, who reminded Dolly that modesty best suited her in her new role. Did she not remember the female figure of America that Paul Revere had engraved for all to see? She had been dressed for both prayer and battle, and Dolly should do the same. John Hancock needed her steady by his side: as "he appears to rise higher, the greater the burdens," Edmund Quincy wrote, and she, his beloved daughter, should do all she could to support him.[11]

John Hancock was busier than ever as keeper of the town, both in politics and in public works. He was on more committees than any other member of the Massachusetts House of Representatives, overseeing everything from land disputes to Hutchinson's letters to street lighting, colonial appointments, and repairs to public buildings. He continued to drill his eighty Cadets on a weekly basis, and his commitment to the entertainments of the citizens of Boston continued as well, with refreshments and music supplied for celebration days, including the commemoration of the king's thirty-fifth birthday on June 4, 1773.

In July, John sat alongside Aunt Lydia and Dolly in a prominent pew of the Brattle Street Church to hear Dr. Cooper's sermon. The church bell, paid for by Hancock, rang out, celebrating the consecration of the newly built church. Hancock had arranged for the bell's inscription: "I to the church the living call / And to the grave I summon all."[12]

But it was the church elders who had provided the engraving on the cornerstone of the new church: HON. JOHN HANCOCK. A mark of thanksgiving, to be seen by all who walked by. Sam Adams had written to a fellow patriot in April 1773 that Hancock was a man to be counted on, for he made his mark everywhere, as benefactor of the town and man of the people.

Hannah Lincoln returned to Braintree in late July 1773 to live once more with her father. Her husband, Bela, had died on Georges Island on July 16 and was buried "among the grazing farm animals" in the burial grounds behind the Old Ship Church in Hingham, where the Lincoln family had lived for generations.[13] The couple had never had children, and it made sense for Hannah to return to live with her father. Her health had suffered during the long months she spent caring for her cantankerous patient, as had her spirits during the years she spent married to him. Living in Josiah's house, with its wide windows overlooking the countryside and the seashore, and now free to do as she wished without criticism or insult, just might restore both her health and her spirits, giving back to Hannah what marriage to a difficult and abusive man had taken away.

Josiah Jr., home again with his wife, Abigail, in Boston, continued to correspond with those he had met during his travels through the South, tightening the connections he had forged and seeking to bolster patriotic fervor wherever he had seen a southern spark of it. He was gratified to receive letters that proved to him that the network was there; he believed that political unity was possible, even across the divides of cultural, religious, and what he deemed "moral" differences (his abhorrence of slavery not abating).

George Clymer from Philadelphia wrote to him in July, "your Patriotism is the greatest Support of the common cause, and I trust will in Time diffuse itself so universally as to make all Attempts against American Liberty as vain as they are wicked."[14] Clymer referenced New Yorkers as unstable supporters of the patriot cause, but Josiah answered promptly: "Instability is not peculiar to New Yorkers: it is characteristic of men in all ages and nations. Let us forgive each other's follies and unite while we may."[15]

The issue that would prove to be the catalyst to union was already in play, a new act devised by Parliament to reap taxes from the colonists, while boosting the East India Company, an English trading company on the verge of bankruptcy. Passed by Parliament in May, the Tea Act of 1773 gave the company the exclusive right to supply tea to the colonies; although duties would be paid on every cargo of tea arriving in the colonies, the Act also provided for a drastic reduction in the price of tea by eliminating duties paid in England. The East India tea was to be sent directly to only East India–approved colonial merchants, to be sold only by those consignors. There would be no incentive for independent merchants to smuggle in tea, for who would buy any other tea, when the East India tea cost so little?

The Tea Act created a monopoly, plain and simple, and would cause the ruin of independent merchants everywhere. From the northern colonies to the southern, protests broke out, with New Yorkers vowing: "The Americans will convince Lord North, that they are not yet ready to have the yoke of slavery rivetted about their necks, and send back the tea from whence it came."[16] From North Carolina came news of the Edenton Tea Party, a collective action taken by the women of that colony, who pledged to boycott all tea coming from England. In South Carolina, Charles Cotesworth Pinckney vowed that tea shipped to Charleston from England would never be allowed to land. The groundwork Josiah Quincy Jr. had laid was beginning to bear fruit.

Patriots in Boston quickly joined in the protests, promising to "oppose the vending of any Tea, sent by the East India Company . . . with our lives and our fortunes."[17] And the best way to prevent any tea being sold was to prevent it from ever reaching the colonial markets. If the tea never made it onshore, there would be no taxes collected, no profits for the East India Company—and no further trouble.

The Massachusetts Committee of Correspondence sent missives to all colonial port towns, declaring that "this tea now coming to us, [is] more to be dreaded than plague or pestilence"; exhorting all colonists to come together "in a most zealous and determined manner, to save the present and future generations from temporal and (we think we may with seriousness say) eternal destruction"; and urging that no cargoes of tea be allowed to unload anywhere in the colonies.[18]

James Scott, captain of John Hancock's fleet, was in London that fall, loading up the *Hayley*, fulfilling orders made by Hancock earlier in the year. When approached by the East India Company to carry a consignment of tea, he flatly refused. But the company had no trouble tracking down other vessels to carry its bales and chests of "weed" (the colonists' dismissive term for tea) to the colonies. The company was willing to pay over-the-top fees to any shipowner willing to take on its cargo; these prices were so high that the Sons of Patriots called them bribes. And, of course, there were shipowners who succumbed.

By the end of October, close to two thousand chests of tea on four separate ships were on their way to Boston. Among the consignors designated to receive and sell the tea in Massachusetts were the two sons of Governor Hutchinson, Thomas and Elisha. The Sons of Liberty saw these contracts as further evidence of treachery on the part of the governor, this "government and guidance which his Excellency hath with two of the Tea-Consignees, and the influence he hath over the rest," and more reason than ever to oppose the landing of the tea at Boston.

On November 2, signs went up on posts "at almost every corner" throughout the town, inviting "Freemen of this & the neighboring Towns . . . to meet at Liberty Tree" to bear witness as "the Persons to whom the Tea is shipped by the East India Company, make a public Resignation of their

Office as Consignees upon Oath & also swear that they will reship any Tea that may be Consigned to them by said Company by the first Vessell sailing for London."[19] *Come see the consignors reject their commission,* advertised the signs; but first the consignors had to be scared into doing so.

Letters were sent to the homes of each merchant consigned to sell the East India tea, including the two Hutchinson brothers. The letters demanded mandatory attendance at the Liberty Tree on November 3 in order to "make a public resignation" of the commission of tea, because receiving and selling such tea "is destructive to the happiness of every well wisher." A warning was added at the end: "Fail not upon your peril."[20] No signature was attached to the letters, nor to the bills posted throughout the town—nor was any claim to authorship necessary.

Sam Adams, John Hancock, Josiah Quincy Jr., Joseph Warren: any one of them could have penned the words on behalf the colonists of Boston— and Governor Hutchinson suspected every one of them of doing so, and of fomenting trouble that he would be hard put to control.

With a limited number of troops now stationed on Castle Island and little support from the tea merchants themselves—they were asking him for protection!—what could Governor Hutchinson possibly hope for in landing tea at Boston? Any attempted unloading of tea cargo was sure to turn violent. Yet he refused to back down: the tea would be landed, he vowed, and the duties collected. After that point, the fate of the tea was not his concern.

By noon on November 3, 1773, over five hundred Sons of Liberty, accompanied by Sam Adams, John Hancock, and Dr. Joseph Warren, had gathered at the Liberty Tree on Orange Street to witness the consignors' resignation of their commissions. Josiah Jr., home convalescing, waited restlessly in his library for news. On Orange Street, the men at the Liberty Tree also became more restless as time passed and no merchants arrived to make their resignations.

The crowd, agitated and grumbling, began to move toward the store of Richard Clarke, a tea merchant and designated consignor. They rallied outside the doorway, shouting for him to come outside and speak to them. Inside, Clarke hunkered down with the Hutchinson brothers, along with Benjamin Faneuil, another designated tea seller. The four men had been meeting, trying to come up with a plan for landing their tea; they had no intention of resigning their commissions. Despite the loud cries from outside, the merchants refused to budge from their seats. The front door of the shop remained closed and bolted.

The crowd dispersed, only to gather again two days later at a town meeting where John Hancock was appointed head of a committee to procure the resignations of the tea sellers. But once again, the tea merchants proclaimed they could not resign their commissions; the tea was already on its way, and they had contractual obligations to sell it.

While publicly defiant, in private the tea agents continued to send desperate letters to Governor Hutchinson, begging him for protection of their homes, their cargoes, and their own selves. The best Hutchinson could offer was refuge on Castle Island, as well as his prayers that all would go as well as it could.

By the end of November, the Sons of Liberty were losing patience with the tea merchants and the governor. The first vessel bearing tea, the *Dartmouth*, had arrived in Boston Harbor. John Rowe, owner of the *Eleanor*, another vessel expected any day now, wrote in his diary, "The worst of Plagues, the detestable Tea . . . is now arrived."[21] Abigail Adams described the tea as "that bainfull weed . . . this weed of Slavery" and despaired of the "direfull consequences" that lay in store for her colony.[22]

All of Boston lay in wait, anticipating the arrival of more tea ships from England. The Sons of Liberty and their supporters haunted the harbor front, keeping vigilant watch, determined to prevent any tea cargoes from being unloaded. The tea merchants remained behind closed doors, equally vigilant and determined: they vowed that nothing would stop them from taking ownership of their cargoes, off-loading the tea, and selling it at the prices set in the Tea Act.

19

Tea, That Baneful Weed

The Spirit of Liberty is very high in the Country . . .

—JOHN ADAMS

At 9:00 a.m. on November 29, 1773, church bells began to peal throughout Boston. The call was not to come to church but to come to a protest. Signs had appeared on every post and corner of the town: "Every friend to his country, to himself and posterity, is now called upon to meet at Faneuil Hall at 9 o'clock this day (at which time the bells will begin to ring) to make a united and successful resistance to this last, worst, and most destructive measure of administration."[1]

More than one thousand people gathered at Faneuil Hall. The building couldn't hold so many people, so the meeting was moved to the Old South Meeting House. By the afternoon, the number had swelled to more than five thousand people, almost one in three Bostonians protesting the landing of East India Company tea—and growing increasingly resolved to fight such landing at any cost.

Messengers were chosen, excellent horsemen all, and told to be ready to leave at any moment, bound for the committees of correspondence in other colonies with news from the citizens of Massachusetts. The meeting ended with the exhortation issued by John Hancock: "My Fellow Countrymen, we have now put our Hands to the Plough and Woe be to him that shrinks or looks back."[2]

Governor Hutchinson had no troops in the city to break up the crowd. He demanded that John Hancock, as commander of the Cadets, call out his men and see to the dispersal of the crowd. Hancock refused; instead he directed the Cadets to assemble promptly at Griffin's Wharf and there to guard against the *Dartmouth* unloading any of its cargo. A twenty-four-hour watch was set up, manned by the Cadets, Paul Revere, and other Masons from St. Andrew's Lodge to ensure that no tea was landed.

On December 1, a meeting was once again convened in the Old South Meeting House and once again, the large crowd called for the East India Company tea to be returned to England. The sheriff for Boston, Stephen Greenleaf, made his way into the church and demanded that the crowd leave the premises, as it was an unlawful meeting. But the thousands gathered there jeered at him and chased him out into the street. By this time, Elisha and Thomas Hutchinson Jr., along with Richard Clarke, had fled with their families to Castle Island. Safe there, they refused to back down from their tea commissions.

But who would unload the vessels? The *Dartmouth* had been joined by the *Eleanor* at Griffin's Wharf; the *Beaver*, with its cargoes of "smallpox and . . . tea" was due any day.[3] John Rowe lamented ever allowing his vessel, the *Eleanor*, to carry tea: "I was very sorry [to have] any Tea on Board—& which is very True for it hath given me great Uneasiness."[4]

Rowe's ship, along with the others, was held hostage in the standoff between Governor Hutchinson and the Sons of Liberty. While the colonists refused to let the tea be landed, the governor let it be known that no tea-bearing vessel would be allowed to leave the harbor before they had unloaded their cargoes—and paid their duties. Hutchinson ordered British warships, armed and ready, to guard the mouth of the harbor to prevent any departures, while the armed citizens on shore were just as determined to prevent the cargoes from landing.

Town meetings continued. Negotiations began between customs officers and other Crown officials, town and colony representatives, shipowners, and tea merchants in an effort to come up with a way of allowing ships to off-load cargo other than tea. Hutchinson wrote later that he never suspected the colonists would destroy the tea cargoes, "there being so many men of property active at these meetings."[5]

And it was true that for the organizers of the meetings at Old South Meeting House, maintaining order and respecting property were both vital concerns: support of the other colonies might well turn on the manner in which the ban on tea off-loading was implemented in Boston. The other colonies, and all of England, were watching—and care would be taken.

But at the same time, the organizers were becoming frustrated. Negotiations were proving fruitless, and as the impasse wore on, it was becoming more and more difficult to contain the anger of agitators who gathered almost every day to protest the Tea Act and the presence of the vessels tied up at Griffin's Wharf. All the pistols in Boston had been "bought up, with a full determination to repell force with force," and every day more men arrived from the surrounding villages, including Roxbury, Dorchester, and Cambridge, ready to fight.[6]

Already the home of Richard Clarke, purveyor of tea, had been attacked and all its windows broken. Hancock, Warren, Sam Adams, Josiah Quincy Jr., and others met night and day, debating a course of action: there must be a way to both vent the anger of the impassioned colonists and control it.

The morning of December 16, 1773, dawned cold but bright, the sun rising in a cloudless sky. Another meeting began at the Old South Meeting House, with speeches and questions, debates and proposed resolutions, continuing on all day. By the afternoon, almost seven thousand people had squeezed into or stood huddled by the doors of the meeting house. Francis Rotch, representative of the family who owned both the *Eleanor* and the *Dartmouth*, had been called to attend the day's meeting, to answer why his ship still stood tied up; he tried to argue that his hands were tied, as Governor Hutchinson refused to let his vessels go.

Try again, he was advised, and off he went.

But as evening began to close in, it became clear to everyone gathered in Old South that the only way through the impasse was a path of radical, and determinative, action. Josiah Quincy Jr., who had rallied his strength to travel the few blocks to the meeting house, and then to climb the stairs to the upper gallery, rose now from his seat to speak. He began to list, in thorough detail, all of the encumbrances laid on the colonists of Massachusetts by the English Parliament. Harrison Gray, a wealthy merchant and Loyalist, interrupted Quincy, and warned him against speaking treason. Josiah didn't flinch.

"If the old gentle man on the floor intends, by his warning to 'the young gentleman in the gallery,' to utter only a friendly voice in the spirit of paternal advice, I thank him," Josiah Jr. said. But, "if his object be to terrify and intimidate, I despise him. Personally, perhaps, I have less concern than any one present in the crisis which is approaching. The seeds of dissolution are thickly planted in my constitution. They must soon ripen. I feel how short is the day that is allotted to me."[7]

With that, Josiah announced to the world that his consumption had returned, and that he had little to lose and everything to gain by securing the liberty of his fellow colonists against British tyranny forever and for good. And so, when he saw a group of men enter the hall, dressed as Mohawk

Indians, he knew the time had come. He and his fellow patriots had devised a plan to overcome the impasse of tea ships tied up at the wharves, British guns positioned at Castle Island, and raging colonists on shore.

The plan was simple: the tea was to be launched, bale by bale, into the freezing waters of Boston Harbor. There would be no unloading and no returning, no payment of duties and no capitulation to Parliament. Josiah drew a deep breath, willing himself not to cough and fighting against the dizziness that now accompanied him every day. He looked down at the gathering of men below and saw John Hancock already rising from his chair. The plan was in play.

"I see the clouds which now rise thick and fast upon our horizon, the thunders roll, and the lightnings play." Josiah spoke in a rising crescendo of certainty. "To that God who rides on the whirlwind and directs the storm I commit my country."[8]

John Hancock, down on the floor, met the gaze of Josiah, then turned around to take in the sight of the crowd gathered in the meeting house, overflowing and ready to spill out into the night. He pronounced the words that would release these men into history: "Let every man do what is right in his own eyes."[9]

John Rowe, seated close to Gray, was heard to murmur, "Who knows how tea will mix with salt water?"[10]

Josiah Quincy Jr. fell back into his seat, exhausted, while all around him, men surged down the stairs, out the doors, and into the night.

A crowd of two thousand and more swarmed down to the harbor, following a legion of men dressed as Mohawks. The costumed men, along with many others, boarded the tea-bearing vessels tied up at Griffin's Wharf, located the chests containing tea, and broke them apart, gathered up the tea in armfuls, and threw it overboard. All in all, it took about sixty men little more than three hours to destroy 342 chests and release 46 tons (92,000 pounds) of tea into the sea.

The work was completed quickly and methodically; as one participant recorded it, "We mounted the ships and made tea in a trice. This done, I took my team and went home, as an honest man should."[11] Any cargoes other than tea were left undamaged in the ships; the ships themselves were not damaged in any way, other than a small padlock broken on one door, which was replaced the next day by anonymous delivery to Captain Bruce of the *Eleanor*.

As John Adams reported to Joseph Warren, "The Town of Boston, was never more Still and calm of a Saturday night than it was last Night. All Things were conducted with great order, Decency and perfect Submission to Government."[12]

For days after, engorged wads of tea washed up along a fifty-mile stretch of shoreline, including the beaches of Dorchester, where it was gathered up and burned so that nobody could attempt to dry and drink the tainted "weed of slavery."[13] One full chest of tea washed ashore at South Boston, where it was retrieved and then carried by wagon all the way back to Boston to be set afire on the Common.

John Hancock came out from his mansion to watch the tea burn; joined by Dolly, he descended from the house to walk the public paths he had paid for. The couple took in deep lungfuls of fragrant, wafting smoke, then turned to go back inside the mansion. A passerby let out a deep whoop, imitating Indian war cries. When asked, John Hancock would always deny that he had been present at the dumping of the tea: "The particulars I must refer you to Capt. Scott, for indeed I was not as acquainted with them myself, as to give a detail."[14]

Hancock had already arranged for all the stores of tea in his warehouses to be sent back to England, no matter that it wasn't East India Company tea, and now he wrote to his London agent with glee over the turn of events: "No one circumstance could possibly have taken place more effectively to unite the colonies than this manoeuvre with the tea."

From juggling his duties as a merchant and as a political leader, John had now firmly decided where his loyalties lay: with the people first, and with his business a far second.

When he heard that he and the other leaders of the meetings at Old South would likely be charged with treason, and their arrests arranged by the attorney general, Jonathan Sewall, Hancock responded that he "was for having a Body Meeting [a public accounting] to take off that Brother in Law of his."[15] He was not yet married to Dolly, sister to Esther Sewall, but he was laying claim to Dolly as his wife, and to America as his country.

Within hours of the Boston Tea Party, messengers on horseback—told days before to be at the ready—rode out to New York, Philadelphia, and beyond, with the news: "We inform you, in great haste, that every chest of tea on board the three ships in this town was destroyed the last evening without the least injury to the vessels or any other property. Our enemies must acknowledge that these people have acted upon pure and upright principle."[16]

From close and distant parts, messages of thanks arrived in Boston, sent to "the worthy Brethren of the Town of Boston, for their unwearied Care and Pains, in endeavoring to preserve our Rights and Privileges."[17]

Throughout the colonies, resolutions were passed that no East India Company tea would be allowed to land, and in Philadelphia, New York, and Charleston, agents for the East India Company were forced to resign their commissions. In New York, "a vast number of the inhabitants, including . . . lawyers, merchants, landowners, masters of ships, and mechanics" together with the "Sons of Liberty of New York" undertook watches to prevent any tea from landing in the colony.[18]

On December 25, the British ship *Polly*, bearing nearly seven hundred chests of tea in its hold, attempted to travel up the Delaware River to Philadelphia. The *Polly* was stopped by a blockade of small boats at Chester, and Samuel Ayres, the captain of the ship, was handed a message: "What think you, Captain, of a Halter around your Neck—ten Gallons of liquid Tar decanted on your pate—with the feathers of a dozen wild Geese laid over that to enliven your appearance? Only think seriously of this—and fly to the Place from Whence you came."[19]

By the next tide Captain Ayres was back on board and the *Polly* was turned round, ready to return to England.

John Adams was away in Plymouth on the evening of the Tea Party. He returned to Boston the next day. He had missed out on all the meetings in the Old South Meeting House; now he sorely regretted not being present as a witness to the dumping of the tea in Boston Harbor.

Writing in his diary about it, Adams was rapturous: "Last Night 3 Cargoes of Bohea Tea were emptied into the Sea. . . . This is the most magnificent Movement of all. There is a Dignity, a Majesty, a Sublimity, in this last Effort of the Patriots, that I greatly admire. The People should never rise, without doing something to be remembered—something notable And striking. This Destruction of the Tea is so bold, so daring, so firm, intrepid and inflexible, and it must have so important Consequences, and so lasting, that I cant but consider it as an Epocha in History."[20]

In a letter to James Warren written that same day, John's excitement continued unabated: "The Dye is cast: The People have passed the River and cutt away the Bridge. . . . This is the grandest, Event, which has ever yet happened Since, the Controversy, with Britain, opened! The Sublimity of it, charms me!"

Abigail rejoiced beside him, admiring both the daringness of the move and the strength of its message: England could not doubt the resolve of the

Americans now. But John and Abigail also worried, for there was sure to be retribution: "What Measures will the Ministry take, in Consequence of this?—Will they resent it? will they dare to resent it? will they punish Us? How? By quartering Troops upon Us?—by annulling our Charter?—by laying on more duties? By restraining our Trade? By Sacrifice of Individuals, or how."[21]

John predicted that the consequences would be largely economic and political: "Individuals will be threatened with Suits and Prosecutions. . . . Charters annull'd—Treason—Tryals in England and all that."

But Abigail foresaw war. It was inevitable, in her view, and might be the only way to secure the rights of the colonists. She shrank from the horrors of it; nevertheless, she hoped her fellow patriots would be as brave in fighting as they had been in protesting: "Altho the mind is shocked at the Thought of shedding Humane Blood, more Especially the Blood of our Countrymen, and a civil War is of all Wars, the most dreadfull. . . . Many, very Many of our Heroes will spend their lives in the cause, With the Speech of Cato in their Mouths, 'What a pitty it is, that we can dye but once to save our Country.'"[22]

Sam Adams wanted the colonists' version of the tea dumping to be the first received on the other side of the Atlantic; he hoped to stave off the worst of parliamentary punishments by ensuring that its representatives had an accurate account of both the events leading up to the Tea Party and the Tea Party itself. In a letter to Arthur Lee, the American representative of colonial trade interests in London, Adams wrote that Governor Hutchinson and his "Cabal" had refused to consider the "conciliatory alternatives proposed" by his group of patriots and declared that Hutchinson himself was "answerable for the Destruction of the Tea."[23]

But Parliament, inundated with reports from both Crown officials (including Governor Hutchinson) and private ship and cargo owners, wouldn't see the events of December 16 in the same way that the Massachusetts colonists did. And when it came to the destruction of the tea, it would be the colonists of Massachusetts, not the governor, who would be made answerable.

What the leaders in Parliament failed to understand was that answering to England was no longer a goal of the New England colonists. What they had been fighting for since the passage of the Stamp Act in 1765 was an acknowledgment of their rights as British citizens, not a reading list of what they owed to England. As Josiah Quincy Jr. wrote back in 1765, "Happy people who enjoy this blessed constitution! Happy, thrice happy people, if ye preserve it inviolate!"

Nine years later, Josiah's admonition proved prophetic: "May ye never forfeit it by a tame and infamous submission to the yoke of slavery and lawless despotism!"[24]

When accused by Governor Hutchinson of being part of the group of traitors who planned the Tea Party, and guilty of "High Treason," Josiah Jr. responded, "Who is the Traitor, who is the Betrayer of Government? He who *openly* assembles with his brethren to consider public affairs; who speaks his sentiments freely, and determines his conduct in the face of all men?—Or he who conspires against the very being of the State . . . and who writes Secret and Confidential letters to the enemies of his country, blasts its reputation with calumny, and points the way to its overthrow and ruin?"[25]

And in an essay widely read throughout the colony, Josiah wrote, "when THIS PEOPLE are driven to desperation, they who thus abuse them, will no longer dwell in safety."[26]

Josiah Jr. must have penned the word "desperation" with a slight puckering of his soul. His consumption had worsened—most likely with the coming of winter and its cold and damp conditions—and the symptoms were as desperate as any man could endure. Daytime chills and coughing spells plagued him, along with nighttime fevers.

Abigail tended to her husband as best she could, following Dr. Warren's instructions, dosing him with steeped Peruvian bark and rhubarb root tea (to ease digestion and increase his appetite) and, when needed, a tincture of opium for the pain. Dr. Warren was careful to call the Peruvian bark by its medical name, cinchona, and not by its more common name, Jesuit's Bark, as Abigail, with her Congregationalist distrust of Catholics, might have waivered from dispensing it.

Earlier in the fall, Samuel Quincy received a letter from a young man, the son of avowed patriots but a hidden Loyalist himself. John Trumbull wrote to Samuel for guidance, declaring, "I am determined to be of no party but of truth."[27] But to which party did truth belong? The spark had been lit, the tea sunk, the lines drawn. Truth was claimed on either side of those lines, while the gap between them only widened.

Sam Quincy watched his brother, his cousins, his father, and his childhood friends plant themselves firmly on the side opposing English rule of the colonies. But Sam couldn't join them; he was convinced, as articulated by

Abigail's cousin Isaac Smith that it was better to live under a "hundred other acts, proceeding from a British Legislature . . . than be subject to the capricious, unlimited despotism of a few of my own countrymen, or behold the soil, which gave me birth, made a scene of mutual carnage and desolation."[28]

For Josiah and Abigail Quincy, John and Abigail Adams, John Hancock and Dolly Quincy, all truth and honor belonged to their side, the side populated by the Sons of Liberty, the Massachusetts Committee for Correspondence, and those who had physically carried out the dumping of the tea. Did they imagine the carnage and desolation to come?

Not yet. Instead, they hoped, these rebels of Braintree, to manage the fire that had started. What they were certain of was that the time had come to claim their liberty—not as a favor to be granted by Parliament but as their inalienable and undeniable right as Americans. Reverend Hancock had preached of liberty as a "solemn covenant"; fulfilling its promise was their sacred duty.

PART THREE

Flame

1774–1776

The flame is lit, and like lightning,
it catches from soul to soul.

—ABIGAIL ADAMS

20

Rocks and Quicksands
on Every Side

A spark of fire inflames a compact building,
a spark of spirit will as soon kindle a UNITED PEOPLE.

—JOSIAH QUINCY JR.

Early in the morning of a cold February day in 1774, Josiah Quincy Jr. opened the door of his office to fellow lawyer John Lowell. The two men had been meeting regularly for the past month; having procrastinated once before, Josiah had promised his father that with the new year he would finally complete a last will and testament, and Lowell was the man to help him. Josiah explained to Lowell that the provisions were simple; but as Lowell explained to Josiah, nothing in estate law was simple, and although what Josiah desired was plain, the language in which his desires had to be couched was not.

All of Josiah's worldly goods were to go to his wife. Abigail would also hold guardianship of all his "political and legal papers," which would pass to his son when he came of age.[1] His son was also to receive Josiah's complete library at age sixteen. "May the Spirit of Liberty rest upon him" with the gift of these books: these were the words he dictated to Lowell.[2] There were other bequests, to Harvard College and also to friends. As for his final wishes, Josiah asked that when he died, he be buried in Braintree beside his ancestors and close by the Third Parish Church.

For the last three months, Josiah's symptoms had not worsened, but nor had they improved. He had grown thinner through the winter. His collarbones jutted out beneath the warming cravat that wound around his throat, and his heavy wool jacket hung loosely on his bony shoulders. But his hand was steady as he reached for the final will prepared by Lowell; the time had come to sign it.

Josiah reviewed all its terms and then wrote his signature at the bottom. Dr. Joseph Warren, William Tudor, and John Gill served as witnesses; they signed after Josiah. By noon Josiah was alone in his office once more and back at work on a matter that pressed more urgently on him than his last will and testament. There was still much to do in the matter of saving his country, his America, and he had no intention of giving in to his illness any-time soon. His sword in the cause was his pen, and he set to it like a man lit by lightning, the quill point leaving a burning mark across ream after ream of paper.

For the first months of 1774, the focus of his ire was Governor Hutchin-son. "Subterfuge and evasion are the true characteristics of a little mind; and so are falsehood and cowardice," he wrote, and then warned, "he who practices the low arts of political cunning, will, in the end, be detected, and sink into contempt." He derided Hutchinson "as the dark assassin of . . . HIS NATIVE COUNTRY."[3]

Soon there would be a greater target for Josiah's anger, and a larger breadth to his arguments. All through February, the newspapers in Boston had been filled with guesses as to what exactly Parliament would do to pun-ish the colonists of Boston for destroying the East India Company's tea. While the severity of the rumored punishments varied, this much was cer-tain: six warships with seven regiments aboard were on their way to Amer-ica, winter seas or not. As reported in the *Boston Evening Post*, "Tea will be forced upon Americans with a fleet and troops."[4]

More reports arrived from England, confirming that John Hancock, Sam Adams, Dr. Joseph Warren, and Thomas Cushing, recognized by the King's Ministry as the organizers of Boston's agitation against the Tea Act, were to be tried for the crimes of "High Treason" and "High Misdemean-ors."[5] Orders for their immediate arrest came from London, to be imple-mented by Samuel Quincy, solicitor general of the colony, and Jonathan Sewall, attorney general.

Josiah Sr. and Jr. both waited to see what Sam Quincy would do. There was no doubt Sewall would secure the arrests if he could—having succumbed to "the vices and treachery which have advanced [him] from Indigence to Opulence"—but what about Sam?

On the morning of March 1, 1774, four days before the third annual com-memoration of the Boston Massacre, John Adams traveled back from Brain-tree to Boston. He was a satisfied man, having now become owner of the house where he'd been born and its large barn, along with thirty-five acres of land. He'd bought the buildings and property from his brother, to add to the small farmhouse and bit of land he'd been left by his father.

"That beautifull, winding, meandering Brook, which runs thro this farm, always delighted me," John wrote in his diary—and now it was his.[6] He had big dreams for how he would improve his expanded Braintree estate: "introduce fowl Meadow And Herds Grass, into the Meadows . . . or still better Clover and Herdsgrass. . . . The Meadow is a great Object . . . and may be made very good. . . . Flowing is profitable, if not continued too late in the Spring."[7]

But he had no time to pursue his dreams for the farm in Braintree. Bigger pots needed stirring and John Adams had taken it upon himself to do so.

Adams had come up with a plan to impeach the chief justice of Massachusetts, Peter Oliver. Of the five judges on the bench of the High Court, Oliver was the only one who proudly and publicly announced that he would receive his salary directly from the king. Oliver's declaration had brought the wrath of the people down on his head; there were even threats of taking him out to the Liberty Tree and letting him swing.

But John Adams could not countenance threats of physical violence against a judge, no matter how crooked the judge might appear. The law must take its course against Justice Oliver, and the method to do so was impeachment.

There was no precedent for impeachment by the Massachusetts House of Representatives. Adams, undaunted, set himself to researching how it might be done, using impeachment cases that had been pursued in England as his model. He very likely consulted Josiah Quincy Jr. as well, who had studied Blackstone's *Commentaries* as diligently as John had and knew a bit about English impeachment practices in the House of Commons.

John Hancock was chosen as orator for the third annual commemoration of the Boston Massacre, to be held in Faneuil Hall. It was a paramount goal of the planners that the commemoration be peaceful and respectful while also reminding colonists of what they were fighting for. But two days before the event, Andrew Oliver died. Oliver—Peter Oliver's brother and Hutchinson's brother-in-law—had served as lieutenant governor under Hutchinson. Colonial leaders feared that his funeral would bring out a mob of protesters, especially following so closely on the heels of the commemoration.

The nonviolent execution of the Tea Party had been the hallmark of the policy carefully crafted by Joseph Warren, Josiah Quincy Jr., and Sam Adams, of holding only orderly and legal protests against British tyranny. The approval and support that had come into Boston from all over Massachusetts, as well as from the other colonies, following the tea dumping, was due in large part to its sober execution. It was imperative to maintain that support as well as to encourage pro-colonial forces in Parliament—and the behavior of local rebels had to be kept in check.

Fearing violence, Chief Justice Peter Oliver and many of Andrew's friends had announced their intention to stay away from the funeral. Samuel Quincy was outraged: Andrew had been a close friend. Just weeks earlier Sam had addressed him in a letter as his "most amiable, patriotic, musical, philosophical friend." He had ended his letter to Andrew with the wish, now never to be fulfilled, that "we may both live to See the Return of those Halcyon days, when both private and public confidence shall be restored; and yes the period when the Lion shall lie down with the Lamb, and every one Lies Secure under his own Vine, & under his own Fig-tree."[8]

Samuel announced that he would attend the funeral of his close friend and honor the man who had been such a sincere and concerned citizen of his native country.

On the afternoon of March 5, 1774, John Hancock stood before a packed Faneuil Hall to give his Boston Massacre commemoration speech. He began with a quiet nod to the teachings of his father, taken in years ago on a sunny slope overlooking the bay waters of Massachusetts: "I have always from my earliest youth, rejoiced in the felicity of my Fellow-men, and have ever considered it as the indispensable duty of every member of society to promote, as far as in him lies, the prosperity of every individual, but more especially of the community to which he belongs."[9]

The "vast crowd" with "rainy Eyes" listened, silent and rapt, to Hancock's every word as he continued, turning next to the duty of government to oversee and foster community.[10] "I am a friend to righteous government, to a government founded upon the principles of reason and justice," he explained. "But I glory in publicly avowing my eternal enmity to tyranny."[11]

The crowd erupted in cheers and then fell silent again. Hancock's "composition, the pronunciation, the action, all exceeded the expectation of everybody," John Adams noted. "They exceeded even mine, which were very considerable."[12]

Hancock called for a union of the colonies and the establishment of a militia, and for a meeting of a "general Congress of Deputies from the several Houses of Assembly on the Continent, as the most effectual method of establishing such an Union. . . . At such a Congress, a firm foundation may be laid for the security of our Rights and Liberties; a system may be formed for our common safety . . . [so] we shall be able to frustrate any attempts to overthrow our constitution; restore peace and harmony to America, and secure honor and wealth to Great-Britain."[13]

In closing, Hancock exhorted the crowd, "I conjure you, by all that is dear, by all that is honorable, by all that is sacred, not only that ye pray, but that you act; that, if necessary, ye fight, and even die for the prosperity of our Jerusalem."[14]

Thoughts and prayers were not enough: action was necessary, and by the roars of the crowd, it was clear: action would be taken.

That night, John Hancock celebrated with a small group of friends and allies at the Bunch of Grapes, with salutations made and drinks taken, and backslapping all around. Sam Adams, who had written much of the oration, was proud and happy with how well it had been delivered and sat back in the tavern, satisfied.

That evening John and Abigail Adams, and Abigail's cousins Katy and Dolly, were invited to the home of Edmund Quincy. There they toasted the health of John Hancock and sang forth praises for his speech: "The Happiness of the Family where I dined, upon account of [Hancock's] justly applauded Oration, was complete," Adams wrote in his diary. "The Justice [Edmund Quincy] and his Daughters were all joyous."[15]

The morning of Andrew Oliver's funeral three days later was cold and wet, one of those New England March days when the world seemed to be rewinding back to winter. Rain mixed with snow began to fall midday as temperatures dropped. But the anger of the mob who had turned out to watch the procession of Oliver's coffin was only just heating up.

As the crowds grew restive, preparing to bring down on the passing procession not only catcalls and jeers but also projectiles of dung, snow, and rocks, suddenly John Hancock appeared. Dressed in his officer's uniform, he led his eighty Cadets to fall in and march behind the wagon carrying Oliver's coffin. In solemn and regulated lines, they followed it all the way to the burial grounds.

As Governor Hutchinson wrote in a letter, Hancock's decision to offer respect and honor at the funeral of his political enemy constituted "unaccountable conduct"—and drew the admiration of all who witnessed the parade of his Cadets, and all who heard about it in the coffeehouses and taverns of Boston and beyond.[16] John Hancock had become even more of a hero to the people of Boston, a paragon of decency, bravery, and goodness.

John Adams, having carefully crafted his plan for impeaching Chief Justice Peter Oliver, set it in motion in late March 1774. One night at a dinner party attended by Adams and several members of the General Court, the dilemma of paying royal salaries to colonial judges came up. As the men lamented this "fatal Measure [that] . . . would be the Ruin of the Liberties of the Country," John piped up that he just might have the answer to the problem.[17] He "told them . . . there was one constitutional Resource . . . nothing more nor less than an Impeachment of the Judges by the House of Representatives before the Council."[18]

When the men of the General Court asked Adams—as he knew they would—for his help in drafting up articles of impeachment against Peter Oliver, Adams graciously agreed. For the next few days and nights he worked on the articles while members of the Massachusetts House hovered over him. As he recalled later, "One Morning, meeting Ben. Gridley, he said to me Brother Adams you keep late Hours at your House: as I passed it last night long after midnight, I saw your Street door vomit forth a Crowd of Senators."[19]

Such a "Crowd" and yet it was John himself who crafted the articles of impeachment. He used the history of the colony and its charter, and the facts of Oliver's "false Representations and evil Advice," as well as his "corrupt Administration of Justice," to argue that impeachment was not only possible but necessary.

Because Oliver accepted the "Sum of four Hundred Pounds Sterling, granted by his Majesty"—and furthermore, hoped for its "Augmentation"—John argued that Oliver had committed the "high crimes and misdemeanors" of taking "a continual Bribe in his judicial Proceedings" in clear "Violation of his Oath." He had been compelled into "accepting and receiving the said Sum" by the "the Corruption and Baseness of his Heart, and the sordid Lust of Covetousness."[20]

The House of Representatives approved John's articles of impeachment and quickly moved to have them published and widely disseminated. Governor Hutchinson, however, refused to recognize either the merits of the claims against Oliver or the legality of the process of impeachment. He declared that Chief Justice Oliver would not be removed, no matter how the Massachusetts House of Representatives had voted.

John Adams did not despair; he knew that a judge without jurors could do little, and the jurors were all colonists with minds and hearts of their own. They would never serve under a man like Peter Oliver; John was sure of it.

In early May 1774, the vessel *Harmony* arrived in Boston. Captain Shayler scurried off deck as soon as the boat docked and hurried to bring news of the "the Severest Act that was ever penned against the Town of Boston" directly to John Hancock.[21] By the afternoon, the town was buzzing with the news of the Boston Port Act, which had been passed in retaliation for the Boston Tea Party. This was the just the first of a series of acts that Parliament called the "Coercive Acts" but would come to be known in the colony as the "Intolerable Acts."

The act provided that starting on June 1, there would be a complete blockade of goods coming into or leaving Boston, to be enforced by troops already on their way. The blockade would continue until a full reparation had been made to the East India Company for the tea destroyed on the evening of December 16, 1773. The intent of the act was clearly stated: to punish the citizens of Boston for their "dangerous commotions and insurrections."[22] The impact was equally clear: with no food or fuel arriving in port, but instead only more troops, the people of Boston were to be starved, frozen, and beaten into submission.

Within days of the *Harmony*'s arrival, the British navy ship *Lively* sailed into Boston Harbor. Armed and ready to enforce the Boston Port Act, she carried on board General Thomas Gage, commander in chief of British forces in America. He had been appointed by Parliament to take Thomas Hutchinson's place as governor of Massachusetts. Hutchinson was ordered to England, to answer for his mishandling of the colony. But for now, Gage and Hutchinson would stay together on Castle Island, conferring over how best to subdue the rebellious colony of Massachusetts.

Gage had already announced that the seat of government would be moved over the next month from Boston to Salem; the Governor's House would be relocated there, and all meetings of the General Court of Massachusetts would convene there. The reasoning was simple: with no goods allowed to land in Boston, how could the work of governing the entire colony be fueled?

John Adams wrote to Abigail in Weymouth, where she had gone to stay with her parents for a brief visit. "We live my dear Soul, in an age of Tryal. . . . The town of Boston must suffer martyrdom: It must Expire. And our principal Consolation is, that it dies in a noble cause." But just as quickly as he seemed to give up on Boston, he urged his wife to dig in and fight. "We must continue to many ways as we can to save Expences, for We may have Calls . . . to prevent other very honest, worthy people from suffering."

Then he assured her, "I can truly say that I have felt more Spirits and Activity since the Arrival of this News, than I had done before for years. I look upon this as the last Effort of Lord North's Despair. And he will as surely be defeated in it, as he was in the project of the Tea."[23]

All the measures Hancock had proposed in his Boston Massacre speech—a union of the colonies, the establishment of a militia, a meeting of a "general Congress"—seemed more necessary than ever. Boston could not oppose Britain and its harsh Port Act on its own. The networks Josiah Quincy Jr. had identified in the South had to be notified, as well as local and colonywide committees of correspondence in both the North and the South.

Unity of action throughout the colonies was needed: "Let us catch the divine enthusiasm . . . of changing the hoarse complaints and bitter moans of wretched slaves, into those cheerful songs, which freedom and contentment must inspire," John Hancock proclaimed. "Let us humbly commit our righteous cause to the great Lord of the universe, who loveth righteousness and hateth iniquity."[24]

No matter how Gage and his troops intended to enforce the Boston Port Act, Samuel Quincy quietly announced to his family that neither he nor Jonathan Sewall would execute arrest warrants on John Hancock or any of the others indicted in England for treason. There was no need to further excite raised emotions, he explained. As things stood, the tension was high enough, and the point of no return was too close for Sam's comfort.

Even after becoming solicitor general, Samuel Quincy had successfully straddled the line between colonists protesting for their liberty and the royal administrators charged with implementing Parliament's orders. He balanced himself there with the certainty that he was serving his duty to both. As he wrote to Josiah Jr., "A consciousness . . . of having done his duty will support every man against the attacks of obloquy and reproach."[25]

But the time was fast coming when he would have to choose. He would have to land on one or the other side of the line he so carefully straddled, and no one who knew him well—much less those many others who gossiped blindly about him—could predict where he would finally end up.

Four days after receiving news of the Boston Port Act, Josiah Quincy Jr. published an eighty-two-page critique of it, titled *Observations on the Act of Parliament Commonly Called the Boston Port-Bill*. Addressed to "the FREE-

HOLDERS AND YEOMANRY of my country . . . in you . . . do I place my confidence, Under God," Josiah beseeched his fellow colonists to acknowledge the "insidious arts, and . . . detestable practices . . . used to deceive, disunite and enslave the good people of this Continent," and warned them that "the extirpation of bondage, and the reestablishment of freedom are not of easy acquisition . . . trial and conflicts you must endure; hazards and jeopardies—of life and fortune—will attend the struggle."[26]

But he also reminded them that "nothing glorious is accomplished, nothing great is attained, nothing valuable is secured without magnanimity of mind and devotion of heart to service . . . dedicate yourselves at this day to the service of your country; and henceforth live A LIFE OF LIBERTY AND GLORY."[27] His rhetoric enflamed all who read it, of all classes, infuriating the Loyalists and encouraging patriots across the board.

Copies of Josiah's essay flew around Boston and out to the villages and towns of Massachusetts. Messengers on horseback, just returned from delivering news of the Port Act itself to points south, including New York City and Philadelphia, now turned around and went back again, this time carrying satchel-loads of Josiah's pamphlet. Reprints made in Philadelphia found their way farther south, to Maryland, North Carolina, and all the way to South Carolina.

Within a few weeks, Ben Franklin in London received his copy of Josiah's pamphlet, which he then reprinted and circulated widely to the colonies' supporters and sympathetic members of Parliament; nonsympathetic members had to wait a bit longer, but soon they too would read Quincy's scathing attack on Parliament and on those "Legislators, who could condemn a whole town."[28]

Josiah's final warning was lost on no one, from Boston to Charleston to London—and Castle Island, where Gage still remained holed up with the former governor, Thomas Hutchinson: "America hath . . . her Patriots and Heroes, who will form a BAND OF BROTHERS: men who will have . . . courage, that shall inflame their ardent bosoms, till their hands cleave to their swords—and their swords in their Enemies hearts."[29] Josiah still used the word "sword" as a metaphor, the pen being his favorite weapon and the field of public opinion his favorite battleground.

Josiah was certain that Hutchinson, with his false tales and exaggerated accounts of what was going on in Massachusetts, had been behind the harsh retributions passed by Lord North and Parliament. If leaders in England could be shown the true facts of what had been occurring in Massachusetts and understand how determined the colonists were in retaining their rights as English citizens—and at the same time, how much they wished to contribute to the British empire of trade and its promulgation of freedom and liberty, reason, and intellect—Josiah was certain that peace between the mother country and its colony could be reached.

Josiah still believed in England, and through his pen, he sought to make the English lords and legislators, the Crown and all his advisers, still believe in Massachusetts.

21

Punishment and Indignation

Does not every man, who feels one ethereal spark
yet glowing in his bosom,
find his indignation kindle at
the bare imagination of such wrongs?

—JOSIAH QUINCY JR.

On June 1, 1774, the port of Boston was closed. Bells tolled, merchants closed and bolted their shop doors, and colonists wore funeral bands around their arms and observed fasts, while sending imploring prayers to heaven. But no measures undertaken by the citizens of Boston—no amount of praying or fasting or public mourning—could prevent the blockade of their port. Eight British warships were deployed to strategic points around the harbor, with the largest vessel, the *Captain*, settling in between Hancock's Wharf and Long Wharf. The warship straddled the lanes in and out, its British guns fixed on Boston.

"Poor unhappy Boston," lamented merchant John Rowe. "God knows only thy wretched fate. I see nothing but misery will attend thy inhabitants."[1] As the days of June passed, the sun growing hotter and the air heavier, the docks remained quiet: no shuffling of crates and boxes, no mainsails raised with a clanging of bells, no shouting of shipmates or horns blasting news of arrival or departure. Only the crowing of seagulls echoed down the silent rows of dry-docked boats, listless wharves, and deserted moorings.

How different the harborside had been just two weeks earlier, when Thomas Gage finally arrived in Boston for his swearing-in as governor of the colony. Large crowds gathered on King Street, from the Town House down to Long Wharf, to welcome him to town. It seemed as if all of Boston had turned out that day, from judges to dockworkers, from merchants to street vendors, from wives of the wealthy to fishmongers' daughters. There had been hope then, some lingering optimism, that Gage would not impose the blockade; that he would recognize the woes of Boston and moderate the fury of Parliament.

John Hancock was at the head of a delegation sent to greet Commander

Gage, leading his Corps of Cadets to the foot of Long Wharf. There, as Gage descended from his warship, the Cadets raised their guns and shot a salute into the air.

Gage presented the Cadets with a banner richly embroidered with his own coat of arms. The banner was hoisted up and displayed to the crowd. Gage stood back, a smile across his face, prepared to accept from the Cadets both their thanks and their allegiance to him, as his official bodyguards.

But when Hancock failed to salute the new governor, an accepted protocol that signaled both allegiance and obedience, Gage's smile turned to a grimace. He waved Hancock away and proceeded up King Street to the Town House of Boston. Accompanied only by local Crown officials and his own British advisers and officers, Gage entered the building, where he was sworn in as governor of Massachusetts.

At the celebration held later at Faneuil Hall, "a good dinner" to which "but very few gentlemen of the town" were invited, toasts were given and cheers made.[2] When Gage insisted on giving a tribute to departing Governor Hutchinson, the "toast was received with a hiss," merchant John Andrews, one of the partygoers, noted: "such was the detestation in which that tool of tyrants is held among us."[3] Gage assessed the crowd and then reassured them that he was in Massachusetts to perform his duty "as a servant to the Crown [but] would do all in his power to serve" the colonists. John Andrews was not alone in his sentiments, which he expressed as "a little doubtfull."[4]

Andrews' doubts were valid, as Gage immediately set about imposing Parliament's restrictions on Boston's trade, even going beyond what Parliament had dictated as just punishment for the town. Regiment after regiment of troops was moved into the city, to be quartered on Boston Common. Not only would they live on the Common, but they would go through their daily training exercises there, in full view of the citizens of Boston. Any deserters caught and tried would also be shot on the Common, again in full view of all.

Having deployed his warships to strategic points in the harbor, Gage announced that the scope of their enforcement would include prohibiting any movement by boat, from skiffs on up, within harbor waters. Although Parliament had provided that fuel and certain foodstuffs could proceed by water into the town, Gage forbade it.

All necessities, along with everything else, would have to be carted in on wagons from the ports of Salem or Marblehead to the north, a journey of thirty miles that some predicted would cost as much as the journey from England to America. The Boston Neck, the narrow strip of land that connected Boston to the mainland, would be the only entry into the city.

For a town whose economy revolved entirely around the movement of goods through its docks, shutting down harbor trade meant desolation and ruin. By the end of June, close to one-third of Boston's population had fled, desperate for work, food, and salvation. Shops were closed, and those few that remained open would soon have little to sell.

What goods did arrive in Boston from ports to the north were costly, given the expense and difficulties involved in delivering them by wagonload to town. The narrow Boston Neck was clogged with traffic: citizens desperate to leave and merchants' cartloads of goods lining up to be brought in.

John Adams lamented to Abigail that his legal business was sure to fail due to the "unfortunate Interruptions" and that all his recent purchases— "books . . . a Pew . . . [our] House in Boston"—would be "almost fatal" to their financial stability.[5] He vowed to hang on as long as he could, with clients still to represent at court sessions scheduled for the summer.

But he worried about his own future, and that of his colony: "We have not Men, fit for the Times. We are deficient in Genius, in Education, in Travel, in Fortune—in every Thing. I feel unutterable Anxiety.—God grant us Wisdom, and Fortitude!"[6]

He began to think of leaving Boston once again, and returning with his family to Braintree. As always, the peace and beauty of Braintree called to him: "My Fancy and Wishes and Desires, are at Braintree, among my Fields, Pastures and Meadows."[7] Life on the seaside farm, with its resources of wood, milk, fish, and vegetables, would be easier than scrambling for expensive food and fuel in the blockaded city.

Rumors abounded of further strictures to be placed on Massachusetts by Lord North. John could not imagine just how far Parliament might go: "I confess myself to be full of fears that the Ministry and their friends and Instruments will prevail, and crush the Cause and Friends of Liberty."[8] Abigail, burdened by the daily search for open stores and markets, was also eager to leave. She missed her sister and her gardens and the Braintree farmhouse she considered home.

As summer settled in, news of more Intolerable Acts promulgated by Parliament arrived. The measures were harsh: the Massachusetts Charter had been revoked; town meetings were limited to just one a year; colonists would no longer elect their legislative representatives but instead a mandamus council appointed by the Crown would run the colony; any British officer or soldier accused of a crime would no longer be tried in colonial courts but would be sent to British courts overseen by British judges; and British soldiers were now allowed to live in uninhabited houses, barns, and warehouses, as well as in private houses when necessary.

Josiah Quincy Jr. was stunned by these wide-ranging acts. But he was also energized, because as harsh as they were, he could use their clear purpose—to intimidate all the colonies of America—to rally support to the cause of the New Englanders. Parliament was likely to extend the measures to cover Connecticut, New York, Pennsylvania, South Carolina—or any of the other colonies where tea ships had been sent back, their cargoes undelivered, and where tea agents had been bullied into resigning or Loyalists harassed.

Josiah would warn all Americans that what had happened in Boston could happen to them. The response to such threats from England must be not a lessening of their protests, but rather an increase; the colonists must show unity against the oppressions of Parliament. Messengers, led by Paul Revere, were sent out to towns and villages throughout the colony and America, to spread the word about Parliament's new measures and urge support from all quarters for poor, beleaguered Boston.

Josiah set to furious writing again, both for the press and in private letters to men he had met on his travels south, exhorting colonists everywhere to unite. He urged that the proposal to hold a colonial congress be taken seriously; now was the time to join together and collectively address Parliament's oppressions of liberty. As an active member of the Boston Committee of Correspondence, he promoted a "Solemn League and Covenant" to boycott all British goods and trade "until the . . . Act for blocking up the . . . Harbour shall be repealed, and a full restoration of our Charter Rights be obtained."⁹

Only by uniting in "our indispensable duty to lay hold of every Means in our Power to preserve and recover our much injured Constitution," Josiah argued, would the rights of the colonists be restored, and war avoided: "no [other] alternative between the horrors of slavery or the carnage and desolation of a civil war" exists but to engage in "this peaceable measure . . . to break off all trade, commerce, and dealings" with Great Britain.¹⁰

Boycotts had worked before, against the Stamp Act and against the Townshend Acts—surely, they would work again. If only all the colonies of the continent could meet in a congress and agree to such financial measures, Josiah prophesied, misery for all America might be averted.

Sympathy for Boston, and gifts for its besieged inhabitants, poured into the town: "11 wagons' load of the riches of the Banks [over 20,000 pounds of fish], one cask of the fatness of Spain [oil], some cash,"[11] from Marblehead; 33 barrels of pork, 58 barrels of bread, 56 barrels of flour, 330 bushels of wheat, and 142 bushels of corn from Virginia; and 3,000 bushels of corn, along with various supplies as well as money, sent from Maryland with the message "Words are said to be cheap but it is universally allowed, that when a man parts with his money, he is in earnest."[12]

With the 258 sheep that arrived from Windham, Connecticut, came a vow of allegiance: "we hereby assure you, that to the utmost of our power we will assist you in every measure necessary for the common safety. . . . This town is very sensible of the obligations we, and with us, all British America, are under to the Town of Boston . . . generous defenders of our common rights and liberties."[13]

But help didn't come only from well-wishers beyond the Boston Neck. At a town meeting held in Faneuil Hall in mid-June, Josiah Quincy Jr. proposed that the well-to-do of Boston contribute resources to help feed the poor, whose numbers were doubling every week as more businesses closed and work became hard to find. Josiah's proposal was met with jeers until John Adams, acting as moderator of the meeting, stepped in and scolded the men for their swinish behavior; quoting a favorite poet, he accused them of acting like "owls and cuckoos, asses, apes, and dogs."[14] Josiah's motion was reconsidered, and silk-lined purses were opened.

Josiah was appointed head of a town committee to oversee all the donations coming into Boston, as well as locals' contributions. His father-in-law, William Phillips, joined him on the committee, and together they converted substantial portions of donated goods to cash, which was then used to fund public works in Boston, employing as many jobless workers as possible.

Josiah also found himself in charge of preparing all the citizens of Boston for possible violence when he was appointed to lead the newly created Safety Committee. The committee ran drills and organized the buying and storing of both arms and ammunition; if the British troops (more arriving every week) sought to impose Parliament's measures through force, the towns-people would be ready.

By mid-June, the idea of a continentwide congress had taken hold in the colonies. John Dickinson, the Philadelphia farmer, wrote in a letter to Josiah Quincy Jr., "I have been able to collect the sense of the Colonies, [and] they are very unanimous in the Measure you mentioned of a Congress."[15] Messages passed back and forth between leaders of the colonies, and finally a date and place were chosen: September in Philadelphia. By the end of the summer, all the colonies, with the exception of Georgia, would agree to attend the Continental Congress.

John Adams, Josiah Quincy Jr., John Hancock, and other members of the Boston Committee of Correspondence moved quickly to ensure their colony's participation in the congress; they knew they had to act before the mandamus council was appointed to run the colony. Congressional representatives would have to be proposed and approved during the meeting of the General Court set for June 7, but Gage could not be told of the plan: if he were to suspect, he would suspend the meeting of the General Court.

In order to appease any suspicions Gage had concerning their motives, the Massachusetts legislators showed up in Salem for the meeting of the General Court without making a single protest as to its new location. They began their business as usual, and proceeded to follow a routine agenda considering various colonial issues. With the intent of boring the spies they were sure that Gage had sent to the meeting, and fooling them into leaving, the legislators droned on and on over insignificant matters.

Then, as evening approached, the true purpose of the meeting was put up for debate. Five men were proposed as representatives to attend the Continental Congress on behalf of the colony of Massachusetts. In addition, a request for funds was made to cover the expenses of the congressional delegation.

Gage had indeed sent spies to the meeting, who raced to the Governor's House to inform him of the plan to send delegates to the congress. Gage quickly sent an emissary to disband the meeting and suspend all further sessions of the General Court.

But it was too late: the door was locked against the emissary and he read his official message out of doors, to the wind, with no one paying any attention at all. Meanwhile, inside the building a vote was taken on the appointments and the funding. Both proposals were resoundingly approved.

John Adams was chosen as one of the delegates for Massachusetts, along with James Bowdoin, Thomas Cushing, Sam Adams, and Robert Treat Paine. John Hancock had withdrawn his name from consideration—his gout had returned with a vengeance in the spring—but he vowed to continue in his role as protector of Boston while the others represented the colony's interests at the congress.

That night all the men, along with their wives, gathered at the home of Joseph Warren to celebrate. Only John Hancock stayed away, reduced to bed rest for a fortnight, to be cared for by Dolly and Aunt Lydia. Abigail Adams must have wondered—for just a moment—if it might have been better for her John to be ill instead of going far away and leaving her alone once again to manage finances, home, farm, and family.

Yet she couldn't help but feel excited for her husband. They both understood that John had been given a great opportunity: "here is a new, and a grand Scene open before me—a Congress . . . an assembly of the wisest Men upon the Continent." But John also felt nervous: "[I] feel myself unequal to this Business. . . . What can be done?"

All he knew for sure was that "deliberations alone will not do. We must petition, or recommend to the Assemblies to petition, or [make] Spirited Resolves—[or pursue] bolder Councils."[16] It was a great honor to be asked to represent his colony, and an honor he would do his best to fulfill.

His old friend Jonathan Sewall tried to convince John to refuse his appointment when the two men met up while attending court in Portsmouth, Maine. At Sewall's request, the men took an early-morning walk together on the hill overlooking Casco Bay. The day was just warming up as they walked, with a mist rising off the water. Sewall asked John to stay away from Philadelphia, counseling him that "Great Britain was determined on her system; her power was irresistible and would certainly be destructive . . . to all those who should persevere in opposition to her designs."[17]

John answered that he was just as determined: "I had passed the Rubicon; swim or sink, live or die, survive or perish with my country, was my unalterable determination."[18]

The two men parted that day, both with heavy hearts. They knew their friendship was at its end, perhaps never to be renewed; such a sad farewell was "the sharpest thorn on which I ever sat my foot," John recalled later.[19] Such separations between friends, and even within families, were occurring throughout the colony; sides chosen and painful breaches made.

Josiah Quincy still held out hopes that his son Samuel would choose the right side; after all, Samuel was known to spout that "the House of Commons had no Right to take Money out of our Pocketts, any more than any foreign State" and to repeat "large Paragraphs from a Publication of Mr. Burke's in 1766 [protesting English overreaching], and large Paragraphs from Junius Americanus [essays by patriot Arthur Lee]."[20] When other Loyalists were attacked, at home, on the street, and even in church, Samuel remained unmolested and above reproof. There was hope for him, his father was sure of it, as was Josiah Jr., who continued to share his writings and his thoughts with his older brother.

Hannah was less convinced that her brother would eventually align himself with his father and brother. She understood Samuel better, she thought, because of their similar dispositions. While Josiah Jr. had come to accept radical actions to protest what he saw as Parliamentary wrongs, neither Hannah nor Sam trusted mobs; like Samuel, Hannah was wary of an opposition that utilized intimidation and chaos to achieve its goals. Mercy Otis Warren, a friend to Hannah, had scolded her for her temerity in condemning "the calamities of our unhappy country" just because Hannah disapproved of "some rash and unjustifiable steps" taken against ministerial authority.

Hannah saw another similarity between herself and her brother: they were both comfortable with keeping things the way they were. Having escaped the tyranny of her husband, Bela, Hannah had found peace again in Braintree with her father—and she feared any event that might disturb their happiness. Samuel had his love of "ease and retirement, though not idle nor unemployed in the valuable purposes of life."[21] Hannah doubted whether her brother, comfortable in his wealth and happiest with constancy in life and love, would ever join a group that was intent, above all else, on change.

John Hancock had been expecting a rebuke for his snub of Governor Gage, especially as the snub had been given in front of all the Cadets and the many Bostonians who had come out to the wharf that day. He was not surprised when, in late June 1774, he received a short letter of barely two lines, written and signed by Gage's secretary, Thomas Flucker, removing Hancock from his command of the Corps of Cadets.

But when the corps of eighty men heard the news, each and every one of them resigned their commissions, surprising not only Hancock but also Governor Gage. William Palfrey, Hancock's clerk and also a member of the Cadets, reported to Sam Adams that the resignations had been undertaken without Hancock's knowledge: "Had he known our intention he would have prevented it. . . . I was highly pleased to find out that we had out-Generaled the General."[22]

The Cadets further surprised Hancock by naming him their representative to Gage, charging him with returning not only their commissions but also their certificates of rank, along with the embroidered banner Gage had presented to them back in May. Their splendid uniforms were given to Hancock to keep safe until the unit might come back together again some day.

While many of those who had the resources to leave Boston did so, Edmund Quincy and his family stayed put. Edmund had lobbied for and received appointments to a number of the new committees sprouting up to run things in Boston, and he took great pride in his role as a justice of the peace. His daughter Katy was invited to join her sister and brother-in-law, Sarah and William Greenleaf, in Lancaster, a small village to the west, but Katy demurred, preferring to stay with her father and Dolly, who still flitted between the modest Quincy dwellings on Kingston Street and the Hancock mansion on Beacon Hill. Although the long dinner parties and afternoon outings were a thing of the past, Dolly found that her new role as nurse, companion, and even confidant to John suited her well.

Josiah Sr. and Hannah Quincy Lincoln must have wanted Josiah Jr. and his wife, Abigail, to return to Braintree, where his health could be better served by fresh air, fresh food, and ample rest. But Josiah Jr., busy with his many committees, as well as with his commitments as a lawyer, was feeling stronger, thanks in part to the invigorations of his many patriotic duties; in part to the ministrations of Dr. Warren; and in part to the care taken by his wife in preparing his daily doses of alleviating herbs and tinctures of opium.

Abigail was pregnant with the couple's second child, due at the end of the summer. Josiah promised his father and sister that changes in domicile would be made then—but the changes to come would not be what either Josiah Sr. or Hannah had anticipated.

August 1774 was hot and dry across Massachusetts: crops wilted, dust stirred, food supplies shrank, and tempers flared. Even as other towns and villages in Massachusetts (including Braintree) and in other colonies announced their boycotts of British goods, the merchants of Boston refused to sign on to the far-reaching boycott Josiah Quincy Jr. had proposed in his "Solemn League and Covenant."

Their businesses were already reeling from the port's closure, the failure of crops due to the hot summer, and the high costs of transporting goods from ports north to Boston. Without the participation of the Boston merchants, Quincy's proposals for economic warfare against England were stalled—for now.

Instead of instigating financial reprisals, the focus of the Boston patriots turned to dismantling British institutions in the colony, including the courts, the system for tax collecting, and the local militias. Colonists vowed to oppose "every civil officer now in commission in this province . . . [and] any said officers [who] shall accept a commission . . . or in any way or manner whatever assist . . . in the assault now making on our rights and liberties."

Defiantly, they declared, that "no obedience" was owed to anyone who accepted royal commissions or salaries.[23] Colonists refused to pay their taxes to royally appointed officials, and the men in charge of village militias resigned their posts rather than serving under commissions confirmed by Gage. The militias were a colonial tradition: local volunteers participated in regular draining drills on town greens—and in Boston, on the Common— and had been doing so for one hundred years.

But now new militias were formed, no longer under the control of the royal administration; they transformed from groups united to protect British authority to groups united to protest against British oppression. These newly motivated militias were captained now by independent leaders, many of them veterans of the Seven Years' War—and none of them beholden to any entity other than the colony they loved.

Colonists also refused to participate in a court system tainted, as John Adams had predicted, by an impeached chief justice. Even when Chief Justice Peter Oliver stayed away from court, they refused to sit as jurors and declined the oath of service. John Adams and Josiah Quincy Jr. were on the court circuit that summer—"Quincy and I have taken a bed together," John wrote to Abigail in early July—and they bore witness as, from Worcester to Charlestown to Plymouth, jurors refused to serve.

When the Superior Court opened in Boston in late August, it quickly became apparent that few cases would be heard. One by one, the jurors called forward by Chief Justice Oliver refused to take the oath, stating, "we believe in our consciences, that our acting in concert with a court so constituted . . . would be betraying the just and sacred rights of our native land . . . [which we need to preserve for] our posterity."[24]

John Adams had planned for this to happen, and yet with no courts in session, his legal work would end. There would be no money coming in to cover the expenses of keeping up a home, an office, and law clerks in Boston. John proposed that the family move back to Braintree, and once again Abigail agreed. When John left for Philadelphia to attend the Continental Congress, she took the children and returned to the farm in Braintree.

Governor Gage was desperate to come up with candidates to serve as mandamus councilors, men suitable to serve as the new governing body of Massachusetts. Just as desperately, the Loyalists of Massachusetts struggled to keep their names off the list of candidates, knowing that being named to the council was an open invitation for trouble. "Our fowling pieces are ready while our fishing lines are in hand" threatened a band of fishermen from Gloucester; they would not hesitate to act against those "stupid villains endeavoring to aid in fastening to our necks and that of our posterity the yoke of bondage."[25]

When the names of the thirty-six potential councilors were finally revealed, only twenty-five agreed to serve. Life for those twenty-five became very hard, very quickly, and for anyone who associated with them. Mandamus councilors and their Loyalist supporters were shunned on the streets where they lived or, worse, verbally "pelted and abused." Their offices were sullied with dirt and feces; and in church, hymns led by Loyalists were met with studied silence. Their homes were fired into, their cattle were driven off, their horses painted in colors, and the tails of their horses sheared to stubs.[26]

On the morning of August 10, the Massachusetts delegation to the first Continental Congress gathered in Boston, close to the home of John Hancock. Five regiments of British troops were running drills on the Common, its green grass long churned to dust under the feet of the soldiers and the summer's unrelenting heat.

But no one who passed along the Common and walked up Beacon Street even glanced at the Redcoats with their guns and bayonets, parading back and forth. All attention was focused on the small group at the top of the hill loading up a carriage with trunks and satchels, while offering handshakes and hugs all around.

John Adams took a moment to grasp Abigail by the shoulders, the older children clustered around her skirts and little Thomas in her arms. Then he turned away and climbed into the carriage, "a coach and four, preceded by two white servants well-mounted and armed, with four blacks in livery, two on horseback and two footmen."[27]

The delegation was to travel in style and now, in plain sight of both the

British troops drilling on the Common and the clusters of colonists gathering in the streets to wish them off with all the best, they set off. They stopped only to pick up Thomas Cushing at his home on Beacon Street, and then they proceeded on their way.

Within days, Abigail, back now in Braintree, wrote to John. She missed him so much; although he had traveled often during the years she had known him, he had never gone so far away. The distance made time stretch: "It seems already a month since you left me."[28] She wrote of her fears: "The great anxiety I feel for my Country, for you and for our family renders the day tedious, and the night unpleasant. . . . What course you can or will take is all wrapt in the Bosom of futurity."[29] An unknown future, for her family, her husband, her country.

Marshaling her study of history, she sought to gird herself, and John, for the necessary battle ahead: "we are told that all the Misfortunes of Sparta were occasioned by their too great Solicitude for present tranquility, and by an excessive love of peace, they neglected the means of making it sure and lasting."[30]

Seated at a window that looked out over the warm, quiet fields of the Braintree farm, Abigail couldn't imagine anything more valuable than peace. Much-needed rain had finally fallen in the night, and the air was sweet-smelling from clover, marsh grasses, and the revived clusters of lavender planted by the back door.

The means to secure peace, she knew, could be—and might well prove to be—brutal and would require "shedding Humane Blood, more Especially the Blood of our Countrymen." War was coming to America; she was sure of it.

By the end of the letter, Abigail regained her composure and understood her role: as the true compass, pointing the way for John. "I long impatiently to have you upon the Stage of action. The first of September or the month of September, perhaps may be of as much importance to Great Britain as the Ides of March were to Caeser. I wish you every Publick as well, as private blessing, and that wisdom which is profitable both for instruction and edification to conduct you in this difficult day."[31]

John would take her advice to heart, as her ambitions so neatly matched his own, for himself and for their country. From Princeton, where he received her letter, he wrote to her, "I have the strongest Hopes, that We shall yet see a clearer Sky, and better Times."[32] Then he climbed back into the black carriage and, with the other delegates, continued on his way south.

It would take the Massachusetts delegation three weeks to arrive in

Philadelphia, refusing as they did to travel on the Sabbath and taking time to stop in nearly every town they passed through to shake hands, wave to supporters, and partake of the local delicacies. They finally arrived at the end of August, in plenty of time for the start of the congress in September, and settled into their rooms on Arch Street in a boardinghouse run by a Miss Jane Port.

Together with the other delegates from the twelve colonies, the Massachusetts contingent voted against holding their meetings in the grand State House of Pennsylvania; in its grandiosity, it was simply too *British*. Instead, they chose to convene the Continental Congress in the more humble Carpenter's Hall.

22

Grand Object of Their View

*May a double Portion of the Genius and Spirit
of our forefathers rest upon us and our Posterity.*

—JOHN ADAMS

Even as the delegates were heading to Philadelphia and Carpenter's Hall, Josiah Quincy Jr. was deciding on a journey of his own. It was a hard decision to make, with his little boy at home, another child soon to arrive, and his father in Braintree growing older. How could he leave his growing children and aging father? And then there was Abigail, patient, resolute, stronger than he was in so many ways; he trusted her above everyone else, addressing her as "My Very Dear Friend," "my bosom friend," and "my political confidant."[1] He was not eager to take another voyage like the one he had taken through the southern colonies and to once again be away from her for far too long.

Unrelenting heat and sun had returned to Massachusetts; the skies were pale and empty, the ground was hard-packed, and the soil turned gray. As grasses faded to yellow, so the hopes of the colonists faded. With rumors swirling everywhere about the men in Philadelphia—had progress been made?—nerves were tight and fears grew. Fear that England would never back down, fear that the colonists would be punished with no mercy, and fear that no one in England really understood the situation in the colonies that had led to the dumping of the tea in the first place.

Someone had to go to England to argue the cause of the colonists—to demonstrate to parliamentary leaders that the colonists' complaints were reasonable and to correct "those who may have been led into wrong sentiments of the people of Boston." Someone who was respectable, eloquent, and persuasive was needed to achieve "a general change in the prejudices of the people of England with regard to us Americans and our claims."[2]

Josiah Quincy Jr. would be that man. As he confided to a small circle of friends and family at the end of August 1774, "at the urgent solicitation of a great number of warm friends to my country, and myself, I have agreed to relinquish business, and embark for London."[3] He had demonstrated his diplomatic skills with the Southerners, and he was intelligent and well-bred enough to impress an English audience.

As Sam Adams put it, Quincy, with his "glowing reputation and dignity," could be "a valuable weapon" in the cause of "saving his Country."[4]

"I am flattered by those who perhaps place too great confidence in me," Josiah wrote to John Dickinson in Philadelphia, "that I may do some good the ensuing winter at the court of Great Britain."[5]

Josiah hoped to tell the true stories of New England to a responsive audience in Great Britain and change their hearts and minds and attitudes toward the colonies as a whole. He had read in the *Boston Gazette* of Edmund Burke's rebuttal of Parliament's harsh measures against Massachusetts: "You will . . . irrevocably alienate the hearts of the colonists from the mother country," Burke had warned. "The bill is unjust. . . . Bostonians will not give up quietly . . . you will find their obstinacy confirmed and their fury exasperated."[6]

Now Josiah would seek out those willing to listen and demonstrate not obstinacy but a willingness to compromise. Through informal conversations and scheduled meetings, he was certain that the union between mother country and colony could be preserved, and that the rights of colonists could be restored under their charter and under the British Constitution he so revered.

The dangers in undertaking a diplomatic journey across the Atlantic were real, not only to Josiah's health, in that a long journey over rough seas could prove debilitating to a man with his condition, but also to his personal safety. Josiah knew that "enemies here would be as indefatigable and persevering to my injury as they have been to the cause in which I am engaged heart and hand."[7]

Already spies were reporting to Gage that a patriot was setting sail for England, with "something mysterious concerning the object of his voyage."[8] No doubt there would be plans in England to have Quincy arrested once he landed: as his father wrote in great fear, "as soon as your arrival [in London] is known, you will be apprehended and secured."[9]

The Loyalists, once they heard about Josiah's departure, predicted an even worse fate: once arrived in England, Josiah would be hanged.

But Josiah saw the journey as necessary to fulfill his long-stated mission of "dedicating myself wholly to the service of my country." Such a journey with such a purpose was the fulfillment of his ambitions to create a legacy for his children—"let [liberty] never perish in your hands but piously transmit it to your children"—and inspire in his progeny their own commitment to family and country.[10]

And now he had two children who would receive his legacy: Abigail had given birth to a daughter in early September. Josiah insisted the baby be named Abigail after her mother.

At the end of September, while the Continental Congress met in Philadelphia, Josiah quietly set sail from Salem on a ship bound for England; "My design is to be kept as long a secret as possible, I hope till I get to Europe."[11] The husband Abigail had taken care of so diligently, guarding his health like treasure, was gone, taking his chances with the sea and what lay on the other side of the Atlantic's stormy expanse.

Even as he became absorbed in the work of the Continental Congress, John Adams found the time to send a note to Josiah before he sailed, wishing him "a prosperous Voyage and much of the exalted Pleasure of serving your Country." As for his own work on behalf of the country, he reported to his kinsman that "We are not idle here. But how long it will be before the World will know our Meditations I cant Say."[12]

Meetings were interrupted on September 7 when John and the other delegates received word that Governor Gage had ordered British troops to seize colonial stores of gunpowder stored in Charlestown and bring the powder back to Boston. It was rumored "that the Soldiers had fired on the People and Town at Boston" in what came to be called "the Powder Alarm." As Thomas Paine recorded in his diary, all of Philadelphia was in an uproar: "in great Concern, Bells muffled rang all PM."[13] Delegates called out for "War! War! War!" on the floor of Carpenter's Hall, and resolutions were debated on taking momentous steps to stop the British.[14]

John wrote in desperation to his Abigail, terrified of "what Scenes of Distress and Terror" were now taking place in Massachusetts. "We have received a confused Account . . . of a dreadfull Catastrophy. The Particulars, We have not heard. We are waiting with the Utmost Anxiety and Impatience, for further Intelligence."[15]

Such intelligence finally arrived days later, when Paul Revere rode into Philadelphia bearing news and a satchel full of messages. Revere assured the delegates that not only had there been no bombing of Boston, there had been no casualties at all resulting from Gage's seizure of the powder.

Although a significant amount of ammunition had been taken, large stores of gunpowder from other depots and hiding places were still held by the colonists, and in fact, a large supply of gunpowder was on its way to the colony, carried by none other than Captain Scott, John Hancock's faithful steward.

John Adams took the opportunity of Paul Revere's return ride to Boston to send notes to his wife and other friends up north. It was vital that correspondence be entrusted only to such men as Revere; Loyalist scouts and British spies were on the roads, ready to waylay potential messengers. Only the most speedy and the most savvy could travel the roads between Massachusetts and Pennsylvania without getting caught.

John's letters to Abigail expressed his many frustrations in attempting to achieve any progress in the Congress, when so many interests of the various colonies conflicted, one against the other. The Powder Alarm and its specter of war had united them but just as quickly now, they could come apart once again. Would it take another assault by Gage, and possible bloodshed inflicted on the colonists of Massachusetts, to bring negotiations to a head?

Reports—and rumors—continued to arrive in Philadelphia, of Gage fortifying Boston, sending his troops out on missions, preparing for something terrible. Abigail wrote to John of cannons being mounted on Beacon Hill, entrenchments dug at the Neck, and cannon and troops stationed there as well: "The people are much alarmed," she wrote.[16] Clashes between rebel colonists and Crown Loyalists and officers were increasing; passions were "all in flames . . . [and only] The importance with which they consider the meeting of the Congress, and the result thereof to the community, withholds the arm of vengeance already lifted."[17]

John Andrews, a Boston merchant, recorded stories of provincial colonists coming into town and heading to the Boston Common to taunt soldiers or bribe them into deserting. Hale and hearty farmers provoked the soldiers, grown thin and sickly on rations, about all the good food out in the countryside. They also boasted about having ample stores of weapons in the countryside and their expertise in using them. One day a villager came to Boston and joined in target practice alongside the British, outshooting them all. Then he announced, "I have a boy at home that will toss up an apple and shoot out all the seeds as it's coming down."[18]

When Gage tried to enlist local carpenters to build much-needed housing for his soldiers, he found his efforts stymied by John Hancock, who told Gage that the carpenters had come to him protesting of hunger. How could they be expected to work when they had barely enough to eat to sustain themselves or their families? Gage offered to have food brought in just for them, but Hancock refused the exchange of food for work when the work was on behalf of the British troops.

In the end, Gage had to send to Halifax for workers to complete the shelters (and Hancock found other work for his carpenters). In the meantime, British soldiers shivered and, in increasing numbers, they deserted. As far away as Braintree, Abigail made note of a deserting soldier who appeared lost and woebegone on the village common, then disappeared again into the woods.

From Philadelphia, John advised Abigail that the colonists needed to stay vigilant. "Let them exercise every day in the Week, if they Will, the more the better. Let them furnish themselves with Artillery, Arms and Ammunition. Let them follow the Maxim, which you say they have adopted, 'In Times of Peace, prepare for War.'"[19]

John had no need to worry, Abigail answered. She and her fellow villagers were well advanced in preparing for war. The local militia drilled every fortnight; vigilant watches were kept in the countryside and along the shoreline; the village stores of gunpowder had been carried away and hidden for safekeeping; and village leaders, including Josiah Quincy Sr. and Norton Quincy, were monitoring activities in Boston. From his perch at the top of his home, Josiah could keep an eye on British ships patrolling the harbor, and on clear days, he could see troop movements in the town itself.

Governor Gage might have banned all town meetings, but, as Abigail reported with a note of pride, in Braintree, "they have had their Town meeting here which was full as usual, chose their committee for the County meeting, and did Business without once regarding or fearing for the consequences."[20]

She also sent John updates about the farm: "The drought has been very severe. My poor Cows will certainly prefer a petition to you . . . they are become great Sufferers . . . by reason of the drought. . . . They Humbly pray that you would consider them, least hunger should break thro the Stone walls." Of their family, she wrote, "Our little flock are well, and present their Duty to their Pappa."[21]

Through all of Abigail Adams' letters ran the thread of her desire to have John with her again: "I dare not express as a distance of 300 miles distance how ardently I long for your return"; and her loneliness without him: "The tenderest regard evermore awaits you."[22]

John's letters in return were full of regrets that he could not write more, but there was so much work to do: "It is a great Affliction to me that I cannot write to you oftener than I do. But there are so many Hindrances, that I cannot. . . . We have so much Business, so much Ceremony, so much Company, so many Visits to receive and return, that I have not Time to write."[23]

In his diary, John recorded the many feasts he attended as a delegate. At the home of Quakers, he'd partaken of "Ducks, Hams, Chickens, Beef, Pigg, Tarts, Creams, Custards, Gellies, fools, Trifles, floating Islands, Beer, Porter, Punch, Wine,"[24] and the very next evening, he'd enjoyed "A most sinfull Feast again! Every Thing which could delight the Eye, or allure the Taste, Curds and Creams, Jellies, Sweet meats of various sorts, 20 sorts of Tarts, fools, Trifles, floating Islands, whippd Sillabubs &c. &c.—Parmesan Cheese, Punch, Wine, Porter, Beer."[25]

But to Abigail he offered no details as to the meals he was enjoying, writing in only one letter of the "incessant Feasting I have endured ever since I left Boston,"[26] and instead focusing on his very busy schedule: "My Time is totally filled from the Moment I get out of Bed, untill I return to it. Visits, Ceremonies, Company, Business, News Papers, Pamphlets &c. &c. &c."[27]

He answered her affections with his own, much less ardently stated: "My Compliments, Love, Service where they are due." Perhaps he was worried about his letters being intercepted, as he wrote, "There is so much Rascallity in the Management of Letters, now come in Fashion, that I am determined to write nothing of Consequence, not even to the Friend of my Bosom, but by Conveyances which I can be sure of."[28]

The lack of warmth, much less passion, might have left Abigail feeling dissatisfied with the already too infrequent letters from her husband. Charged with keeping the farm going and taking care of a house full of children, and answering daily inquiries from neighbors curious for news from Philadelphia, she might have welcomed a more amorous declaration from John. But she continued doggedly with her duties to farm, family, and community, whether John appreciated her hard work or not.

23

In the Cause of Liberty

That Americans know their rights . . .
and defend them, are matters of which I harbour no doubt.
Whether the arts of policy or the arts of war will decide the
*   contest,*
are problems we will solve at a more convenient season.

—Josiah Quincy Jr.

Throughout the fall of 1774, threats against the Massachusetts Loyalists mounted as fears of Gage's next steps increased. Those colonists still loyal to Parliament, or still in their pay, were viewed as collaborators to the oppressions imposed by Gage and were to be punished. John Hancock had threatened Jonathan Sewall before—"he was all for a mob to take off that brother-in-law of his"[1]—but his words had been in jest.

When the real threats arrived at Sewall's door, Hancock was horrified—especially because it was Dolly's sister Esther who bore the brunt of the attack, not her husband. Esther was home alone the day the mobs arrived, with just her three young children and a few servants. Jonathan had fled to Boston the day before, after hearing rumors that colonists, angered over the Powder Alarm, were plotting revenge against those they deemed responsible. Jonathan stopped in at the home of Edmund, his father-in-law, but when Edmund asked him to spend the night, Jonathan had refused and left to find refuge with a Loyalist friend.

Edmund wrote to his daughter Katy, who had finally gone to stay with her sister Sarah in Lancaster, that he blamed Sewall for bringing such shame on the entire family, and such misery to the entire colony; but he consoled himself that with Sewall gone into hiding, Esther would be safe from the mob: he was certain "no hurt will come to her or her house."[2] He was wrong.

By midday on September 1, men and boys from Cambridge and Charlestown, and even some coming from as far away as Roxbury and Dorchester, had gathered on the Cambridge Common. Dust billowed around the feet of the growing mob, turning shoes and pant legs gray; throats grew parched in the rising heat of the day. Barrels of cider and beer were rolled out, and drinks taken to stem the growing thirst.

Then the crowd moved away from the Common, marching up Tory Row. William Brattle was the initial target of the mob, for it was he who had alerted Governor Gage to the gunpowder stored in Charlestown, thereby setting off the raid by the British and putting into motion the hysteria and fears that Gage intended to launch an all-out bombardment of Boston. Even when the fears subsided, the anger remained.

But Brattle was not at home when the mob surrounded his house, nor were any of his family. The ire of the crowd next turned to Sewall, a known favorite of the new governor and a longtime Loyalist. The frustrated men and boys of the crowd began to march toward his house, shouting all the way. Esther, hearing the cries of the mob, drew close to the windows of her drawing room. Her two boys were with her, ages four and seven, and they too ran to the windows to see what was happening.

Suddenly, a barrage of rocks came flying, hurled against the closed windows. Glass shattered on the floor all around her, and Esther shouted to her children to move back as far as they could up against the walls of the room. With no thought to her own safety, Esther ran to the front door of her home.

She threw the heavy wooden door wide open and stepped through, standing on the brick stoop and facing the crowd. Stunned by her appearance, the crowd stopped its shouting and lowered the missiles intended for the remaining unbroken windows of the house.

Esther called out that their assault was without merit, that her husband had nothing to do with the seizure of ammunition, and in any event, her husband was not at home and she had children in the house. She told the men that if they left her in peace and her home unharmed, they could help themselves to refreshments from the family wine cellar.

Casks were hauled out into the yard and broken open. Men and boys of the mob drank their fill and then retreated back down the street, leaving the empty casks in their wake. All of Esther's strength—inviting the men into her home, leading them down to the cellar, watching resolute and still as they drank from the broken casks—was now gone. She had managed it all on adrenaline alone; with the retreat of the mob, the adrenaline failed and she fell, exhausted and trembling, into a chair. Her son Jonathan lay prostrate in fear on the floor; as a grown man he would never forget the humiliations of that day. He changed the spelling of his last name to the English way—Sewell—and vowed undying hatred for Americans.

Jonathan Sewall, hearing of the attack on his home, immediately sent for his wife and children. Within days, he had everything of value removed from their home. For now, they would stay in Boston, safe under the watchful eyes of the British troops. Edmund Quincy quailed at having his town become the "City of Refuge" for the Loyalists—and prayed for Parliament to retract its Intolerable Acts and "save Great Britain and the colonies."[3]

Samuel Quincy, still drawing his ample salary as solicitor general for the Crown, welcomed the Sewalls to Boston. But while Jonathan Sewall continued to rail in the press against rebel agitators, Samuel never published a single political essay or went on record for or against the colonial protesters. His wife, Hannah, was beginning to wish that he would stand up for their fellow colonists. It wasn't that she didn't enjoy the luxuries of their Boston home, paid for by her husband's Crown salary, or their social life, enlivened by high-ranking British officers and their fashionable wives. But Hannah had grown increasingly uncomfortable with the punishments levied on the colony by Parliament.

Samuel was just as concerned as his wife, and in private railed against overreaching and illegal parliamentary measures. Nevertheless, he wouldn't involve himself in the public fight against England, and he wouldn't step down from his position in the royal government. What he hoped for most of all—and there were many who joined him in his wish—was a peaceful reconciliation between the colony and the mother country. He doubted there was anything he could do to influence the course of events but wanted to wait and see what the future might bring. As he wrote to his wife later, "I am but a Passenger and must follow the fortunes of the day."[4]

Josiah Sr. held a dinner party in Braintree in mid-September. Samuel stayed away, but his wife, Hannah, attended. She enjoyed herself, not realizing it was a send-off for Josiah Jr.—the secret of his journey would be kept until after he sailed. But politics did come up, and Hannah distanced herself from the balancing act still carried out by her husband. Abigail Adams was there and wrote later to her husband John that there had been "a little clashing of parties you may be sure. Mr. Sam's Wife said she thought it high time for her Husband to turn about, he had not done half so clever since he left her advice."[5]

Throughout the fall of 1774, Governor Gage and his troops continued to tighten their clamp on the colony. Over a dozen more cannon and iron artillery pieces were rolled out to the Boston Neck, and the walls along the town gate were fortified. Gage, having suspended any meetings of the General Court, moved government offices back to Boston from Salem. He renewed Parliament's prohibitions against town meetings being held there or anywhere else in Massachusetts. Control over the colony was to be absolute, backed up by a dramatic show of weaponry.

But the colonists in Massachusetts were not intimidated by Gage's authority, his troops, or his weapons. In September, a countywide meeting was convened, led by Joseph Warren. Technically, Gage had only banned town meetings, not county meetings, and representatives from all over Suffolk County flocked to the village of Milton.

In long work sessions, they set about writing up a list of resolutions, which came to be known as the Suffolk Resolves. The preamble to the numbered resolutions, eighteen in all, stated that having witnessed "the power but not the justice, the vengeance but not the wisdom of Great Britain," it was imperative for the colony to govern itself, arm itself, and communicate and organize with other assemblies throughout the continent to oppose unfair British rule.[6]

The resolves called for a boycott of all British goods; a courier system to improve communication among the colonies; and a prohibition of all mob actions on the part of colonial rights. The fight for their rights would be orderly, with emphasis on economic pressures on England.

Once printed up, copies of the resolves were sent throughout the colony, as well as to the Continental Congress in Philadelphia. The congress voted to endorse them in a unanimous show of support for Massachusetts. That day, wrote John Adams in his diary, was "one of the happiest Days of my life."

Overwhelmed by the "generous, Noble sentiments, and Manly eloquence" of his fellow delegates, Adams joyfully wrote, "This day convinces me that America will support Massachusetts or perish with her."[7] When Gage heard about the Suffolk Resolves, and read all of its resolutions, he condemned it as an act of treason.

While Joseph Warren organized the county, John Hancock convened all willing legislators of the Massachusetts General Court to meet in what he called "a Provincial Congress." Two hundred sixty men agreed to attend, representing towns and villages throughout Massachusetts. Governor Gage condemned the congress as another act of treason, but there was little he could do to stop the assembly from taking place.

Gage didn't want to start a violent confrontation between his troops and the colonists. In any event, he couldn't move his troops against the colonists without parliamentary approval, and communication between the colony and England was torturously slow. Gage sent spies to infiltrate meetings of the Provincial Congress, biding his time for now and waiting for instructions from England.

Hancock was aware of Gage's watchful eye and his legion of spies. The location of the Provincial Congress's meetings was changed without warning to keep spies away, moving from Salem to Concord, and then to Cambridge. In Cambridge, they met one day in the small courthouse off the Common and the next day they met across the street, in the First Church of Cambridge.

From place to place, village to village, Hancock arrived in his fine carriage, his jacket always freshly brushed and the buttons on his breeches rubbed to gleaming, his shoes polished to shining and a sprightly ribbon holding back his hair. He felt it was his duty to appear strong and unfazed by pressure, secure in his place and ready to lead. When he was elected president of the Provincial Congress of Massachusetts, he relished his new title, which he felt was well deserved. And when he was named chairman of the Committee of Safety, charged with raising a militia of twelve thousand and securing arms and supplies for defending the colonists against British aggression, his satisfaction was complete.[8]

Hancock committed a huge amount of his own money to pay for supplies for this new army, including firearms, bayonets, knapsacks, cartridges, and balls. But his personal fortune would not be enough, nor would it be appropriate for this new entity, this Provincial Congress of Massachusetts, to be dependent upon the wealth of one man.

In order to pay for the militia and supplies, a new tax system was put into place. For the first time in the history of the colonies in America, taxes were to be collected and managed by a government independent of the king and Parliament. The first step to independence, a leap into fiscal management and responsibility, had been taken.

John Hancock was at the top of Gage's catalog of political enemies and the focus of the ire of Loyalists and British troops alike. Along with Josiah Quincy Jr., Hancock's name appeared on a list of men to be apprehended "the instant rebellion happens," and then to be put "immediately to the sword." Death would not be enough: the order was to "destroy their houses and plunder their effects; it is just they should be the first victims to the mischiefs they have brought upon us."[9]

Death threats to Hancock arrived as anonymous missives left in the middle of the night at the door of the Beacon Hill mansion or printed up in bills that were then posted throughout Boston. A bounty was placed on his head. Both he and Joseph Warren were threatened with death by assassination, but one British officer claimed that it would be "a pity for them to make their exit that way, as I hope we shall have the pleasure of seeing them do it by the hands of the hangman."[10]

Throughout the fall of 1774, John Adams was hard at work on the committee charged with drafting a declaration of rights and grievances, as well as the committee preparing the articles of association. The declaration would set forth the reasons why the colonists were implementing actions against England, and the articles would list the nature of those actions.

At first John found the work energizing and inspiring, the debates most "ingenious and entertaining."[11] But as the days passed, and September turned to October, impasses over minor details and major points multiplied; it seemed as if the members of the committee could not agree on anything, not only about the grievances themselves but also about what actions to take against British oppression, including a boycott, training local militia, and raising funds to pay for it all.

John grew discouraged by "the nibbling and squibbling" of the delegates and the deliberations that "spun out to an immeasurable Length."[12] He complained of having to submit to the "Mortification [of having] to sit with half a dozen Witts" who considered themselves "refined Genius's."[13] He knew that many of the other delegates feared that the Massachusetts contingent were radicals, fanatics for independence who were set on a course that would lead to war. But Adams did not want war, nor was he advocating independence—not yet.

What John Adams wanted was resolution, and he wanted it now. Too much time had been wasted; too many weeks had passed since he'd left Abigail and the children. He had recently received a letter from his son, John Quincy: "I hope I grow a better Boy and that you will have no occasion to be ashamed of me when you return."[14] John longed to return, to be home with his family on his farm in Braintree.

Finally, on October 14, 1774, the full Continental Congress approved the committee's Declaration of Grievances. The declaration excoriated the Intolerable Acts, which were deemed "impolitic, unjust, and cruel, as well as unconstitutional, and most dangerous and destructive of American rights."[15] The declaration then defined what these "American rights" were. Numbering ten in all, the defined bill of rights included the right to peaceably assemble; the right to government by their own representatives (no taxation without representation); and the right to life, liberty, and property.

With the declaration approved, work returned to finalizing the Articles of Association, a list of actions to be undertaken by the colonists to secure their rights. On October 20, the articles were approved by the full congress. The articles provided the framework for implementing and enforcing what Josiah Quincy had been advocating since the spring: an economic boycott of Great Britain. Tea was banned immediately, and all other goods from Britain were subject to boycott as of December.

The Continental Congress passed other measures that were designed to help colonists survive the boycott—measures that promoted thrift and austerity, along with local manufacturing. Shop owners were prohibited from raising prices for limited goods; sheep were to be protected, in order to ensure that enough wool was available to meet colonists' needs now that British wool was no longer available; expensive or wasteful entertainments, such as horse racing, cockfighting, and plays, were to be suspended; and extravagant funerals were forbidden.

One significant provision of the Articles of Association was the ban on the slave trade: as of December, the importation and purchase of slaves would be prohibited. This measure may have been enacted because of threats by both free and enslaved blacks that they would join whichever side promised freedom, whether it be the British or the Americans.

Abigail was heartened by the news of the ban when she read it. "I wish most sincerely there was not a Slave in the province," she wrote to John. "It always appeared a most iniquitious Scheme to me—fight ourselves for what we are daily robbing and plundering from those who have as good a right to freedom as we have." She added in her note to John, "You know my mind upon this Subject."[16]

And well he did. John agreed with her, and neither he nor his father had ever owned slaves. While Abigail's father owned slaves, as did other members of the older Quincy generations, she and her cousins, along with John Hancock (who freed his uncle's slaves upon Thomas's death) were all in agreement about the evils of slavery.

In celebration of having approved the Articles of Association, the Continental Congress adjourned for the night to "the City Tavern . . . a most elegant Entertainment."[17] Judging by his satisfaction in such a grand meal, John Adams saw no irony in participating in a sumptuous celebration at night while voting for frugality and temperance during the day. Perhaps John was celebrating the fact that he could soon leave Philadelphia and get home to Abigail.

But there was still one more task to be accomplished, and it was not one that the Massachusetts delegates supported. John Dickinson wrote a petition to King George, formulating it as a plea for understanding, patience, and support: "We ask but for peace, liberty, and safety . . . [and] beseech your majesty that your royal authority and influence may . . . procure us relief." In closing, the petition from the Continental Congress offered the hope that "your majesty may enjoy a long and prosperous reign, and that your descendants may govern your dominions with honour to themselves, and happiness to their subjects."[18] Grudgingly, the Massachusetts delegates, along with the rest of the congress, agreed to the petition being sent.

Now John Adams could finally return to Braintree.

When the Massachusetts delegates arrived back in Boston on November 9, 1774, church bells were set pealing in greeting. Where the journey had begun, it now ended, and the travelers were invited into John Hancock's mansion for a celebratory meal.

John Adams was not with them, however; he had left the entourage at Cambridge and traveled to Braintree on a hired horse. He had had his fill of meals, wine, toasts, and talk. His eyes hurt, turned swollen and red in the dust brought up by the horses; his head ached from the rolling of the carriage; his arms longed for his wife and children. Traveling alone by the Plymouth Road, he arrived at nightfall to his farmhouse by the sea.

There would be no rest for him there. A constant stream of friends and family—his brothers, his mother, his in-laws—came by the house to see John, to hear stories of the Continental Congress, to pull hope from his words and thereby sustain themselves through what was sure to be a long, cold winter. Within days of his return, a call came for him to attend the Provincial Congress, now meeting at the First Parish Church in Watertown (still evading Gage's spies as best they could). John agreed to come, and binding up his aching eyes in lavender-soaked bandages, he hired a man to take him by wagon to Watertown.

The sight that greeted him, of 260 men from all across the colony, made him stop at the door and draw breath. Men of every trade and station, from

John Hancock, the wealthiest man in the colony, resplendent as always in a jacket of deep maroon, to men dressed in muslin and patched wool: John Adams came forward to meet them all.

He learned that they were blacksmiths and bakers, fishermen and farmers, tradesmen and tailors, shopkeepers and men who had lost their shops—and yet still they came, confident and determined, ready to build together a legitimate government in the void created now that the royal government was an entity to be disdained and ignored.

What a piece of work is man, Josiah Quincy Jr. would have whispered in his ear, if only he had been there at Watertown with John. John missed his friend and colleague, a man so wise in law, justice, and Shakespeare. He wished that Josiah could see for himself the resolution of his fellow New Englanders, hard at work creating a new government in this old meeting house in Watertown.

Abigail Adams, just miles away, knew John would soon return to her. Abigail Quincy, staying with her father in Boston, wondered if her husband, Josiah, ever would. She had yet to hear from him, and she didn't know if he was in England or at the bottom of the sea or lying ill somewhere in between.

24

On This Island, This England

It is yourselves, it is yourselves must save you;
and you are equal to the task.

—JOSIAH QUINCY JR.

John Hancock presented the annual Thanksgiving Day proclamation for Massachusetts, taking over the role always assumed in the past by the governor. The Provincial Congress had just voted to send Hancock to the Second Continental Congress, to be held in Philadelphia in May 1775. His army of "minutemen" was swelling with volunteers, and training of the men had started. And now, he would give thanks for all the colony, serving as the representative of their gratitude as well as of their dreams. Hancock gloried in the role.

For the first time in the history of the colony, the name of the king was not mentioned in the Thanksgiving Proclamation. No sovereign existed but the will of the people, united against oppression: "a Union which so remarkably prevails not only in this Province, but throughout the Continent."[1]

With December came snow, every day more snow. December 25 was not a holiday celebrated by the colonists of Massachusetts, but a day for work like any other unless it happened to fall on the Sabbath, and this year, it did. There was meetinghouse in the morning, a long lunch, and then back to meetinghouse in the afternoon. The Third Parish Church in Braintree was full that day. Anthony Wibird was in the pulpit; he continued his ministry of the church and was as well loved as ever by his congregation, although his sermons were less than compelling (Abigail Adams described him as "our inanimate old bachelor").[2]

Abigail Quincy attended the day's sermons with her father-in-law, having come out to Braintree with her children for a long visit. News had finally arrived of her husband's safe arrival in Falmouth, from a captain who had been there to see it. But still no word from Josiah himself. Until she heard from him, she could not be sure of his safety; until then, Abigail would continue to write to Josiah, the letters sent care of a trading agent in London, an old colleague of John Hancock.

The letters were never easy to begin. What to write? Abigail couldn't help but fear that her words would never be read by their intended recipient. But fear was no excuse, and she knew what she had to do.

Dearest Friend, she began. And from there, the words flowed.

At the end of the year, Edmund Quincy wrote to his daughter Katy, who was on a brief visit to Lancaster. John Hancock had been to the house on Kingston Street and "spent a Sociable evening of 2 hours . . . I should be glad to see him often." Dolly and Hancock were still "entwined," and yet no date had been set for the wedding, with "how things are here." The scourge of the British was haunting all aspects of colonial life, and now a perhaps even greater threat had appeared in Boston: "the most threatening evil among us . . . small pox." Edmund urged Katy to get herself inoculated, along with her sister and nieces and nephews. Quoting scripture, he advised her to take care of her "Vineyard . . . and [follow] the *Truth* of *Righteousness*."[3]

Smallpox had indeed come to Boston, infiltrating the British troops first and then spreading to the civilian population. The selectmen of Boston, still working despite the prohibition against town meetings, moved quickly to contain the illness. Stricken parents and children, along with British soldiers, were sent to a special smallpox hospital to recuperate or die. For those who refused to move from their homes, a fence was erected in the street around their dwelling and "Flags hung out to give notice of the Distemper."[4]

Despite the efforts at containment, concerns multiplied that by spring, Boston "will be filled with Pestilence and a consequent degree of Famine."[5]

But by early February 1775, William Cooper, town clerk and avowed patriot, announced that "after Strict Enquiry no person is found to have small pox in this town."[6] As welcome as the news was, townspeople only shifted their vigilance elsewhere, their fear of contagion quickly replaced by other, equally frightening worries.

Finally, in January 1775, Abigail Quincy received word from Josiah. The letter had been written in early November from aboard the ship on his way to England and was just now delivered back to America. "Dear Partner of my Life," Abigail read, "when removed from you I most sensibly feel how dear you are to me. . . . I look toward you as my most valuable treasure."[7]

She read through quickly, looking for the news she sought most desperately, and she found it: "no one on board feels freer [than me] from disorder and none most certainly in better spirits."[8] Josiah was well. He was healthy. Abigail felt herself breathe again.

A flow of letters began to arrive, letters for Abigail and Josiah Sr., as well as letters to be forwarded on to Joseph Warren, John Dickinson, James Lovell (an old friend from school, whose father was a Tory but who himself was a devoted patriot), and others. Details of the last few months of Josiah's life were filled in, the voyage, the landing at Falmouth, and the journey on land to London.

Josiah had taken his time traveling up-country; this was his first time in England and he wanted to take in all the sights. He was awed by the farms—"the cultivation of the land can scarcely be realized by a mere American . . .'tis an amazing perfection"—as he traveled up to the port of Plymouth. There the great number of docks, busy and bustling, so impressed him that he wrote in his journal, "My ideas of the riches and powers of this great nation are increased."[9] He also noticed the many gunships docked there, with firepower enough to wipe out Boston, if they so desired to try it.

He traveled to Exeter, where he toured the cathedral ("Amazing work of superstition!"), and then continued on toward London, stopping for a day in Stonehenge—"a wonderful piece of workmanship and antiquity."[10] He finally arrived in London on November 17. He moved into a house on Arundel Street, near Fanton Square and Haymarket. That very afternoon he had tea with Ben Franklin.

Josiah had long suspected Franklin of playing both sides of the controversy between England and the colonists. But it took only that one meeting on the first day to convince Josiah that he had been wrong. Franklin quickly became one of Josiah's most visited and relied-upon friends in London: "Dr. Franklin is an American in heart and soul."[11] Franklin lived just a short stroll away from Josiah's London home, and the two would spend many hours together over the weeks to come.

Within just a few days of his arrival in London, Josiah met with the British prime minister, Lord North. North was a "heavy booby-looking sort" but his "blubbery" looks belied his sharp-edged tenacity.[12] Josiah saw only warmth in North's greeting of him, and was heartened by their meeting, in which he told North that the cause of "our political evils" was "gross misrepresentation and falsehood" concerning events in Massachusetts and the alleged motives of the colonists.

He spoke with Lord North about the Boston Port Act, and "upon this subject I received much pleasure," Josiah wrote in his journal, adding, "His Lordship several times smiled and seemed touched." At the same time, Lord North stressed to Josiah the superior powers of Great Britain and "the determination . . . to effect the submission of the colonies."[13]

Thomas Hutchinson, living now in London, renewed himself as Josiah's nemesis within his first days in London. Reports reached Josiah, via a number of different people, that Hutchinson continued to insist that "a union of the colonies was utterly impracticable; that the people were greatly divided among themselves in every colony; and that there could be no doubt that all America would submit, and . . . soon."[14] Infuriated, Josiah Quincy Jr. sought to persuade the influential Englishmen he met that the colonies were united, resolute, and stubborn.

During those early weeks he spent in London, Josiah's hopes for a peaceful resolution of the conflict between England and America grew: "I find every day more reason to think that multitude of fervent friends to America reside on this Island." And to Abigail, he wrote of finding "people . . . who revere, love, and heartily wish well to us . . . it is the interest, the highest private interest of this whole nation to be our fast friends."[15]

He was confident that he himself was serving to ignite even further love and support for the Americans: "I feel the ardour of an American; I have lighted up the countenances of many. . . . I am infected with an enthusiasm I know to be contagious."[16]

With great optimism, he sallied forth, scheduling meetings with William Pitt (Earl of Chatham, member of the House of Lords) and Sir George Savile (baronet and member of the House of Commons). The two men could not have been more different. Pitt, a former prime minister, was elegant and outspoken, while Savile was self-effacing and quiet; yet both were firm friends to the colonies, and both had opposed Lord North's punitive acts against Massachusetts.

Josiah also met with Lord Dartmouth, secretary of state for the colonies, who complimented Josiah on his pamphlet attacking the Boston Port Act but promised nothing; and Corbyn Morris, a member of the ministry, who advised him, "your Countrymen must fail in a contest with this great and powerfull people . . . you ought to write to your friends this intelligence and endeavor to influence them to their duty."[17]

Josiah recorded Morris' advice in his journal, followed by exclamation marks; but he did not intend to share this unwanted counsel with his compatriots in America. Instead, he would focus on Morris' request for a list of starting points from which a reconciliation between the colonies and England could begin.

As long as his health held up, he would not stop striving, in meeting after meeting, to rally enough support for the colonists so that Lord North and his ministry would be forced to change course. Josiah prayed for a rescission of the Port Act and all the other Intolerable Acts, and a suspension of the tax on tea. Most of all, he hoped for a smooth return to those times when, before the Stamp Act, the American colonies and England existed in a happy equilibrium of mutual support and benefit.

What Josiah did not know was that Thomas Hutchinson had poisoned the way for him, setting both Lord North and Lord Dartmouth against him even before they met. Lord Dartmouth had initially believed Josiah was a man who could bring about reconciliation between the colonies and England, but then Hutchinson gave him a copy of Josiah's pamphlet on the Port Bill[18]—the very pamphlet Dartmouth later duplicitously complimented Josiah on—and after reading it, Dartmouth doubted anything could be accomplished via negotiations with such a man.

After meeting with Josiah, Lord North reported back to Hutchinson that Quincy was "a bad, insidious man" who had pretended to come to England for his health but now spent all his time in pursuit of political advantages.[19] And Corbyn Morris never intended to take Josiah's list for opening negotiations seriously; instead, he tried to convince Josiah of England's great poverty and its great need of the tax revenues from the colonies.

In early December, Quincy's tiring schedule in London resulted in a relapse of his consumption. "Incessant application, incessant talking . . . has brought me a little fever and a raising of blood."[20] In the evenings, he left his windows open while he slept in a vain effort to catch what fresh air he could in a London swathed in fog, and he suffered daily chills and fever. With the decline in his health came a decline in his outlook: not only had he begun to see how difficult it was to negotiate with people who refused to speak the truth with him or take his positions seriously, but disturbing rumors had begun to arrive in England of mayhem and destruction in Boston. His worries for America manifested themselves physically: coughing, chills, blood on his pillow.

On December 7, he wrote to Abigail that he had heard "BOSTON WAS

NOW IN ASHES." Was it true? He was frustrated by the lack of solid news, having received no letters from anyone in Boston, Braintree, or Philadelphia. Instead, he told her, he was taunted in a coffeehouse that any day now, the news would be "that you are all subdued and in deep humiliation."[21]

He refused to believe the coffeehouse predictions—and yet he feared what lay ahead for America. Rumors had been circulating of parliamentary plots to divide the colonies, to bribe delegates to the Continental Congress, to grant concessions to the southern colonies so they might turn away from New England. He warned that above all else the colonies must stay united: "Prepare, prepare, I say, for *the worst*." As John Adams had counseled his Abigail, now Josiah counseled: "Weigh, commune, consider, and act."

To show unity was paramount: "when once there is a conviction that the Americans are in earnest, that they are resolved to endure all hazards with a spirit worthy of the prize for which they content . . . [then] you will have many firm, active, persevering, and powerful friends, in both Houses of Parliament."[22] It was more important now than ever, for the colonies to present a unified and strong front to Lord North if they hoped to achieve a successful reconciliation with the mother country.

But Josiah had begun to wonder if reconciliation was possible or even desirable. The vast space between America and England, not only politically but also physically and atmospherically, had awoken doubts about whether the American colonies were still British at all. England was a strange place in so many ways, with such disparities of opulence and poverty, so much frivolity and entertainments on offer, and everywhere he looked, "extended miseries of enormous wealth and power," including immorality and corruption.[23]

London was very different from Boston and another universe entirely from Braintree. Josiah went one evening to the playhouse at Covent Garden, which only confirmed his opinion that "the stage is the nursery of vice, and disseminates the seeds of it far and wide, with an amazing and baneful success."[24]

Even the English that was spoken in London was different from the language he was used to. In the mid-eighteenth century, the upper classes in England began to speak in a new way, broadening out their *a*'s, slurring their *s*'s and changing both idiom and intonation, in a conscious effort to sound distinctly elegant and refined.[25] The change in speech may have been due in part to the influence of the actor David Garrick, whom Josiah had seen perform at Drury Lane (and whom he called "a most surprising fellow").[26] Garrick's elocution was widely admired in London—and imitated everywhere.

To Josiah's ears, the language seemed both "contrived and pretentious,"[27] yet another example of "that pageantry I see . . . [which] makes me every day more attached to the simplicity of my native soil."[28]

Perhaps his native soil should separate from England and declare its independence from the British Empire. Josiah wasn't quite ready to accept such a conclusion—but he had begun to think about it.

Josiah continued to write to friends and family in America, hopeful that his letters were traveling safely by transatlantic packets and eager to finally receive return letters from home. Most of his letters were to Abigail, and he instructed her to share the news carefully with his "political friends . . . they must consider my letters to you as intended for them."[29]

But there were also words in those letters that were meant only for her: "My whole heart is with you; my whole time is employed in endeavoring to serve my country. . . . My heart feels for you all very exquisitely when I think of you, which is eighteen hours out of the twenty-four. Adieu, my best friend."[30]

As winter, damp and cold, settled on London, Josiah's energy lagged. He felt disillusioned by the hypocrisy of those British representatives who spoke of a reconciliation between the colonies and England, while at the same time Lord North and his ministry pursued an ever harder line against America. But what depressed Josiah most of all was his growing awareness that King George shared Lord North's punishing view of the colonies.

For so long, Josiah and other New Englanders had believed that their sovereign would listen to them, that he would be eager to know the truth of what was going on in America, and that he would support them in their petitions for fair treatment. Instead Josiah found King George to be as prejudiced against the colonists of Massachusetts as his prime minister, Lord North.

The king had opened Parliament in late November with a speech in which he asserted the power of Parliament to rule over all "the Dominions of my crown, the maintenance of which I consider as essential to the dignity, the safety, and the welfare of the British Empire."

The colony of Massachusetts, he declared, was home of the "most daring spirit of resistance and disobedience to the law," with ever more "fresh violences of a very criminal nature." He promised to punish all who "attempt to weaken or impair the supreme Authority of this Legislature over all the Dominions of My Crown" and directed Parliament to do what was necessary to demonstrate to the colonies "due Reverence for the Laws, and a just Sense of the Blessings of our excellent Constitution."[31]

The irony was not lost on Josiah. His own deep reverence for the "excellent Constitution" led him to the opposite conclusion of the king's; and for the king he held no "due Reverence" at all: "in his robes and diadem . . . surrounded with his nobles and great officers. I was not awe-struck with the pomp."[32] For so long he had such high hopes for his monarch, but now he had almost none.

All around him, men kept blaming Thomas Hutchinson for all the troubles of Massachusetts—Josiah recorded more than six instances of being told of Hutchinson's treachery in one month—but Josiah began to think that the problem ran much deeper than one man's misrepresentations of a colony; the distrust and scathing disregard for the colonies started at the top with the king, and then spread wide and ran deep.

As Josiah's hopes for a peaceful resolution faded, he saw a new purpose in the unification of the colonies; unity would be the sword necessary to cut, once and for all, the cords binding America to the Old World. He wrote to Abigail in mid-December of his conviction that his "countrymen must seal their cause with their blood. . . . I see every day more and more reason to confirm my opinion." He urged Abigail to tell the colonists of America, "acknowledge your ability to save your country if you have but union, courage, and perseverance."[33] Union to achieve more than just a boycott and to make more than just resolutions: union to make war.

Three days later he wrote to Joseph Reed, a fellow lawyer and patriot he had met while in Philadelphia. His missive to Reed held the same message that he had sent to his wife: "my countrymen . . . must yet seal their faith and constancy to their liberties with blood." He felt war was a curse but at times a necessity: "[War] is distressing . . . indeed! But hath not this ever been the lot of humanity?"[34]

In mid-December, rumors began to fly around London. News had arrived from America concerning the Continental Congress held in Philadelphia in the fall. Josiah rushed to Franklin's home to learn what the older statesman knew. Franklin told Josiah that the Continental Congress had enacted a boycott of all British goods, proclaimed a Bill of Rights for the colonists, and rejected Parliament's right to tax the colonies. Committees to enforce the boycott had been formed in all the colonies and militias would be trained. A petition to the king had been written and signed by representatives from twelve of the thirteen colonies, all those present at the Continental Congress. Ben Franklin was instructed by the delegates to make sure the petition was delivered to the king himself.

Josiah was stunned. He had yet to receive a single letter from America and was not prepared for the enormity of what the Continental Congress had achieved. Another boycott? Militias? It was as if America were declaring war. In fact, Horace Walpole, past member of Parliament who opposed Lord North's policies, declared: "The long-expected sloop is arrived at last, and is indeed a man of war!"[35]

But when Franklin shared with Josiah the contents of the petition, Josiah saw that despite the measures undertaken by the congress, such as the boycott and militia and committees, their petition to the king was both moderate and conciliatory. The Americans asked for relief from their revered sovereign in a humble way and expressed no threat of rebellion or any kind of violence at all: "so far as promoting innovations, we have only opposed them . . . and can be charged with no offence, unless it be to receive injuries and be sensible of them."[36]

Lord Dartmouth agreed to pass the petition on to the king but could not promise that King George would receive it, much less read it. With Christmas coming, Parliament was disbanded and would take up the problems of America in the new year.

Ben Franklin met with Lord Richard Howe on Christmas Day, in an effort to work with him to formulate a plan for reconciliation between the colonies and England. Josiah was not invited, but he would not have come if he had been. He was desperate to leave London, to get away from the damp chill and dirty air of the city. He passed the New Year's holiday in Bath and spent hours on end wandering the hills that surrounded the ancient city. He was anxious for news from across the sea; he waited for instructions on what to do now, for his colony and his country.

On both sides of the Atlantic, fear was growing that battles, not of words but of guns and swords, would have to be fought to resolve the conflict between England and America. And not just battles, but a war.

25

Sharpening Quills and Swords

We have too many high sounding words,
and too few actions that correspond with them.

—ABIGAIL ADAMS

John Adams was hard at work in Braintree in the early days of 1775, holed up in his corner office while the winds howled off the sea a mile away and snow piled up against the farmhouse, rising to a height just below the window ledges. The snowfall had been unexpected and would melt within days under the sunny skies to come. But for now, roads were impassable and Braintree felt isolated and quiet, a village alone along the sea.

During the past weeks, a spate of letters had come out in the *Massachusetts Gazette*, all purportedly the writings of an anonymous Tory who went by the pen name "Massachusettensis." The letters praised parliamentary rule in the colonies and warned against the "proliferation of Committees" (a direct attack at both the Provincial Congress and the Continental Congress); the writer warned that the protests against England would lead to annihilation: "With the British navy in the front, Canadians and Savages in the rear, a regular army in the midst, desolation will pass through our land like a whirlwind, our houses burnt to ashes, our fair possessions laid waste."[1]

Well-written and hugely popular—John Adams himself described the letters as "shining like the moon among the lesser stars"—the letters offered support to those colonists who feared that protests against parliamentary authority were going too far and who believed reconciliation was only achievable through reasonable concessions made on both sides.[2]

Eventually, it would be revealed that the letters had been penned by Daniel Leonard, an old friend of John who had become a confirmed Loyalist; Adams blamed Thomas Hutchinson for having "seduced from my Bosom, three of the most intimate Friends I ever had in my Life, Jonathan Sewall, Samuel Quincy, and Daniel Leonard."[3]

But for a long time, John was convinced that Jonathan Sewall had written the letters. He took the essays as a personal attack by his old friend, a public retaliation for John's refusal to take Jonathan's advice those long months ago, when they walked together on the hill overlooking Casco Bay. John decided he had to answer the letters with ones of his own; he would respond to the points made by Massachusettensis and go even further, to prove once and for all that he, John Adams, had made the right choice in attending the Continental Congress and choosing a unified America.

In his essays, penned under the name "Novangelus," he emphatically refuted that colonists opposing parliamentary oppression were seeking an independence from England. But even as he wrote these words, the idea of a unified and independent country began to grow—and would be seeded in the minds of his readers: "The patriots of this province desire nothing new— they wish only to keep their old privileges. . . . They were for 150 years allowed to tax themselves, and govern their internal concerns . . . [while] Parliament governed their trade. . . . This plan, they wish may continue forever. But it is honestly confessed, rather than become subject to the absolute authority of parliament, in all cases of taxation and internal polity, they will be driven to throw off" any continued oversight from England.[4]

John had not quite issued a call for independence—but he had come close.

Josiah Quincy Jr. finally received a packet of letters from America when he returned to London from Bath in the new year. He dug into the pile, reveling in hearing once again his friends' voices and feeling the love of his wife and family. From his wife came concerns for his well-being and news of the children. From his father, a wish that his son's health was vibrant; hearing good news on that score "would be almost as joyful and reviving to your aged Father, as to hear that through your Mediation, Peace and Harmony were restored between the Parent State and her injured and oppressed children."[5]

From Dr. Joseph Warren came advice that was both radical and reasonable: "If the late acts of Parliament are not to be repealed, the wisest step for both countries is fairly to separate, and not spend their blood and treasure destroying each other."[6] Josiah found it hard to believe there might a peaceful, bloodless solution to the conflict—and like Warren, he saw independence of the American colonies as a real possibility, not just an idea. He had seen for himself what he considered to be a corrupt regime controlling Parliament, and believed that separating America from England might be necessary to protect not only the liberties of the colonies but their sanctity as well.

In return for all the letters he received, Josiah consigned to his local agent a large number to be sent to America. On most of his correspondence, he used an assumed name, "Henry Ireton," fearing that his own name would excite too much interest and possible interception of his mail. In a letter to his father, Josiah made a joke about the possibility of his correspondence being confiscated: "This letter is intended to contain nothing but what spies of the ministry may be willing to let pass; and having gratified their own curiosity, I wish they may also be candid and generous enough to let my friends gratify theirs too."[7] But his humor barely disguised his concerns.

He was right to be worried. There were those in the British government heavily advocating a policy of screening all letters carried by packet ships to and from the American colonies. Although official action on the proposal wouldn't take place for months, Josiah correctly suspected that agents of Parliament had already begun searching the mail of known agitators. Josiah Quincy Jr. was known to be one such agitator—within days of his arrival in London, he was denounced in Parliament as a man "walking the streets of London . . . [who instead] ought to be in [the prisons] Newgate or Tyburn."[8] It would be easy enough to steal letters from a packet sailing to America, and Josiah had to be very careful not only how he signed his letters but how he sent them.

He grew increasingly certain that letters addressed to him had already been confiscated, having received no news at all from Sam Adams, John Adams, or any of the other delegates to the Continental Congress. He wrestled with what to do, unsure of his role or purpose now that a boycott had started and a petition had been sent to the king. Was he to negotiate some kind of peace with England or resign himself and his country to war?

When Parliament began meeting again, in January 1775, Josiah was unexpectedly buoyed by the valiant and moving speeches he heard there. Friends in Parliament finally came to the floor to argue on behalf of the colonies, and Josiah, overjoyed, enthusiastically recorded their speeches word for word.

Lord Chatham, Lord Camden, Lord Shelburne—all gave rousing orations asking for consideration of the complaints made by the colonists, and suggesting avenues for peaceful resolution of the disputes between colonies and Parliament. They also predicted grave consequences if no resolution could be reached. "You cannot force a form of Government upon any people," the Duke of Richmond said. "You may spread fire, sword, and desolation, but that will not be government."[9]

Josiah wrote home to Abigail that the colonies' commercial pressures might prove enough after all to both stave off war and propel Parliament to rescind the Intolerable Acts: "The people of this country must be made to feel the importance of their American brethren . . . must feel it at every nerve. . . . The cause of the colonies grows every day more popular; that of the ministry, more desperate. There can be no doubt that the peaceful, spiritless, and self-denying warfare [the boycott] would yield an ample victory."[10]

As his spirits rose, his health improved; "I never enjoyed greater health or spirits," he wrote to his wife.[11] He urged her to spread the message that if Americans continue to "withstand the blandishments of luxury, and the delusions of false pride, they may purchase liberty . . . they must soon make their election, the loaf of slavery or the sword of blood."[12]

He suddenly had real hope that the sword of blood could be avoided. There seemed to be so much support in Parliament for rescinding the Port Bill's harsh measures against Massachusetts, and even removing troops from the colony. And petitions were pouring in from manufacturers all over Great Britain pleading for a resolution with the colonies and a return to full trade and commerce.

But all too soon, Josiah's hopes were dashed. Behind the scenes, the ministry had been planning a program to annihilate colonial resistance all along. At the end of January, Josiah Quincy Jr. sat stock-still, listening to the roll call of votes offered on Lord Chatham's motion to withdraw all British troops from Boston: it was defeated, 69 votes against to 18 in favor. Another vote was taken, on a proposal to hear pro-American petitions from the merchants of London: it was also defeated.

Josiah realized then that all his allies in Parliament could not help America: they were too few, and the ministry and Lord North were too powerful. He returned to his rooms, disheartened, and wrote in his journal, "This debate and division show that if King, Lords, and Commons can subdue America into bondage against the almost universal sentiment, opinion, wish, and hope of the Englishmen of this Island, the deed will be done."[13]

That evening, Josiah once again fell ill. His fever returned, and with it, a cough so deep and rough that blood came up. He retreated to his bed for days.

Visitors came by daily, bringing updates on Parliament, each new item more disturbing to Quincy than the one before: Lord Dartmouth had sent instructions to Governor Gage to arrest the principal rebels, including John

Hancock and Sam Adams. More troops were on their way to Boston. New bills were being crafted that would proclaim Massachusetts to be in rebellion and punish the colony by exacting even more punitive measures, including imposing bans on fisheries under British control. And Lord North planned on offering conciliatory measures to certain factions in America in an effort to divide the colonies. If Massachusetts could be isolated and its rebellious factions destroyed, Lord North was sure that the rest of America would bow down to parliamentary control and pay obeisance to the Crown.

At the beginning of February, as Josiah Quincy Jr. lay sick and exhausted in London, John Hancock called to order the second meeting of the Massachusetts Provincial Congress. Close to three hundred delegates and observers crowded into the meetinghouse in Cambridge, assembling on the hard pews. The odor of wet wool and sweat mixed with the scent of burning wood, as the woodstove worked overtime against the freezing temperatures seeping in through the slats of the walls and the high windows.

Rumors now abounded throughout the colony: more British troops would arrive any day; Hancock and Adams, along with other patriot leaders, were to be arrested and possibly condemned to hang; and new, even more punitive measures were being considered by Parliament for the already heavily burdened New Englanders.

On February 2, the *Massachusetts Spy* printed the full text of King George's speech given at the opening of Parliament in November, in which he denounced the colonists of Massachusetts and deemed them guilty of treason. The colonists were at last learning what Josiah Jr. had already come to understand: the king was against them.

Abigail Adams was horrified: "Yesterday brought us such a Speach from the Throne as will stain with everlasting infamy the reign of George the 3 . . . the most wicked and hostile measures will be persued against us—even without giving us an opportunity to be heard in our defence. Infatuated Brittain! poor distressed America. Heaven only knows what is next to take place but it seems to me the Sword is now our only, yet dreadful alternative."[14]

The specter of the King's Speech hung over the Provincial Congress. In addressing the gathered representatives, Hancock counseled that the time to prepare for war had come. A motion was made and quickly passed, re-electing Hancock president of the congress. Calling on Sam Adams and Joseph Warren to help, Hancock began to form committees, which in turn would take on responsibility for carrying forward measures that would ensure the colony was ready for whatever was coming next from Britain, including civil war.

A plan was put forth for manufacturing firearms in the colony and safeguarding existing stores of arms and ammunition. Vigilant watch was to be kept on British movements in Boston. The citizens of the colony were to be educated as to "the imminent danger they are in, from the present disposition of the British ministry and parliament . . . there is reason to fear that they will attempt our sudden destruction . . . inhabitants of this colony [are] to prepare themselves for the last event."[15]

John Adams in Braintree was relieved to receive news of another item that had been considered and then approved by the Provincial Congress: each delegate to the Continental Congress would be paid, both for past service and for the upcoming session scheduled for May. With few legal clients, and little income from the farm because of the previous season's drought, the money would be welcome in the Adams household. John may have suspected that part of his salary would be paid out of Hancock's own coffers, but Adams still bristled at the wealth of his childhood friend, and he failed to acknowledge Hancock's generosity in sharing what he had. The colony struggled to gather the funds needed to keep their fledgling—and illegal—government going, and Hancock continued to help as much as he could.

Across the Boston Neck, "a great uneasiness" had settled on the town.[16] The number of Redcoats seemed to exceed the number of locals, as so many Bostonians had fled to the countryside and those who remained avoided public venues, fearful of encounters that could quickly turn ugly.

Abigail Adams wrote to her friend and mentor, Mercy Otis Warren, about an incident involving a drunken soldier who started a melee that in the end involved nine more British officers, all "pretty well warmd with liquor . . . who fell upon the [Town] Watch."[17] Abigail, hearing of the altercation with a "good deal of pertubation of Spirits," waited for news from Boston, to "relieve me from my apprehensions." But she noted that the fight had been spontaneous; it did not appear "that there was any premediated design to raise a Tumult."[18]

Nevertheless, such incidents were occurring with greater frequency in Boston and its surrounding villages as more soldiers arrived in Massachusetts. Finding life in the colonies difficult, with meager rations and inadequate housing, the British troops resorted to hanging out in taverns to stay warm and drinking rum to dull hunger; drunken brawls between soldiers and colonists was the all-too-common result.

"Thus are we to be in continual hazard and Jeopardy of our lives from a Set of dissolute unprincipald officers," Abigail complained to Mercy; "subjected to "an Ignorant abandoned Soldiery who are made to believe that their Errant here is to Quell a Lawless Set of Rebels." She added at the end, "who can think of it without the utmost indignation."[19]

Dolly Quincy, her sister Katy, and her father, Edmund, remained in Boston but spent as much time as possible in the Hancock mansion with Aunt Lydia, feeling secure on Beacon Hill. Even the rumors of John Hancock's imminent arrest didn't alarm them. As James Lovell had written in a letter to Josiah Quincy Jr., the feeling among the patriots of Boston was that despite his early and harsh restrictions in the port, Governor Gage was turning out to be a reasonable man: "we know [his] Conduct has fallen vastly short of the bloody expectations of those Villains who surround him."[20]

After all, Gage had court-martialed the British soldiers who attacked the town watch in January. He had started to allow the movement of certain goods into harbor waters. And as a man seasoned by brutal war (having served in battles in the Netherlands and Scotland, and also in the Seven Years' War in America, alongside a young George Washington), he was loathe to start another one. He wouldn't seek out the arrest of Hancock or Sam Adams, knowing that such a move would surely spark insurrection throughout the colony.

But then another threat appeared on the streets of Boston. By early March 1775, cases of smallpox were once again being reported, both in private homes and in the barracks; the scourge had also appeared in the surrounding towns of Roxbury, Cambridge, and Mendon. The town selectmen, led by Hancock, imposed quarantines and required that all affected homes be treated by a smoking out of the interiors. Both town leaders and Governor Gage were intent on keeping the number of cases down, in the already miserable town.

In London, Ben Franklin was worried for Josiah Quincy Jr., his young friend. He had been coughing up blood for days and was too weak to leave his rooms even to attend Parliament: "It is a thousand pities his strength of body is not equal to his strength of mind. His zeal . . . will, I fear, eat him up."[21]

Franklin called in a doctor to look after Josiah. Dr. John Fothergill was well known throughout London as an excellent doctor; he was personal physician to Lord Dartmouth and a number of other worthies. He was also a devoted and active friend to America, and as a Quaker, he hoped for a peaceful resolution to the present conflict. He visited Josiah a number of times over the winter and refused payment every time: "I consider this as a public cause to which we must all contribute."[22]

Upon Fothergill's advice, Quincy moved to Islington on the outskirts of London, to stay with his wife's uncle, Thomas Bromfield. He recuperated there, dining on fresh vegetables and hearty broths and taking walks in quiet lanes. As his strength came back, he even ventured out on horseback into the surrounding countryside. "Rode out for the fourth time on horseback, about 12 or 14 miles," he wrote in his journal on February 26. "Evidently better when I am in open air, and the motion of the horse not fatiguing."[23]

He continued to meet with friends and allies, turning increasingly to two American brothers, William and Arthur Lee, and two Englishmen, Joseph Priestley and Richard Price, all of them men whom Franklin considered both too radical and too militant in their ambitions for America. Josiah, however, found their resolve matched his own. Liberty for America was their cause, and they encouraged Josiah in his growing certainty that the only way to achieve liberty was through an absolute independence from England.

And the only way to win independence, Josiah was convinced, was for the colonies to fight as one country, a unified coalition of north and south, farmer and lawyer, fisherman and merchant. Josiah understood that Lord North also saw danger in a union of the colonies, and that was why he would do all he could to divide them, one from the other.

Josiah wanted to get the message to his countrymen to stand strong and stand together. But the mail was less secure than ever, and he'd been warned against conveying anything in writing that might be construed as instructions of rebellion, for then he would be immediately arrested.

Should Josiah himself return to America to deliver the message? Dr. Fothergill and Ben Franklin advised against it, but the Lee brothers and other radicals encouraged him to do it. As Josiah wrote in his journal, "they insist upon my going directly to Boston: they say no letters can go with safety; and that I can deliver more information and advice viva voce, than could or ought to be wrote. They say my going now must be (if I arrive safe) of great advantage to the American Cause."[24]

Only Josiah could reveal the full magnitude of Lord North's plans, and he must do it face-to-face with his colonial compatriots in America.

The March 5 anniversary of the Boston Massacre fell on a Sunday in 1775. Because of the Sabbath, the annual oration would take place the next day. Monday dawned unseasonably warm, and already by early morning, crowds began filling the streets of Boston, as if all those who had remained in town were determined to attend. By midday a large number of people had gathered at the Old South Meeting House, and when the doors opened, they swarmed inside.

Joseph Warren was the chosen orator for the commemoration, and all were eager to hear him. Five years had passed since the bloody clash between troops and townspeople. Now even more Redcoats lived in Boston, walked its streets, and patrolled the ports. Freedoms in politics, trade, and social life once taken for granted now seemed dear. Warren was known as a healer; surely he could bring some hope to Boston after a long winter and with little respite from hardships in sight.

At one end of the Old South Meeting House, by the pulpit, a low platform had been set up. John Hancock took his place there beside other town leaders, nodding to Edmund Quincy, who was seated to the side with a good view of the stage. The crowd was loud, their chatter anxious and eager, as they waited for Warren to arrive. In the house on Beacon Hill, Dolly and Aunt Lydia were also anxious, seated together in the drawing room of Hancock's mansion, waiting for news.

They were right to be anxious. A group of British troops appeared at the door of the Old South Meeting House. More than three dozen in all, they pushed their way in, looking for seats. Sam Adams invited them to sit at the very front, and room was made for them.

One of the men held an egg in his pocket. The plan agreed to by the Redcoats—but unknown to their commander, Governor Gage—was that if Warren were to make any treasonous statement against the king, the egg would be thrown at him, signaling to the other soldiers "to draw swords." A soldier later reported the plot to Thomas Hutchinson in England, adding, "they would have massacred Hancock, Adams, and hundreds more."[25]

But it was not Warren's intent to speak ill of King George. Instead, he wished to appear to all the crowd as a sage, imparting wisdom and advising both courage and restraint. To further the image of sage, when Warren finally arrived, climbing over rows of people to get to the pulpit, he was dressed not in topcoat and breeches but in a toga.

The symbolism was not lost on anyone: Warren was dressed as Cicero, a wise man of ancient Rome. Only citizens of Rome could wear togas; slaves and soldiers were forbidden the honor. Now as wise man and citizen, Warren spoke to his fellow colonists.

"Our country is in danger, but not to be despaired of," he proclaimed.

"Our enemies are numerous and powerful; but we have many friends, determining to be free, and heaven and earth will aid the resolution. On you depend the fortunes of America. You are to decide the important question, on which rest the happiness and liberty of millions yet unborn."[26]

The crowd was rapt, listening to every word, colonists and troops alike.

"Act worthy of yourselves," Warren advised.[27] The egg remained in the pocket of the soldier; the swords of his compatriots, sheathed. The oration proceeded peacefully.

But after Warren's oration ended and Sam Adams rose to speak, the soldiers in the front row grew restive and belligerent. They began to shout and bang their heels. Sam Adams had been denounced by Governor Gage as "flagitious," a villain and a traitor, and they could not allow him to speak.[28]

"Fie! Fie!" they yelled out, trying to drown out Adams' words.

Up in the gallery, the words yelled by the soldiers were heard as "Fire! Fire!" Mayhem broke out. Those seated in the upper galleries flung themselves through windows and landed on the roof, flailing as they spun downward; the crowds below surged to the doors to get out. A regiment of troops passing by on the street and marching to the beat of drums only added to the noise and confusion.

As Edmund related it later to Dolly and Lydia, the mayhem might have turned to murder but for the restraint shown by all. How much longer could such restraint last, Edmund wondered.

Hancock prophesied that it would not last long on either side. Warren had claimed in the crowded hall that "an independence on Great Britain is not our aim. No, our wish is, that Britain and the colonies may, like the oak and the ivy, grow and increase in strength together."[29] But Hancock knew that behind closed doors, away from prying English eyes and ears, Warren, Sam Adams, and now he too, believed that a separation was necessary, lest the English ivy choke the American oak.

To achieve such separation would require an unshackling of all restraint, Hancock believed, and an unbridled bravery concomitant with utter fearlessness: the path to independence would be "through fields of blood."[30] As Warren proclaimed that day in the Old South Meeting House, what glory for all of them if they could achieve a new country, with the "adored goddess Liberty . . . on the American throne. . . . Even the children of your most inveterate enemies . . . [who] in secret curse their stupid, cruel parents, shall join the general voice of gratitude to those who broke the fetters which their fathers forged."[31]

Edmund had nodded at the words. He too believed that in the "present expected contest" there was a God-given "Glorious" plan for a new country to be born: "ye Kingdom of Christ is to be erect, here, in the Western Hemisphere, called yet by some, 'the New World.'"[32] A new world of guaranteed liberties, blessed under God and protected by the people of America—and the Old World left behind once and for all.

26

Ship in a Storm

Heaven grant that a grand constellation
of virtues may shine forth
with redoubled lustre,
and enlighten this gloomy hemisphere!

—JOSIAH QUINCY JR.

On March 4, 1775, Josiah Quincy Jr. boarded a ship in Plymouth, England, bound for America. He went charged with the mission to warn Americans that Britain had no intention to reconcile with the colonies, but instead, as William Lee insisted, "the Ministers, with their leader are violently blowing the coals into a flame, that will lay waste the whole British Empire."[1]

Josiah also carried with him details about secret plans being hatched in England to help the colonists in the fight for their rights. Those plans, treasonous and detailed as they were, were too explosive—and dangerous to creators and sharers alike—to be penned in a letter, or even written about in his journal. The only way to share them was to keep the details memorized and then reveal those details to his fellow patriots in person. Josiah was on his way to America to do just that.

For over a week his ship stayed in the harbor at Plymouth, as late winter storms ravaged the Atlantic, making travel dangerous. Josiah wrote to Thomas Bromfield, whose house in Islington had been his refuge during the worst of his illness, "The sea runs high, and I can scarcely write legibly. . . . My cough is far from better, though in the day-time I am troubled a very trifle with it. . . . I wrote you I had been ill-used and deceived. I discover every day more instances of it. . . . I am perplexed much what I ought to do. The sea runs so high."[2]

Fevers again set in, and Josiah found he was becoming confused and uncertain; it was hard to focus on the tasks at hand. Who had "ill-used" him? Did he feel betrayed by friends in England—or by the enemies to America that he found there? Before arriving in London, he believed that all British citizens were brothers under the skin, and that once he appealed to those in England who had misunderstood the motives and desires of the colonists, all peace and harmony between England and America would be restored. He had been wrong.

His cough worsened as he waited at anchor for the ship to set sail. Dr. Fothergill had warned him against traveling and advised him to rest awhile in a seaside town before attempting the return home. Josiah wondered if he should try to disembark—"I have a thousand minds to go to Bristol"[3]—but then he thought of his secret mission, and he resolved to stay aboard and see the journey through.

All he wanted were the means and fortitude to carry out his plan of "preventing calamity and producing much good to Boston and the Massachusetts Bay, and in the end to all America."[4]

Finally, on March 18, the vessel left Plymouth and began its trip across the sea. Just days later, Ben Franklin would follow his young friend. During Josiah's journey west, the weather on the open ocean turned every day more miserable, the air wet and cold, the waters rough and the wind hard. Josiah had no choice but to remain below deck in the putrid atmosphere of his cabin, growing more ill by the day. He longed to go on deck at night and see the stars overhead, guiding him home, but he hadn't the strength to rise from his bed.

The Massachusetts Provincial Congress moved to Concord for their March meetings; Cambridge was too uncomfortably close to Governor Gage and his increasingly large army. John Hancock, along with Sam Adams, was invited to stay at the parsonage in Lexington, six miles to the east, where he had lived for a brief time as a boy. The bishop of Lexington had died long ago and now the Reverend Jonas Clarke, married to Hancock's cousin Lucy Bowes, lived in the manse.

John Adams had not been invited to participate in this third meeting of the congress, and although it irked him to be left out of the proceedings, he wrote to James Warren, husband of Mercy Otis Warren: "I was much averse to being chosen, and shall continue so, for I am determined, if Things are Settled, to avoid public Life. I have neither Fortune, Leisure, Health nor Genius for it. . . . I cannot help putting my Hand to the Pump, now the Ship is in a storm, and the Hold half full of Water. But as soon as she gets into a Calm and a Place of Safety, I must leave her."[5]

As soon as peace returned to his province, John intended to once again settle down into the private life of a village lawyer and gentleman farmer. He had made duty to his country a priority, but he had to make money again, as he found himself "a Man of desperate Fortune, and a Bankrupt in Business."[6]

But no one in the colony expected a swift return to peace. In Boston, signs were everywhere that Gage was preparing for something big. As the *Massachusetts Spy* reported, "the army in this town seem to be preparing for a matter & considerable number of wagons are made and now ready for their use."[7] Longboats were deployed in the harbor, the kind used to bring troops from ship to shore. Training drills on the Common were intensifying. And newspapers reported everything from the number of hogs being sent from England to feed the troops to warnings of royal seizures of colonists' arms and powder. There was no doubt that Gage intended to engage his troops in some kind of military maneuver—but to what purpose? And where?

Unbeknown to the colonists—and to Josiah Quincy Jr., whose ship they overtook and easily passed—two British warships were crossing the Atlantic. The *Nautilus* and the *Falcon* carried on board arms, ammunition, troops, horses, food supplies, and detailed orders for Governor Gage from Lord Dartmouth. Lord William Howe (younger brother to Lord Richard) was also due to arrive any day aboard the *Cerberus* from Portsmouth, with regiments of horses and additional supplies for the troops stationed in Boston.

Rumors of the ships' arrival began to circulate. Josiah Quincy Sr. kept watch from the monitor atop his roof in Braintree; frustrated and angry, and worried for his colony, he wrote to Ben Franklin, "Are we Bastards, and not Children, that a Prince, who is celebrated as the best of Kings, has given his consent to so many and such unprecedented Oppressive Acts?"

Then he asked, "Who are answerable for all the horrid consequences of a long and bloody civil War?—They, who from Motives of Avarice and Ambition, attack, or They, who from a Principle of Self-preservation, defend?"[8] He wondered where his son Josiah was now, whether he was still seeking negotiations with England alongside Franklin or whether he was on his way home to Massachusetts.

As head of the Committee of Safety, John Hancock ordered six additional companies of Massachusetts artillerymen to be ready to go. Medical supplies, canteens, and other supplies were purchased, "sufficient for an army of fifteen thousand to take the field."[9]

Hancock also ordered that four brass fieldpieces and a pair of mortars currently under Loyalist command in Boston be seized and spirited away before such arms could be turned over to Gage. The two cannons were subsequently named "Adams" and "Hancock" in honor of Sam and John; the one named Adams would explode within weeks, but the Hancock endured through many a battle to come.[10]

Hancock knew what an army needed to get ready for war. He'd learned from his uncle Thomas, who had made a vast fortune outfitting English troops in their various campaigns throughout Canada and New England. Now Hancock would use that knowledge, along with some of his fortune, to make sure his men were properly supplied for war.

With so much of his time taken up by the Committee of Safety, Hancock resigned the presidency of the Provincial Congress to Joseph Warren. He had become, in essence, commander in chief of the Massachusetts militia, charged not only with outfitting the militia and training them but also with calling them out to battle.

But the Provincial Congress did not give Hancock absolute powers to wage war. He was only permitted to call out militiamen if "the Army under Command of General Gage . . . shall march out of the Town of Boston, with Artillery or Baggage." Furthermore, the Massachusetts men were only to fight against such forces "on the defensive so long as it can be justified on the principles of reason and self-preservation."[11]

The Massachusetts representatives did not want to be accused of having started a war, so they made sure their instructions were clear and well known: the militiamen could defend the rights of colonists but were prohibited from mounting an offensive against England.

Even amid the nonstop work of building up and supplying an army, Hancock still found time to write to Dolly. From Concord, Hancock wrote of his regrets at being held there by "Business of utmost importance." He promised to "return as soon as possible."

Writing to her from a room "full of Committee Men," he wrote nevertheless of matters close to his heart: "no Person on Earth can be possess'd of greater affection & regard for anyone, than I have for the Lady to whom I address this, & be fully convinced that no Distance of Time or place can ever Erase the Impressions made & the determinations I have formed of being forever yours, in that Confidence & Expectation I close. . . . My Dear Dolly, Yours forever in every respect."[12]

The letter was signed with his name, the signature large and the flourish below it bold.

John Hancock returned to Boston, but as March turned to April, it became apparent that life in the town was becoming too dangerous for him, and for Dolly and Lydia. In early April, a small band of British soldiers approached the Beacon Hill mansion and began hacking away at the surrounding fences "in a most scandalous manner."[13]

Two days later, they returned and, surveying Hancock's stables, poked around in the grass and hay and knocked on the doors and walls of the building. When Hancock approached them, they told him they were "seeing if his stables would do for barracks."[14] Hancock told them to leave immediately, and they replied that soon enough all the land and the buildings on it would be under their control.

Hancock lodged a formal complaint with Governor Gage, and his fence was promptly repaired and the soldiers disciplined. He nevertheless feared another assault could come at any time and be of much more serious consequence. The repeated calls for his assassination, in flyers posted around town and letters left at his doorstep, were less easy to shrug off now that tensions in the town were so high and the work he was doing so potentially treasonous.

As he wrote to Dolly's father, Edmund, who was considering leaving to go stay with his daughter Sarah in Lancaster, "I am not at liberty to say what I know . . . but pray . . . remove immediately from Boston. . . . Things will very soon be serious."[15]

Aunt Lydia met with Edmund and arranged for Dolly to be evacuated from Boston with her; the two women would travel together to Lexington, where they would stay at the old parsonage while Hancock continued his work with the Provincial Congress. All agreed that the wedding between John and Dolly would take place as soon as possible; Aunt Lydia hoped for June, but John Hancock, apprised daily of the military preparations being mounted by Governor Gage, dared not set a date for fear of tempting fate against them both.

Dolly settled into the Clarke parsonage with little trouble. Lexington reminded her of her hometown, Braintree, and the parsonage was as nice a home as the former Quincy home had been. Thomas Hancock built the parsonage for his father, the bishop of Lexington, in 1738, and it was spacious and airy, with plenty of room for the exiles of Boston currently taking refuge there. Although far inland, and thus with none of the sea views Dolly associated with Braintree, the village's lively green, easily viewed from the front windows of the parsonage, was familiar to her.

She heard from her father; he told her he was still in Boston but promised her that soon both he and Katy would leave, bound for Lancaster. A letter from her cousin Helena Bayard offered a contrary view, that neither Katy nor Edmund seemed in a hurry to leave. As for Helena herself, she had been assured by British officers that she would be well taken care of in Boston; scornful of the promises, she wrote to Dolly, "I am, you will say, wicked, but I wish the small pox would spread" and take all these British away.[16]

Hancock left Boston just in time. On April 16, from his monitor in Braintree, Josiah Quincy Sr. spotted the British warship *Falcon* and then, two days later, the *Nautilus*, arrive in Boston Harbor. Josiah descended the stairs as rapidly as he could and set out for the home of Norton Quincy, the house of the selectman being the first stop in spreading the news to all of Braintree. John Adams, recently reelected to the town meeting and now in charge of encouraging local men to sign up for the militia, would be visited next. Soon the whole town would know. Warships had arrived; could war be far behind?

The *Nautilus* and the *Falcon* carried identical messages for Governor Gage, the orders coming directly from Lord Dartmouth. Gage was to delay no longer in arresting "the principal actors and abettors in the Provincial Congress." Dartmouth also ordered Gage to protect those colonists who were loyal to the Crown; as for those colonists who rose up against the royal government in Massachusetts, "Force should be repelled by Force."

General William Howe arrived within days to help Gage carry out the orders from England. The rebels of Massachusetts were deemed to be in rebellion; pursuant to the Massachusetts Charter, Governor Gage was empowered to use "martial law," and all that such tactics and measures implied, to fight the rebellion.[17]

Gage understood what he was being told to do: to start a war against the rebelling colonists while protecting the Loyalists and preserving the royal government in the colony. He had no desire to start a war but agreed that loyal colonists must be protected, the Provincial Congress must be shut down, and the military stores of the rebels confiscated. The first order of business was to arrest Hancock and Sam Adams and secure the arms and ammunition that had been hidden away by the Massachusetts militia under Hancock's command.

Through a network of spies, Gage learned that he could take care of both tasks with one focused blow. John Hancock and Sam Adams were staying in Lexington, just down the road from a hidden depot of ammunition, cannons, and food supplies in Concord. Gage reasoned that he could take a small but formidable force of troops out to Lexington, capture the rebel leaders, then continue to Concord and capture the supplies. He knew that Hancock had been restricted by the Provincial Congress to call up his militiamen only if Gage was seen marching out of Boston fully geared for battle ("artillery and baggage").[18] Gage decided he would send troops without either and try to disguise the planned military maneuver as a simple training drill.

But the colonial leaders had their spies as well. They realized that Concord's stockpile of arms and supplies would be a target, especially given its proximity to the Provincial Congress meeting place. They quickly transferred most of the weaponry, including cannons and powder, out of its hiding place in Concord and moved it to safekeeping elsewhere.

Colonial lookouts, on duty every minute of the day, reported back to Joseph Warren, still in Boston, news of the first patrol that Gage sent out early on the morning of April 18. The patrol was small but their movements were suspect. Warren sent messages to the Provincial Congress, and to John Hancock in particular: *Be on your guard.*

By the evening of April 18, it was clear that Governor Gage was intending a military operation outside of Boston, most likely to be directed at the Provincial Congress and its leaders, including Hancock. But when such attack would take place was still unclear. As night fell, eight armed men from the Lexington militia were posted outside the parsonage in Lexington, charged with protecting Hancock, Sam Adams, Aunt Lydia, and Dolly, along with the Clarke family. Thirty more Lexington minutemen convened at Buckman's Tavern down the road, preparing to stay up all night in anticipation of whatever might be coming down the road from Boston.

It was just after midnight, the earliest hours of April 19, 1775, when Paul Revere came galloping up the turnpike to Lexington from the direction of Charlestown. The guards posted at the parsonage of Reverend Clarke came forward to greet him as he dismounted from his horse, but they didn't know who he was and were uncertain whether he was enemy or friend.

William Munroe of the Lexington guard took charge, admonishing Revere to keep down the noise or he would wake the people sleeping within.

"Noise!" spluttered Revere. "You'll have noise soon enough before long. The regulars are coming out."[19]

He was right: Redcoats were on the march, eight hundred in all, armed and ready. They'd rowed from Boston to Lechmere's Point in Cambridge in the dead of night, but they'd been spotted by colonial watchmen and Revere had been alerted. One if by land, two if by sea. They came by sea and now were heading to Lexington.

Hancock's head suddenly stuck out of an upper-floor window. "Come in, Revere," he said, adding, in order to set Munroe and the militiamen at ease, "We are not afraid of you."[20] After a few moments, the front door opened and Paul Revere went inside.

27

Lexington and Concord

We are determined that, wheresoever,
whensoever, or howsoever
we shall be to make our exit,
we will die freemen.

—Josiah Quincy Jr.

Dolly would later recount the events of April 19 without much show of emotion—she was very good at both self-effacement and understatement—but from the moment that Paul Revere had come into the parsonage the night before, she had felt the charge in the air all around her: change was coming. When Hancock heard from Revere that British troops were on their way, he "gave the alarm and the Lexington bell was rung all night."[1]

Then, as Dolly looked on, Hancock "was all night cleaning his gun and sword . . . determined to go out to the plain by the meeting house to fight."[2] He told Dolly of his concerns for the men gathering in the rising daylight on the green; he knew they had the heart to fight but worried that they were "but partially provided with arms and those they had were in most miserable order."[3]

Hancock wanted to join the countrymen on the field of battle. If he had his musket, he declared, he would lay waste to the Englishmen now coming over the rise into town.[4] But Sam Adams refused to let him go. Adams reminded Hancock of their duties to the colony; taking up arms against the Redcoats "is not our business. We belong to the Cabinet."[5] Rather than fight, Sam persuaded John that they had to flee Lexington and get to someplace where they would be safe from arrest—or worse. Aunt Lydia and Dolly would stay with Jonas Clarke and his family and join them later when all danger was gone and the coast was clear.

Dolly didn't mind being left behind; she knew she was far safer in the care of a minister than in the company of a rebel wanted for treason. Aunt Lydia was less sanguine about the matter; as Clarke's daughter, Elizabeth, told the story, "Aunt [Lydia was] crying and wringing her hands . . . [while]

Dolly [was] going round with father to hide money, watches, and anything down in the potatoes or up in the garret."[6]

Just after dawn, British troops appeared at the far end of the Lexington green. Dolly could see their uniforms, bright red against the lightening skies behind them. She drew back from the window, suddenly frightened. Huddled close to Clarke's daughter, and with her arm around old Aunt Lydia, Dolly listened intently to the sounds coming from outside. She heard drums, feet shuffling, a rumble of jumbled voices. Then she heard a voice calling out, ordering the militiamen to withdraw: "Lay down your arms, you damned rebels, and disperse."[7]

All was quiet and then a shot rang out. Dolly rushed to look out the window as the fighting began. For how long she stood there, she couldn't say; shouts, drums, musket shots, and cries of pain were the background to gray smoke against a vivid blue sky; black boots on green grass; and wounds that dripped red blood from a torn brown coat.

Dolly stood back as two wounded men were brought into the parsonage. She bent down to see what she could do for them. Suddenly, one of the "British bullets whizzed by old Mrs. Hancock's head as she was looking out the door. 'What is that?' she cried out [and we] told her it was a bullet and she must take care of herself."[8] Rising to her feet, Dolly took Aunt Lydia's arm and led her to a back room, away from the windows and the danger of an errant bullet, away from the sight of the wounded men bleeding on the floor of the parsonage.

In Boston that morning of April 19, John Lovell, schoolmaster of the Boston Latin School in Boston where John Hancock and the Quincy brothers had been students, stood on the steps of his schoolhouse, located on the south side of the Boston Common. From there he had a good view of Lord Percy leading his brigade of a thousand footguards down to Orange Street, which led to the Neck and out of Boston. The rumors circulating since morning were true; he saw the proof himself now as line after line of armed Redcoats marched on their way out of Boston. He returned to the classroom and announced that his students were dismissed and the school was now closed. "War's begun and school's done," he declared, then added in Latin, *"Deponite libros."*[9] Put down your books. Boys grabbed their bags and ran for the doors, and home.

Early in the afternoon of the same day, Abigail Phillips Quincy gathered her son, Josiah, in her arms. For the past two weeks both of her children had been ill. On April 13, little Abigail died and was buried in the Granary Burying Ground, with only a small stone and a fading stand of daffodils to mark her grave. Josiah was feeling better but he was still too weak to walk more than a few steps, so Abigail carried him from the Quincy home on Marlborough Street to her father's house on Beacon Street. A carriage waited for them there, along with Abigail's two sisters, Mary and Hannah.

William Phillips, patriarch of the family, looked tired, but when Abigail insisted that he flee Boston with them, he shook his head. Patriots like him and Joseph Warren had to stay in town as long as possible, to protect those Bostonians who had neither the means nor the will to leave their hometown. He would join them in Connecticut as soon as he could, he promised. Abigail's brother, William Phillips Jr., was already in Norwich, waiting for his sisters. The family would be safe there.

The carriage made its way through the crowded streets to the Boston Neck. There they were stopped by a sentry of British troops. As Josiah Quincy III remembered it many years later—it was his first memory, that of a child just three years old—everyone in the carriage was "made to descend and enter the sentry-box successively. On each side of the box was a small platform, round which each of [us] . . . was compelled to walk, and remain until our clothes were thoroughly fumigated with the fumes of brimstone cast upon a body of coals in the centre of the box." With smallpox loose in Boston, "This operation was required to prevent infection."[10]

Thoroughly fumigated, the party was allowed to travel on, to leave Boston and get as far away in one day's travel as they could. In a few days they would be in Norwich, settled in the large and stately childhood home of Benedict Arnold.[11] William Phillips promised Abigail he would send any letters from Josiah Jr. as soon as they arrived; she in turn promised to let Josiah Sr. know where she had gone with his grandchild. He would understand why she had left Boston: she had to keep what remained of his family safe for her husband, Josiah.

But where was her husband? Was he still in London, she wondered, or was he finally on his way home to her?

The British soldiers who stumbled back into Boston late in the afternoon of April 19 were exhausted and disheartened by the day's battles. Almost half of Gage's troops had been either injured or killed. The whole day had been a terrible awakening as to the capabilities of the Americans. Thousands upon thousands of colonists had shown up to fight, and they appeared to be disciplined, determined, and fearless. As reported by Lord Percy, "The

Rebels attacked us in a very scattered, irregular manner, but with persever-ance & resolution. . . . Whoever looks upon them as an irregular mob, will find himself much mistaken."[12]

The next morning, the troops and their commanders woke up to find that the Cambridge coastline facing Boston was lined with over fifteen thou-sand American militiamen. They had come from all over Massachusetts, as well as Rhode Island, Connecticut, New Hampshire, and Maine. Struggling to get past the crowds of militiamen were streams of Loyalists, eager to get away from the mainland and into Boston; on the other side of the Boston Neck, Bostonian rebels lined up to leave the town, fearful of what the British troops might do to anyone who failed to vow allegiance to the king.

Meeting with the remaining selectmen of Boston, Gage worked out an arrangement whereby anyone seeking to leave Boston would be allowed to do so, as long as they carried no weapons or ammunition on their person or in their baggage. Loyalists who wished to enter Boston were allowed in; they settled in homes abandoned by departing rebels and hoped for the best. The siege of Boston had begun.

Who had fired the shot that started the battle at Lexington? No one could be sure, but both sides were quick to blame the other. Edmund Quincy, who had been nowhere near the scene, was nevertheless certain the shot had come from "a Number of Tory villains, some Irish and some others . . . [hid-ing] in a blind" who had fired upon the Americans as they were retreating; he condemned such "unheard of Villainy and Baseness!"[13]

John Adams was determined to saddle up his horse and ride to Lexing-ton to see for himself what had happened there. Every day more and more refugees from Boston passed through Braintree, seeking shelter, food, and some direction as to where they should go now. They brought with them such a variety of reports of the battles of April 19 that John couldn't make sense of what had happened. When Abigail asked, he agreed that she should open their home to refugees they knew. Then he rode away, leaving his wife alone at the doorway.

Over the coming days, Abigail Adams would take in a number of friends and family; Josiah Quincy Sr. was forced three times to evacuate his mansion overlooking the sea when British man-of-war ships came close to his shore-line, frightening the entire family and sending them running for safety.

In the coming weeks, Abigail would also take in strangers; her home was open to anyone fleeing the British and their horrors. "What a scene has opened upon us . . . a scene as we never before Experienced. . . . If we look back we are amazed at what is past, if we look forward we must shudder at the view," Abigail wrote in a letter to Mercy Otis Warren in early May; "O Britain Britain how is thy glory vanished—how are thy Annals stained with the Blood of thy children."[14]

The Provincial Congress met on April 20 and ordered that depositions be taken from as many witnesses as possible as to the day's events. The depositions were then collected in a pamphlet and also printed in the *Essex Gazette*.[15] The newspaper account and the depositions were sent to England on the *Quero*, the fastest ship the colonists could find, in order to ensure that the Americans' version of events would be the first news Englishmen received of the battle.

In the summary of the depositions provided, the Provincial Congress asserted that while "The inhabitants of Lexington and the other towns were about one hundred, some with and some without fire arms . . . [and were] far from being disposed to commit hostilities against the troops of their sovereign," the British troops, "seeming to thirst for BLOOD, wantonly rushed on, and first began the hostile scene by firing on this small party, in which they killed eight men on the spot and wounded several others before any guns were fired upon the troops by our men."[16]

The *Quero* would reach England by the end of May. Within days, the account prepared by the Provincial Congress was printed in newspapers; when the British version of events finally arrived two weeks later, the horrors and losses of the battles were the same as those recounted by the Americans. As Thomas Hutchinson wrote in his diary after reading both accounts, "The material difference is the declaration by . . . the commander . . . that the inhabitants fired first."[17] The answer to the question of who fired first would, in the end, remain unknown.

On the night following the Battles of Lexington and Concord, John Hancock and Sam Adams were on the run for hours before finally finding refuge in Billerica, a small village north of Concord, on a small farm owned by Amos Wyman. Wyman was a patriot, and his isolated homestead, surrounded by dense woods and with only one narrow path winding its way in, was the perfect hiding place. Word was sent to Dolly and Aunt Lydia, still in Lexington. The gilded Hancock carriage, its woodwork now sullied with dust and its wheels muddied, brought the women to the farm as first sunlight broke through the trees.

Dolly was sick with worry for her father and sister, and insisted that she be allowed to take the carriage and return to Boston for them. But John Hancock wouldn't hear of it; as his known fiancée, the British might use Dolly as bait to make Hancock return to Boston, where he would be arrested and most certainly executed. He'd heard the ballad sung outside his windows in Boston and knew that with the first shots of war having been fired, the Redcoats would not hesitate to kill him; "As for their King, that John Hancock, / And Adams, if they're taken, / Their heads for signs shall hang up high, / Upon the hill called Beacon!"[18]

"No, madam," he told her, "you shall not return as long as there is a British bayonet left in Boston."

Dolly, scared for her family and exhausted after twenty-four hours of alternating hell and tedium while she waited for word from Hancock, lashed out.

"Recollect, Mr. Hancock, I am not under your authority yet. I shall go to my father's tomorrow!"[19]

But in the end, as more reports reached the farmhouse in Billerica of the mayhem around Boston, Dolly agreed to travel with John and the others to Worcester. She could only pray that her father had left Boston in time; Hancock promised messages would be sent in an effort to find out. They remained for a few days in Worcester, while John and Sam waited for the arrival of the other Massachusetts delegates to the Second Continental Congress, due to meet in Philadelphia in June.

From Worcester, Hancock wrote a letter to the Provincial Congress meeting again in Watertown, asking for news—"I beg to hear from you. . . . Are our men in good spirits? For God's sake do not suffer the spirit to subside"—and hoping that Boston had not been burned to the ground by the British: "Boston must be entered; the troops must be sent away . . . our country must be saved."[20]

Hancock also asked about the other delegates: Where were they? Cushing, Paine, John Adams—he needed all the delegates together for the long trip to Philadelphia so that they would have time to plan for the future: the future of their colony, now engaged in war, and the future of their country.

Hancock and Adams couldn't wait any longer for the other delegates; it was just too dangerous to remain in Massachusetts, with the price on their heads getting higher by the hour. They decided to move on to Hartford in Connecticut and wait there for the other delegates before going on to Philadelphia. Aunt Lydia and Dolly would go to Fairfield, Connecticut, and find refuge in the home of Thaddeus Burr, a wealthy patriot, sheriff of Fairfield

County, and friend to John Hancock. Lydia no longer thought of a June wedding; the nuptials could wait.

Abigail Phillips Quincy arrived safely in Norwich, as did little Josiah and Abigail's two sisters. Josiah had passed the journey in his mother's lap, his fever of the past weeks returning during the long flight to safety. It continued unabated for days. Abigail worried for her son, and thought of her daughter. Forty-nine Americans had been killed during the Battles of Lexington and Concord, and seventy-three British. She prayed her son, Josiah, would not become yet another victim of the growing conflict between England and America, joining the men laid dead by musket shot, blunderbuss, and bayonet.

And what of her husband? She'd received no word from him for weeks.

John Adams rode his horse slowly along the road that led from Lexington to Concord. It was a battlefield that he rode through under damp and heavy skies, a descent into a hellish world of grays and browns, pounded dirt mixed with blood, rotting carcasses of horses, and torn garments, bloodied and burnt with powder, remnants of the injured and the dead. The edging of bright green spring grass seemed cruel in its taunting promise of life when everywhere around him were signs of death.

He spoke to men and women he met on the way, who told him they had fought against terrible odds: "if We did not defend ourselves they would kill Us." John became convinced that "the Die was cast, the Rubicon passed," and a civil war had begun.[21]

As he wrote later, "The Battle of Lexington on the 19 of April, changed the instruments of warfare from the pen to the sword."[22] He would never again write as Novangelus; but would he fight? He had a role to play, but not on the battlefield. John turned his horse around and returned to Braintree, feeling sick to his stomach all the way, with all that he had seen and heard.

He arrived at home "seized with a fever, attended with allarming Symptoms." But there was no time to convalesce; he was "determined to go" to the Continental Congress in Philadelphia; there was so much now for him to do there.[23]

Abigail worried for him; as she wrote to him later, "I feared much for your health, when you went away." But she understood "the Duty you owe your Country," and it was that consideration—their country—that "prevaild with me to consent to your departure." She would be left home alone, again, and "in a time so perilous and so hazardous to your family," but what was to happen at Philadelphia was too important for John to miss.[24]

For John too, it was that consideration of what he owed his colony that drove him on, first to Hartford to meet up with John Hancock and Sam Adams, and then on to Philadelphia. He was heartened to find that his fellow delegates were also in favor of pursuing an aggressive agenda to protect their colony: creation of a strong army, formalizing the union of the colonies, and forcing Governor Gage to withdraw his cannons from the perimeter of Boston.

While there would be no talk of independence yet, the idea was already percolating in the minds of the New Englanders. Blood had been drawn of their own brethren; reconciliation with the perpetrators seemed a violation of the duty they owed to their threatened, and hurting, colony.

The ship carrying Josiah Quincy Jr. from England arrived in Gloucester Harbor on April 26 (three days before the *Quero* left for England to deliver news of the Battles of Lexington and Concord). Josiah was too ill to disembark, or even be carried to land. He died on board that evening, without learning of the battles or about the death of his infant daughter.

Five days earlier he had dictated his last words to a sailor, who recorded them dutifully as best he could. Josiah was already hovering toward death then, vacillating between consciousness and delirium. But the sailor was patient and sat beside Josiah for hours, taking down what Josiah whispered to him word by word, and then waiting through periods of silence until Josiah was ready to speak again. For his vigilance at the side of the dying man, Josiah's family would always be grateful.

Josiah's final sentence was for his wife: "my most Dear and Beloved wife will Consent to her being Laid by me at her Death . . . for it is the last Desire of a Dying Man the Last Request [of] that Expiring Husband that she may Lay by my side at her Death."[25]

And what of Josiah's secret messages, to be entrusted only to certain trusted patriots? The sailor copied down Josiah's words stating that his intention had been "Immediately upon my Arrival to Assemble Certain Persons to whom I was to Communicate my trust." But the passage to America proved both too rough—"Most Inclement and Damp"—and too long: "Had Providence been pleased that I should reach America Six days ago I should have been able to converse with my friends." Josiah resigned himself to his fate: "This Voyage and Passage [have] put an End to my Being. His Holy

Will be done."[26] There would be no final messages for the patriots. The knowledge that he brought home from England—information of "Extreme Urgency"—died with him, never to be shared.[27]

The selectmen of Gloucester sent messages to Braintree and Boston, in an effort to contact Josiah's father and wife. But no response came, and after a few days, Josiah was buried in the public burial ground at Gloucester. When Abigail finally arrived in the port town, having traveled from Connecticut with her sister Mary, all that remained for her were Josiah's trunks and a thick envelope.

The trunks were filled with his clothes and books, his journals, and inside a round box, the rings he had made in England for her and for his father; the ring for Abigail was set with diamonds, and the one for Josiah Sr. was engraved with the image of the woman Liberty leaning against the urn of disease, a dagger at her feet. Above the urn was a circle, symbolizing immortality. Inside the ring was inscribed the motto, *Oh, save my country!*

The thick envelope was handed over to Abigail. Inside she found ribbon-tied bands of golden red curls, shorn from her husband's head before he was buried. His hair was so similar to that of his son, Josiah III. The boy had recovered from his fever and was doing well in Norwich. Abigail's eyes closed: her son would never see his father again.

Abigail hoped to meet the sailor who had sat beside her husband for all those long hours, but he had gone again to sea. One more item was handed over to Abigail: the parchment paper on which the sailor had written Josiah's final words. Abigail took the paper, the packed trunks, and the envelope of hair and began her journey back to Norwich.

28

Clouds over Boston

I have no reason to doubt the zeal
of my fellow countrymen in the cause of freedom,
and their firmness in its defense.

—Samuel Quincy

Abigail Adams opened her door in Braintree to find Abigail Phillips Quincy on her doorstep, her sister Mary at her side. Abigail Quincy appeared wan and shrunken; her eyes were bloodshot and underscored by dark shadows. Mrs. Adams drew Mrs. Quincy to her as tenderly as if the woman were her own child and brought her inside. The rumors were true: Josiah Quincy Jr. was dead.

John had written from Hartford that he had heard news of Josiah's death: "a Man came in and inform'd us. . . . Proh Dolor!"[1] *Alas, what grief.* He added, "I am wounded to the Heart." After Mrs. Quincy's appearance on her doorstep, Abigail wrote back to John, confirming the news. Her letter was punctuated by grief: "Mr. Quincys Death . . . a most melancholy Event . . . his distressed widow. . . . Poor afflicted woman, my heart was wounded for her."[2]

Letters of condolence began to arrive for the Quincy family, for "the disappointed father, the weeping sister, and the still more afflicted wife."[3] The loss of such "a warm, unshaken friend" was felt from South Carolina all the way to Massachusetts and farther abroad to England; and the realization of what such a loss meant was shared: "America [is] Deprived of his assistance when . . . had his life been spared, he might have rendered his country very eminent service."[4]

Letters addressed to Josiah himself continued to arrive, a crushing reminder of how dependent so many had become on his counsel—and now he was gone. A letter from William Lee from London was especially hard for the widow Abigail to read, for Lee had written to Josiah with such expectations of joy: "I hope the sea air, and exercise will restore you to a perfect state of health and that you will have a happy meeting with your family."[5]

Edmund Quincy finally left Boston on April 30, stopping overnight in Cambridge to stay with his daughter Esther and her husband. Jonathan and Esther were in the midst of packing up their remaining belongings to move to Boston, the only place where such a prominent Loyalist as Jonathan could feel safe. Edmund kept his opinion to himself but both Jonathan and Esther knew of his pro-colonial leanings.

Edmund wrote later to his son Henry of his sadness in missing Dolly before she left Massachusetts and ventured on to "Fayrefield" under the protection of John Hancock and his aunt Lydia; "I don't expect to see her until peacable times are restored."[6] What he couldn't have known then was that he would never see Esther again; ignorant of what the future held, he offered Esther only a simple farewell before traveling with Katy to the home of his daughter Sarah in Lancaster.

As the Massachusetts delegation traveled south to Philadelphia, everywhere they went they were met with an outpouring of colonial support, approbation, and adulation. In New York, as John Hancock described in a letter to Dolly, "we were Met by the Grenadier Company and the Regiment of the City Militia under Arms, Gentlemen in Carriages and on Horseback, and many Thousands of Persons on Foot, the Roads fill'd with people."[7]

John Adams wrote to Abigail that it "would take many Sheets of Paper, to give you a Description of the Reception, We found here [in New York City]. The Militia were all in Arms, and almost the whole City out to Meet us. . . . Our Prospect of a Union of the Colonies, is promising indeed."[8]

The support and spirit continued as they traveled farther south, and when they arrived in Philadelphia, all the city bells rang out in welcome. Coming out from their homes and businesses, people swarmed the streets to greet the Massachusetts delegates.

John hoped the fervency of the crowds would be reflected in the makeup of the congressional delegates themselves, and that progress could be made toward establishing a union of the colonies that would be both lasting and effective; but his hope was tinged with anxiety: "I feel anxious, because, there is always more Smoke than Fire—more Noise than Musick."[9]

Perhaps his apprehensions were tied to his health. Neither John Adams nor John Hancock felt physically well; Hancock was once again suffering from gout, and his "Face and Eyes are in a most shocking situation, burnt up and much swell'd and a little painfull."[10] And John Adams, sick when he left Braintree, continued to complain of "miserable health and blind eyes," and feeling "not well," "quite infirm," and "weak in health."[11]

Fortunately, due to the grave events preceding the Second Continental Congress, the opulent meals and nightly socializing of the First Continental Congress were not repeated. The delegates still met—all fifty-six of them— every Saturday evening for a meal, but the seven-course dinners that ended with toasts and rich desserts were a thing of the past. Food was dear, money was tight, and a budding nation demanded the delegates' full—and sober— attention. Now meeting two blocks up on Chestnut Street, in the State House, the work at hand was as demanding and fractious as the meetings of the First Continental Congress had been.

Despite their physical ailments, the two Johns, raised on the same sermons of community obligation and self-sacrifice, soldiered on; they both understood it was their duty to "keep about and attend Congress very constantly," as John wrote to Abigail.[12] Both Hancock and Adams played leadership roles, with Hancock assuming the very public responsibility of president of the Congress (pending the convalescence of Virginia delegate Peyton Randolph, who previously held the position), while Adams managed things behind the scenes, cajoling, calculating, and threatening, to get things moving along.

Georgia had finally sent one delegate to Philadelphia, Dr. Lyman Hall from the Parish of St. John's. Hall came on his own, covering over eight hundred miles on horseback, determined to represent his county, if not his entire colony, in the Congress.

Hall was originally from Connecticut, and his first wife was Abigail Burr, sister of Thaddeus Burr of Fairfield, with whom Dolly and Lydia were now staying. He was a friend to New England, just when the Massachusetts delegates needed friends in Congress. Some of the other delegates were distancing themselves from the men from Massachusetts, whom they considered too radical; at the same time, there was growing support for John Dickinson from Pennsylvania and James Duane from New York, who both favored a reconciliation with Great Britain.

Although there seemed to be agreement about establishing a continental army and also creating a working union of colonial governments, there was no agreement in Congress as to how hard a line such a union should hold against Parliament and the Crown. The two Adams, Sam and John, were viewed as radicals for pushing offensive action against Gage's fortification of Boston.

John Hancock, on the other hand, was considered a moderate, because instead of voicing strong opinions in Congress, he felt it was his duty as president to manage disparate viewpoints, temperaments, and desires. As the weeks went by, Sam Adams, and even John Adams, began to doubt that Hancock would carry out the agenda agreed upon by the Massachusetts delegation—but there was no denying that Hancock was very good at getting everyone to the table to at least discuss the New England initiatives.

Once at the table, however, the "wasting, exhausting Debates of the Congress" could go on for days; as John Adams lamented, "Oh, that I was a soldier!"[13] Going to battle seemed easier to him than participating in Congress. He was finding it difficult—and tiring—to be a politician, a tactician, a coaxer, and at times even a bully, in trying to get things done.

The heat and humidity of a Philadelphia summer arrived early, with temperatures in May already reaching July highs. Tempers at the Congress grew short and energies flagged, slowing down the Massachusetts agenda even more; "Our Debates and Deliberations are tedious. . . . Our Determinations very slow," John wrote to Abigail.[14]

Not a breath of air came in through the opened windows of the State House, and when the delegates went outside, heat rose in damp mists off the cobblestones. Even in the shade of trees, men broiled in their breeches, jackets, and wigs. Requests were made to move Congress to a meeting place farther north; Hartford in Connecticut was suggested.

But the delegates remained in Philadelphia, sweaty and grim, and with, as John Adams described it, "an amazing Field of Business, before us." If only he could push resolution of the "Business" toward his goals of unified resistance to Britain.[15]

Aaron Burr arrived in Fairfield in the middle of May to pay a visit to his cousin Thaddeus; he had traveled from Litchfield, Connecticut, where he was studying law under the guidance of Tapping Reeve. Thaddeus Burr wrote to Reeve about the effect of having such a handsome, charming, and young man under his roof: "Mrs. Hancock [Lydia] is vastly pleased with him. And, as to Miss Quincy, if Mr. H. were out of the way I don't know but she would court him."[16]

Dolly found Aaron fascinating, and according to a friend of Dolly, "he was much charmed with Miss Quincy."[17] Summer was settling in and the pair found themselves spending the lengthening days together. Eyebrows were raised, along with concerns. In the end, Aunt Lydia had to step in: "Madame Hancock kept a jealous eye on them both and would not allow any advances . . . toward the prize reserved for her nephew."[18]

The careful aunt might also have written to John, urging him to set the date for the marriage and make Miss Quincy a married woman. Perhaps under Lydia's prodding, Thaddeus Burr ushered his cousin along, urging him on his way. By mid-June, Aaron Burr was gone.

All this time John was writing to Dolly and sending her gifts from the elegant shops of Philadelphia: silk stockings, satin shoes, a hat, a cloak, caps, a fan. He asked for nothing in return but a letter: "I have asked a million questions and [received] not an answer to one. . . . I really take it extremely unkind. . . . I beg my dear Dolly, you will write me often and long letters. I will forgive the past if you will mend in the future." And just one more thing: he asked that she make for him "a watch string . . . I want something of your doing."[19]

Her words to ease his heart and her handiwork to hold fast his watch— Dolly felt the justice of his requests, and perhaps a bit of guilt for her dalliance with Burr. She wrote to John and sent him a watch string she had made out of scarlet- and gold-colored ribbons. But the letter she penned was not long enough for John and he wrote back to her: "I dearly love you should be particular, pray write me one long Letter, fill the whole paper, you can do it if you only set about it." He signed, as he always did, "Yours forever."[20]

Aunt Lydia, intent on making their union fixed, still hoped for a summer wedding. But so much stood in the way: the workings of Congress; Governor Gage and his troops; and the uncertain future of Massachusetts, its villages under threat and Boston under siege. She prayed that peace and normalcy could return, if only long enough to allow her John to marry his Dolly.

On May 21, 1775, Abigail Adams woke to the ringing of church bells and the beating of drums. Tumbling down the stairs, she heard shouts and screaming, and then the firing of guns. Abigail recognized the signal of the alarm shots. Braintree was under attack—or was it Weymouth from whence came the ringing of the bells? Were her parents in danger?

Abigail ran to the front door of the farmhouse and looked toward the sea. She saw neither ships on the coast nor British soldiers marching up the Plymouth road. She sent Isaac, one of her tenant farmers, to the village green for news. He brought back the news, and just moments later, a message arrived from her mother: "3 Sloops and one cutter had come out, and dropped anchor just below Great Hill. It was difficult to tell their design, some supposed they were coming to Germantown others to Weymouth." The Smiths were all in "great distress" and her aunt Tufts had become hysterical; she "had her Bed thrown into a cart, into which she got herself, and orderd the boy to drive her off to Bridgwater which he did."[21]

The alarm, which "flew like lightning," brought militiamen from all around Braintree, including one company led by Elihu Adams, brother of John. Elihu met his men on the training field beside the old burying ground and then marched south to Weymouth.

As they walked along the coast, they could see the British troops, going from their sloops to the shores of Grape Island off Weymouth. The small island was owned by a local Loyalist, Elisha Leavitt, who used it for storing forage for cattle and horses. It was clear what the British were up to: they needed food for their horses.

Meeting up with the Weymouth militia, the colonists now numbered close to two thousand. They broke up into groups and spread out along the Weymouth shoreline; at the signal, they began to fire at the British, who had landed on the island and were dragging large bales of hay down to the edge of the water to load onto their boats. The British returned fire, but the distance between the island and the shoreline was too far for either side to make contact. Nevertheless, the exchange of shots drove the British back to their boats and kept them from returning to the low barn filled with dried grasses and the rows upon rows of hay stacked outside.

A slew of Braintree men finally loaded onto a boat, and while the others kept firing at the British, they landed on the far side of Grape Island. They shimmied through the grass and bushes and set fire to the rows of piled forage. The fire burned through the bales of dried herds-grass and clover; then the barn caught fire. It burned for hours, until only a shell of charred wood remained. The British returned to Boston with only a meager supply of hay for their horses, and the men of Braintree and Weymouth called it a victory for their side.

Abigail rejoiced in their success but feared more attacks from the British were on the way: "We know not what a day will bring forth, nor what distress one hour may throw us into."

A steady stream of people continued to arrive at the farmhouse, so close to the Plymouth road that led south out of Boston. Colonial soldiers came for "lodging, for Breakfast, for Supper, for Drink," along with scores of "refugees from Boston tired and fatigued," seeking shelter "for a Day or Night, week." She wrote to John, "you can hardly imagine how we live" and prayed that she could maintain both her "calmness and presence of Mind," while chaos seemed always at the door.[22]

Not only chaos but hunger: Abigail feared that another dry summer was on its way, as no rain had fallen for weeks. If her early crops failed, there would be less to eat, and less to sell or barter. Her tenant farmers paid her little respect, and she feared they might abandon their parcels, leaving her to farm the fields on her own. The farm, the children, the tide of refugees seeking food and shelter: it was all too much. She begged John to write to her. Was there any good news to bring her solace, fortify her reserves? "I have not heard one Syllable from Providence since I wrote you last. I wait to hear from you."[23]

As difficult as life was in Braintree, life in Boston was even harder. Abigail heard the stories from those fleeing the city and wrote to John that the "Distresses of the inhabitants of Boston are beyond the power of language to describe."[24] In addition to the growing scourge of smallpox, municipal services were nonexistent: the streets were filled with filth; grass grew wild and tall between buildings, while the previously lovely Common had become a dusty, pock-ridden pit; public and private buildings were falling into disrepair.

The firing of arms could be heard all day long. There were skirmishes between British troops, lighting on islands like Hog Island and Noddle Island in search of supplies of food and forage, and the colonists who defended the islands and their resources from ravenous Brits. And the British Army carried out drills to the beat of drums throughout the day. Accompanying the sound of drums and gunfire were the church bells, which rang with regularity to mark yet another death in the town. Only at night, with the curfew imposed by Gage's martial law, was there silence.

Worse than the crumbling conditions or pervasive noise was the constant spectre of hunger. Farmers feared approaching the city and no longer sent supplies of eggs, vegetables, and meat; as one British soldier wrote home, "with no market, the inhabitants are starving."[25] The British themselves weren't faring much better, suffering from scurvy, malnutrition, and a rising sense of futility.

Jonathan Sewall somehow remained optimistic. He and Esther had settled with their children in a large and "convenient house . . . with a garden . . . [and all were] in good health and spirits."[26] With his wealth, he was able to secure foodstuffs enough; the garden could be cultivated, if necessary.

Sewall managed to ignore the fact that his family was captive in Boston. But Esther could not forget that her father and siblings were outside the fortifications surrounding Boston; inside those walls she was lonely, with little social life to be enjoyed, no evening parties or afternoon teas. The children were home all the time, with no schools in session and nowhere to go in Boston for an outing or fresh air.

The days passed, and while Jonathan admitted that in fact their confinement in town had been "a long, dark, stormy night," his optimism persevered; by early June he was insisting that he could "see daylight . . . I begin to hope the storm has almost spent itself."[27] He was sure that soon things would return to normal.

Other Loyalists were not so sure. They were leaving Boston for Canada or England by the boatload. John Rowe recorded in his journal weekly departures of men he had known for years but now would never see again: "I sincerely wish their prosperity and happiness."[28]

The British occupation drove Samuel Quincy to make a fateful decision; he would leave Boston to go to England on his own, while his wife, Hannah, and their three children went to Cambridge to live with her brother, Henry Hill, and his wife, Amelia. Sam wrote in a letter to Henry Hill that his journey was "to hazard the unstable element . . . to change the scene. Whether it will be prosperous or adverse is not for me to determine. I pray to God . . . that my deportment may be guided by that Wisdom, 'whose Ways are Ways of Pleasantness, and all her paths, Peace.'"[29]

He promised that "if I cannot Save my country, which I shall endeavor to the utmost of my Power, I will never betray it."[30] What was his meaning? Was Sam finally choosing a side—or was his goal to promote peace between the colonies and England, no matter the cost?

His brother had failed to secure peace for the colonies while in England; Samuel perhaps thought that he would not fail, that he would be able to get through to the English leaders and barter some kind of reconciliation: "There never was a time when sincerity and affectionate Unity of Heart could be more necessary than at present . . . in the midst of the Confusion that darkens our native Land, we may . . . by a rectitude of Conduct, entertain a rational hope, that the Almighty Governor of the Universe, will in his own time, Remember Mercy."[31] And the king of England might too be merciful—if approached the right way. Samuel intended to try.

Hannah Quincy Lincoln wrote to her brother from Braintree, furious with Sam for what she saw as an abandonment of family and country. "You are my only brother . . . our two departed brothers died upon the seas; you will perhaps say your body is sound, it may be so, but [you are] sick in mind."

Extolling the virtues of her two dead brothers, both with hearts "inflamed with patriot zeal," she scorned Samuel for leaving Boston; "Let it not be told in America, and let it not be published in Great Britain, that a brother of such brothers fled from his country . . . to enlist as a sycophant under an obnoxious Hutchinson."[32]

She saw no possibility of success in any alleged petition for peace from North and prophesied that Sam's entreaties would be "blown aside with a cool, 'tomorrow Sir.'" She urged Samuel to stay home, seeking no greatness in politics but instead "greatness of soul."

There was no country better than America, she counseled—"a land flowing with milk and honey; and in which as yet iniquity of all kinds is punished and its Religion as yet free from Idolatry." Hannah feared that Samuel would become lost in England, a victim to its labyrinths of corruption, greed, and evil: "Can you take fire into your boson, and not be burned?"[33]

But even as Hannah wrote her lengthy, beseeching letter, she knew her brother would go. Her heart ached at the thought of yet another leave-taking in the family, another ending she could not attend to. Her mother's grave in Boston, behind enemy lines. Her brother Josiah's grave in Gloucester, more than a day's ride away. Her brother Edmund, buried at sea. And now Samuel leaving, and she would not be able to visit him in Boston before he left; perhaps she would never see him again. "I take a long farewell," Hannah wrote at the end of her letter; "and wish you success in every laudable undertaking."[34]

Leaving his family "wounded me to the heart,"[35] Samuel wrote to Henry Hill. Maybe he would never win the approbation of his father, always reserved for his older brother, Ned, and the youngest, Josiah. Maybe Hannah was right, that his business as "a seeker" in England would come to nothing.[36] But he would do his best to serve America with integrity, determination, and with "love of my country . . . to use my best endeavors to bring about a reconciliation."[37]

At the end of May, Samuel boarded a ship bound for England, sure that he would be back in Boston by the fall. But he never set foot in America again.

Governor Gage offered an amnesty to all the colonists of Massachusetts: "a pardon to all persons who shall forthwith lay down their arms and return to their duties as peaceable subjects." Only two men in all the colony were to be exempted from the offer of amnesty: Sam Adams and John Hancock, "whose offenses are too flagitious a Nature to admit of any other Consideration than that of condign Punishment."[38]

Hancock received the news in Philadelphia within a few days, a messenger from Boston having brought the announcement to him, along with updates on the outfitting of militia (thousands of men now camped out in Cambridge); and the ongoing fortifications of Boston being undertaken by Gage (including a battery of cannons on top of Copp's Hill, overlooking the Charles River and Charlestown). Hancock made his reports to the other delegates, updating them on news received but passing over his ineligibility for amnesty without a thought; he'd been on Britain's hit list for so long, it no longer mattered to him.

The ongoing debates at Congress took all his energies now, as divisions solidified between those who wanted to send a so-called Olive Branch Petition to the king, and those, including John Adams, who absolutely opposed such a gesture. The First Continental Congress had tried a petition to the king and it had failed. To pursue another petition was, in Adams' opinion, a "Measure of Imbecility" that was taking up an inordinate amount of time in debates, motions, and committees, while "In the Meantime the New England Army . . . were left, without Munitions of War, without Arms, Cloathing, Pay or even Countenance and Encouragement."[39]

John Adams was right. Powder, arms, food, and uniforms were all in short supply in Massachusetts; and the soldiers' unmet needs were leading to falling morale and disorder in the ranks. A commander was needed to reestablish order, funds were needed to pay for supplies, and moral support from Congress, displayed through messages and resolutions, was also needed if the disjointed groups of militias from all over New England were to be turned into a united army.

On June 17, 1775, Abigail Adams was shaken awake by her son, John. She sat up in bed and heard cannons firing, louder than anything she had ever heard before. Dressing quickly, she and John scurried outdoors, following other neighbors to nearby Penn's Hill. From there, they could see all the way to Boston. What they saw horrified them.

Colonial forces on Breed's Hill in Charlestown, who had built a fortification overnight, were being bombarded by British cannon fire. The fighting continued as the day wore on; suddenly all of Charlestown was on fire, the flames lighting up Bunker Hill, Breed's Hill, and the entire peninsula. Then everything was covered in smoke, billowing clouds of it, and the people gathered on Penn's Hill in Braintree could see nothing at all.

As a grown man, John Quincy Adams would always remember the terror he felt standing beside his mother and watching as Charlestown burned and clouds of smoke rose up. What would come out of that horrible morass of fire and smoke? He was sure that British troops were on their way to Braintree, "to butcher them in cold blood."[40] The next day, his mother told him the terrible news: Dr. Joseph Warren, their close friend and family doctor, was dead. He'd been killed on Breed's Hill, one of the last Americans to retreat from his position fighting the British forces, run through by a bayonet and left to die.

"My bursting Heart must find vent at my pen," Abigail wrote to John the next day. "I have just heard that our dear Friend Dr. Warren is no more but fell gloriously fighting for his Country. . . . Great is our Loss." Before sending the letter, she added, "I wish I could contradict the report of the Doctors Death, but tis a lamentable Truth, and the tears of multitudes pay tribute to his memory."[41]

As for what would come to be known as the Battle of Bunker Hill, Abigail wrote, "Charlestown is laid in ashes. . . . How many have fallen we know not—the constant roar of the cannon is so distressing that we cannot Eat, Drink or Sleep. May we be supported and sustained in the dreadful conflict."[42]

Messengers were already on their way to Philadelphia with the news. Along with Joseph Warren, 140 other colonists had been killed in the battle; close to 300 were wounded. The toll on the British was even greater: 226 dead and over 900 wounded. The British had won the day, but even they knew, as General Howe so succinctly stated, "The success is too dearly bought."[43]

Messengers carrying the grim letters sent from Massachusetts passed by messengers traveling north, carrying letters from Congress to Massachusetts, including letters written to the now-deceased Joseph Warren. John Adams and John Hancock had written to him in separate letters to share the news that George Washington had been appointed commander in chief of the Continental Army. Five hundred other commissions had also been approved, naming officers under Washington's command.

Adams, who had negotiated Washington's nomination, wrote of Hancock's disappointment at not being named head of the army and his "mortification and resentment"[44] when Washington was confirmed. But it wasn't likely that Hancock, hobbled with gout, would have wanted a position that required riding out on horseback and other physical activities. In fact, Hancock appeared—to all observers other than Adams—to be pleased with having George Washington as commander of the army.

Hancock wrote to Joseph Warren that Washington was "a gentleman you will all like." He then asked that Warren provide "a suitable place for his residence and the mode of his reception . . . such as to do . . . the Commander-in-Chief great honor."[45] But unbeknown to Hancock, Warren lay behind enemy lines, his dead body interred in a mass grave where it fell. General Washington would have to see to his own residence and reception.

John Adams was stunned by the news of Warren's death, following so quickly on the loss of Josiah Quincy Jr.: "two characters, as great in proportion to their age, as any that I have ever known in America. . . . They were both my intimate friends, with whom I lived and conversed, with pleasure and advantage. I was animated by them, in the painful dangerous course of opposition to the oppressions brought upon our country; the loss of them has wounded me too deeply, to be easily healed."[46]

Josiah Quincy Sr., mourning the loss "of a Warren and a Quincy, who have [both] perished in the Storm of Tyranny and oppression," wrote to Sam Adams in Philadelphia, urging the Congress to persevere: "may God . . . preserve the Lives of our remaining skillful pilots, and enable them to steer the shattered Bark into the Harbor of Peace Liberty and Safety! So well constructed a ship, and so richly laden, ought not to become the Prize of Robbers and Pirates. Before that should happen . . . we would maintain the conflict to the last man."[47]

Washington received news of the terrible Battle of Breed's Hill while he was in New York on his way to Cambridge, where he would take over command of the New England militia. The sealed message had been addressed to John Hancock, but Washington, sensing its importance, opened it. He read of the two thousand British troops that had stormed colonial fortifications and forced the Americans to retreat from Charlestown. He asked the messenger if "the provincials stood the British fire" during the battle. The messenger assured him that they had. "Then the liberties of our country are safe," Washington replied.[48] And he continued on his way to Massachusetts.

Edmund Quincy was in the crowd that gathered on the Cambridge Common on July 3, 1775, to greet General Washington. He'd traveled in from Lancaster with his son-in-law, Will Greenleaf, to bear witness as the general from

Virginia took command of the Americans' army. In the past few days, rain had finally come to Massachusetts, pummeling down in a steady downpour, but the morning of July 3 dawned sunny and clear. Drum and fife played as Washington inspected the gathered soldiers of New England. The men wore clothing of all kinds and in all states of disrepair; their weapons were just as varied, from trusty muskets to knifes rigged to poles to Indian tomahawks.

Edmund marveled at the number of men who had come together to fight for Massachusetts—and not just from Massachusetts but from Vermont, New Hampshire, Rhode Island, Connecticut, and as far away as Maine. Edmund realized the fight was not for just one colony; the fight was for all the colonies of America, all oppressed under British rule. He felt both humbled and empowered by what a unified Congress had created, and what these gathered men would fight for: "the remarkable instrument . . . confirming and establishing the liberty of America."[49]

Washington, tall and erect on his horse, trotted to the front of the rows of men and then turned his mount around so that he faced the soldiers square on. Drawing his sword from its scabbard, he raised it and held it aloft for all to see. These men were his soldiers now; they were the first regiments of what Washington would call "the troops of the United Provinces of North America." He vowed that "all distinctions of colonies will be laid aside," for they were all of one country and together, they would fight for one country.[50]

Edmund joined in the cheering that broke out, the crowd's loud hurrahs joining with the hearty banging of the drums. The noise grew even louder, rising up like a cloud and traveling on the wind to Boston, just a few miles east. Notice had been given: the war was on.

29

The Unhappy Contest

*I view the dangerous and doubtful struggle
with fear and trembling.*

—Samuel Quincy

Abigail Adams went through her meager collection of pewter pieces, picking out those spoons sturdy enough to withstand the heat: Elihu, John Adams' brother, was coming to the house to melt them down for bullets. Abigail had her bullet mold ready, its hinges open and the curved insides waiting for liquid pewter to be poured in. All over Massachusetts, metals were being melted down to make bullets, direly needed by the American army. Josiah Quincy Sr. went to the old Burying Ground and, with the help of a chisel, broke off a lead plaque with the Quincy coat of arms from one of the family gravestones. It too would be added to the caldron for melting, then poured into molds for bullets.

Josiah was desperate to help the cause any way that he could, from spying on the British from the monitor on the rooftop of his house and sending detailed reports to John Hancock in Philadelphia, to using his position as justice of the peace for Braintree to chase down colonists supplying the British with goods.

"Have you not been repeatedly derided and warned not to go on board or to have any Commerce with the People on board his Majesty's ships as it would be inimical to the Disposition of your Country?" he thundered at a laborer who had brought provisions to British soldiers aboard the *Mercury*. John Spear pleaded ignorance—"not to my remembrance," he answered—but Justice Quincy fined him anyway and threw him in jail for a few days to ponder his sins.[1]

By the end of July 1775, George Washington was settled into his headquarters on Brattle Street, in the imposing mansion left behind by the Loyalist John Vassall (Vassall, like Jonathan Sewall and Andrew Oliver, had fled Cambridge for Boston). From the top floor of his new home, Washington could see Boston. He marveled at how close the British forces were to his American troops in Cambridge—two bitter enemies, "almost near enough to converse."[2]

Sniping between the two forces went on with regularity; one of many diarists of the time recorded that "an Exchange of Shot is very frequent,"[3] and another wrote, "At one time a horse would be knocked on the head, and at another a man would be killed."[4] But Governor Gage and General Howe seemed in no hurry to begin a true battle with General Washington and the colonists.

Washington was happy for the standoff. He needed time to bring order and discipline to the troops he increasingly despaired of; he complained to his brother of these "provincials" and tried to discipline them in everything from cleanliness to subservience to unity.[5] While the troops continued to admire, and even revere, him—"General Washington fills his place with vast ease and dignity and dispenses happiness around him"[6]—the feeling was not mutual.

Washington did not especially like or trust the New Englanders, and he included both John and Sam Adams in his assessments. But he did like John Hancock; he respected him as a man of good breeding, solid wealth, and honorable reputation. In time, Martha Washington and Dorothy Hancock would get to know each other, and the same feelings of respect and liking would grow between the two women.

Throughout the summer and into the fall of 1775, skirmishes continued between the British troops and the local militia up and down the coast of Massachusetts, with both sides raiding coastal islands in search of supplies, including livestock and forage. The colonists went further, setting fire not only to buildings where supplies were stored but also to lighthouses on various islands.

The lighthouses were crucial to the safety of the ships that continued to arrive from Britain, carrying more troops and supplies. When a band of militia set fire to the Boston lighthouse, Governor Gage immediately sent carpenters out to repair the structure and get it working again. A week later, the colonists, under the cover of night, returned to the island; fighting off the British guards, they raided the storehouses for oil and other supplies, then set fire to every structure on the island. The buildings, including the repaired lighthouse, burned to the ground by morning.

After they retreated from the island that night, the buildings aflame behind them, British troops set out in pursuit. A number of men were wounded, and one was killed—"an unhappy youth," Abigail Adams wrote to John, "who received a Ball thro the temples as he was rowing the boat." His funeral was held in Braintree, presided over by Reverend Wibird, who "made the best oration . . . I ever heard from him."[7]

In attendance at the funeral were four wounded British soldiers who had been captured by the colonists. Abigail wrote to John that they had asked to come to the services at the North Parish Church, where they "appeared affected" by Reverend Wibird's sermon. When Abigail asked them why they "should be obliged to fight their best Friends," they answered that "they were sorry—they hoped in God [that] an end would be speedily put to the unhappy contest."

The men were just pawns in a battle designed by others, Abigail observed; she wrote to John that "they were told if they were taken alive, they should be Sacrificed by us"—but now understood that they had been "deceived" and "express'd gratitude at the kindness they received" at the hands of the colonists of Braintree.[8]

Whatever pity Abigail felt for the captured soldiers—and she did—that sympathy did not extend to the deserters from the British Army who continually passed through Braintree. Just in the past week, five had appeared, Abigail wrote to John, and not one of them could be trusted: "no one can tell the secret designs of such fellows whom no oath binds. . . . Those who do not scruple to bring poverty, Misery, Slavery and Death upon thousands will not hesitate at the most diabolical crimes—and this is Britain. Blush o! Americans that ever thou derivest thy origin from such a race."[9]

John had come to rely on Abigail's letters not only as a source—and sometimes the *only* source—of information about Boston but also as an inspiration. He wrote to her, "You are really brave, my dear, you are an Heroine. And you have Reason to be. For the worst that can happen, can do you no Harm. A soul, as pure, as benevolent, as virtuous and pious as yours has nothing to fear, but every Thing to hope."[10] He felt her hope extending across the hundreds of miles to him.

He tried to reciprocate, offering both empathy and advocacy in the same breath: "Your Description of the Distresses of the worthy Inhabitants of Boston, and the other Sea Port Towns, is enough to melt an Heart of stone. Our Consolation must be this, my dear, that Cities may be rebuilt, and a People reduced to Poverty, may acquire fresh Property: But a Constitution of Government once changed from Freedom, can never be restored. Liberty once lost is lost forever."[11]

While Abigail soldiered on in Braintree, he would be soldiering on in

Congress. But at times, the odds against him in that forum seemed to be just too much: "There are some Persons [from] New York and Philadelphia, to whom a ship is dearer than a City, and a few Barrels of flower, [worth more] than a thousand Lives—other Men's Lives I mean."[12] It was then he turned to Abigail's fortitude to console him, and drive him on: "I am charmed with [your] Admirable Fortitude . . . I cannot express the Satisfaction it gives me, nor how much it contributes to support me."[13]

John listed for Abigail all the work still to do at Congress: "a Constitution to form . . . a Country of fifteen hundred Miles extent to fortify, Millions to arm and train, a Naval Power to begin, an extensive Commerce to regulate, numerous Tribes of Indians to negotiate with, [and] a standing Army of Twenty-seven Thousand Men to raise, pay, victual and officer." And there was still the confounded—to John Adams—Olive Branch Petition to deal with, a petition for mercy and conciliation created by John Dickinson to be sent to the king.

After the carnage of Bunker Hill, John Adams and all the other members of the Massachusetts delegation were even more opposed to sending a petition to England. The discussions between John Adams and John Dickinson became acrimonious. Dickinson threatened Adams that if "you New Englandmen" did not support the Olive Branch Petition, "I, and a Number of Us, will break off, from you . . . and We will carry on the Opposition by ourselves in our own Way."

Adams refused to respond to the warning but walked away, furious over Dickinson's "rude lecture."[14] Over three hundred New Englanders had died since hostilities began—and Dickinson wanted to barter those deaths for peace? Abigail had asked in a letter, "Does every member feel for us? Do they realize what we suffer?"[15] The answer seemed to be no.

Blaming Dickinson for what had been destroyed between them—"the Friendship and Acquaintance was lost forever"—John stewed over the nasty exchange for days.[16] Fed up not only with Dickinson's imperious attitudes but also with the petty squabbling of other delegates, he finally gave vent to his feelings in an angry letter to Abigail, in which he referred to the "fidgets, the whims, the caprices, the vanity, the superstition, the irritability" of his fellow delegates.[17]

He then wrote a letter to his good friend James Warren, husband of Mercy, in which he denounced Dickinson as "A Certain great Fortune and piddling Genius, whose Fame has been trumpeted so loudly, [and who] has given a silly Cast to our whole doings."[18]

Adams complained to Warren of the sacrifices that had to be made to get anything accomplished, but added that he understood Warren himself was making sacrifices, in having to deal with the eccentric and capricious Charles Lee, army officer and inveterate dog lover, now settled in Cambridge. "But you must love his Dogs if you love him," advised John, "and forgive [Lee] a thousand whims for the Sake of the Soldier and the Scholar."[19]

Feeling quite calm now, and satisfied as well, John sent his letters off and went to bed. The repercussions of his words could not have been imagined by the gently snoring man—but would be felt soon enough.

A compromise was finally reached between those opposing the Olive Branch Petition and those supporting it: a declaration of war would be drafted, and once approved, sent to all the colonies as well as overseas to England. This document, a "Declaration of the Causes and Necessity of Taking Up Arms," laid out the reasons why the colonies had formed a continental army, but it also emphasized their desire to lay down arms "when Hostilities shall cease on the part of the Aggressors."

Dickinson, one of the two authors of the declaration, made clear that "We have not raised Armies with ambitious designs of separating from Great-Britain, and establishing Independent States."[20] The second author, Thomas Jefferson from Virginia, added both force and heat to the document, making it somewhat more palatable to New England: "Our Cause is just. Our union is perfect. Our internal resources are great, and if necessary, foreign Assistance is attainable." After threatening alliances with other countries, Jefferson also warned that the Americans were not afraid to fight until the bitter end; "[We are] resolved to die Freemen rather than to live slaves."[21]

The declaration was approved by Congress on July 6, 1775, two days after it approved the Olive Branch Petition. The petition would be sent to London by courier (Richard Penn, son of William Penn) and handed over to Arthur Lee, its seal unbroken, who would then ensure delivery of the petition to the king himself.

As for the declaration, it was printed up and then sent out for publication throughout the colonies. The hope was that the document would encourage fearful colonists and shore up their determination and resolution. Life was becoming more difficult by the day, with basic goods in short supply and no end in sight to the boycott, the blockade of Boston, or any of the other burdens and sacrifices in the battle for colonial rights.

While the colonists suffered, the militias grew, and Washington's army trained, Congress had to get back to a full agenda of work: appointing officers, setting and paying salaries, and assuring the supply of foodstuffs, uniforms, and weapons for the soldiers. And to pay for all these measures, they had to set up a system of taxation, leveling the burden among the colonies. In addition, Congress had to follow through on nascent negotiations with the Indian nations in order to get their support; build up domestic manufacturing of goods and supplies; and establish a safe system for sending mail.

John Hancock, who bore the brunt of moving the work forward in Congress, was feeling the strain. His gout flared with frequency, causing a terrible burning in his joints for which there was no remedy. After Congress finally approved the five hundred officer commissions to support Washington in the field, it fell to the president, John Hancock, to sign every one of those commissions. His wrist ached for days.

But the mental demands, even more than the physical ones, exacted the hardest toll of all on the president. The psychological acrobatics required to referee debates between delegates, soothe wounded egos, come up with compromises—or at least identify possible areas of agreement—were demoralizing and exhausting.

At one point, Hancock became so weary of it all that he sent to George Washington a heartfelt request to be taken on as a soldier; "I am determined to act under you, if it be to take a firelock and join the ranks as a volunteer."[22]

Gout or no, he wanted out of Philadelphia. He wanted someone else calling the shots and ordering him around. He wanted rest from the bickering, grandstanding, and endless talking of Congress. To be a soldier would seem like a rest cure after the past months spent leading Congress.

General Washington answered Hancock's letter promptly (much more quickly than his dear Dolly, who had yet to answer a single letter). Washington graciously declined Hancock's offer to serve—"so little is in my power to offer to Colonel Hancock's merits, and worth his acceptance"—and signed off as "your most obedient and very humble servant."[23] John Hancock could not throw off the mantle of president so easily; he would be held to his duty.

The temporary desire to flee faded, and Hancock once again accepted his obligation to his country, to be met not on the battlefield but in Congress. He got back to the work at hand and took over lobbying every colony in America to send whatever funds, arms, goods, and soldiers they could to support the new government.

For Hancock, it was not just a temporary administration he was working toward; it was a new country, and he would do everything he could to ensure its survival. "Let us . . . exert every Nerve to distinguish ourselves. I entreat you to quicken your Preparations, and to stimulate the good people of our Government," he wrote in letter after letter to representatives of the colonies. He was intent on garnering the men, supplies, and monetary support needed to carry the new government and its army forward to freedom.[24]

Washington must have been relieved to receive the letter from his good friend Benjamin Harrison, fellow Virginia delegate to the Congress: "Our President is . . . Noble, Disinterested, and Generous to a very Great Degree."[25] Keeping Hancock out of the army and firmly in charge of Congress had been the right thing to do.

Following the Battle of Bunker Hill, living conditions in Boston deteriorated even further. So many people were dying in Boston, including soldiers wounded in battle, that Governor Gage forbade the ringing of bells to announce a death. George Washington heard from his spies of "the great mortality" of British soldiers, due not only to wounds but also to "the want of fresh vegetables and meat."[26]

And soldiers weren't the only ones dying. "The Condition of the Inhabitants detained in Boston is very distressing," Washington wrote to John Hancock, "they are . . . destitute of the Comfort of fresh Provisions, & many of them are so reduced in their Circumstances, as to be unable to supply themselves."[27]

Abigail Adams heard from a fisherman who had recently escaped from Boston by boat that "all the fresh provisions they can procure they are obliged to give to the sick and wounded." Milch cows were being killed and their meat sold at precipitously high prices, too dear for most to afford.[28]

Governor Gage began arresting more and more citizens of Boston, taking them into custody on charges of treason and promoting rebellion; "such Suspicion & Jealousy prevails, that they can scarcely speak, or even look, without exposing themselves to some Species of military Execution."[29] James Lovell, Josiah Quincy Jr.'s good friend (and son of John Lovell, Tory schoolmaster of Boston Latin School), was arrested along with Peter Edes, son of the publisher of the *Boston Gazette*. They languished in prison, enduring miserable conditions, fearful of death by infection, or lack of food, or a wound left untreated; they knew that of the nineteen wounded colonists taken after Bunker Hill, every one of them had died in the British prison.

The Old South Meeting House was turned into a riding school for the

British officers, and the pews and galleries torn out and burned for heat; other churches were turned into barracks. The houses of rebels and Loyalists alike were plundered to the needs of the soldiers and citizens; ransacked for what supplies the homes might contain, and bits and pieces hacked away for fuel, barter, or simply out of malice.

Abigail wrote to John that she had heard that General Burgoyne, who had taken over the home of Samuel and Hannah Quincy, treated the belongings with little care; "raw meat [was] cut and hacked upon her Mahogonay Tables, and her superb damask curtain and cushings exposed to the rain as if they were of no value."[30]

Somehow, Hancock's mansion on Beacon Hill remained intact; probably because it had been appropriated by the British general Henry Clinton, an opinionated and quarrelsome man who nevertheless insisted on a gentleman's code of conduct at all times, even during war.

The earlier optimism of Jonathan Sewall had evaporated in the gloom of hunger, death, and despair: "Funerals are now so frequent that . . . you meet as many dead folks as live ones in Boston Streets," he wrote to a friend, "and we pass them with less emotion and attention than we used to pass dead sheep and oxen in days of yore."[31] Still displaying his wry sense of humor, he added, "Musketry, bombs, great guns, redoubts, lines, batterys, enfilades, battle sieges, murder, plague, famine, rebellion, and the Devil have at length brought me to a determination to quit the scene." Jonathan, Esther, and the children would be leaving Boston as soon as Jonathan could find them a ship out.

When dysentery descended on the town, Sewall grew even more desperate to leave; "I have seen, heard and felt enough of the rabies—I wish to be out of the noise," he wrote in mid-August. By the end of the month, he and the family were aboard a ship sailing for London.[32]

Edmund Quincy wrote to Dolly in Fairfield, to tell her of Esther's imminent departure; "I wish them a safe journey, and peace and comfort to Esther, for of late, she could not enjoy any great share."[33] But for all his wishes for her happiness, he also grieved to think he might never see his daughter again: "I was afraid I should lose a Daughter to the quarrel: But we must learn to submit to whatever way be the will of Heaven concerning us or ours."[34]

In early August, the Second Continental Congress adjourned for the summer, to meet again in the fall. King George's response to their petition would determine Congress's next steps; many were hopeful that a conciliation still might be possible, forestalling all the proposals made by the New England delegates for outfitting the army, creating a navy, and other plans that had more to do with war than peace. But John Hancock and Sam and John Adams knew that the colonists had to be prepared for the worst. It would do no harm to ensure the colonies' strong position in the event of a proposed compromise from the king; and if instead of peace, the king pursued war, the colonists would be ready.

Abigail rejoiced when she heard John was finally coming home—"The return of thee my dear partner after a four months absence is a pleasure I cannot express"—but in fact, there would be no rest for either John Adams or John Hancock.[35] Both would spend the summer shoring up support throughout their province and New England for a coming confrontation with Great Britain.

John Adams would do it from the very cramped quarters of his home in Braintree. Refugees from Boston were still ensconced in rooms of the farmhouse, from the attic on down, and even in the barn; to make room, Abigail had removed all the trappings of John's office into her own chamber, where she slept now with the children, John's books, and stacks of paper.

As happy as John was to be home again, it must have been with some relief that he left again to attend the Provincial Congress meeting in Watertown, where he would enjoy a quiet room of his own. And Abigail, invited to join him there, was very pleased to do it. To have time alone with her husband, away from the demands of the farm, was a needed indulgence.

Abigail was with John when the news broke that two of his letters from Philadelphia to Massachusetts had been intercepted, taken from the messenger who carried them and then printed in Tory newspapers. One was the letter in which John had spoken of Dickinson as "a piddling genius" and belittled other delegates for their "Whims, Caprice, and Vanity," while also expressing his desires for all-out preparation for war. The other letter was the one he had written to James Warren, in which he had made fun of General Charles Lee.

The letters were published not only in America but also in England. In Boston, beleaguered Loyalists responded with fury and ridicule, while in England, Adams' letters were held up as proof of the colonists' perfidy and their treasonous desires for war. Within days of the letters' publication in London, King George received the Olive Branch Petition sent by Congress; although he was already prepared to ignore it, Adams' letters were further proof that a desire for conciliation was not universally felt on the part of the colonists.

But for the most part, the letters did little to hurt John either politically or personally. Although his relationship with Dickinson was further damaged, he had never really thought it might be repaired after all the rancor shared in the spring. Surprisingly, John found both a fan and a friend in General Lee, who wrote to Adams thanking him for the moniker of "eccentric," which he took as a compliment, adding, "my love of Dogs passes with me as a still higher complement."

Lee added, in explanation, "when once I can be convinced that Men are as worthy objects as Dogs I shall transfer my benevolence" to them, but until that point, dogs would remain his favorites. Lee called John an excellent "biped," endowed with "generosity, valor, good sense, patriotism and zeal for the rights of humanity," and he promised John his own lasting "friendship and passion." He closed the missive by sending the love of his dog Spada, who was very grateful for Adams' published letter, as the little black Pomeranian now enjoyed ample petting and caressing "by all ranks, sexes, and Ages."[36]

John Hancock wrote to Dolly that he would be on his way to Fairfield just as soon as he took care of some essential business, including reporting to the Provincial Congress in Watertown; delivering half a million dollars to George Washington in Cambridge so that Washington could pay army salaries (the money came from taxes collected from the colonies, and from Hancock's own coffers as well); and picking up Dolly's trunks, which had been left in Worcester after the flight from Lexington.

But then, he promised, he would "ride on to Fairfield as quick as I can . . . as I am very desirous of being with you soon."[37]

Everywhere he went, Hancock was met with admiring crowds. Newborn babies were held up to him; he was surprised to learn how many had been named after him, a whole legion of infant John Hancocks. Dolly's sister Sarah had named her baby boy, born in April, John Hancock Greenleaf, and in July, Edmund wrote to Dolly that Mrs. Rice, a friend of the family, gave birth to twins: the boy and the girl had been named John and Dorothy, respectively.

Hancock continued to write his messages pleading for support as he traveled north. He asked his colonial compatriots for their support, not only spiritual but also material, in the form of concrete contributions, such as much-needed gunpowder and always welcome arms and other supplies. Stockpiles of powder were dangerously low, and Hancock received almost weekly requests from George Washington begging for more gunpowder to be sent, and soon.

By the end of the summer Hancock would write to the legislative assembly of every single colony, beseeching them for funds and supplies in the name of "the Liberties of your Country, and the Happiness of Posterity" and reminding them that "you stand engaged in the most solemn Ties of Honour to support the Common Cause."

And the colonies responded: Pennsylvania, South Carolina, and Maryland all sent arms and powder, supplementing reserves sent earlier by Connecticut, Rhode Island, and New York. The colonies were joining together, not just in words but in deeds. Josiah Quincy Jr. had planned for this joint effort on behalf of liberty—and now the seeds he had planted were producing fruit, even though he was not there to see it.

In mid-August, John Hancock finally arrived in Fairfield. And on August 28, 1775, in the home of Thaddeus Burr, the long-awaited wedding between John and Dolly finally took place. People from the village stood by the fenced garden, eager to catch a look at the festivities. One onlooker reported, "Silver buckles, white silk stockings, knee breeches of various hues, scarlet vest and velvet coats with ruffled shirts and broad fine neckwear adorned the masculine fraternity, while the ladies were radiant in silks and laces, lofty head-dress, resplendent jewelry and the precious heirlooms of old families."[38]

With John Hancock a wanted man, and British spies everywhere, there were many who marveled at the couple marrying in such public circumstances. John and Dolly were heralded for their bravery, their romance, and their patriotism for "marrying now, while all the colonies are as much convulsed as Rome when Hannibal was at her gates."[39]

Edmund Quincy, still in Lancaster with his daughter Sarah, would have no inkling of his daughter's change in status until he received a letter on September 8, dated August 29 and sent from John Hancock. The letter was cosigned, the writing at the bottom of the note clear and strong: *Dorothy Hancock.*

It was a gift from daughter to father. In July, Edmund had written to Dolly, "I hope in some months to see you with a new name."[40] Now, seeing her signature at the bottom of the page, Edmund understood that his wish had been granted. As he wrote to Aunt Lydia, in undisguised relief and muted joy, it was thanks to the letter lately received that he "became acquainted with their being married on the evening before."[41]

Edmund had also expressed in that July letter the equally fervent "wish [that] peace may by that time be restored to our Israel, but let us wait patiently."[42]

His second wish, for peace, would not be granted so easily.

30

Complications of Evil
and Misfortune

The Critical Period has arrived, that will seal the fate,
not only of ourselves, but of Posterity.

—John Hancock

Abigail Quincy took her time going through her husband's travel chests. For the first weeks after she finally arrived back in Norwich, the chests had remained in the back hall of the house, an obstruction to all who entered that way. But no one said a word to Abigail. The annoyance was too small, and her grief too large. Finally, as June gave way to July, she asked that the chests be brought upstairs to the sunny room she had hoped to share with a returning husband. She would share it with him still, she vowed, and slowly, slowly she began to go through the contents of the chests, one by one.

She marveled over the "curiosities" he had picked up in London, worn volumes of history and philosophy.[1] Packets of pamphlets on political issues. Stacks of letters, tied with ribbons. Sheets of drawing paper, revealing the long hours he had spent designing the rings for his father and her. She wore her ring now as the symbol of immortality he had planned for it to be. He had known when he commissioned the ring in February that he might not make it back to her. But then, she had known as well.

"Everything in his chests [were] safe except his watch which I suspect was stolen as one of the chests was broken open," she wrote to her father-in-law, Josiah Quincy Sr., "but in the same chest I found near one hundred £ sterling in cash, and it seems strange they should take a watch and leave the money."[2]

She promised to send her father-in-law all the pamphlets that his son had collected in England, along with the books he'd purchased—except for those too fragile to make the now perilous and uncertain trip into Massachusetts, "for fear of their being damaged."[3]

Abigail spent over a month reading through Josiah's London journal.

"Spent the evening at Covent Garden," he wrote in December, "Milton's *Masque of Comus* was altered much for the worse; and no part was performed well but the part by Ms. Catley, which being wanton was done admirably by her."[4] It was like having a conversation with her husband, and she must have felt like answering, *But you never trusted the theater, did you, my Josiah?*

It took Abigail close to another month to read the speeches made in Parliament that Josiah had copied out, word for word (and from memory), given on behalf of the colonies in Parliament by Lord Chatham, Lord Cambden, Lord Shelburne. With such friends in Parliament, how could the cause of American liberty fail? And yet even Josiah had noted that such friends had not power enough to override the will of the king, Lord North, and those in Parliament intent on punishing the American colonists for daring to talk "about their natural and divine rights, their rights as men and citizens; their rights from God and nature."[5]

Abigail took special notice of Josiah's mentioning an evening in which Ben Franklin told the story when, decades earlier, Charles Pratt (who would become Lord Camden) predicted the colonists would "one day throw off . . . dependence upon this Country and . . . set up for Independence." Franklin had countered then—and still believed now—only if England "grossly abuse" the colonists.[6]

For the next few weeks, Josiah's chests remained closed, their contents hidden away. Abigail needed breathing room to think about all she had read. And then her son fell ill. It was the end of summer, with thunderstorms raging over the Connecticut fields, and her child lay in bed with a high fever and splotches of red on his cheeks.

Josiah Quincy Sr. wrote from Braintree, "The Dysentery has lately prevailed in the neighboring Towns & especially in the Army; has proved mortal to some: I hope not too many & that you & all the Family have escaped it."[7] John Adams' brother Elihu died of the "bloody flux"—dysentery—in mid-August. Elihu had caught the illness in the army camps at Cambridge; by the end of summer, hundreds of New Englanders, soldiers and civilians alike, would die of it.

Abigail Quincy sat beside her child in his bed and prayed for the "goodness of God" to carry him through.[8] She could not bear another loss.

Once settled in London, Samuel Quincy found that his presence went largely unnoticed by the men to which he'd hoped to plead the American cause. He was just one American in a sea of indifferent British. Even Thomas Hutchinson, with all his connections, lamented that "we Americans are plenty here and very cheap. Some of us at first coming are apt to think ourselves important but other people do not think so and few if any of us are consulted or enquired after."[9]

Samuel sought what comfort he could find in the company of old friends at the newly formed New England Club. The club, an invitation-only fraternity for Americans, met at different taverns and coffeehouses every week. There, the exiled men shared what little news they'd received from Massachusetts—the news of Bunker Hill was a terrible shock—and together fretted over the fate of their country.

"Everything is peace here, and I wish it may soon return to my dear, dear country," Samuel wrote to his wife. He ruefully noted that he was becoming acquainted with all the respectable watering holes in town—Paul's Head Tavern, the Crown & Anchor, the Adelphi—but had yet to see the inside of a lord's home or office. There was little he could do here in London for his country, and having heard of the utter misery of Boston and the surrounding villages, he was "peculiarly anxious" to hear from his wife; "it is now five months since I saw you, and more than three since I heard from you. . . . Next [to] the pleasure of seeing you, is that of seeing your handwriting; next to hearing you, hearing from you."[10]

To his brother-in-law Henry Hill, Sam wrote of the futility of his mission to England: "every proposal of hope . . . to alter the measures of Government & redress the Grievances . . . is spurned at . . . the People of this Country are united in their attachment to the reigning Prince and his illustrious family. . . . The political subordination of the Colonies is in this island a sacred tenet."

The Battle of Bunker Hill only ignited further passion on the part of the British to tighten the screws on the colonies, Samuel warned; and "more ships and troops, every species of ammunition and warlike implements . . . are already embarked" for Boston.[11]

Depressed by the likelihood of a bloody war in which many of his friends would die—and which would threaten his own wife and children as well—Samuel felt useless and emasculated. "To stay longer in England, absent from my friends and family with a bare subsistence, inactive, without prospects, and useless to myself and the world was death to me."[12]

To his wife he lamented, "The continuance of our unhappy separation has something in it so unexpected, so unprecedented, so complicated with evil and misfortune."[13]

Sam turned his lost hope for peace into fervent prayers for a short war;

it was the best outcome he could imagine. He wrote to Henry Hill, it is "my duty patiently to submit to the event as it may be governed by the all-wise counsel of that Being who ruleth in the heavens, and is the God of armies."[14]

Meanwhile, his wife, Hannah, lived with her brother in Cambridge, the center of the war in America. George Washington's headquarters on Brattle Street were just a few blocks away, and the thousands of New England soldiers encamped nearby could be heard and smelled from the garden of the Hill home. The sounds of the militias were bad enough—the daily drills and actual sniping, shots and balls fired across the water at Boston, the incessant drumming, a tattoo of impending battle always rattling in her brain.

But the smells were even worse—the reek of untended latrines; the lingering odors of sickness and the scouring sharpness of vinegar used to cleanse sickness away; the terrible stench of cooking, as every varmint that could be caught was roasted over an open fire—Hannah and the other inhabitants of the house held a handkerchief to their faces when they went outside to ward off the smells that would never fade away.

The second meeting of the Second Continental Congress began in Philadelphia on September 5, 1775. John Hancock and his new wife, Dolly, had settled into rooms on Arch Street, in the house they shared with the other Massachusetts delegates. John was once again suffering from gout and Dolly's attention was focused on his comfort; she left their trunks and furnishings untouched as she sought out new doctors in Philadelphia. But there was little to offer John in terms of treatment, and he took to his bed to endure in silence the severe burning and swelling of his joints.

The pain was so bad that for the first weeks of Congress, John could not attend most meetings, although he hid the severity of the illness as best he could: "Mr. Hancock having a Touch of the Gout, there was no President in the Chair," wrote Richard Smith, delegate of New Jersey. Smith noted the absence with a note of melancholy; support for Hancock's continued presidency of the Congress remained strong, and most of the delegates eagerly awaited his return.

Even Peyton Randolph, the first president chosen, had no problem with Hancock continuing in the role. John Adams, however, wrote to James Warren of his disapproval: "Mr. Randolph, our former President is here, and Sits very humbly in his Seat, while our new one, continues in the Chair, without Seeming to feel the Impropriety."[15]

Soon enough, Randolph once again succumbed to illness while Hancock improved in health, and by the middle of September, Hancock was firmly in charge once again. (Randolph died on October 17 and his funeral took place one week later; this was the only day off that Congress had the entire fall.) Hancock's duties were many, and included signing off on, and then assigning responsibility for, the implementation of legislation and resolutions passed by Congress, such as securing ammunition and arms, and setting up a navy. He also had to write out and sign requisitions for all the money needed to implement congressional actions, such as army salaries and funds for supplies. As president, he was charged with initiating negotiations for support from France through letters and petitions, and had to approve and write up officers' commissions by the dozens.

But now he had help. Dolly took on the responsibilities of clerk for her husband. She was kept busy "trimming off the rough edges of bills of credit issues by Congress and signed by the President," she recalled later, "and packing them up in saddle bags to be sent off to various quarters for use by the army."[16] She also took on responsibility for sending out the officers' commissions signed by her husband and taking notes of the daily meetings, as dictated by Hancock to her late at night.

Even John Adams had to admit that Dolly was a welcome addition to the delegation from Massachusetts—"she lives and behaves with Modesty, Decency, Dignity and Discretion I assure you. Her Behaviour is easy and genteel"—although he did not go so far as to acknowledge her assistance to the actual workings of Congress: "She avoids talking upon Politicks. In large and mixed Companies she is totally silent, as a Lady ought to be."[17]

Ignoring her work as clerk, he instead appreciated the respectable socializing she'd instigated, breaking up the ten-hour days, six days a week, of congressional meetings, with "after-hours caucusing and conversation."[18]

But Dolly's work was acknowledged in another way. At the beginning of November, good news was received from Canada, where the Continental Army was engaged in a battle to conquer the Province of Quebec. Fort Chambly on the route to Montreal had been taken by the Americans, and a number of English troops from the Seventh Regiment (Royal Fusiliers) had been taken prisoner.

The flags of the Royal Fusiliers were sent to Philadelphia, and in a short but moving ceremony, presented as a gift to Dolly. They were hung ceremoniously in the rooms she shared with her husband, where they were displayed "with great Splendor and Elegance."[19] While the victory in Canada would be short-lived, the flags remained, a tribute to Dorothy Hancock's contribution to the cause.

Within a week of John Adams leaving Abigail in Braintree en route to Philadelphia, the scourge of dysentery arrived in the village. Abigail was the first to fall ill in her household; she even considered writing to John and asking him to return, but she worried that if he came back to the village, he "should be a partaker of the common calamity"—and she wanted her man to stay healthy.

After a few days, Abigail began to feel better, but then one of her servant girls fell sick, and then another did. And then little Tommy became feverish and splotchy. Abigail wrote to John that their youngest child "lies very ill now—there is no abatement at present of his disorder. . . . I hope he is not dangerous."[20]

Tommy recovered within a week of falling ill—although "was you to look in upon him you would not know him, from a hearty hale corn fed Boy, he is become pale lean and wan"[21]—but the servant Patty suffered throughout September, her symptoms turning her into what Abigail described as "the most ghastly object my Eyes ever beheld."

Because Patty was "continually desirous of my being with her the little While she expects to live," Abigail tended to her, even when she became "such a putrid mass" that no one could bear to come near her, much less "do their Duty towards her."[22]

All of Braintree suffered the horrors of the disease. Abigail wrote to John: "18 have been buried since you left us. . . . [There have been] 4, 3 and 2 funerals in a day for many days. . . . Mrs. Randle has one child that is not expected to live out the night, Mrs. Belcher has another, Joseph Bracket another. . . . Mr. Wibird lies bad. Major Miller is dangerous. Revd. Mr. Gay is not expected to live. . . . So sickly and so Mortal a time the oldest Man does not remember."[23]

Two weeks later, the illness still raged: "Some poor parents are mourning the loss of 3, 4 and 5 children, and some families are wholly striped of every Member."[24]

Abigail's home was turned into a hospital. She nursed on her own, "such is the distress of the neighborhood that I can scarcely find a well person to assist me in looking after the sick."[25] The only help she had was from her mother, who traveled every day from Weymouth to do what she could for her daughter and for the household.

But then Abigail's mother fell sick; "She has taken the disorder and lies so bad that we have little hopes of her Recovery. She is possess'd with the Idea that she shall not recover, and I fear it will prove but too true," Abigail wrote mournfully to John at the end of September.[26]

By mid-September, Abigail Quincy's son, Josiah, was well on his way to recovery. Abigail Quincy wrote to Josiah Sr. in Braintree that her little boy's fever had passed and he was feeling so much better that he was now going out on horseback rides through the countryside: a relief for both mother and grandfather that this one child survived.

Abigail Quincy also wrote of her continuing sorrow over the loss of Josiah Jr.; her love for her "dear husband," she wrote to his father, "will remain till I cease to breathe the vital air."[27]

And even after—for Abigail was resolute in her desire that in death, she and her husband be reunited, his body exhumed from its grave in Gloucester and the two of them laid together, as he had wished, in the burial grounds at Braintree.

Abigail Adams' mother died on October 1, 1775. Abigail wrote to John, "How can I tell you (o my bursting Heart) that my Dear Mother has Left me . . . she left this world for an infinitely better [one]. . . . Almighty God restrain the pestilence which walketh in darkness and wasteth . . . and which has laid in the dust one of the dearest of parents."[28]

Her father, who had administered the final blessing on his wife, was devastated. "Child, I see your Mother, go to what part of the house I will," he told Abigail.[29] He would not remarry but would hold Elizabeth Quincy Smith in his heart as his only love until he died, nine years later.

Patty, Abigail's servant girl, whom she considered "one of my own Family," died on October 8; "she made the fourth Corpse that was this day committed to the Ground" in Braintree.[30] Abigail had written back in September that "the desolation of War is not so distressing as the Havoc made by the pestilence."[31] She prayed to "the Father of Mercies" now to keep her remaining family well and safe and wondered if the twin plagues of illness and discord would ever end.[32]

On October 10, 1775, Josiah Quincy Sr. sat in a chair at his window overlooking Boston Harbor. Another royal governor was leaving Massachusetts, and Josiah wanted to watch him go. Governor Gage had been recalled to

England, blamed by Parliament for the losses suffered at Bunker Hill and for failing to take decisive action against the colonists earlier in the year. Sir William Howe replaced Gage as commander of the British forces in New England. Lord North was hopeful that Howe would be able to crush the colonists there, and splinter all support in Congress for war against England.

Josiah took a knife from the table beside him, used for peeling the apples that were picked every morning, still wet with dew, from the orchards that grew up and down the hillsides of his property. Carefully, he carved into the glass of his window with the point of his knife: "Oct. 10, 1775. Governor Gage sailed for England with a fair wind."[33]

He laid the knife back down. His heart was heavy. Fair winds blew for Gage, but he knew storm clouds, fomented by Howe, would soon be descending over all of New England.

British forces, in the form of four hulking navy ships, approached the port town of Falmouth on Cape Cod early in the morning of October 17. In weeks past, a few shots had been fired from Falmouth toward passing British vessels. Howe was now determined to deliver a message, not only to the rebels of Falmouth but to all New Englanders, that any aggressive acts against Britain would be punished.

A messenger from the English ships rowed to shore and delivered Howe's ultimatum to the people of Falmouth: rebel leaders, along with all town munitions, were to be surrendered immediately or Falmouth would be destroyed.

No surrenders were made and the following day, the English fired an eight-hour barrage of cannonballs, bombs, and incendiary shells into the town. When townspeople were spotted trying to put out fires, a landing party of British soldiers pushed them back, ensuring that the fires burned through the day and night.

By dawn the next morning, more than three hundred buildings, along with wharves, warehouses, and fishing boats, lay in ruins, reduced to ashes and charred beams. With a long winter on its way, the residents of Falmouth were left without homes or food, and without boats to secure sustenance from the sea. A flood of refugees made its way inland, seeking shelter.

In Braintree, John Adams' mother was worried that the British Navy would next travel to Philadelphia and bombard that town, placing her son in danger. Abigail, however, incensed as she was over "Poor Falmouth [which] has shared the fate of Charlestown," worried less about John and more about the future of her colony: "are we become a Sodom? I would fain hope we are not."[34]

More and more, Abigail was beginning to think that the only path to salvation was through independence: "Unsearchable are the ways of Heaven who permitteth Evil to befall a city and a people by those very hands who were by them constituted the Guardians and protecters of them," she wrote to John.[35] England no longer protected the colonies, but instead hurt them; and the colonies must separate from such evildoers.

Two weeks later, as more details of the bombing of Falmouth came out and the miseries of Boston multiplied ("Poor poor inhabitants of Boston, what will be their fate?"), Abigail became certain of her position.[36] She opposed any "reconciliation between [the] tyrant State, and these Colonies."

She proclaimed to John: "Let us separate, they are unworthy to be our Brethren. Let us renounce them and instead of supplications as formerly for their prosperity and happiness, Let us beseech the almighty to blast their counsels and bring to Nought all their devices."[37]

Independence! This was her rallying cry now.

George Washington, stunned by the "cruelty and barbarity . . . revenge and malice" in the bombardment of Falmouth, saw the British military action as "proof of the diabolical designs" of Lord North and his ministry.[38] He demanded that Congress now allow Americans to engage in privateering—the capturing of enemy boats at sea—as both retaliation for the bombing of Falmouth and to secure much-needed supplies for the colonists.

Although Congress would not officially condone privateering for months, the leaders of Massachusetts directed its colony's vessels to attack and capture any passing British ship; prizes could be claimed for the goods found on board, and any army supplies would go to the continental forces. By the end of October, a fleet of scrappy New Englanders in their humble boats set sail, intent on their prey; they aimed their schooners, sloops, and brigs at the navy ships of England, the most powerful armed vessels in the world.

In November, the Continental Congress in Philadelphia received word from London. The king had responded to their Olive Branch Petition by declaring them all to be in "open and avowed rebellion . . . traitorously preparing, ordering, and levying war against" England. King George vowed that there would be "condign punishment [for] the authors, perpetrators, and abettors of such traitorous designs."[39]

On October 26, the king, in opening Parliament, once again declared the colonies to be in rebellion and vowed that England would "put a speedy end to these disorders by the most decisive exertions of force." He alluded to additional armed support from "foreign assistance," that is, mercenaries.

Although he promised to pardon the "deluded multitude . . . sensible of their error," the leaders of the treasonous conspiracy against England would be punished without mercy.[40]

The Olive Branch had been swatted away. England had declared war on its colonies in America.

John Adams, in responding to the king's rejection of the petition, stayed away from words like *independence* and *separation*. And yet he was already beginning to devise a system of government that, as he wrote to Richard Henry Lee, "is most readily and easily adopted by a Colony, upon a Sudden Emergency"—such as the sudden emergency of finding itself independent. He offered details to Lee of a "a Legislative, an Executive and a judicial Power" with a "balancing each of these Powers against the other two" in order to check the impulse "in human Nature towards Tyranny" and to preserve Freedoms as guaranteed in "the Constitution."[41]

Adams' vision of this "emergency" government would prove to be the framework of the new nation—but a nation that now he could see only in his dreams and speak of only in private.

As usual, Abigail both dreamed and spoke more freely. She had put much thought into how a new country would be best governed and shared with her husband her concerns; "if we separate from Britain, what Code of Laws will be established. . . . How shall we be governed so as to retain our Liberties? Can any government be free which is not administered by general stated Laws? Who shall frame these Laws? Who will give them force and energy?"[42]

She had formed her own ideas on how best to govern people, to nudge them toward good behavior and reward them for loyalty and hard work—and her plans applied not only to white men, but to all the population. She saw merit in every human being and would try over the coming months to get John to see things the way she did, especially in terms of the rights of blacks and women.

Unbeknown to her when she wrote in early December, John was finally on his way home. He had asked leave from Congress—as he was "worn down with long and uninterrupted Labour"—and it had been granted; on December 9 he left for Massachusetts; he would finally arrive in Braintree on

December 21.[43] Abigail longed to see him: "I have been like a nun in a cloister ever since you went away. . . . My Evenings are lonesome and Melancholy."[44]

She wanted her John back in the flesh again; his words scrawled hastily across paper were never an adequate substitute. To have him with her, to hold and to talk to, and to persuade as best she could to her point of view on independence for everyone.

In early December 1775, John Hancock received word from George Washington that the British brig *Nancy*, an ordnance ship, had been captured by the *Lee*, a small schooner captained by the "rough and ready" Boston shipmaster John Manley.[45] The British ship carried tons of ammunition, thousands of muskets, several brass cannon, one hundred thousand flints, and a three-thousand-pound mortar that would later be called "the noblest piece of ordnance ever landed in America."[46]

Not only would the British be denied their arms and ammunition, but with that one capture, the Americans had landed supplies they desperately needed. Ammunition stores had fallen so steeply that Congress was considering outfitting soldiers with bows and arrows—but the capture of the *Nancy* would help toward refilling empty coffers.

John Hancock quickly shared the news of the *Nancy*'s seizure with Congress. Cheers rebounded around the meeting room in the State House. Hope once again flourished; more prizes would be secured on the high seas, the delegates were sure. In addition, Hancock reported, Henry Knox, a twenty-five-year-old former bookseller from Boston, had formulated a plan, approved by George Washington, to travel to Fort Ticonderoga in upper New York and steal away the fifty-nine cannon and mortars that were held there by the British and bring them back to army headquarters in Cambridge.

But the optimism brought by the seizure of the *Nancy* was short-lived. The final weeks of 1775 brought an almost constant barrage of bad news, day after day, week after week. Lord Stirling of New Jersey, an English nobleman who had joined the rebels, wrote to John Hancock about how Tory opposition forces were strengthening in New Jersey, supported by the royal governor William Franklin (son of Benjamin); having acquired both arms and ammunition, "the Tories . . . assume fresh courage and talk very daringly."[47]

News came from Virginia that John Murray, Earl of Dunmore, Loyalist royal governor of the colony, had declared martial law; established a Loyalist army; proclaimed all revolutionaries to be traitors; and offered freedom to any slaves willing to fight on behalf of England. The news struck terror into the hearts of Southerners, fearful of uprisings; John Hancock condemned the "horrid attempts . . . to excite domestic insurrections."[48]

George Washington wrote to Hancock of the imminent depletion of his fighting forces. The terms of enlistment for over ten thousand men now serving were coming to an end, and most planned on leaving the army to return home to farms, families, and avocations. Not only was the number of soldiers set to fall precipitously, but once again, rounds of ammunition and stores of gunpowder were running perilously low. Washington also needed money, he wrote to Hancock, to pay for salaries, food, and other supplies.

To increase the number of troops, Washington made the unilateral decision to allow blacks to fight for the American cause. Ignoring Congress's previous instructions barring them from service, he wrote diplomatically to John Hancock that he had "presumed to depart from the [congressional] resolution, and have given license for their being enlisted."[49] After all, it was a black man, Salem Poor, who had shot and killed Major John Pitcairn at the Battle of Bunker Hill, landing a terrible blow to the British forces even as they claimed their hollow victory.

John Adams had argued against blacks being allowed into the army last spring. But in the dead of winter in Braintree, far away from the debates in Congress, he found himself agreeing with Washington's decision. Slowly, slowly, he was edging closer to his wife Abigail's position on the manumission of blacks; she always understood that a passion for liberty for one sort of man must be aligned with a passion for liberty for all.

Desperate for a victory, George Washington repeatedly wrote to Hancock asking for Congress's approval to launch an offensive against British forces in Boston. He could not understand why Howe had not attacked the colonists and hoped that it might be because Howe's troops were just too weak and too low on supplies, and therefore vulnerable themselves to attack.

In fact, Howe had planned to evacuate Boston by the end of the year, moving the British forces to New York to fight there. But parliamentary approval to leave Boston didn't arrive until December, and by then winter had arrived in full force, making travel difficult. In addition, the number of boats available to General Howe were too few to allow all the troops to leave.

Howe knew that winter in Boston would be miserable, long, and cold. Snow had fallen early in November, wet and heavy, icing streets and making already damp shelters even chillier. Bitterly cold winds blew off the harbor, and more snow fell as December settled in. Scurvy, smallpox, and dysentery took its toll on British soldiers and Americans alike.

Every week, scores of people died in the besieged town; Boston had become "the grave of England and the slaughterhouse of America."[50] With fuel low (the Old North Church had long been busted up, its planks, pews, and beams burned for heat, and most of the trees of Boston cut down, including the Liberty Tree) and food stores depleted, the misery would only grow worse as winter dragged on. But there was nothing Howe could do. In mid-December, he announced to his officers that they would remain in Boston until early spring.

John Hancock urged Congress to send more money to Washington and to work harder to find more supplies for what army he did have. He also spoke in favor of Washington's proposed attack on Boston, despite the dangers that such an attack posed to his own interests there.

"It is true nearly all of the property I have in the world is in houses and other real estate in the town of Boston," he told his fellow delegates. "But if the expulsion of the British army away from it—and the liberties of our country—require their being burnt to ashes, issue the order for that purpose immediately."[51]

While there were a few who opposed the offensive (on the grounds that such an attack would be an act of war against Britain—these delegates still hoped for a peaceful reconciliation with England), on December 22, Hancock was able to send the directive to Washington, giving him congressional approval to proceed and offering the sincere hope that "God crown your attempt with success. I most heartily wish it, though individually I may be the greatest sufferer."[52]

When she heard the news, Dolly was shaken by the prospect of her husband losing everything he owned: his mansion on Beacon Hill and other properties, all the furnishings of the buildings, his warehouses, and whatever goods remained stored there. She had lived through changes of fortune before and the possibility of genteel poverty didn't scare her. But she worried about how John and Aunt Lydia would fare, losing everything they had.

On the morning of December 23, she went to a Quaker meetinghouse not far from the Arch Street home of the Massachusetts delegation. She stayed there throughout the afternoon and into the evening, praying. She asked God to keep both the inhabitants and the properties of Boston safe. As for the British, she begged for their departure, the sooner the better.

31

Surrender of Boston

Hath not blood and treasure in all ages
been the price of civil liberty?
Can Americans hope . . .
that the best of blessings will be obtained
and secured without the sharpest trials?

—JOSIAH QUINCY SR.

Abigail Quincy read through the letters her father had shared with her, missives from friends and neighbors who used to live close to them in Boston but were now scattered far and wide, having taken refuge in villages and towns throughout New England. How everyone missed the homes they'd left behind! And how they wished they had taken with them more of their belongings, for now all of those homes and belongings—and memories held therein—were threatened. Not by the British, who had certainly done their worst, but by American forces intent on retaking Boston.

Abigail knew that the world she had grown up in, and then lived in as a married woman, would never survive the onslaught of a bombardment against Boston. But unlike her neighbors, Abigail felt only relief, for she would be spared reminders of her husband if she never saw Boston again. "I dread the thought of going among my friends that were his friends & acquaintances—as though they were enemies—and feel a secret pleasure in thinking we are not likely to see Boston this winter."[1]

She, like John Hancock, was ready to see the enemies brought to battle and, with God on their side, defeated. As Josiah had written years earlier, "we fear not the hour of trial, though the hosts of our enemies shall cover the field like locusts."[2]

Samuel Quincy spent Christmas with Jonathan and Esther Sewall—in England, the day was celebrated with feasting and drinking—and he enjoyed the festivities as best he could, given the separation from his wife and family. He missed them and hoped that he would not become a hazy figure in their memories; in his letters to his wife, Hannah, he asked her to send him details of "how you live, what intercourse you have with one another, and whether my friends round you ever talk or think of me."[3]

Sam especially worried that his children, Sam and Tom, might not remember him, "as I do them, that is, with great Tenderness and Affection, and an earnest Solicitude to see them."[4]

Samuel was certain that war would be fought, and that the British would win. He only hoped it would all be over quickly, with as little blood spilled and lives lost as possible. Until then, "God preserve you all," he wrote to Hannah, thanking her for her letters, which gave him "evidence that you were still in life."[5] He worried that he—or any member of his family—might not survive the coming war to see each other again and prayed that their separation could end soon.

Samuel's hopes for a short war disintegrated as reports began to arrive in England: there had been a British victory in Canada, the Americans held back from entering Quebec City in a crushing defeat of their forces. The American general, Richard Montgomery, was dead, along with fifty other Americans; close to forty men had been wounded and over four hundred Americans had been taken prisoner. And yet still the Americans hung on, camped out at the gates of the city in a brutal winter.

Samuel had long known of Montgomery's military exploits, and having heard his brother Josiah speak highly of Montgomery's Whig politics, he wrote a poem in honor of the slain general.

> Oh, Spirit of the Truly Brave
> From thy obscure, sequestered grave
> Arise! Montgomery, arise!
> Thy immortal name
> bid the Youth Aspire
> Like Thee, on Glory's Wing to rise.[6]

In his diary, Samuel admitted now that the civil war would be long and bloody. He grieved over his separation from friends and family; how he longed to see them all and be back in the Boston he feared would soon be destroyed, and gone forever.

Jonathan Sewall had no desire to ever see Boston again; he might "wish it well," but he would never return to that place where "Rebellion and Fanaticism are engendered"—and instead would "shun it as I would a country infested with the plague."[7] His wife Esther, however, missed her old friends and her family; she was lonely for their company and also worried for their safety. No one knew for sure what was happening in Boston; too many rumors flew around London, and too few facts. What she wanted most of all was to return to her native country and see for herself what was going on. She missed her house in Cambridge and the quiet life she had led there until all the troubles began.

John Adams left Braintree in early January 1776 to return to Congress. But first, he traveled to Cambridge to meet with General Washington and to see the new flag that had just been hoisted to fly over army headquarters. Accompanied by a thirteen-gun salute, the flag, with the cross of St. George and St. Andrew in one corner and thirteen stripes for the thirteen colonies, was raised high above Prospect Hill. Its brilliant white and red stripes could be seen as far away as Boston, and that was the intention.

America had not only its own army now—the Continental Army, as Washington had formally named it—but also its own flag. When British lookouts first spotted it, they thought it was a signal of surrender. But a closer examination with their telescopes revealed the details of the new flag—and destroyed any hope that the rebels might be laying down their arms and returning to the fold of Great Britain.

In an attempt to stir dissension in the American ranks, British officers had copies of the King's Speech from October printed up and sent through enemy lines for wide distribution among rebel forces. In his speech, the king had offered pardon to those who laid down arms and promised merciless destruction to those who did not. The British were certain that once the rebels knew what the king had promised, there would be a wave of desertions from the American cause. After all, the offer of mercy from King George III was just too good to pass up.

But wherever the printed speech made its way, the reaction was the same: soldiers tore their copies of the speech into shreds and threw the bits and pieces into the campfires, turning the King's Speech to ashes.

By late January 1776, Washington reported to John Hancock that he had between eight and ten thousand men in his army, with more men reenlisting than he had anticipated. But he told Hancock only the number of men, not their quality, perhaps to ensure that Congress would continue to support his plan to attack Boston.

In a letter to his friend Joseph Reed, Washington was more honest: he admitted that fewer than half the men were actually battle-ready; even worse, the amount of ammunition held by the army was too paltry, and the number of weapons were too few, to mount any kind of attack. "The reflection upon my situation and that of this army produces many an uneasy hour when all around me are wrapped in sleep. Few people know the predicament we are in."[8]

Washington, however, would not back down from his plan to attack Boston: "no opportunity can present itself earlier than my wishes."[9] In a council of war with his generals, to which John Adams (as representative of the Massachusetts Provincial Assembly) was invited, Washington told Adams to convey to Congress how urgently he needed arms and ammunition to mount the offensive. John promised he would deliver the message to his fellow delegates, unaware that Washington had another plan for securing weapons: Henry Knox, the young man he'd sent to upstate New York, should be returning soon.

On his way south to Philadelphia, John Adams stopped in New York, intent on finding copies of a recently published pamphlet that was receiving much praise and publicity. John found what he wanted and purchased two copies; he would keep one copy of Thomas Paine's *Common Sense* for himself and send the other one home to Abigail. He was sure she would enjoy it.

As for his own perusal of the pamphlet, John Adams appreciated the "manly and striking style" exhibited by Paine's writing, yet believed he himself could have done a better job "if I had undertaken such a Work." He understood how to construct the government of a new nation; whereas Paine "seems to have very inadequate Ideas of [how] to form Constitutions for single Colonies, as well as a great Model of Union for the whole."[10]

Abigail had no such complaints about Thomas Paine or his pamphlet. She quickly read through her copy, then read it again, before taking it upon herself to "spread it as much as it lay in my power." Everyone in the village, she wrote John, "assents to the weighty truths it contains. I wish it could gain Credit enough in [Congress] to be carried speedily into Execution."[11]

Abigail felt as if Thomas Paine had taken the words from her own mouth when he wrote, "We have every opportunity and every encouragement before us, to form the noblest purest constitution on the face of the earth. We have it in our power to begin the world over again."[12]

She agreed as well with the method he proposed for beginning the world over again: "Everything that is right or reasonable pleads for separation,"

Paine wrote, "Wherefore, since nothing but blows will do, for God's sake let us come to a final separation."[13] Abigail prayed that Congress would do whatever had to be done to bring such a goal to fruition. To turn the world upside down, start over again, and do it right.

And yet she feared for her colony, as the battle for Boston loomed. "The preparations increase and something great is daily expected, something terrible it will be. I impatiently wait for, yet dread the day."[14] She and John had their own property interests in Boston, nothing compared to what John Hancock laid claim to, just a small building containing the remains of John's Boston law practice. Nevertheless, for them it was where they had shared so much time living and working together in the same house, with their children underfoot; and it was together in Boston that the first spark of their joint passion for the rights of their colony had been lit, first by Parliament's interference and then by the events of that cold March day, almost six years ago.

What would their present times look like if on March 5, 1770, no young rascal had taunted Hugh White on his officer's failure to pay a wig bill? The escalation of events from that point—had it been unstoppable or inevitable? For Abigail, her resolution for independence from England had started with the Battles of Lexington and Concord, when she feared that any colonist could be next in the line of fire.

And then the siege of Boston, with all the pestilence that such an occupation released: the misery of being held hostage, of being separated from fellow colonists; the lack of food and supplies, the starvation; the illnesses that multiplied in crowded, miserable conditions; the constant vigilance against an uncertain threat; and the oppression of spirit that came from having an enemy in line of sight, just across the water.

The enemy held Boston, and Boston was a symbol to the colonists. The city on a hill, where those escaping oppression came to be both free in spirit and certain of their duty. Now they were again oppressed—and by the same tyrant, England—and their duty was more certain than ever. And so, once again, they would escape the tyranny of the mother country, but this time, they had to do it for good. As Abigail wrote to John, "may justice and righteousness be the Stability of our times, and order arise out of confusion. Great difficulties may be surmounted, by patience and perseverance."[15]

Abigail Adams in her home by the sea, Josiah Quincy Sr. in his rooftop guard post, Edmund Quincy in Lancaster: they anticipated the roll and thunder of cannon fire any day now, and the sight of flames and smoke rising over the city on a hill.

"I expect soon to hear the Bombardment and Cannonading of poor Boston!"[16] Edmund wrote as the winter dragged on. Across the colony, he was not alone.

At the end of January, John Hancock met with Benjamin Franklin after a long day of congressional committee meetings. Franklin had joined his Pennsylvania delegation the summer before and was proving to be a trusted ally to Massachusetts. He had long discarded hopes for reconciliation with England and was now fully committed to the path laid out by his former mentor, Josiah Quincy Jr.: the path to independence. In the summer of 1775, he had made his feelings clear when he declared, in a widely shared letter, that England, having "begun to burn our towns and murder our people," was the "enemy." The enemy to be fought against, and separated from, forever.[17]

Neither Franklin's commitment to the cause of independence nor his enthusiasm could be dampened by the recent bad news of defeat and losses in Canada. In fact, as British incursions increased over the coming months, his resolve did as well: "Forces have been sent out and towns have been burnt. We cannot now expect happiness under the domination of Great Britain. All former attachments have been obliterated."[18]

And yet John Hancock knew that the report he had received that day from Lord Stirling in New Jersey might very well cloud the countenance of the old diplomat. Stirling had good news, that the Tories in New Jersey had been subdued. But as part of the measures taken against New Jersey Loyalists, Governor William Franklin was put under armed guard and held prisoner in his home. It would be up to Hancock to tell Benjamin Franklin of his son's fate.

Franklin took the news stoically and agreed with Hancock that the best place for his son would be far from New Jersey, thereby preventing him from associating with Loyalist friends and family. Franklin had tried to convince William in December to come over to the cause of liberty, but he had failed. Benjamin Franklin wouldn't see his son again for almost a decade, and left nothing to him in his will when he died.

The winter in Philadelphia was so much milder than what those in New England were suffering through, and yet John Hancock's gout returned; it was less dependent on the weather than on the amount of stress under which he labored—and those stresses were steady. Every meeting of Congress had to be presided over by Hancock; every document issued by Congress had to be signed by Hancock; every colony had to be persuaded to contribute men, supplies, and money by Hancock; and every visitor to Congress had to be greeted, listened to, and sent on their way—by Hancock.

Edmund Quincy wrote to Dolly that all the ailments of Hancock were to be pitied but "especially that it should affect . . . his eyes since the Clearest Sight of every American Patriot is [so] critical . . . and more so [for Hancock] than any other member of the most important political Council now existing on the Globe."[19] With such expectations upon him, no wonder John Hancock felt such strain and such pressure.

Henry Knox and his nineteen-year-old brother made it back to Massachusetts from Fort Ticonderoga in mid-February. With the help of the dozens of volunteers who came out of small towns and villages all along the way, the two brothers dragged, carried, rowed, pushed, and pulled forty-two sledges and wagons carrying fifty-eight howitzers, mortars, and cannons across three hundred miles. The weaponry weighed close to sixty tons, the journey took more than fifty days, and the weather the brothers endured included rain, ice, snow, and hail. It was an awesome feat and a signal to Washington of the heart and resolve of his New England troops.

Washington now had the guns he needed. But what he would do with them would surprise many. As he confided in a letter to John Hancock, he admitted that the plan to attack Boston was perhaps more hazardous "than was consistent with prudence."[20] Having been counseled by his war generals "to take possession of Dorchester Hill, with a view of drawing out the Enemy," he now found himself agreeing to a different plan of warfare.[21]

While the new plan was seen by some as a bizarre engineering stunt, Washington was convinced that the idea of building in one night an entire fort out of hay and sticks might be just the trick to intimidate the British and allow the Americans to appear stronger than they actually were. The plan had been conceived by Rufus Putnam, a self-taught engineer, after he happened upon the idea in a book about military maneuvers.

The fort—or two forts, as it turned out—would be built on Dorchester Heights, a no-man's-land that looked out over Boston from a great height. Putnam oversaw the engineering of premade frames of light wood and twisted hay bales, which could then be dragged uphill and quickly arranged into a wall of what would appear to be a solid fort. To distract any British soldiers who might be watching, Knox's cannons would be placed at Cambridge and Roxbury, from which points they would launch balls and fire at Boston, raising all kinds of hell.

The night chosen for building the fort was March 4. For the two nights before, the Americans shot cannon at Boston, but the attacks were moderate and largely harmless. Then, on the evening of March 4, as the true cannonade began, three thousand American soldiers began carrying their prefab forts of sticks and straw up the hill.

The next morning, on the sixth anniversary of the Boston Massacre, the British were amazed to see towering atop Dorchester Heights two brand-new forts, as if magically conjured. One faced Castle Island, and the other faced out over Boston. The misty morning added to the sense of unreality, but at the same time, General Howe was very sure of what he was seeing. "Howe was seen to scratch his head and heard to say by those that were around him, that he did not know what he should do," a local minister reported, "that the provincials . . . had done more work in one night than his whole army would have done in six months."[22]

The forts were so high up that it was impossible for British guns to reach them, although the British tried, again and again, with a barrage of fire and shot. Meanwhile, the cannonade from Cambridge and Roxbury continued to rain down upon the town. The long-awaited battle for Boston had begun but in a way no one had anticipated.

Abigail in Braintree wrote nonstop to John in Philadelphia, as she heard the cannon roar and as rumors flew, and with no certainty as to what was happening, who was winning, or what the outcome would be. She had no idea if her letters would get through to John but she had to write, to share with him the terror of the ensuing battle.

Already on March 2, the night of the first barrage, she wrote, "hark! the House this instant shakes with the roar of Cannon. I have been to the door and find tis a cannonade from our Army. . . . No Sleep for me to Night." She laid blame on the English for the carnage she was sure was about to ensue: "the miserable wretches who have been the procurers of this Dreadful Scene and those who are to be the actors, lie down with the load of Guilt upon their Souls."[23]

All night long, her "Heart Beat pace with" the cannon fire; "what tomorrow will bring forth God only knows." She left the house at dawn and made her way, along with almost the entire village, to Penn's Hill, from where they could look out over Boston. A haze lay over the water, and smoke still rose in columns, obscuring the hills of Dorchester and the town beyond.

That afternoon, she returned to Penn's Hill and stayed until once again she heard "the amazing roar of cannon. . . . The sound I think is one of the Grandest in Nature."[24]

But as she began her walk down the hill toward home, the cannon, "now an incessant Roar," seemed less grand and more a terrible harbinger of things to come: "O the fatal Ideas which are connected with the sound. How many of our dear country men must fall?"[25]

That night, the night of March 4, Abigail put her children to bed, unaware of the thousands of men now working their way up the slopes of Dorchester to build their fort out of hay, sticks, and hope. Her home was her own again, the many refugees having moved on, and she paced the silent rooms, unable to rest; "I could no more sleep than if I had been in the engagement," she wrote to John.

Once again, a bombardment had started: "The rattling of the windows, the jar of the house and the continual roar of 24 pounders, the Bursting of shells."[26] She went again and again to the windows of her farmhouse, looking out into a dark night. The moon was full, but its light obscured by the fog rising off the sea.

On March 5, Abigail, groggy with little sleep yet still anxious and nervous for news, again found herself walking out to Penn's Hill. It had become the meeting ground for all the neighbors, the new village green where news was shared and fears exchanged. The haze over Boston was thicker than ever, the sun rising to the east, just a dim light wrapped in fog and smoke. A heavy mist rolled off the sea, enveloping all of Braintree in a damp and salty gloom.

Then shouts echoed from down below, and the sharp report of hoofbeats was heard coming down the Plymouth Road. A messenger had arrived from Cambridge to deliver in a staccato of short sentences an account of all that had happened between the Americans and the British. He returned to his saddle, refusing even a draught of cider, and sped again on his way, to continue south to the chain of towns waiting for news.

Abigail returned home, shaken by the news; certainly, it was good that "we got possession of Dorchester Hill Last Night. 4000 men upon it to day— lost but one Man. The Ships are all drawn round the Town."

But still she had no idea what would happen next. Her only certainty was that the battle for Boston was not over. "Tonight we shall realize a more terrible scene still. I sometimes think I cannot stand it—I wish myself with you," she wrote to John. Even more, she wished she could write that the battle was finished and that victory belonged to the Americans: "I hope to give you joy of Boston, even if it is in ruins."[27]

For two days more, shots and cannon continued to be lobbed back and forth between Boston and Cambridge. Abigail despaired that all the days of bombardment had resulted in so little: "from all the Muster and Stir I hoped and expected more important and decisive Scenes; I would not have suffered all I have for two such Hills."

And still it continued. On March 10, Abigail wrote to John that all of Braintree was "assaulted with the roar of Cannon. . . . My Hand and heart will tremble, at this domestic fury, and fierce civil Strife, which encumber all our parts. . . . I feel for the unhappy wretches who know not where to fly for safety. I feel still more for my Bleeding Country men who are hazarding their lives and their Limbs."[28]

Abigail did not know that two days earlier, on March 8, the British forces holding Boston had offered George Washington a truce: if they were allowed to evacuate the town, taking what time they needed to gather their supplies, load their vessels, and also accommodate all the Loyalists who wished to evacuate with them, the British promised they would not burn Boston to the ground before leaving. Washington agreed to the terms of their departure.

Over eleven thousand people were to be loaded up on one hundred British ships, including close to nine thousand troops and over a thousand Loyalists. Howe had arranged passage not only for Loyalists wishing to leave Boston but also for his American prisoners; John Lovell, Loyalist schoolmaster of the Boston Latin School, took a berth, but it is not known whether he went in search of his son James, a prisoner of the British since winter and now confined in the cargo hold of one of the British ships leaving Boston.[29]

Josiah Quincy Sr., sitting in his monitor, saw for himself the British ships loading up with passengers, barrels and crates of supplies, horses, trunks, and chests and then moving out of the harbor toward Castle Island, where more people and bundles were picked up. Then finally, the ships set sail, pitching forward into the welcoming swells of the Atlantic and leaving Massachusetts behind.

Overwhelmed with gratitude and writing with "a trembling hand," Josiah Sr. wrote to George Washington in Cambridge, expressing his "compliments of Congratulation, which are due to you from every friend to liberty and the rights of mankind, upon your triumphant and almost bloodless victory, in forcing the British . . . to a precipitate flight from the capital of these colonies."[30]

"The more I think of our Enemies quitting Boston, the more amazed I am," Abigail Adams wrote to John. "Shurely it is the Lord's doings and it is Marvelous in our Eyes."[31] Their son Charles, age five, had a different take on the departure; he called the British "cowards for they have stood it but one year, and we would have stood it three."[32] John celebrated the "Joy of Boston and Charlestown, once more the Habitations of Americans."[33]

Safe but uneasy in Norwich, Abigail Quincy was grateful for the minimal lives lost in securing the British surrender of Boston; but mixed in with her solemn gratitude was her fervent desire, the "energetic principle beating in [her] heart," of seeing independence from England declared.[34] Edmund Quincy had the same idea; while he praised the "Glorious defensive Struggles we have made under the Severe attacks of the British wicked Ministry," he also prayed, "May we deserve a Continuance of the Protections of Heaven and may there soon be an Accommodation of Separation."[35]

At the end of March, Abigail Adams, accompanied by Mercy Otis Warren and her husband, James, climbed once again to the top of Penn's Hill to watch "the last division of the British fleet" sail away from Boston: "about sixty or seventy sail. . . . What their destination is we are not able to ascertain."[36]

Mercy wrote to Dolly Hancock of the "dead silence" that now surrounded Boston—and then assured Dolly that the Hancock mansion was safe; "your own delightful residence . . . to the surprise of everyone has escaped the outrages of the enemy."[37]

John Hancock had already heard from George Washington of the generally good state of his mansion ("no damage worth mentioning . . . the family pictures are all left entire and untouched").[38] From his steward Hancock heard that his wine cellars were emptied and his backgammon table was missing, but everything else seemed in order. However, the engraving of his name at the foot of Brattle Square Church had been chiseled away from the stone. No great loss: what had been broken away could be chiseled again into the stone.

Despite the months of occupation and the days of incessant shelling, Boston was not in as bad shape as everyone had anticipated, but still, destruction was everywhere in evidence. North Meeting Church was gone, torn down for firewood, and the Old South Meeting House had been damaged by its use as a riding ring. A number of houses lay in ruins, destroyed by looters, including Samuel Quincy's mansion on Hanover Street.

Abigail Adams had little pity for Samuel's loss, his house having fallen victim to his "own merciless party." Apparently even the Redcoats felt "a

Reverential awe for Virtue and patriotism, whilst they Detest the paricide and traitor,"[39] she wrote to John, referring not only to Quincy's destroyed home but Hancock's preserved one.

John Adams felt as little remorse for the fate of Samuel Quincy as Abigail did. "Let Us take Warning and give it to our Children. Whenever Vanity, and Gaiety, a Love of Pomp and Dress, Furniture, Equipage, Buildings, great Company, expensive Diversions, and elegant Entertainments get the better of the Principles and Judgments of Men or Women there is no knowing where they will stop, nor into what Evils, natural, moral, or political, they will lead us," he lectured to Abigail.

But he prefaced his lecture against Samuel Quincy with mercy for his family: "I pity his pretty Children, I pity his Father, and his sisters."[40]

Both John and Abigail were grateful for the survival of the small building they'd called home on Queen Street, which was intact (although "very dirty"). "I look upon it as a new acquisition of property," Abigail wrote, "which one month ago I did not value at a single Shilling, and could with pleasure have seen it in flames."[41]

The worst destruction to Boston's buildings and furnishings, according to John Rowe, who had remained in town through the entire siege, had occurred in the final days when British soldiers rampaged through the streets and along the wharves, "taking all things . . . never asking who is the owner or whose property, making havoc in every house. . . . There never was such destruction and outrage."[42]

The greatest desolation seemed to be to the people of Boston themselves, who greeted their liberators with a weary joy; skinny and malnourished, unkempt in well-worn clothing and leather shoes bound together by twine, the survivors of the siege welcomed the gifts of fish, bread, meat, cider, and beer to feast on, and warm clothes and wood for their fireplaces. Even John Rowe, who had spent the entire siege in Boston in relative comfort, welcomed the gifts offered by returning friends, having lost all provisions and most of his warehoused goods in the ransacking of the final days.

After the final British vessel left the harbor, John and Eben Warren, brothers to Dr. Joseph Warren, made the trek from the close streets of Boston to the slopes of Breed's Hill. They were accompanied by their longtime compatriot, Paul Revere. Under a blue April sky and with cool breezes coming off the sea, the brothers and the silversmith walked amidst dozens of shallow graves, searching for their fallen brother and compatriot.

It was a gruesome task but the men were determined; they sifted through remains, in grave after grave shared by a number of dead, until they found what they believed to be Joseph's body. It was badly decomposed but identifiable through the scraps of a familiar waistcoat and the remains of a canvas smock on the body beside him; the brothers had been told Joseph was buried beside a farmer wearing just such a smock.

Paul Revere knelt to the ground to examine the skull. He saw in the jaw, still firmly attached with gold wiring, the ivory dentures he'd crafted for Warren in the early 1770s, an upper left canine and a first premolar. He looked up and nodded to John and Eben: the corpse before them was their brother. The men wrapped Joseph Warren's body in canvas sacking and carried him down the hill, back to Boston.

A few days later Joseph Warren was buried in the Granary Burying Ground adjacent to the Boston Common, after a funeral service in King's Chapel. Abigail Adams, having heard from those who were present, described the scene for her husband. "The Masons walking in procession from the State House, with the Military in uniforms and a large concourse of people attending . . . the Dead Body like that of Caesars before their Eyes."[43]

William Phillips was there in King's Chapel. He had traveled from Norwich to attend the service in honor of his daughter Abigail and her love for Dr. Warren, who had kept her husband alive as long as he could; and in memory of his son-in-law. Like Joseph Warren, Josiah was a man taken too young, who gave his all for a nation yet to be born.

In one of his last letters to his wife, Abigail, Josiah had written, "O my dear friend! my heart beats high in the cause of my country. Their safety, their honor, their all, is at stake! I see America placed in that great tide in the affairs of men, which, taken at the flood, leads on to fortune. Oh, snatch the glorious opportunity!"[44]

The time had come to take the opportunity. Time to make that new nation. All eyes turned to Philadelphia, and to the men in Congress.

32

Debating Separation

The People grew more and more sensible
of the Wrong that was done them . . . ,
more and more impatient . . . ,
and determined at all Hazards
to rid themselves of it.

—JOHN ADAMS

Toward the end of February 1776, John Adams returned from an evening of caucusing with Sam Adams and Richard Henry Lee. They had met to discuss the working paper recently introduced into Congress by John Dickinson and James Wilson of Pennsylvania, William Hooper of North Carolina, and James Duane of New York. To Adams' disgust, the paper laid out in no uncertain terms that while the colonies sought redress from England for wrongs committed against them, independence was in no way their goal.

John knew that the time for reconciliation between colonies and the mother country was long past. There was no support for it in England; not from Parliament, nor from the Crown, nor from Lord North. Did John Dickinson really believe that the clock could be turned back, that all would be forgiven on both sides of the Atlantic and things would return to how they had been before the Stamp Act? Too much blood had spilled, and too many lives lost.

Although the hour was late, John set himself to work, determined to stay strong against those waffling legislators who dared not demand independence. He began to write a list of all that he wanted achieved in Congress over the coming weeks. "Government to be assumed in every Colony. . . . Coin and Currencies to be regulated. . . . Forces to be raised and maintained," and so the list went on, every measure a step toward the self-sufficiency and self-defense of the American colonies.

And then he wrote, in a quick scribble, almost an afterthought, which he quickly followed with other measures, "Declaration of Independency."[1]

But it was no afterthought. A Declaration of Independence, the document itself, and everyone in Congress signed on to it—was the crucial cornerstone to every plan of action he had listed. Define the new nation by its goals. State the reasons for it, the need for it, and the God-willed and man-made beauty of it—and everything else would follow.

He had just one more letter to write before his day was done. A letter to Abigail, laying out a recipe for saltpeter. It was important that all the colonists do their bit to increase the amount of gunpowder available to the army, and so he carefully wrote, "Earth dug up from under a Stable [so as to be full of horse urine and feces], put into a Tub. . . . Filled with Water. Stand 24 Hours. Then leaked off Slowly. Then boil'd for one Hour. Then run thro another Tub full of ashes. . . . Then put into a Kettle and boiled, until it grows yellow. Then drop it on a cold stone or cold Iron, and it will christallise for a Proof. Then set it by in Trays in cool Places. . . . And the Salt Petre is formed."[2]

John folded the letter up and added it to a pile he hoped to have go by messenger to Boston the next day. He rose from his chair and made his way to bed.

Abigail answered his request for saltpeter with a soft jibe—"I find as much as I can do to manufacture clothing for my family which would else be Naked"—and then she turned the tables, telling John that she had "seen a small Manuscript describing the proportions for the various sorts of powder, fit for cannon, small arms and pistols." She offered, "If it would be of any Service your way I will get it transcribed and send it to you."[3]

John was very busy at Congress, but Abigail was very busy at home; if he supposed her to have time to make gunpowder, she supposed he might have the time to do the same.

Abigail's confidence and frustrations had grown side by side in the past few years: she was responsible for so much at home, with the finances and in management of the farm, and yet she was too often denied decision-making power in any of those realms. She sacrificed as much for her colony as her husband had, but she doubted that she would enjoy the same freedoms and liberties that he was expecting as the just rewards for his sacrifices.

Turning again to her letter, she wrote to her husband that in creating new laws for a new country, he should "Remember the Ladies. . . . If particular care and attention is not paid to the Ladies we are determined to foment a Rebellion, and will not hold ourselves bound by any Laws in which we have no voice, or Representation."

Thinking perhaps of her friend and cousin, Hannah Quincy Lincoln,

Abigail gave an example of just how poorly women faired under the current legal system—"the vicious and the Lawless [are able] to use us with cruelty and indignity"—and suggested that the pursuit of happiness ought to be as protected for women as for men.[4]

A few days later, Abigail wrote again, perhaps to massage her request a bit and give it more context: she wrote about her busy days, so "encumbered about many things and scarcely know which way to turn myself. I miss my partner, and find myself unequal to the cares . . . of our Husbandry and farming."

She ended the note referring to the intimacy that passed between them— "to wake the Soul by tender strokes of art . . . to Ruminate upon happiness we might enjoy."[5]

She loved John, she missed him, and she acknowledged both the loneliness she suffered with him gone and the many inadequacies that plagued her as she attempted to carry on the farm without him. But all her sentiments only served to shore up her main argument: that women, in feelings and thoughts, physically and mentally, deserved the same respect and privileges as men.

John answered her plea for equal rights with laughter and incredulity— "As to your extraordinary Code of Laws, I cannot but laugh"—and then compared her claims to those made by "Children and Apprentices . . . Indians . . . and Negroes" and concluded that "your Letter was the first Intimation that another Tribe more numerous and powerful than all the rest were grown discontented."[6]

Abigail was not amused: her husband had managed to insult not only women, but also Indians and blacks in just one paragraph. She reached for paper and pen and wrote her response.

John's final word on her suggestions for laws that recognized the rights of women—"We know better than to repeal our Masculine systems"—was answered by her with indignation: "you insist upon retaining an absolute power over Wives. But you must remember that Arbitrary power is like most other things which are very hard, [that is,] very liable to be broken."[7]

And a few days later, she added in another note to her husband, "a Government of Good Laws well-administered should carry with them the fairest prospect of happiness to a community, as well as to individuals."[8]

How disappointing for Abigail to discover that John's interests, in recognizing the rights of women, "when weigh'd in the balance," were found wanting.[9] But with no voice in government, nor any expectation of being given such a voice (her husband would argue vigorously to keep all voting rights reserved only to men of property), there was little Abigail could do to assert her own rights and those of all women.

Nevertheless, she continued to write to John with advice for Congress, everything from military maneuvers in Massachusetts to the necessary optics in declaring independence to the price of tea. After all, she told John quite plainly, "notwithstanding all your wise Laws and Maxims we have it in our power not only to free ourselves but to subdue our Masters, and without violence, throw both your natural and legal authority at our feet. . . . 'Charm by accepting, by submitting sway / Yet have our Humour most when we obey.'"[10]

Her influence was greater than he might admit, and Abigail would exercise all her rhetorical skills to bring John to see things from her point of view.

After the surrender of Boston, George Washington reached out to Josiah Quincy Sr., asking for his help in monitoring the coastline of Massachusetts: "there is one evil I dread," he wrote, "and that is . . . spies." He asked that "the most attentive watch . . . kept to prevent any discourse with the [British] ships and the main land. . . . I wish a dozen or more honest, sensible, and diligent men were employed to haunt the communication between Roxbury and the different landing places . . . in order to question, cross-question, etc, all such persons as are unknown, and cannot give an account of themselves in a straight and satisfactory line."[11]

This request was right in Josiah's bailiwick—questioning alleged evildoers—and he set himself to the task with all the diligence Washington had wanted. Within the month, Washington was thanking Josiah "for the intelligence" he'd shared.

Josiah also received a letter from his old friend Benjamin Franklin, advising him to stay industrious on the part of the colonists and ever alert to acts of "increasing enmity."[12] Franklin added that in the end, nefarious acts committed by the British served the best goal of all: "every day furnished us with new causes . . . and new reasons for wishing an eternal separation; so there is a rapid increase of the formerly small party who were for an independent government."

Franklin was right: the number of delegates speaking out in favor of independence—and speaking on behalf of the colonies that they represented—was growing steadily in the spring of 1776. The provincial legislatures of South Carolina, North Carolina, Rhode Island, and Virginia all sent instructions to their delegates to pursue whatever means were necessary to protect the colonies and support the workings of Congress.

Consensus was growing that the contract between the king and his colonies was broken past repair and that independence was the logical next step. South Carolina created its own state constitution and elected a governor; it was the first colony to make such a stand, and John Adams was overjoyed when he heard about it. "The News from South Carolina, has aroused and animated all the Continent," he wrote to James Warren; "and if North Carolina and Virginia should follow the Example, it will Spread through all the rest of the Colonies like Electric Fire."[13]

To encourage the creation of new provincial governments, John wrote up a paper outlining his ideas on how to structure such government, all concepts that he had shared with Richard Henry Lee in the fall; the paper was passed around to various delegates and then published by Lee, with the title *Thoughts on Government*.[14]

Adams was sure that as more colonies dissolved their royal governments, established provincial governments, and created their own constitutions, support for the final break from England would grow. But patience was required, as Adams wrote to Warren; the other colonies "are advancing by slow but sure steps, to that mighty Revolution, which You and I have expected for Some Time."[15]

John Hancock worried that the Continental Army was running out of time; the sooner the colonies acted to both unite and declare independence from England, the sooner he could appeal to foreign nations for much-needed help to fight the British.

When rumors began to arrive in the colonies that Britain had hired German mercenaries to swell its ranks of soldiers to well over forty-five thousand men, Hancock became exasperated with the slow pace of Congress. In hiring mercenaries, the "Tyrant of Britain and his Parliament have proceeded to the last extremity," he declared in a letter to the Massachusetts Assembly. He set to work once again cajoling and bullying the various colonial assemblies to send supplies and soldiers to help General Washington fight the English.[16] The next stage of battle was certain to be New York, and Washington needed all the men who could be roused to defend against the British troops bearing down on the American colonies.

"Our continental troops alone are unable to stem the torrent," Hancock wrote in a desperate appeal to the assemblies of the colonies, asking that they send local militia to help: "They are called upon to say whether they will die slaves or die free men . . . the cause is certainly a glorious one."

Waste no more time, he scolded, but "Quicken your preparations and stimulate the good people of your government." Together, he promised, we will be able to "lead them to victory, to liberty, and to happiness."[17]

Dolly Hancock told John the good news in April, that she was pregnant with their first child and expected to give birth in the fall. Elated, John looked for more spacious accommodations for his wife and him; in addition to the baby, Dolly's sister Katy was coming to Philadelphia to "accompany and be a comfort to" Dorothy in her confinement, and Aunt Lydia was also certain to come.[18] John found a "large and roomy" house for them to move to, in "an airy, open part of the city, in Arch and Fourth Streets."[19]

Increasing tensions between John Hancock and the two Adams cousins might have been another reason for the change in habitation. John Adams was irked that Hancock had taken the side of Robert Treat Paine in a dispute between Paine and Adams, and Sam Adams had always disliked Hancock's compromising with recalcitrant delegates.

In November, when Dolly Hancock had planned a ball to celebrate the arrival of Martha Washington to Philadelphia, Sam Adams was outraged by the impropriety, in his view, of spending money for gaiety and dancing during wartime when soldiers were starving and without needed supplies. The ball was canceled, and hard feelings remained between the Hancocks and the Adamses.

Never mind that Sam's portrait still hung side by side with John Hancock's in the Hancocks' Beacon Hill mansion (and had survived the siege miraculously unscathed); Sam Adams was no longer a fan of the man who had been his protégé at one time and his financial savior many other times.

But Hancock didn't have the time or the inclination to assuage the egos of men in his own delegation; it was exhausting and time-consuming enough to have to worry about all the delegates from other colonies. Removing himself from the same domicile as the two Adamses would relieve the strain, Hancock reasoned; they all had the same goal, after all, and would continue the fight toward independence together but on separate paths.

For the first time in five years, there had been no March commemoration of the Boston Massacre; perhaps the raising of forts on Dorchester Heights had been sufficient memorial—a military maneuver instead of an oration marking the date. But on April 19, a date Abigail Adams described as "ever memorable for America as the Ides of March to Rome and to Caesar," a ceremony was held to remember the Battles of Lexington and Concord one year earlier.[20]

The Reverend Jonas Clarke of Concord, with whom Hancock had sought refuge, gave the sermon, which he titled "The Fate of Blood-Thirsty Oppressors." In it, he described the arrival of the British troops on the Lexington green, just outside the windows of his parsonage. "They approach with the morning's light, and more like murderers and cutthroats, than the troops of a Christian king, without provocation, without warning, they draw the sword of violence upon the inhabitants of this town."

Such ravages against an innocent people would never be forgotten, he thundered from his pulpit, and would certainly be punished: "Surely there is one that avengeth, and that will plead the cause of the injured and oppressed; and in his own way and time, will both cleanse and avenge their innocent blood."[21]

No commemoration of the battles was held in Congress, and the date of April 19 went by unmarked. Business went on as usual, and there was much to do: fund the war through setting taxes; buy supplies and pay soldiers; build a navy; and employ diplomatic envoys to secure foreign support. Silas Deane had been sent to France to start forging ties between France and the colonies. But without a formal declaration of independence, support for the Americans would be limited. France could not take the chance that the colonies would reunite with England; nor would any other nation. The colonies had to make their intentions clear to all the world.

At the end of April, Lydia Hancock died in Fairfield after suffering a stroke. When he received the news a few days later, John was heartbroken. He had been "the object of her fondest affection on this side of heaven."[22] She had been for him his staunchest defender, tenderest caretaker, and most devoted counselor. Without Lydia, he might never have been taken in by his uncle Thomas or given the education and opportunities that he had; he might not have married Dorothy Quincy, or become a leading advocate for colonists' rights, or been elected to serve the people of Massachusetts. John knew all this better than anyone, and his tears mixed with gratitude in thinking of his seemingly unstoppable and indefatigable aunt.

In her will, Lydia finally did what Hancock had been urging her to do for years: she freed her slaves, and left them money to begin their new lives.

She also left a bit of money to friends and a small donation to the Brattle Square Church. But the rest of her estate was left to John.

Dolly promised her husband that if the new baby they were expecting was a girl, she would be named for Aunt Lydia. And when the times allowed, she and her husband would travel to Fairfield and visit the grave; but almost sixteen years would pass before a marker was laid there, commemorating the life of Lydia Henchman Hancock.

The momentum for independence in the middle and southern colonies continued to build, as news filtered out to towns and villages of England's intent to close the seas to all colonial vessels (thereby threatening to destroy all trade that was the lifeblood of port towns up and down the coast). Rumors of the thousands of mercenaries the Crown had contracted with to fight against its own subjects also galvanized support for separation, as did the knowledge that if independence was declared by the Americans, France was sure to support the new country in its fight.

John Adams was heartened by the growing tide of support. "The Passion, Feeling, Sentiment, Principle and Imagination, were never in more lively Exercise than they are now, from Florida to Canada," he wrote to Abigail.

Knowing that she was longing "to hear you have declared an independency," he promised her, "We are hastening rapidly to great Events. . . . Governments will be up everywhere before Midsummer, and an End to Royal style, Titles, and Authority."[23]

To push the creation of provincial governments further along, John Adams proposed a resolution in Congress urging the colonies to form their own independent governments as quickly as possible, in order to "promote the Happiness of the People."[24]

In the preamble to his proposed resolution, Adams argued that the nature of England's oppression, the failure of the king to protect his colonies from such oppression, and indeed, the forces called out by the king to enforce the oppressions, indicated that the time had come: "Every kind of authority under the said crown should be totally suppressed, and all the powers of government [should be] exerted under the authority of the people of the colonies."[25]

Congress approved the resolution, together with its preamble. John wrote with exultation to Abigail that now there would be a "complete Separation, a total Independence, not only [from] Parliament, but [from the] Crown."[26]

And yet John knew that for all its voting for and approving of various steps toward independence, Congress had yet to reach the point of unanimous support for a declaration of independence. He noted in his journal that James Duane of New York had called his resolution "a Machine for the fabrication of Independence." John knew he was right, but independence would truly be proclaimed only when "We must have it with more formality,"[27] in both a resolution for independence and a declaration setting forth the reasons for it.

Pennsylvania, with John Dickinson leading the way, was sure to vote against any proposed resolution for independence, and Adams couldn't be sure of Delaware, Maryland, or New York (whose delegates were personally all for independence but who could not vote for it without explicit authority granted to them from their provincial assembly). South Carolina had led the South in creating its provincial government and promoting separation from England, but would its delegates follow through with a vote for independence? In his letters to Abigail, John feigned certainty, but in private and on his own, he worried.

Two weeks later, on June 7, 1776, Richard Henry Lee of Virginia submitted a resolution to Congress. He could wait no longer, he told John Adams; the time had come to vote on independence from England.

Invited to the dais by John Hancock, Lee stood silent for a moment, surveying the room. He was a slim man, always elegantly dressed. His left hand was usually wrapped in a black cloth to hide its disfigurement; he had lost all his fingers on that hand in a riding accident. But this morning, both hands were free. With his right hand, he held the resolution he had prepared, while his left hand he held over his heart.

Sure of the attention of all, Lee read his resolution aloud: "That these United Colonies are, and of right ought to be, free and independent States, that they are absolved from all allegiance to the British Crown, and that all political connection between them and the State of Great Britain is, and ought to be, totally dissolved."[28]

John Adams immediately rose to second the resolution, and debate was scheduled to begin the next day, a Saturday. For two days the arguments went back and forth, with John Dickinson proclaiming that the people "were not yet ripe for bidding adieu to [the] British connection" and John Adams responding, "The people wait for us to lead the way."[29]

Delegates asked for time to return home and confer with their people there; an agreement was reached to consider the resolution again on July 1.

Thomas Jefferson and four others, including John Adams, were appointed to a committee to prepare a written declaration in time for the July 1 meeting, laying out the reasons why the united American colonies sought separation from England. The resolution and the declaration could then be considered together by Congress.

Representatives from the Iroquois Confederacy were present during many of the congressional debates that occurred during May and early June of 1776. The Native Americans had been invited to see for themselves how the American colonists governed in the wake of the dissolution of British control. Concerns had been raised on the part of the Iroquois as to the role of "president" in such proceedings; within their own administrative and political structure, the Iroquois Confederacy used two branches of legislative power, but there was no third branch with an executory role.

The Native Americans were lodged on the second floor of the State House, making it easy for them to attend the various proceedings in Congress. They paid special attention to John Hancock, watching how he maneuvered within Congress, when he stepped in and when he stepped back again.

On June 11, as their sojourn in Philadelphia was drawing to a close, a number of Iroquois chiefs were invited to a ceremony held by Congress in their honor. Colonial delegates made speeches in which they promised continued friendship with the Native Americans. When Hancock rose to offer official goodbyes, he was surprised by a request made by an Onondaga chief, that he be allowed to give Hancock an Indian name. John Hancock was then adopted into the Iroquois Confederacy under the name Karanduawn, meaning "the Great Tree."[30]

On that same day, Thomas Jefferson set to work drafting the Declaration of Independence. In the days since Congress had recessed, he had met with the four other men chosen with him to draft the declaration, and it quickly became evident that the task would not be shared among them. Ben Franklin was feeling too ill-disposed to work on a draft, and as he later revealed to Jefferson, "I have made it a rule, whenever in my power, to avoid becoming the draughtsman of papers to be reviewed by a public body."[31]

Roger Sherman of Connecticut and Robert Livingston of New York also declined to write the declaration, so Jefferson turned to Adams.

John Adams knew that a text produced by a Southerner like Jefferson would be more likely to be approved than one coming from (what many still perceived as) the radical fringe of New England. John was also confident that Jefferson would write a persuasive and eloquent exposition on the whys and wherefores of independence. He told Jefferson that while he would happily offer comments on whatever Jefferson produced, he would leave the writing of the document up to him. Jefferson agreed to take on the project by himself.

Adams was tempted to visit the younger man as he worked but he hung back. He left Jefferson alone in his rooms on Market and Seventh, writing away on the small lap desk he'd had specially made. While Adams waited to see what the Virginian came up with, he kept himself busy with a variety of committees, all needing his attention. He also churned out a record number of letters, including one to Abigail, in which he cryptically revealed, "Great Things are on the Tapis"—a kind of slang for *something big is about to happen*.[32]

By June 13, Jefferson had a completed draft for Adams to read. Composed of twenty-four paragraphs—many of them bullet points listing the wrongs committed against the Americans—and close to two thousand words, it was as passionate a work of patriotism, spirit, and determination as Josiah Quincy Jr. himself might have turned out. Adams reckoned that Josiah—or any New Englander—might have put more God into the text, but he was not disappointed with Jefferson's work. "I was delighted with its high tone, and the flights of oratory with which it abounded, especially that concerning negro slavery, which though I knew his southern brethren would never suffer to pass in congress, I certainly never would oppose."[33]

The paragraph Adams referred to was one in which Jefferson had put some of his most angry rhetoric; so much of the text was passionate, with Jefferson listing in detail allegation after allegation of abuse committed by the Crown and Parliament. But in the paragraph on slavery, Jefferson went even further. He denounced King George for having "waged cruel war against human nature itself, violating its most sacred rights of life and liberty in the persons of a distant people who never offended him, captivating & carrying them into slavery in another hemisphere or to incur miserable death in their transportation thither."[34]

Not only had King George brought, through forcible violence, unwilling workers to America, but "he is now exciting those very people to rise in arms among us, and to purchase that liberty of which he has deprived them, by murdering the people on whom he also obtruded them: thus paying off former crimes committed against the Liberties of one people, with crimes which he urges them to commit against the lives of another."[35]

It was this paragraph on slavery—with its "most Manly Sentiments," as she termed it—that would please Abigail so much when she read it, copied in John's hand; he'd written the entire declaration out for her and sent it for her perusal.[36] She thought John had written it himself and was so proud of her husband.

She felt her hopes rise, as pride in her husband swelled. Perhaps the time had come when what Abigail had long dreamed of would finally arise: a country ruled by the "generous and christian principal of doing to others as we would that others should do unto us."[37] A world of independence for all.

33

The Signature of Independence

The set time is come wherein Providence
has appointed the Flourishing States
to withdraw themselves from the Control of all others.

—EDMUND QUINCY IV

Congress began meeting again on July 1, 1776. By the end of that first day, John Hancock felt both tired and hopeful. He waited in his president's chair as the chamber emptied out. Only the secretary of the Congress, Charles Thomson, remained, and he would soon leave after sorting through his notes. John looked down at the document that lay on the table before him.

It had been another very warm day, with temperatures outside reaching well into the nineties. With the windows kept closed to preserve the secrecy of congressional debates, the chamber had been sweltering during the day. But as the afternoon wore on, the skies had filled with dark clouds—so dark that candles were lit in the room.

During John Dickinson's long harangue against independence, the sun had beat hard against the windows, but when John Adams began his defense of Lee's Resolution for Independence, the clouds began to roll in. As he went on and on with his arguments, speaking not from any notes but from his heart and mind, the thunder had joined in, punctuating his points.

While Dickinson had pointed out the dangers of independence, Adams instead underscored its necessity. Richard Stockton from New Jersey, who arrived late and asked Adams to begin again—which he did—pronounced Adams in his oratory to be "the Atlas of American independence." Thomas Jefferson lauded Adams as the "ablest advocate and defender" of independence; and a southern delegate, in describing Adams' performance that afternoon, said it was if "an angel was let down from heaven to illumine Congress."[1]

For nine hours the debate on the Resolution for Independence had continued. When it came time to vote, John Rutledge from South Carolina rose up from his seat and asked for a postponement until the next day. Hancock polled the delegates, and all agreed to wait a day before voting on the resolution. Hancock adjourned Congress until the next morning.

With the delegates gone, the windows to the chamber had finally been opened and cooling breezes were coming in, along with the occasional slap of moisture from the rain pouring outside. Hancock again looked down at Richard Henry Lee's resolution. By now most every member of Congress knew the words by heart: "That these United Colonies are, and of right ought to be, free and independent states."

Hancock wasn't worried about Lee's resolution. After Adams' oration, he was certain that the delegates would, in the end, vote for it. But he had heard rumors of last-minute dealmaking among the delegates to make changes to Thomas Jefferson's Declaration of Independence. Hancock had read it, as had all the delegates. He approved of every bit of it; Jefferson had done a magnificent job laying out in clear terms the reasons why America was declaring itself a new nation.

"We hold these truths to be self-evident: that all men are created equal; that they are endowed by their creator with inalienable rights; that among these are life, liberty & the pursuit of happiness. . . . When a long train of abuses & usurpations . . . evinces a design to reduce the people to absolute despotism it is their right, it is their duty to throw off such government, & to provide new guards for their future security. . . . The history of the present king of Great Britain is a history of injuries and usurpations, all having in direct object the establishment of an absolute tyranny over these states."[2]

There would be few who could argue with the power of Jefferson's words. But what about his angry paragraph denouncing King George for imposition of the slave trade: Would the southern colonies back out at the last minute from voting for independence? And if the paragraph were taken out to secure necessary votes, would the new country of America become complicit in slavery, even as it fought for freedom?

Hancock rose from his seat and left the chamber, leaving the resolution on the desk but carrying his notes on Jefferson's declaration home with him. Walking the few blocks to his rooms on Arch and Fourth, he was impervious to the rain, his mind taken up with thoughts of tomorrow.

The next morning John Adams woke early. He heard the rain outside the windows. He hurried from his bedsheets and dressed quickly, deciding to forego breakfast at the tavern across the street. Today the vote on Lee's

Resolution for Independence would be taken. He couldn't get to the State House fast enough.

By eleven in the morning, the business of Congress had turned to Lee's resolution. Colony by colony, Charles Thomson called on the delegates to make their vote, which he then recorded. Adams rested easy during the calling on Connecticut, Rhode Island, Massachusetts, New Hampshire, and Virginia: he knew all those delegates would vote for independence. Maryland voted for independence, as did New Jersey, while New York's delegates were forced by their circumstances to abstain, as they were still awaiting formal approval from the New York Assembly back home.

When it was Delaware's turn, Adams was surprised to see that the delegate Caesar Rodney was in attendance; he'd been absent for weeks, but now here he was. His clothes were damp, even more so than John's or the other delegates who had scurried through rainy streets to arrive at the State House.

The story passed down the aisle: Rodney had ridden on horseback, covering sixty miles in twelve hours, in the dark and in the rain, to arrive in Philadelphia in time to vote. The "oddest-looking Man in the World" (as Adams described him) joined his fellow delegate, Thomas McKean, in voting for independence.[3]

Another surprise came when Pennsylvania was called upon. John Dickinson and Robert Morris had both decided to abstain from the vote. Pennsylvania approved the resolution, with its three remaining delegates—Ben Franklin, James Wilson, and John Morton—voting for independence.

When it came time for the southernmost colonies to vote, John Adams found the breath in his lungs contracting. His hands fidgeted in his lap and his left heel tapped on the floor. John Hancock sat motionless on the dais, to the side of Secretary Thomson. Adams and Hancock did not look at each other, or at the delegates from the South. Instead they kept their eyes riveted on Thomson as he called the name of the delegates from each of the three southern colonies.

All three of the Georgia delegates in attendance voted for independence, as did the two delegates present from North Carolina. All four delegates for South Carolina voted for independence as well, although the evening before Rutledge had seemed to be leaning the other way.

Adams narrowed his eyes for a moment but then let his anxiety go. He took a deep breath, refilling his lungs. The important thing was that independence had been approved. Unanimously, with just one abstention—and that accord would be coming soon, the New York delegation promised.

The crowd of delegates broke out in hurrahs, until Hancock called their attention back with a smack of the gavel. There was more work to do; the resolution they had just agreed to needed to be backed up with a statement of their reasons *why* all connections with Britain were being severed.

With only a few hours left in the afternoon, debate on Jefferson's Declaration of Independence began. But it soon became clear to Hancock and everyone else that the debate would have to be continued the next day. Again, a night would pass in which deals were made, disagreements ironed out, and, hopefully, accord found.

Again, the delegates filed out, leaving Hancock alone at his desk. There was no going back on independence: votes had been taken. The delegates who had voted today would no longer be representing colonies but instead would be representing states. Now it was Hancock's duty to sign their resolution to separate from England and execute history.

A gift had recently arrived at the rooms Hancock shared with Dorothy, a token of remembrance sent after the death of Aunt Lydia. The gift consisted of a packet of pamphlets containing sermons of Reverend Hancock, John's father. One of the sermons had been given on September 16, 1739, on the hundredth anniversary of their Parish Church in Braintree. John himself would have been just two years old at the time, a babe on his mother's knee.

The anniversary sermon was a lengthy one, and touched on the role of each individual in his community, not only the community of God but the community of man: "I am sensible of the Darkness and Difficulty with which some of the Affairs of Government are perplexed at this Time; the Province is in great Affliction, but yet we are not in Despair, so long as our wise Men that are among us are our Pilots, and rule with GOD."

How clearly his father's voice still resonated: "public charitable Spirit would greatly contribute to extricate us from all our Difficulties and Dangers . . . prove your selves good and useful Members of the State."[4]

John bent to the paper before him and signed the Resolution of Independence with a flourish.

Back in his rooms on Arch Street, John Adams wrote to Abigail in a flurry of excitement, excited to finally tell her that all political connections between the colonies and Britain had been dissolved: "the greatest Question was decided, which ever was debated in America, and a greater perhaps, never was or will be decided among Men."[5]

He predicted that the "Second Day of July 1776, will be the most memorable Epocha, in the History of America. I am apt to believe that it will be celebrated, by succeeding Generations, as the great anniversary Festival. It ought to be commemorated, as the Day of Deliverance by solemn Acts of Devotion to God Almighty. It ought to be solemnized with Pomp and Parade, with Shews, Games, Sports, Guns, Bells, Bonfires and Illuminations from one End of this Continent to the other from this Time forward forever more."[6]

But he tempered his joy at passage of the Resolution for Independence with an edge of wary pragmatism: "the new Governments we are assuming, in every Part, will require a Purification from our Vices, and an Augmentation of our Virtues or they will be no Blessings. The People will have unbounded Power. And the People are extremely addicted to Corruption and Venality. . . . I am not without Apprehensions from this Quarter."[7]

Adams' fears would be realized in the morning, when debate over Jefferson's Declaration of Independence started up again. But first, there was other congressional business to attend to: letters had to be sent out to the assemblies of Pennsylvania, Delaware, and Maryland requesting that more troops be supplied for Washington's defense of New York; money had to be found to pay for a fleet to protect the northern border, particularly along Lake Champlain; and reports from committees had to be heard, including on relations with Native Americans and the making of an American seal (which would appropriate Native American imagery).[8]

Finally, the Declaration of Independence was taken up for discussion, and once again the editing began. Over the next two days, delegates took apart Jefferson's work, everyone wanting their say on matters as insignificant as inserting the word "certain" before "inherent and inalienable" and then taking out "inherent;" while other delegates demanded the deletion of entire paragraphs.[9]

As painful as the editing of the declaration was for Adams, for Jefferson it was pure agony. Ben Franklin, seated beside Jefferson in the council chamber, sought to console the young man by telling him an amusing story of a hat seller whose sign is edited down from "John Thompson, hatter, makes and sells hats for ready money" to just Thompson's name and a picture of a hat.[10]

Jefferson appreciated the attempt at humor, but it was John Adams who earned Jefferson's deep gratitude during those two long days. Adams fought "fearlessly for every word" that Jefferson had written; he was "the pillar of [the declaration's] support on the floor of Congress, its ablest advocate and defender against the multifarious assaults encountered."[11]

But there was no standing against the demands made by the southern delegates; Jefferson wrote later that the paragraph "reprobating the enslaving the inhabitants of Africa, was struck out in complaisance to South Carolina & Georgia, who had never attempted to restrain the importation of slaves, and who on the contrary still wished to continue it."

Jefferson placed the blame for removing the antislavery provisions from the declaration not only on the Southerners but on New Englanders as well: "Our Northern brethren also I believe felt a little tender under those censures; for tho' their people have very few slaves themselves yet they had been pretty considerable carriers of them to others."[12]

Nothing Adams or Jefferson could do would save the clause, and both acknowledged that compromise was the only way to ensure passage of the declaration as a whole. Adams understood "the haste" with which they were working; "Congress was impatient . . . [and] cut off about a quarter of it, as I expected they would; but they obliterated some of the best of it."[13]

For Adams, the most important aspect of the Declaration of Independence was that it "will cement the union."[14] He simply could not foresee the effect slavery would ultimately have on such union. Jefferson, however, having grown up in the South, had a stronger understanding of the severe impact slavery had on democratic institutions.

As Josiah Quincy Jr. had observed, during his two-month sojourn through the South, slavery poisoned every person and place it touched: "The brutality used towards slaves . . . and the laws [controlling them] . . . will stand as eternal records of the depravity and contradiction of the human character. . . . These are but a small part of the mischief of slavery—new ones are every day arising—futurity will produce more and more greater."[15]

But there was little Jefferson could do to save his antislavery provisions. Left with no recourse but to remove the offending clause, Jefferson nevertheless made sure his efforts to prohibit slavery, and the actions of others to prevent him from success, would be recorded for posterity: "As the sentiments of men are known not only by what they receive, but what they reject also, I will state the form of the declaration as *originally reported*," he wrote in his notes on the proceedings.[16]

By the afternoon of July 4, Thomas Jefferson's Declaration of Independence was finally ready to be voted upon by Congress. Charles Thomson stood to read the document in its entirety—it had been pared down to just about fourteen hundred words—and then a symbolic roll call was taken. Every state voted "Yea," and the Declaration of Independence was approved.

The windows to the chamber were thrown wide open, now that the debates had ended, and fresh air streamed in. The delegates in the chamber, according to Thomas Jefferson, walked one by one to the desk on the dais and affixed their signature to the handwritten copy, the agreed-upon changes marked clearly across the pages.[17] This was the final step in the process of disunion with England, and the moment must have weighed heavily upon them all. With their vote of affirmation, and now their signature, they had committed themselves entirely to the independence of the thirteen states of America.

The sanctity of that commitment was underscored by the declaration's final sentence: "for support of this declaration, with a firm reliance on the protection of Divine providence we mutually pledge to each other our lives, our fortunes & our sacred honour."[18]

John Adams had supported the addition of "Divine providence" to the oath, knowing the hold such a vow would have over both the men who signed the declaration and the public who would read it. As Josiah Quincy Jr. had always asserted, "the God of armies on our side, even the God who fought our fathers' battles" would lead the Americans to victory: "While we have equity, justice, and God on our side, Tyranny, spiritual or temporal, shall never ride triumphant."[19]

All the men of Congress knew that their signature was akin to signing "our own death warrants."[20] On August 2, when they were asked to sign again (this time the document they signed had been beautifully printed on a sheet of stiff parchment), John Hancock was heard to say, as he began the flourish of his large signature, "There must be no pulling different ways; we must all hang together." Franklin retorted, "Yes, we must, indeed, all hang together, or most assuredly we shall all hang separately."[21]

Benjamin Harrison from Virginia turned to Elbridge Gerry and noted that he would have an advantage over Gerry "when we are all hung. . . . From the size and weight of my body I shall die in a few minutes, but from the lightness of your body you will dance in the air an hour or so."[22]

But it was John Hancock who was in the most danger of hanging. Within days of the signing on July 4, copies of the Declaration of Independence were making their way across the city, then the colony, and farther out, to every colony in America, and then to the world. This version of the signed

Declaration of Independence had only one signature on it. Underneath the words "signed by order and on behalf of the Congress," writ large across the bottom of the page, was *John Hancock*.[23]

In Massachusetts, the Declaration of Independence was read aloud from the balcony of the State House in Boston on July 18. William Greenleaf, the husband of Dolly's sister Sarah and the new sheriff of Boston (replacing his brother, Stephen Greenleaf, a Loyalist), was charged with reading the document aloud.

Abigail Adams had come to Boston days earlier, together with "not less than 30 people from Braintree," in order to undergo inoculation for small-pox.[24] The effects of the smallpox dosage had left her feeling queasy, but when hearing that the Declaration of Independence was to be read aloud from the balcony of the State House, Abigail vowed she would attend, even if she had to be carried there.

As it turned out, on the morning of July 18 she felt strong enough to walk out on her own. Accompanied by Hannah Quincy Lincoln, who was also undergoing smallpox inoculation, Abigail made her way to King Street to hear the reading. Joining the "multitude" that had gathered there, Abigail and Hannah listened with "great attention . . . to every word."[25]

Because William Greenleaf's voice was too weak to carry over the crowd that had gathered, he asked his friend Colonel Thomas Craft to "be his herald." Standing together on the balcony of the State House, Greenleaf murmured the sentences of the declaration, one by one, and then Craft repeated each sentence with his mighty elocution. When Greenleaf offered the final words, Craft echoed them down the streets and alleyways: "we mutually pledge to each other our Lives, our Fortunes and our sacred Honor."[26]

A rousing cry rang out: "God Save our American States!" A torrent of cheers, and then "the bells rang, the privateers fired, the forts and Batteries, the cannon were discharged, the platoons followed and every face appeared joyful." A bonfire was built on King Street, and all of "the king's arms were taken down from the State House and every vestige of him from every place in which it appeared" was thrown into the blazing fire, to be burned down to ashes and coal.[27]

Decades earlier, standing in his pulpit in the Third Parish Church of Braintree, the Reverend John Hancock spoke of the "solemn covenant" laid by his ancestors, a covenant which promised "Liberty" in the new world.[28] The sons and daughters of his congregation strove, each in their own way, to secure that promise of liberty. Now the promise was written into the Declaration of Independence.

"Thus ends royal Authority in this State," Abigail wrote to John; "and all the people shall say Amen."[29]

Epilogue: Friends to Mankind

Every man died a hater of tyrants,
an abhorrer of oppression,
a lover of his country,
and a friend to mankind.

—JOSIAH QUINCY JR.

In the fall of 1776, Dorothy Hancock gave birth to a baby girl. She was named Lydia Henchman Hancock, in honor of John's aunt. The child died in the summer of 1777 and was buried in Philadelphia, in a "Mohogany Coffin 2 feet six inches long."[1] The couple had another child, in 1778, a boy they named John George Washington Hancock. He died eight years later when he fell through an iced-over pond and drowned.

John Hancock remained president of the Continental Congress until 1777; he served as president again during the Confederation Congress but had to resign due to ill health. He was elected first governor of the state of Massachusetts in 1780 and was elected again in 1787; he served as governor until his death in 1793, at the age of fifty-six.

In 1796, Dolly married James Scott, Hancock's longtime confidant and captain of many of Hancock's vessels. Dolly and James were married in the Brattle Square Church; as they left the church, the bell that John Hancock had paid for decades before pealed in celebration. Dorothy Quincy Hancock Scott died on February 3, 1830, at the age of eighty-two.

John and Abigail Adams continued to spend many years of their married life apart, when John served as commissioner to France, minister to the Netherlands, and then minister to Great Britain. Abigail finally joined John in Paris in 1784 and traveled with him to England. John served as the first vice president under President George Washington and was elected the second president of the United States in 1796.

During his presidency, Abigail took such a public and active role in advising her husband and supporting him that she was called Mrs. President.[2]

After Adams lost his bid for a second term, the couple returned to the large estate they had purchased in Braintree, which they called Peacefield.

Abigail Adams died at Peacefield on October 28, 1818, at the age of seventy-three. In the days preceding her death, John Adams wanted only "to lie down beside her and die, too."[3] John lived another eight years and died in Braintree on July 4, 1826, the date of the fiftieth anniversary of the signing of the Declaration of Independence. Thomas Jefferson died on the same day at his estate, Monticello. Adams was ninety years old, and Jefferson was eighty-three. Two years earlier, John and Abigail's son, John Quincy Adams, had been elected sixth president of the United States.

Esther Quincy Sewall remained in England with her husband until 1787; just before they left, they enjoyed a brief reunion with John and Abigail Adams in London. "Our conversation was just as might be expected at the meeting of two old sincere friends after a long separation," Sewall wrote in a letter.[4] Jonathan Sewall died in 1796, from what John Adams called "a broken-heart."[5] He never felt welcomed in England or in Canada, and had been banished from America. After his death, Esther returned to Cambridge, settling back into her old house. She later returned to Canada to be with her children (her oldest son, Jonathan, was chief justice of Canada, and Stephen was solicitor general). She died in Montreal in 1810 at the age of seventy-two.

Hannah Quincy Lincoln married Ebenezer Storer in 1777. This marriage was a happy one, and they lived together until his death in 1807, at the age of seventy-seven. After she was widowed, Hannah and John Adams met again, sometime in the 1820s. Hannah, visiting Peacefield, was seated in a room when John Adams entered and exclaimed, "What! Madam, shall we not go walk in Cupid's Grove together?" Hannah took but a moment to reply, "Ah, sir, it would not be the first time we have walked there!"[6] Hannah died in 1826 at the age of ninety.

Edmund Quincy never returned to Braintree to live but stayed in Lancaster with his daughter Sarah for the rest of his life, spending his time writing very long letters full of advice and offering praise to God to the very end for every good thing that had ever happened to him. Edmund died in 1788, at the age of eighty-five.

Samuel Quincy was never able to return to America, having been placed on the banishment list in 1778. A review of the archives indicates that he never received a single letter from his father after he left Boston in 1775, but he corresponded regularly with his sister, his brother-in-law Henry Hill, and his wife and children—"I frequently make you vivid, especially when . . . I compose myself to Sleep, perhaps to Dream."[7]

In 1779, Sam was commissioned comptroller of customs in Antigua, West Indies. There, he was finally reunited with his wife, Hannah. He would never, however, see any of his children again. According to a letter he wrote to Hannah's brother, Henry Hill, his wife died in his arms in November 1782. She was forty-eight years old.

Samuel married Mrs. M. A. Chadwell in St. Croix, West Indies, in 1785. By the fall of 1789 he had grown so ill with gout (his second wife claimed it was caused by too much dancing) that he traveled to England in search of a cure. He died while en route and was buried in Bristol. He was sixty-four. The second Mrs. Quincy returned to St. Croix but, in despair over Samuel's death, killed herself in 1790.

Josiah Quincy Sr. lived the rest of his life in Braintree. Throughout the Revolutionary War, he served as lookout from his beloved monitor. He received visits from Ben Franklin and the two men corresponded for years. It was in a letter to Josiah that Franklin declared, after peace with England had been made, "May we never see another war! For in my opinion there never was a good war or a bad peace."[8]

During the war, Josiah arranged to have his son's body exhumed from his Gloucester grave and reburied in Braintree, as Josiah Jr. had wished.

Josiah Sr. died on March 3, 1784, his death caused by going out to sit "upon a cake of ice" in the frozen expanses of the bay beside his house, while "watching for wild ducks."[9] He was seventy-five years old.

Josiah Quincy Sr.'s will provided that his home in Braintree pass to Josiah Quincy III, his grandson. Josiah also left to his grandson the ring that Josiah Jr. had made for him. In his will, Josiah Sr. instructed his grandson to never forget or neglect the motto inscribed on the ring, "Oh, Save My Country," and the duty it imposed. By all accounts, Josiah III wore the ring all his adult life.

Abigail Quincy never remarried. Five years after Josiah Jr.'s death, she wrote, "I have been told that time would wear out the greatest sorrow, but mine I find is still increasing. When it will have reached its summit, I know not."[10] She devoted her life to raising her son and preserving her husband's memory.

Josiah Quincy III spent his life in public service, serving on the Boston Town Meeting, in the Massachusetts House of Representatives, in the U.S.

House of Representatives, and as mayor of Boston. From 1829 to 1845, he was president of Harvard University. Quincy Market in Boston is named for him. Like his father (and his cousin John Quincy Adams), Josiah III abhorred slavery and was an early abolitionist.

Later in his life, Josiah III recalled how his mother had him memorize stanzas from *The Iliad* by Homer (as translated by Alexander Pope) and then recite them for her. She particularly favored the story of Andromache, whose husband, Hector, leaves her and their newborn baby to fight in the Trojan War.

"Her imagination, probably, found consolation in the repetition of lines which . . . seemed to typify her own great bereavement," Josiah III explained. "She identified [these lines] with her own sufferings and seemed relieved by the tears my repetition of them drew from her."[11]

> Too daring prince! ah whither dost thou run?
> Ah too forgetful of thy wife and son!
> And think'st thou not how wretched we shall be,
> A widow I, a helpless orphan he!
> For sure such courage length of life denies,
> And thou must fall, thy virtue's sacrifice.

When Abigail Quincy died on March 25, 1798, she was buried beside her husband, Josiah Jr., in the burial ground at Braintree.[12] Their shared grave lies just across the grassy path from the grave of the Reverend John Hancock, the man whose vision of community and liberty fostered a generation that fought for both.

Acknowledgments

Many people helped me in researching and writing this book. From its first vague outline, the truly marvelous Esther Newberg encouraged me and supported me. I am so grateful to Michael Flamini, my smart, kind, and insightful editor at St. Martin's Press. Thanks are also due to talented book designer Young Lim, who created the beautiful cover; editorial assistant Hannah Phillips, who is patient with me; and Rebecca Lang, Michelle Cashman, and Paul Hochman, who propel my book into the world. Martha Cameron copyedited with an eagle eye and a much-appreciated sense of humor.

My extensive research at the Massachusetts Historical Society in Boston was supported by the Marc Friedlaender Fellowship, which I was honored to receive. The Massachusetts Historical Society is a true gem of a place, not only for its incredible collections and its fellowship opportunities, but also for its community of researchers, librarians, writers, and editors, including Sabina Beauchard, Alexis Buckley, Rakashi Chand, Anna Clutterbuck-Cook, Dan Hinchen, Peter Drummey, Sara Martin, and Conrad E. Wright. Thank you for sharing your collections and your knowledge with me.

Thanks are also due to Maggie Hoffman, for guiding me through the Brinkler Library of the Cambridge Historical Society; and to Elizabeth Rose for her assistance at the Fairfield (Connecticut) Museum and History Center.

Visits to the Dorothy Quincy Homestead and to the Josiah Quincy House were an integral part of my research (along with many, many follow-up emails). I am very grateful to the best guides ever, the women who led me through the rooms, the grounds, and most important, the history of these amazing landmarks: Mary Robinson, Barbara Armenta, Marcia Synott, Jeanne Eckard, Melinda Huff, and Nancy Carlisle.

ACKNOWLEDGMENTS

Anyone interested in the history of the United States should make a pilgrimage to Quincy, Massachusetts, and visit the Dorothy Quincy Homestead, managed by The National Society of the Colonial Dames of America, Massachusetts Society; and the Josiah Quincy House, managed by Historic New England; as well John Adams National Historical Park. I was fortunate to have my great friend Viveca Van Bladel as my traveling companion and will always treasure our time together on the history trail. I will miss Deborah Quinsee and her rebel heart, and am grateful for her support of my work.

Natasha Sankovitch and Charlotte Rogan were more than willing to read through my drafts, and they both offered comments and edits that helped enormously. Dorothy Ko encouraged me in my research and writing. Thank you to these brilliant women.

As always, I am deeply indebted to my parents, Tilde and Anatole Sankovitch, and my sister Natasha; and to my husband, Jack Menz, and our children, Meredith, Peter, Michael, George, and Martin. Thank you to my granddaughter Charlotte for the joy she has brought into all of our lives.

I carry my sister Anne-Marie Sankovitch with me always, and my work is inspired by her dedication to researching and writing the history of our world.

Notes

Prologue: A Village Mourns

1 Ebenezer Gay, "The Untimely Death of a Man of God Lamented in a Sermon Preach'd at the Funeral of the Reverend Mr. John Hancock, Pastor of the First Church of Christ in Braintree; Who Died May 7th. 1744," Hancock Family Papers, Massachusetts Historical Society (hereafter cited as MHS).

2 Elbert Hubbard, *Little Journeys to the Homes of American Statesmen* (New York: William W. Wise, 1916), p. 103.

3 Gay, "The Untimely Death of a Man of God."

4 Ibid.

5 Records of the First Church, North Braintree, quoted in William S. Pattee, *History of Old Braintree and Quincy* (Quincy, MA: Green and Prescott, 1878), p. 218. The date noted by the Reverend John Hancock was in accordance with the Old Style calculation of time (pre-Julian calendar).

6 John Adams to William Tudor, June 5, 1817, Adams Papers, MHS. The Adams Papers include digital editions, microfiche, and original documents of John Adams and Abigail Adams; unless otherwise noted, all footnotes citing the Adams Papers refer to the digital edition of the document cited.

7 John Hancock, "A Memorial of God's Goodness. Being the Substance of Two Sermons, Preach'd in the First Church of Christ in Braintree, Sept. 16th. 1739," Hancock Family Papers, MHS.

8 John Langdon Sibley, *Biographical Sketches of Graduates of Harvard University in Cambridge, Massachusetts,* vol. 3 (Cambridge, MA: Charles William Sever, 1885), p. 109.

9 Clifford K. Shipton, *New England Life in the Eighteenth Century* (Cambridge, MA: Belknap Press/Harvard University Press, 1963), p. 450.

10 Daniel Munro Wilson, *Where American Independence Began* (Boston: Houghton Mifflin, 1902), p. 68.

11 Gay, "The Untimely Death of a Man of God."

12 Hancock, "A Memorial of God's Goodness."

Chapter 1: Founding a Village

1 Also called "Filcher" in some accounts; John Adams refers to him as B. Fitcher in his autobiography, but I could find no record of his first name.

2 Thomas Morton, *New English Canaan of Thomas Morton*, ed. Charles Francis Adams (Boston: Prince Society, 1883), p. 123.

3 Morton, *New English Canaan*, p. 14, 4n.

4   William Bradford, *History of Plymouth Plantation* (Boston: Little, Brown, 1856), p. 238.
5   Morton, *New English Canaan*, p. 180.
6   Bradford, *History of Plymouth Plantation*, p. 237.
7   John Adams, "Notes on the History of Mt. Wollaston, 19 October 1802," *Founders Online*, National Archives, http://founders.archives.gov/documents/Adams/99-02-02-4984.
8   Morton, *New English Canaan*, p. 277; Bradford, *History of Plymouth Plantation*, p. 237.
9   Bradford, *History of Plymouth Plantation*, p. 237.
10 Morton, *New English Canaan*, p. 283.
11 Ibid., p. 280.
12 Bradford, *History of Plymouth Plantation*, p. 241.
13 Morton, *New English Canaan*, p. 287.
14 Ibid., pp. 237–238.
15 Morton returned one more time to the New World. He was arrested yet again, this time for Royalist leanings; this was during the English Civil War, and Puritans in New England were on the side of the Parliamentarians and against the Royalists. Because of his age, Morton was released and died in the wilds of Maine sometime around 1647; he would have been around seventy years old.
16 Thomas Hutchinson, *The History of Massachusetts Bay*, vol. 2 (London: M. Richardson, 1765); Appendix, p. 509.
17 See Chandler, *American Criminal Trials*, vol. 1 (Boston: Timothy H. Carter and Company, 1841), pp. 24–26.
18 See Wilson, *Where American Independence Began*, pp. 42–43.
19 In the late seventeenth century, Daniel Quincy, grandson of the first Edmund Quincy in America, married Anne Shepherd, a granddaughter of Captain Tyng. John Quincy, a child of the marriage, inherited the lands of Mount Wollaston.
20 Hancock, "A Memorial of God's Goodness."

Chapter 2: The Education of Boys

1   "Indenture of Thomas Hancock," *Bostonian Society Publications*, vol. 12, pp. 99–101, cited in William T. Baxter, *House of Hancock* (Cambridge: Harvard University Press, 1945), p. 5.
2   *Boston News-letter*, March 4, 1725, Collections of the MHS, cited in Baxter, *House of Hancock*, p. 6.
3   Thomas Hancock Bookseller Advertisement, reproduced in Baxter, *House of Hancock*, p. 7.
4   Herbert S. Allan, *John Hancock: Patriot in Purple* (New York: Macmillan, 1948), p. 31.
5   Carrie Rebora and Paul Staiti, *John Singleton Copley in America* (New York: Metropolitan Museum of Art, 1995), p. 32.
6   Diary of John Adams, vol. 1, August 14, 1756, Adams Papers, MHS.
7   David McCullough, *John Adams* (New York: Simon & Schuster, 2001), p. 32.
8   Diary of John Adams, December 30, 1758, Adams Papers, MHS.
9   Diary of John Adams, vol. 3, Parents and Boyhood, Adams Papers, MHS.
10 Ibid.
11 Ibid.
12 Ibid.
13 Ibid.
14 Ibid.
15 Ibid.
16 Ibid., vol. 1, A Letter to Richard Cranch About Orlinda, a Letter on Employing One's Mind, and Reflections on Procrastination, Genius, Moving the Passions, Cicero as Orator, Milton's Style, etc., October–December 1758, Adams Papers, MHS.
17 John Hancock to Jonas Clarke, undated, quoted in Allan, *John Hancock: Patriot*, p. 375.
18 Diary of John Adams, vol. 3, Parents and Boyhood, Adams Papers, MHS.

Chapter 3: Worldly Goods, Heavenly Debates

1   Samuel Eliot Morison, *Three Centuries of Harvard, 1636–1936* (Cambridge, MA: Harvard University Press, 1946), p. 60.
2   Jonathan Edwards, *Sinners in the Hands of an Angry God, A Sermon Preached at Enfield, 8 July 1741*, Collections of the MHS.
3   Lemuel Briant, "The Absurdity and Blasphemy of Depretiating Moral Virtue: A Sermon Preached at the West-Church in Boston, June 18th, 1749," p. 23, Collections of the MHS.
4   Ibid.
5   Ibid., p. 7.
6   Captain Isaac Freeman to Messrs. Quincy, Quincy, and Jackson, August 1, 1748, quoted in Robert A. McCaughey, *The Last Federalist* (Cambridge, MA: Harvard University Press, 1974), p. 2.
7   Shipton, *New England Life*, p. 278.
8   Ibid., p. 107.
9   Edmund Quincy IV to Elizabeth Wendell Quincy, undated, quoted in Kate Dickinson Sweetser, *Ten American Girls from History* (New York: Harper and Brothers, 1917), p. 37.
10 John Porter, *The Absurdity and Blasphemy of Substituting the Personal Righteousness of Men in the Room of the Surety Righteousness of Christ, in the Important Article of Justification Before God. A Sermon Preached at the South Precinct in Braintree, December 25th 1749*, Evans Early American Imprint Collection.
11 Jonathan Mayhew to Experience Mayhew, August 21, 1752, Collections of Boston University Library.
12 Diary of John Adams, vol. 3, Harvard College 1751–1755, Adams Papers, MHS.
13 Shipton, *New England Life*, pp. 453–454.
14 Diary of John Adams, vol. 3, Harvard College 1751–1755, Adams Papers, MHS.
15 Diane Jacobs, *Dear Abigail* (New York: Ballantine, 2014), p. 19.
16 *The Report of a Committee of the First Church in Braintree, Appointed March, 1753, to Enquire into the Grounds of Those Slanderous Reports That Had Been Spread Abroad, Respecting Themselves, and the Reverend Mr. Lemuel Briant, Their Pastor*. Collections of MHS.
17 William S. Pattee, *A History of Old Braintree and Quincy, with a Sketch of Randolph and Holbrook* (Quincy, MA: Green & Prescott, 1878), p. 222.

Chapter 4: The Education of Girls

1   Woody Holton, *Abigail Adams* (New York: Free Press, 2009), p. 3.
2   Abigail Adams to Caroline Smith, February 2, 1809, *Journal and Correspondence of Miss Adams*, vol. 1 (New York: Wiley and Putnam, 1841), p. 216.
3   Abigail Adams to John Quincy Adams, December 26, 1790, Adams Papers, MHS.
4   Elizabeth Smith to William Smith, April 28, 1763, Library of Congress, Papers of William Cranch.
5   *New England Chronicle or Essex Gazette*, October 19, 1775, Collections of MHS.
6   Abigail Adams to Abigail Adams Smith, 1795, quoted in Charles Francis Adams, ed., *Letters of Mrs. Adams, Wife of John Adams*, vol. 1 (Boston: Wilkins, Carter, 1848), pp. xxv–xxvi.
7   Abigail Adams to John Quincy Adams, December 30, 1804, Founders Online, National Archives, https://founders.archives.gov/documents/Adams/99-03-02-1372.
8   Abigail Adams to Abigail Adams Smith, 1795, quoted in Adams, ed., *Letters of Mrs. Adams*, pp. xxv–xxvi.
9   Charles Francis Adams, ed., *The Works of John Adams*, vol. 2 (Boston: Little, Brown, 1856), p. 75; Diary of John Adams, vol. 3, Spring and Summer 1759, Adams Papers, MHS.
10 Diary of John Adams, February 11, 1759, Adams Papers, MHS.
11 Josiah Quincy IV, *Figures of the Past from the Leaves of Old Journals* (Boston: Roberts Brothers, 1883), pp. 64–65.

12   Diary of John Adams, vol. 1, A Letter to Richard Cranch About Orlinda, Adams Papers, MHS.

13   Early Diary of John Adams, vol. 1, Letters to Three Friends on Studying Law, October–November 1758, Adams Papers, MHS.

14   Ibid.

15   Diary of John Adams, vol. 3, Parents and Boyhood, Adams Papers, MHS.

16   Diary of John Adams, vol. 1, Tuesday, January 1759, Adams Papers, MHS.

17   Diary of John Adams, vol. 1, Worcester, February 11, 1759.

18   Diary of John Adams, vol. 1, Summer 1759, Adams Papers, MHS.

19   Ibid.

20   Diary of John Adams, vol. 1, October 26, 1758, Adams Papers, MHS.

21   Diary of John Adams, vol. 1, Summer 1759, Adams Papers, MHS.

22   Diary of John Adams, vol. 3, Harvard College, 1751–1755, Adams Papers, MHS.

23   John Adams to William Tudor, November 16, 1816, Founders Online, National Archives, http://founders.archives.gov/documents/Adams/99-02-02-6659.

24   Diary of John Adams, vol. 1, December 1758, Adams Papers, MHS.

25   Jonathan Sewall to Thomas Robie, June 16, 1759, Robie-Sewall Family Papers, MHS.

26   Diary of John Adams, vol. 1, Wednesday, January 1759, Adams Papers, MHS.

27   Diary of John Adams, vol. 1, A Letter to Richard Cranch About Orlinda, Adams Papers, MHS.

28   Diary of John Adams, vol. 1, Wednesday, January 1759, Adams Papers, MHS.

29   Ibid.

30   John Adams, *Diary and Autobiography of John Adams*, edited by L. H. Butterfield (Cambridge, MA: Belknap Press/Harvard University Press, 1961), vol. 1, p. 119.

31   Diary of John Adams, vol. 1, Summer 1759, Adams Papers, MHS.

32   Diary of John Adams, vol. 1, Spring 1759, Adams Papers, MHS.

33   Ibid.

34   Ibid.

35   Ibid.

36   Diary of John Adams, vol. 1, Summer 1759, Adams Papers, MHS.

37   Ibid.

38   John Adams to Abigail Adams, November 4, 1775, Adams Papers, MHS.

39   Diary of John Adams, vol. 1, October–December 1758, Adams Papers, MHS.

40   Diary of John Adams, vol. 1, Letters to Three Friends on Studying Law, October–November 1758, Adams Papers, MHS.

Chapter 5: Changing Fortunes

1   Jonathan Belcher, letter dated August 21, 1755, Jonathan Belcher Letter Books, 1723–1755, vol. 11, Collections of the MHS.

2   Adams, *The Works of John Adams*, vol. 2, p. 76.

3   Edmund Quincy IV to Katy Quincy, undated, Quincy Family Papers, MHS. The Quincy Family Papers are part of the Quincy, Wendell, Holmes, and Upham family papers collection of the MHS.

4   Benjamin Franklin to Edmund Quincy IV, December 10, 1761, ibid.

5   Wilson, *Where American Independence Began*, p. 172, 82.

6   John Adams to Samuel Quincy, April 22, 1761, Founders Online, National Archives, http://founders.archives.gov/documents/Adams/06-01-02-0039.

7   Diary of John Adams, vol. 1, December 2, 1760, Adams Papers, MHS.

8   Ibid.

9   Rebora and Staiti, *John Singleton Copley in America*, p. 190.

10   Ibid.

11   Ibid., p. 187.

12   John Hancock to Thomas Hancock, 1760, quoted in Allan, *John Hancock: Patriot*, p. 69.

13   Allan, *John Hancock: Patriot*, p. 71.

14 Ibid., pp. 69–70.

15 Baxter, *House of Hancock*, p. 144.

16 Ibid.

17 Allan, *John Hancock: Patriot*, p. 74.

18 Adams, *The Works of John Adams*, vol. 10, p. 259.

19 Adams Family Correspondence, vol. 1, Richard Cranch and John Adams to Mary Smith, December 30, 1761, Adams Papers, MHS.

20 John Adams to Abigail Adams, October 4, 1762; Abigail Adams to John Adams, August 11, 1763; Adams Papers, MHS.

21 John Adams to Abigail Smith, October 4, 1762, Adams Papers, MHS.

22 Ibid.

23 Abigail Smith to John Adams, August 11, 1763, Adams Papers, MHS.

24 John Adams, *Autobiography, Part One*, Sheet 8 of 53, 1761–1765, Adams Papers, MHS.

25 Diary of John Adams, vol. 1, Friday, December 29, 1758, Adams Papers, MHS.

26 James Otis, *Against Writs of Assistance, February 1761*, National Humanities Institute, http://www.nhinet.org/ccs/docs/writs.htm.

27 Ibid.

28 Adams, *The Works of John Adams*, vol. 4, p. 7.

29 Otis, *Against Writs of Assistance*.

30 John Adams to William Tudor Sr., March 29, 1817, Founders Online, National Archives, http://founders.archives.gov/documents/Adams/99-02-02-6735.

Chapter 6: Colonial Enthusiasms

1 Allan, *John Hancock: Patriot*, p. 40.

2 Harvard College Library Books Borrowed by Josiah Quincy Jr., 1762–1763, Harvard University Archives.

3 *Proceedings of the Massachusetts Historical Society*, vol. 13 (Boston: MHS, 1875), p. 216.

4 Cover of *Law Commonplace* book, Josiah Quincy Jr., Quincy Family Papers, MHS.

5 Daniel R. Coquillette and Neil Longley York, *Portrait of a Patriot, The Major Political and Legal Works of Josiah Quincy Jr.*, vol. 5 (Charlottesville: University of Virginia Press, 2009), Appendix, "The Legal Maxims of Josiah Quincy, Jr."

6 Ibid., p. 446.

7 Ibid.

8 See Daniel Hannan, "Eight Centuries of Liberty," *Wall Street Journal*, May 30–31, 2015.

9 Oxenbridge Thacher, "Draft of an Address to King and Parliament" [1764], *Proceedings of the Massachusetts Historical Society*, vol. 20 (Boston: MHS, 1884), p. 51

10 Josiah Quincy, *Memoir of the Life of Josiah Quincy, Junior, of Massachusetts, 1744–1775*, edited by Eliza Susan Quincy (Boston: John Wilson & Son, 1874), p. 226, 1n.

11 Ibid., p. 21.

12 Diary of John Adams, vol. 1, August 13, 1769, Adams Papers, MHS.

13 Baxter, *House of Hancock*, p. 223.

14 Abigail Smith to Hannah Quincy Lincoln, October 5, 1761, quoted in Adams, ed., *Letters of Mrs. Adams*, vol. 1, p. 5.

Chapter 7: The Mobs of Boston

1 *Boston Gazette*, February 4, 1765; see also Jayne E. Triber, *A True Republican: The Life of Paul Revere* (Amherst: University of Massachusetts Press, 1998), p. 38.

2 Baxter, *House of Hancock*, pp. 231–232, 21n.

3 John Hancock to John Barnard, April 5, 1765, Letter Book, quoted in Baxter, *House of Hancock*, p. 233.

4 John Hancock to John Barnard, September 11, 1765, quoted in Baxter, *House of Hancock*, p. 233.

5 John Adams to William Tudor, June 1, 1817, Adams Papers, MHS.

6   Harlow Giles Unger, *John Hancock: Merchant King and American Patriot* (New York: Wiley, 2000), p. 89.
7   Coquillette and York, *Portrait of a Patriot*, vol. 5, p. 446.
8   Peter Shaw, *American Patriots and the Rituals of Revolution* (Cambridge, MA: Harvard University Press, 1981), p. 73.
9   Shipton, *New England Life*, pp. 280–281.
10 *Boston Gazette*, December 9, 1765.
11 *Maryland Gazette*, July 4, 1765.
12 *Boston Gazette*, December 9, 1765.
13 Ibid.
14 *Boston Gazette*, September 2, 1765.
15 Diary of John Adams, vol. 1, 15 August 1765, Adams Papers, MHS.
16 John Hancock to Hill, Lemar, and Bissett, November 12, 1767, Letter Book, quoted in William M. Fowler, *The Baron of Beacon Hill* (Boston: Houghton Mifflin, 1980), p. 51.
17 Thomas Hutchinson, *The Correspondence of Thomas Hutchinson, 1740–1766*, edited by John Tyler and Elizabeth Dubrulle (Charlottesville: University of Virginia Press, 2014), p. 12.
18 Governor Bernard to Board of Trade, August 31, 1765, cited in Unger, *John Hancock: Merchant*, p. 92.
19 Thomas Hutchinson to Richard Jackson, August 30, 1765, reproduced in Jonathan Mercantini, *The Stamp Act of 1765: A History in Documents* (Peterborough, ON: Broadview Press, 2017), p. 97.
20 Ibid.
21 Ibid.
22 Ibid.
23 William Gordon, *History of the Independence of America*, 1788, cited and quoted in www.newenglandhistoricalsociety.com/1765-thomas-hutchinson-moves-milton-involuntarily.

Chapter 8: Warmest Lovers of Liberty
1   Diary of Josiah Quincy Jr., reprinted in Albert Bushnell Hart, ed., *American History told by Contemporaries*, vol. 2, *Building of the Republic* (New York: Macmillan, 1919), p. 397.
2   Ibid., p. 399.
3   Ibid.
4   Ibid., p. 400.
5   Ibid.
6   Ibid. This quotation cited by Josiah Quincy Jr. in his diary entry comes from *Cato, A Tragedy*, by Joseph Addison, written in 1712; see *The British Drama* (London: William Miller, Old Bond Street, 1804), p. 354.
7   John Hancock to John Barnard, January 18, 1766, Hancock Family Papers, MHS.
8   Fowler, *The Baron of Beacon Hill*, p. 59.
9   Frederick F. Hassam, *Liberty Tree, Liberty Hall, Lafayette and Loyalty!* (Boston: 1891), p. 1.
10 "Liberty, Property, and No Excise: A Poem," Compos'd on occasion of the sight seen on the Great Trees (so called) in Boston, New England, on the 14th of August, 1765, printed in *The Magazine of History, with Notes and Extra Numbers*, Issue 77, vol. 20.–Issue 84, vol. 21 (Tarrytown, NY: William Abbat, 1922), pp. 135–139.
11 Morison, *Three Centuries of Harvard*, p. 133.
12 *Proceedings of the New York State Historical Association*, vol. 17, p. 72.
13 John Adams, "A Dissertation on the Canon and the Feudal Law," No. 1, Monday, 12 August 1765, Adams Papers, MHS.
14 Ibid.
15 Ibid.
16 John Adams, *Instructions Adopted by the Braintree Town Meeting Braintree 1765 Septr. 24*, Papers of John Adams, vol. 1, p. 137, Adams Papers, MHS.
17 Ibid.

18   Diary of John Adams, vol. 1, December 19, 1765, Adams Papers, MHS.

19   Lorenzo Sears, *John Hancock: The Picturesque Patriot* (Boston: Little, Brown, 1913), p. 101.

20   Baxter, *House of Hancock*, p. 234.

21   John Hancock to John Barnard, October 21, 1765, John Hancock Letter Book, quoted in Baxter, *House of Hancock*, p. 235.

22   Rebora and Staiti, *John Singleton Copley in America*, p. 71.

23   John Hancock to John Barnard, September 30, 1765, quoted in Baxter, *House of Hancock*, p. 233.

24   Thomas Hutchinson, October 26, 1765, *The Correspondence of Thomas Hutchinson*, vol. 1 (Boston: Colonial Society of Massachusetts, 2014), p. 315.

25   Diary of John Adams, vol. 1, Saturday, December 28, 1765, Adams Papers, MHS.

26   Ibid.

27   John Hancock to John Barnard, June 23, 1764, Letter Book, Hancock Family Papers, MHS.

28   Barlow Trecothick to Lord Rockingham, November 7, 1765, quoted in John L. Bullion, "British Ministers and American Resistance to the Stamp Act, October–December 1765," *The William and Mary Quarterly* 49, no. 1 (January 1992), p. 100.

29   Ibid.

30   *Boston Gazette*, May 26, 1766.

31   John Adams to William Tudor, June 1, 1817, quoted in Allan, *John Hancock: Patriot*, p. 96.

32   John Hancock to Harrison and Barnard, May 27, 1766, quoted in Allan, *John Hancock: Patriot*, p. 97.

33   Richard Frothingham, *The Rise of the Republic of the United States* (Boston: Little, Brown, 1873), p. 201.

Chapter 9: A Watchful Spirit

1   Abigail Adams and John Adams to Mary Smith Cranch, January 12, 1767, Adams Papers, MHS.

2   Abigail Adams and John Adams to Mary Smith Cranch, May 26, 1766, Adams Papers, MHS.

3   Abigail Adams to Mary Smith Cranch, January 31, 1767; ibid., October 6, 1766, Adams Papers, MHS.

4   Ibid.

5   Adams, *The Works of John Adams*, vol. 3, p. 488.

6   Ibid., p. 489.

7   Catherine Drinker Bowen, *John Adams and the American Revolution* (Boston: Little, Brown, 1950), p. 308.

8   Abigail Adams to John Adams, September 14, 1767, Adams Papers, MHS.

9   Abigail Adams to Mary Smith Cranch, October 13, 1766, Adams Papers, MHS.

10   Abigail Adams to Mary Smith Cranch, October 6, 1766, Adams Papers, MHS.

11   *Boston Gazette*, March 14, 1768, MHS.

12   "Hyperion," December 5, 1767, in Daniel R. Coquillette and Neil Longley York, eds., *Josiah Quincy, Jr. Political and Legal Works*, vol. 6 (Boston: Colonial Society of Massachusetts, 2014), p. 8.

13   Ibid.

14   Ibid., p. 9.

15   Ibid., p. 10.

16   Clifford K. Shipton, *Sibley's Harvard Graduates*, vol. 13 (Cambridge, MA: Harvard University Press, 1965), p. 480.

17   "Hyperion," December 5, 1767, Coquillette and York, eds., *Josiah Quincy, Jr., vol. 6*, p. 9.

18   Ibid.

19   Ibid., p. 22.

20   "Remarks by Mr. Josiah Quincy," *Proceedings of the Massachusetts Historical Society*, 19 (January 1882), p. 213.

21 Samuel Quincy to Henry Hill, May 13, 1775, Quincy Family Papers, MHS.

22 *Boston Gazette*, March 21, 1768, MHS.

23 Josiah Quincy Jr., "Observations on the Boston Port Bill," *Memoir of the Life of Josiah Quincy*, p. 247.

24 Diary of John Adams, vol. 1, January 30, 1768, Adams Papers, MHS.

25 *Massachusetts Gazette Extraordinary, Number 3351*, December 24, 1767, MHS.

26 Ibid.

27 Unger, *John Hancock: Merchant King*, p. 115.

28 Josiah Quincy Jr., *Boston Gazette*, October 5, 1767, reprinted in Joseph Tinker Buckingham, *Specimens of Newspaper Literature* (Boston: L.C. Little and J. Brown, 1850), pp. 180–181.

Chapter 10: The Arrival of Troops

1 Massachusetts Circular Letter, February 11, 1768, reprinted in William Macdonald, *Documentary Source Book of American History, 1606–1898* (New York: Macmillan, 1908), p. 148.

2 Bowen, *John Adams and the American Revolution*, p. 321.

3 Ibid., p. 322.

4 Customs Commissioners to Lords of Treasury, Mar. 28, 1768, in Public Records Office, London, quoted in Baxter, *House of Hancock*, p. 260.

5 Thomas Hutchinson to R. Jackson, April 17, 1768, in Massachusetts Archives, vol. 26, p. 299, State House, Boston.

6 Abigail Adams to Isaac Smith, April 20, 1771, Adams Papers, MHS.

7 Diary of John Adams, vol. 3, First Residence in Boston, 1768, Adams Papers, MHS.

8 Adams, *The Works of John Adams*, vol. 2, p. 210.

9 Ibid.

10 Samuel Quincy, "Death of a Cobbler," preserved poem found in the Quincy-Hill-Phillips-Treadwell Papers, 1699–1969, Cambridge Historical Society, Cambridge, Massachusetts.

11 Quoted in Allan, *John Hancock: Patriot*, p. 108.

12 Bowen, *John Adams and the American Revolution*, p. 305.

13 John Adams to Dennys de Berdt, September 27, 1768, quoted in Allan, *John Hancock: Patriot*, p. 109.

14 John Rowe, *Letters and Diary of John Rowe, a Boston Merchant*, ed. Anne Rowe Cunningham (Boston: W. B. Clarke Company, 1903), entry dated May 2, 1768, p. 161.

15 *Pennsylvania Chronicle and Universal Advertiser*, February 27, 1769, Library of Congress.

16 Falmouth, Maine's leading seaport, was the only town in Maine to sign a nonimportation agreement in retaliation for the Townshend Acts.

17 Governor Bernard to Lord Barrington, July 20, 1768, William Widman Barrington (Viscount), *The Barrington-Bernard Correspondence and Illustrative Matter, 1760–1770* (Cambridge, MA: Harvard University, 1912), p. 167–168.

18 Quincy, *Memoir of the Life of Josiah Quincy*, p. 14.

19 *Boston Gazette*, February 23, 1767, MHS.

20 Josiah Quincy Jr. to Reverend John Eagleson, September 15, 1768, *Memoir of the Life of Josiah Quincy*, p. 13.

21 *Evening-Post*, October 24, 1768, *The Annotated Newspapers of Harbottle Dorr, Jr.*, MHS.

22 Josiah Quincy Jr., writing as Hyperion, *Appeal, Boston Gazette*, October 3, 1768, reprinted in *Memoir of the Life of Josiah Quincy*, p. 14.

23 Josiah Quincy Jr. to Reverend John Eagleson, September 15, 1768, *Memoir of the Life of Josiah Quincy*, p. 16.

24 John Adams, *Diary and Autobiography*, vol. 1, edited by L. H. Butterfield (Cambridge, MA: Harvard University Press), Adams Papers, MHS, part 1, sheet 16 of 53.

25 Ibid.

26 Baxter, *House of Hancock*, p. 268.

Chapter 11: Portents of a Comet

1   *Boston Gazette*, May 12, 1768, MHS.
2   *Journal of the House of Representatives*, June 27, 1769, MHS.
3   Bowen, *John Adams and the American Revolution*, p. 324.
4   *Boston Gazette*, August 7, 1769, MHS.
5   Diary of John Adams, Monday, August 14, 1774, Adams Papers, MHS.
6   Ibid.
7   Diary of John Adams, August 14, 1769, Adams Papers, MHS.
8   Ira Stoll, *Samuel Adams: A Life* (New York: Free Press, 2008), p. 76.
9   John Dickinson, *The Liberty Song, Boston Chronicle*, August 29–Sep. 5, 1768, Dickinson College Archives.
10 Diary of John Adams, August 14, 1769, Adams Papers, MHS.
11 John Hancock to Barnard & Harrison, February 7, 1765, Hancock Papers, MHS.
12 *New York Journal*, January 18, 1770, cited and quoted in Arthur Meier Schlesinger, *The Colonial Merchants and the American Revolution, 1763–1776* (Washington, DC: Beard Books, 1939), p. 168.
13 Adams, *The Works of John Adams*, vol. 2, p. 226.
14 Ibid.
15 John Adams to Abigail Adams, Adams Family Correspondence, June 29, 1769, MHS.
16 Bowen, *John Adams and the American Revolution*, p. 330.
17 Adams, *The Works of John Adams*, vol. 3, p. 506.
18 See *The Chronicle of Henry of Huntingdon* (London: H. G. Bohn, 1853), p. 148, 212.
19 Quincy, *Memoir of the Life of Josiah Quincy*, p. 21.
20 Josiah Quincy Jr. to Josiah Quincy Sr., December 1768, excerpted in *Memoir of the Life of Josiah Quincy*, p. 20.
21 Ibid., p. 20.
22 Coquillette and York, *Portrait of a Patriot*, vol. 1, p. 100.
23 *A Pride of Quincys*, A Massachusetts Historical Society Picture Book, Boston, 1969, in holdings of the MHS.
24 Edmund Quincy to Dorothy Quincy, undated letter, Quincy Family Papers, MHS.

Chapter 12: Pressing Forward

1   *Boston Gazette*, January 30, 1770, MHS.
2   *Boston Gazette*, February 12, 1770, MHS; see also Quincy, *Memoir of the Life of Josiah Quincy*, p. 23.
3   *Boston Gazette*, February 12, 1770, MHS.
4   Hiller B. Zobel, *The Boston Massacre* (New York: Norton, 1970), p. 172.
5   Edmund Quincy Commonplace Book, p. 34, Quincy Family Papers, MHS.
6   See Nina Sankovitch, *The Lowells of Massachusetts: An American Family* (New York: St. Martin's Press, 2017), p. 147.
7   *Boston Gazette*, February 5, 1770, MHS.
8   Triber, *A True Republican*, p. 73, citing "Journal of Transactions in Boston, January 18, 1770."
9   George Mason to unknown recipient, January 24, 1770, *Narrative of Proceedings at Boston, February 7 to March 14, 1770*, cited in Peter Shaw, *American Patriots and Ritual of Revolution* (Cambridge, MA: Harvard University Press, 1981) pp. 160–161.
10 Ibid.
11 Triber, *A True Republican*, p. 73.
12 Diary of John Adams, February 26, 1770, Adams Papers, MHS.
13 Thomas Hutchinson to Samuel Hood, February 23, 1770, quoted and cited in Zobel, *The Boston Massacre*, p. 173.
14 Ibid., p. 174.
15 Coquillette and York, *Portrait of a Patriot*, vol. 1, p. 24.

16 L. Kinvin Wroth and Hiller B. Zobel, *Legal Papers of John Adams, vol. 3* (Cambridge, MA: Harvard University Press, 1965), p. 266.

17 Rowe, *Letters and Diary*, p. 197.

18 Thomas Hutchinson to Lord Hillsborough, February 28, 1770, cited and quoted in Zobel, *The Boston Massacre*, p. 178.

19 Ibid.

20 Diary of John Adams, February 26, 1770, Adams Papers, MHS.

Chapter 13: Mayhem and Massacre

1 Two weeks earlier, Henderson had married Sally Jackson, previously courted by John Hancock.

2 Adams, *Diary and Autobiography*, vol. 3, p. 291. 12 of 53, pp. 1768–1770.

3 Ibid.

4 "The Bloody Massacre perpetrated in King Street, Boston on March 5th 1770 by a party of the 29th Regiment," Engraving by Paul Revere, Boston 1770, MHS; "A Fair Account of the Late Unhappy Disturbance at Boston in New England," London, printed for B. White, 1770, MHS.

5 Zobel, *The Boston Massacre*, pp. 186–187.

6 Ibid., p. 197.

7 Ibid., p. 198.

8 Ibid., p. 202.

9 Unger, *John Hancock: Merchant King*, p. 145, citing *New York Public Advertiser*, April 28, 1770, New York Public Library.

10 Bernard Bailyn, *The Ordeal of Thomas Hutchinson* (Cambridge, MA; Harvard University Press, 1974), p. 161.

11 *Boston Gazette*, March 12, 1770, MHS.

12 Josiah Quincy Jr. to Josiah Quincy, March 26, 1770, *Memoir of the Life of Josiah Quincy*, p. 28.

13 Ibid., p. 27–28.

14 Thomas Preston to William Pitt, Earl of Chatham, March 17, 1770, quoted in Coquillette and York, *Portrait of a Patriot*, vol. 1, p. 22.

15 "A Fair Account of the Late Unhappy Disturbance at Boston in New England," London, printed for B. White, 1770, p. 9, MHS.

16 Coquillette and York, *Portrait of a Patriot*, vol. 2, p. 19, extracting in its entirety Josiah Quincy's Commonplace Law Book, dated 1770, p. 69.

17 Quincy, *Memoir of the Life of Josiah Quincy*, p. 32.

18 Josiah Quincy to Josiah Quincy Jr., March 22, 1770, *Memoir of the Life of Josiah Quincy*, p. 26.

19 Ibid., p. 27.

20 Ibid.

21 Ibid., p. 28.

22 Adams, *Diary and Autobiography*, vol. 3, p. 294.

23 *Report of the Record Commissioners, Boston Town Records, 1770–1777* (Boston: Rockwell & Churchill, 1887), pp. 31–32.

24 Ibid., pp. 26, 31–32.

25 Thomas Hutchinson to Lord Hillsborough, May 21, 1770, cited and quoted in Zobel, *The Boston Massacre*, p. 228.

26 Quincy, *Memoir of the Life of Josiah Quincy*, p. 50.

27 *Boston Gazette*, March 12, 1770, MHS.

Chapter 14: On Trial

1 Diary of John Adams, June 27, 1770, Adams Papers, MHS.

2 Ibid.

3 Diary of John Adams, June 26, 1770, Adams Papers, MHS.

4 Adams, *Diary and Autobiography*, vol. 3, p. 294.

5   Ibid.
6   Marcia G. Synott and Laurel Sharp, "Women in the Quincy Homestead" (Boston: The National Society of the Colonial Dames of America, 1998), p. 11.
7   Edmund Quincy IV to Katy Quincy, July 31, 1771, Quincy Papers, MHS.
8   Zobel, *The Boston Massacre*, p. 242.
9   Adams, *The Works of John Adams*, vol. 10, p. 201.
10 Broadside titled "On The Trial of the Inhuman Murderers, of the 5th of March 1770," published October 1770, MHS.
11 Zobel, *The Boston Massacre*, p. 259.
12 Ibid.
13 *American History told by Contemporaries*, p. 400.
14 Quincy, *Memoir of the Life of Josiah Quincy*, p. 29, 1n.
15 Diary of John Adams, vol. 2, March 5, 1773, Adams Papers, MHS.
16 Quincy, *Memoir of the Life of Josiah Quincy*, p. 31.
17 Ibid., p. 226, 1n.
18 Ibid., p. 32.
19 Ibid., p. 38.
20 Ibid., p. 39.
21 Ibid., pp. 40–41.
22 Clifford K. Shipton, *Sibley's Harvard Graduates, vol. 15* (Boston: Massachusetts Historical Society, 1970), p. 482.
23 *Legal Papers of John Adams*, vol. 3, "Adams' Argument for the Defense, 3–4 December 1770," Adams Papers, MHS.
24 Quincy, *Memoir of the Life of Josiah Quincy*, p. 48, (mis)quoting from *The Merchant of Venice*, by William Shakespeare.
25 Ibid.
26 Ibid., p. 290.
27 Ibid., p. 291.
28 Ibid., pp. 292–293.
29 Ibid., p. 293.
30 *Boston Gazette*, December 17, 1770, MHS, and quoted in Zobel, *The Boston Massacre*, p. 294.
31 Diary of John Adams, vol. 2, March 5, 1773, Adams Papers, MHS.
32 John Adams to John Lowell, December 15, 1770, Adams Papers, MHS.
33 Samuel Quincy to Robert Treat Paine, December 16, 1770, Quincy Family Papers, MHS.
34 Ibid.
35 Josiah Quincy Jr. as "Marchmont Nedham," in the *Boston Gazette*, December 27, 1773, MHS.
36 Coquillette and York, *Portrait of a Patriot*, vol. 1, p. 22.
37 See Thomas Hutchinson, *The Diary and Letters of His Excellency Thomas Hutchinson, Captain-General and Governor-in-Chief of His Late Majesty's Province of Massachusetts Bay in North America*, vol. 1, edited by Peter Orlando Hutchinson (Boston: Houghton Mifflin, 1884), p. 81.

Chapter 15: Retreat to Braintree

1   Diary of John Adams, vol. 2, February 14, 1771, Adams Papers, MHS.
2   Coquillette and York, *Portrait of a Patriot*, vol. 1, p. 22.
3   Josiah Quincy Jr., *Political Commonplace Book*, p. 192, Quincy Family Papers, MHS; and see Coquillette and York, *Portrait of a Patriot*, vol. 1, p. 170.
4   Josiah Quincy Jr., *Political Commonplace Book*, Quincy Family Papers, MHS, p. 44, and Coquillette and York, *Portrait of a Patriot*, vol. 1, p. 120; see also Quincy, *Memoir of the Life of Josiah Quincy*, p. 51.
5   Josiah Quincy Jr., quoting Sir John Phillips, January 29, 1744, *Political Commonplace*

Book, Quincy Family Papers, MHS, p. 119; and Coquillette and York, *Portrait of a Patriot*, vol. 1, p. 146.

6   *Boston Gazette*, February 11, 1771; see also Quincy, *Memoir of the Life of Josiah Quincy*, p. 51.

7   Triber, *A True Republican*, p. 85.

8   *Boston Gazette*, March 11, 1771, cited and quoted in Triber, *A True Republican*, p. 85.

9   See *Diary of Anna Green Winslow, a Boston School Girl of 1771*, ed. Alice M. Earle (Boston: Houghton Mifflin, 1894), p. 72.

10   John Adams, *Diary and Autobiography*, vol. 1, p. 74.

11   *Massachusetts Spy*, February 27, 1772, cited and quoted in Neil L. York, "Tag-Team Polemics: The 'Centinel' and His Allies in the 'Massachusetts Spy,'" *Proceedings of the Massachusetts Historical Society*, ser. 3, vol. 107 (1995), p. 103.

12   Josiah Quincy Jr. as "Hyperion," *Boston Gazette*, November 25, 1771, MHS.

13   Josiah Quincy Jr. as "Marchmont Needham," *Boston Gazette*, June 6, 1772, MHS.

14   Edmund Quincy III, Letter dated May 11, 1771, recipient unknown, Quincy Family Papers, MHS.

15   John Langdon Sibley, *Biographical Sketches of Harvard Graduates*, vol. 3 (Cambridge, MA: Charles William Sever, 1885), p. 112; quoting *Boston Gazette*, February 27, 1775.

16   William M. Wiecek, "Somerset: Lord Mansfield and the Legitimacy of Slavery in the Anglo-American World," *University of Chicago Law Review*, vol. 42, No. 1 (Autumn, 1974), pp. 86–87.

17   John Adams to Jeremy Belknap, March 21, 1795, Adams Papers, MHS.

18   Ibid.

19   John Adams to Richard Cranch, September 23, 1767, Adams Papers, MHS.

20   Diary of John Adams, vol. 2, May 2, 1771, Adams Papers, MHS.

21   John Adams to Isaac Smith Jr., April 11, 1771, Adams Papers, MHS.

22   Diary of John Adams, vol. 2, April 18, 1771, Adams Papers, MHS.

23   Ibid., May 1, 1771.

24   Abigail Adams to Isaac Smith, April 20, 1771, Adams Papers, MHS.

25   John Adams to Abigail Adams, July 1, 1775, Adams Papers, MHS; and see Diane Jacobs, *Dear Abigail* (New York: Ballantine Books, 2014), p. 43.

26   Abigail Adams to John Adams, August 14, 1776, Adams Family Papers, MHS.

27   Ibid.

28   Ibid.

29   Edmund Quincy IV to Katherine Quincy, July 31, 1771, Quincy Family Papers, MHS.

30   Diary of John Adams, vol. 2, June 13, 1771, Adams Papers, MHS.

31   Ibid.

32   John Adams to James Warren, March 1771, Warren-Adams Letters, MHS.

33   Josiah Quincy Jr. as "Mentor," *Boston Evening-Post*, February 11, 1771, MHS.

34   Diary of John Adams, vol. 2, May 2, 1771, Adams Papers, MHS.

35   John Hancock, Oration, March 5, 1774, as excerpted in *American Patriotism: Speeches, Letters, and Other Papers which Illustrate the Foundation, the Development, the Preservation of the United States of America*, Vol. 1, ed. Selim Hobart Peabody (New York: American Book Exchange, 1880), p. 86.

36   Thomas Hutchinson to Thomas Gage, December 1, 1771, quoted in Allan, *John Hancock: Patriot*, p. 125.

37   Thomas Hutchinson to Frances Bernard, January 29, 1772, quoted in Allan, *John Hancock: Patriot*, p. 125.

Chapter 16: Patriots Assemble

1   Thomas Hutchinson to Francis Bernard, January 29, 1772, quoted in Allan, *John Hancock: Patriot*, p. 126.

2   Sam Adams to Arthur Lee, April 12, 1773, quoted in Allan, *John Hancock: Patriot*, p. 125.

3   Rebora and Staiti, *John Singleton Copley in America*, p. 277.

4   *A History of the Church in Brattle Street, Boston, by its Pastor Samuel Kirkland Lothrop* (Boston: Wm. Crosby and H.P. Nichols, 1851), p. 101.

5   John Hancock to Ebenezer Hancock, January 11, 1771, quoted in W. T. Baxter, "A Colonial Bankrupt, Ebenezer Hancock, 1741–1819," *Bulletin of the Business Historical Society*, vol. 25, No. 2 (June 1951), p. 9.

6   John Adams to Abigail Adams, September 17, 1771, Adams Papers, MHS.

7   Diary of John Adams, vol. 1, February 9, 1772, Adams Papers, MHS.

8   John Adams to Abigail Adams, May Saturday 1772, Adams Papers, MHS.

9   Ibid.

10 John Hancock to George Hayley, August 24, 1768, quoted in Fowler, *The Baron of Beacon Hill*, p. 91.

11 John Hancock to Hayley & Hopkins, November 14, 1771, quoted in Allan, *John Hancock: Patriot*, p. 125.

12 Abigail Adams and John Adams to Mary Smith Cranch, January 12, 1767, Adams Papers, MHS.

13 Diary of John Adams, vol. 2, September 22, 1772, Adams Papers, MHS.

14 John C. Shields, *Phillis Wheatley and the Romantics* (Knoxville: University of Tennessee Press, 2008), pp. 112–113.

15 Josiah Quincy Jr. as "Marchmont Nedham," *Boston Gazette*, 1772, quoted in *Specimens of Newspaper Literature*, vol. 1, ed. Joseph Tinker Buckingham (Boston: C.C. Little and J. Brown, 1850), p. 188.

16 Ibid.

17 Quincy, *Memoir of the Life of Josiah Quincy*, pp. 52–53.

18 Ibid.

19 *The Votes and Proceedings of the Freeholders and other Inhabitants of the Town of Boston, in Town Meeting Assembled* (Boston: Edes and Gill, 1772), p. iii, MHS.

20 "A Letter of Correspondence to the Other Towns, Boston, November 20, 1772," *A Report of the Record Commissioners of the City of Boston*, vol. 18 (Boston: Rockwell and Churchill, 1887), p. 106.

21 *The Votes and Proceedings of the Freeholders*, p. 2.

22 Ibid., p. 35.

23 *The Writings of Samuel Adams, 1770–1773*, vol. 2, ed. Harry Alonzo Cushing (New York: G. P. Putnam's Sons, 1906), p. 372.

24 Diary of John Adams, vol. 2, November 21, 1772, Adams Papers, MHS.

25 Josiah Quincy Jr., *The Southern Journal*, p. 184, Quincy Family Papers, MHS.

26 Josiah Quincy Jr. to George Clymer, August 1773, extracted in Quincy, *Memoir of the Life of Josiah Quincy*, p. 119.

Chapter 17: Branching Out

1   Diary of John Adams, vol. 2, January 1, 1773, Adams Papers, MHS.

2   John Adams to the *Boston Gazette*, January 11, 1773, Adams Papers, MHS.

3   John Adams, "Reply of the House to Hutchinson's First Message, January 26, 1773," Adams Papers, MHS.

4   Ibid.

5   Ibid.

6   Ibid.

7   Josiah Quincy Jr., "Observations on the Port-Bill," *Memoir of the Life of Josiah Quincy*, p. 318.

8   John Adams, "Adams Notes of Authorities, Suffolk Inferior Court, Boston, January 1771," Adams Papers, MHS.

9   Quincy, "Observations on the Port-Bill," p. 355.

10 Boston Town Records, 1770–1777, p. 93; quoted in Fowler, *The Baron of Beacon Hill*, p. 148, and Unger, *John Hancock: Merchant King*, p. 161.

11 See Bowen, *John Adams and the American Revolution*, pp. 426–427.

12 Hutchinson as quoted in Unger, *John Hancock: Merchant King*, p. 162.

13 Thomas Hutchinson to John Pownall, November 13, 1772, quoted in Andrew S. Walmsley, *Thomas Hutchinson and the Origins of the American Revolution* (New York: NYU Press, 1999), p. 136.

14 Thomas Hutchinson to Lord Dartmouth, December 13, 1772, quoted in ibid., p. 137.

15 Josiah Quincy Jr., Southern Journal, p. 3, Quincy Family Papers, MHS.

16 Ibid., p. 1.

17 "Nos patria fines, nos dulcia linquimus Arva," Virgil, Eclogue I; see Coquillette and York, *Portrait of a Patriot*, vol. 3, p. 89.

18 Josiah Quincy Jr., Southern Journal, Quincy Family Papers, MHS, pp. 9–10.

19 Ibid., p. 11, 17.

20 Ibid., p. 24, 28–29, 31.

21 Ibid., p. 25.

22 Ibid., p. 28.

23 Ibid., p. 33.

24 John Adams, "Reply of the House to Hutchinson's First Message, January 26, 1773," Adams Papers, MHS.

25 Bowen, *John Adams and the American Revolution*, p. 426.

26 Ibid.

27 Josiah Quincy Jr. as "Callisthenes," *Boston Gazette*, September 28, 1772, extracted in Quincy, *Memoir of the Life of Josiah Quincy*, p. 52.

28 Diary of John Adams, vol. 2, March 4, 1773, Adams Papers, MHS.

29 Adams, *The Works of John Adams*, vol. 10, p. 162.

30 Josiah Quincy Jr. to Abigail Phillips Quincy, March 1, 1773, extracted in Quincy, *Memoir of the Life of Josiah Quincy*, p. 71.

31 Josiah Quincy Jr., Southern Journal, Quincy Family Papers, MHS, p. 56, 66.

32 Ibid., p. 45, 90.

33 Ibid., p. 89.

34 Ibid., p. 96.

35 Ibid., p. 104.

36 Ibid.

37 Ibid., p. 54; Samuel A. Forman, *Dr. Joseph Warren: The Boston Tea Party, Bunker Hill, and the Birth of American Liberty* (Gretna, LA: Pelican Publishing Company, 2012), p. 100.

38 Josiah Quincy Jr., Southern Journal, Quincy Family Papers, MHS, p. 114.

39 Ibid., p. 95.

40 Ibid., p. 91.

41 Ibid., pp. 142–143, 172.

42 Josiah Quincy Sr. to Josiah Quincy Jr., April 9, 1773, Quincy Family Papers, MHS.

43 Ibid.

44 Josiah Quincy Jr., Southern Journal, Quincy Family Papers, MHS, p. 56, 65.

45 Ibid., p. 174.

46 Ibid., p. 181.

47 Ibid., p. 110, 94, 114.

48 Samuel Quincy to Josiah Quincy Jr., April 13, 1773, Quincy Family Papers, MHS.

49 Diary of John Adams, vol. 2, March 22, 1773, Adams Papers, MHS.

Chapter 18: Anxiety and Apprehensions

1 *American History Told by Contemporaries*, vol. 2, ed. Albert Bushnell Hart and John Gould Curtis (New York: Macmillan, 1901), pp. 421–22.

2 Mercy Otis Warren, *History of the Rise, Progress, and Termination of the American Revolution*, vol. 1 (Boston: 1805), p. 56, 352–53.

3 *Boston Gazette*, July 19, 1773, MHS.

4   Diary of John Adams, vol. 2, April 24, 1773, Adams Papers, MHS.
5   Journals of the House (Boston, 1773), quoted in Fowler, *The Baron of Beacon Hill*, p. 152.
6   Journals of the House of Representatives of Massachusetts, vol. 50, 1773–1774 (Boston: Massachusetts Historical Society, 1981), p. 41.
7   Diary of John Adams, vol. 3, August 1775, Adams Papers, MHS.
8   Abigail Adams to Mercy Otis Warren, July 16, 1773, Adams Papers, MHS.
9   John Quincy Adams to Betsy Cranch, 1773, Adams Papers, MHS.
10 Abigail Adams to Mercy Otis Warren, July 16, 1773, Adams Papers, MHS.
11 Edmund Quincy to Dorothy Quincy, June 18, 1773, Quincy Family Papers, MHS.
12 *The New England Historical and Genealogical Register,* 1874 (Boston: New England Historical, Genealogical Society, 1874), p. 182.
13 See http://www.hinghamcemetery.org/_site/pages/our_history.php.
14 George Clymer to Josiah Quincy Jr., July 29, 1773, Quincy Papers, MHS.
15 Josiah Quincy Jr. to George Clymer, August [no date specified], 1773, Quincy Papers, MHS.
16 Extract of a letter from New York, September 27 (1773), printed in *The Massachusetts Gazette; and the Boston Post-Boy and Advertiser,* Number 842, 4–11, October 1773, MHS.
17 "Proceedings of the North End Caucus," quoted in Triber, *A True Republican,* p. 92, citing Goss, *Life of Colonial Revere,* vol. 2, app. C, p. 641.
18 "IN consequence of a conference with the committees of correspondence for the towns in the vicinity of Boston, November 23, 1773," Broadside, MHS.
19 Rowe, *Letters and Diary,* November 2, 1773, p. 252.
20 Egerton Collection, November 2, 1773, MHS.
21 Rowe, *Letters and Diary,* November 29, 1773, p. 255.
22 Abigail Adams to Mercy Otis Warren, December 5, 1773, Adams Papers, MHS.

Chapter 19: Tea, That Baneful Weed

1   Rowe, *Letters and Diary,* November 29, 1773, p. 255.
2   Quoted in Les Standiford, *Desperate Sons* (New York: HarperCollins, 2012), p. 207, relying on Boston Town Records, 1770–1777.
3   John Rowe Diary, December 8, 1773, p. 257; The fourth vessel, the *William,* owned by the Clarke family, foundered off the coast and would never arrive in Boston; the tea would be off-loaded from the vessel as it lay stuck on a reef.
4   Ibid., p. 256.
5   Thomas Hutchinson to Israel Maudit, December 1773, extracted in "Tea Party Anniversary," *Proceedings of the Massachusetts Historical Society,* vol. 13 (Boston: MHS, 1875), p. 170.
6   *Boston Gazette,* December 13, 1773, MHS; and see Triber, *A True Republican,* p. 94.
7   Quincy, *Memoir of the Life of Josiah Quincy,* p. 125.
8   Ibid.
9   Allan, *John Hancock: Patriot,* p. 139, citing B. B. Thatcher, *Traits of the Tea Party,* pp. 177–178.
10 Charles Augustus Goodrich, *Travels and Sketches in North and South America* (Hartford: Case, Tiffany, 1852), p. 78; see also Nathaniel Philbrick, *Bunker Hill* (New York: Viking Penguin, 2013), p. 100. Although Rowe had scribbled into his diary that he "being a little Unwell" was home on the evening of December 16, there are many who speculate that he added the sentences in to protect himself and that in fact he was present and was overheard speaking about the mixture of tea and salt water.
11 "The Command at the Battle of Bunker Hill, as Shown in the Statement of Major Thompson Maxwell," *New England Historical and Genealogical Register,* vol. 22 (1868), p. 58.
12 John Adams to Joseph Warren, December 17, 1773, Adams Papers, MHS.
13 Abigail Adams to Mercy Otis Warren, December 5, 1773, Adams Papers, MHS.
14 John Hancock, Letter Book, December 21, 1773, quoted in Baxter, *House of Hancock,* p. 283, 11n.
15 Diary of John Adams, vol. 2, December 18, 1773, Adams Papers, MHS.

16   Letter of the Boston Committee of Correspondence, sent to Plymouth and Sandwich, quoted in "Tea Party Anniversary," p. 173.

17   Letter to Boston from Medford, MA, published in the *Boston Gazette*, December 20, 1773, MHS.

18   Unger, *John Hancock: Merchant King*, p. 173.

19   "How the Landing of Tea Was Opposed in Philadelphia by Colonel William Bradford and Others in 1773," *Pennsylvania Magazine of History and Biography* 15, no. 4 (1891): 390–391.

20   Diary of John Adams, vol. 2, December 17, 1773, Adams Papers, MHS.

21   Ibid.

22   Abigail Adams to Mercy Otis Warren, December 5, 1773, Adams Papers, MHS.

23   Samuel Adams to Arthur Lee, January 25, 1774, quoted in John Ferling, *Independence: The Struggle to Set America Free* (New York: Bloomsbury Press, 2011), p. 52.

24   Diary of Josiah Quincy Jr., reprinted in Albert Bushnell Hart and John Gould Curtis, eds., *American History Told by Contemporaries*, vol. 2, *Building of the Republic* (New York: Macmillan, 1919), p. 400.

25   Diary of John Adams, vol. 2, December 18, 1773, Adams Papers, MHS; *Boston Gazette*, December 27, 1773, MHS.

26   Josiah Quincy Jr. as "Marchmont Nedham," December 20, 1773, *Boston Gazette*, MHS.

27   John Trumbull to Samuel Quincy, September 11, 1773, Quincy Family Papers, MHS.

28   Isaac Smith Jr., to Mary Cranch, October 20, 1774, Adams Papers, MHS.

Chapter 20: Rocks and Quicksands on Every Side

1   Last Will and Testament of Josiah Quincy Jr., Quincy Family Papers, MHS.

2   Quincy, *Memoir of the Life of Josiah Quincy*, p. 293.

3   Josiah Quincy Jr. as "Nedham's Remembrancer," *Boston Gazette*, January 10, 1774, and as "Marchmont Nedham," *Boston Gazette*, February 7, 1774, MHS.

4   "Extract of a Letter from London," *Boston Evening Post*, February 15, 1774, MHS.

5   *Boston Gazette*, May 2, 1774, MHS.

6   Diary of John Adams, vol. 2, February 28, 1774, Adams Papers, MHS.

7   Ibid.

8   Samuel Quincy to Andrew Oliver, January 31, 1774, Quincy Family Papers, MHS.

9   John Hancock, An Oration, March 5 1774, Hancock Family Papers, MHS.

10   Diary of John Adams, vol. 2, March 5, 1774, Adams Papers, MHS.

11   John Hancock, An Oration, March 5, 1774, Hancock Family Papers, MHS.

12   Diary of John Adams, vol. 2, March 5, 1774, Adams Papers, MHS.

13   John Hancock, An Oration, March 5, 1774, Hancock Family Papers, MHS.

14   Ibid.

15   Diary of John Adams, vol. 2, March 5, 1774, Adams Papers, MHS.

16   Thomas Hutchinson, *Diary and Letters*, vol. 1, p. 130.

17   Adams, *Diary and Autobiography*, vol. 3, pp. 299–300.

18   Ibid.

19   Ibid., p. 302.

20   *Papers of John Adams*, vol. 2, February 24, 1774, Adams Papers, MHS.

21   Rowe, *Letters and Diary*, May 10, 1774, p. 269.

22   Henry Steele Commager and Milton Cantor, eds., *Documents of American History*, (Englewood Cliffs, NJ: Prentice Hall, 1998), p. 71.

23   John Adams to Abigail Adams, May 12, 1774, Adams Papers, MHS.

24   John Hancock, An Oration, March 5, 1774, Hancock Family Papers, MHS.

25   Samuel Quincy to Josiah Quincy Jr., June 1, 1774, Quincy Family Papers, MHS.

26   Josiah Quincy Jr., *Observations on the Act of Parliament Commonly Called the Boston Port-Bill; With Thoughts on Civil Society and Standing Armies* (Boston: Edes and Gill, in Queen-Street, 1774), pp. 1, 80–81.

27   Ibid., p. 82.
28   Ibid., p. 2.
29   Ibid., p. 82.

Chapter 21: Punishment and Indignation

1   Rowe, *Letters and Diary*, June 1, 1774, p. 273.
2   Ibid., May 17, 1774, pp. 270–271.
3   John Andrews, *Letters of John Andrews, Esq., 1772–1776* (Cambridge, MA: John Wilson and Sons, 1866), May 18, 1774, p. 15.
4   Ibid.
5   John Adams to Abigail Adams, June 29, 1774, Adams Papers, MHS.
6   Ibid., June 25, 1774.
7   John Adams to Abigail Adams, June 23, 1774, Adams Papers, MHS.
8   John Adams to Abigail Adams, July 1, 1774, Adams Papers, MHS.
9   *Massachusetts Historical Society Proceedings*, vol. 12 (Boston: MHS, 1873), p. 47.
10   Ibid.
11   Ashley Bowen, *The Journals of Ashley Bowen (1728–1813) of Marblehead*, ed. Philip Chadwick Foster Smith (Boston: Colonial Society of Massachusetts, 1973), p. 404.
12   *Boston Gazette*, June 27, 1774, MHS.
13   Ellen Douglas Larned, *History of Windham County, Connecticut, 1760–1880* (Worcester, MA: Charles Hamilton, 1880), p. 125.
14   See Bowen, *John Adams and the American Revolution*, pp. 443–444.
15   John Dickinson to Josiah Quincy Jr., June 20, 1774, Quincy Family Papers, MHS.
16   Diary of John Adams, vol. 2, Monday, June 20, 1774, Adams Papers, MHS.
17   Adams, *The Works of John Adams*, vol. 4, p. 8.
18   Ibid.
19   Ibid.
20   John Adams to Abigail Adams, July 7, 1774, Adams Papers, MHS.
21   Samuel Quincy to Josiah Quincy Jr., June 1, 1774, Quincy Family Papers, MHS.
22   William Palfrey to Samuel Adams, September 1774, quoted in Allan, *John Hancock: Patriot*, p. 175, citing First Corps Cadets Papers.
23   *Essex Gazette*, September 6–13, quoted in T. H. Breen, *American Insurgents, American Patriots* (New York: Farrar, Straus & Giroux, 2010), p. 83.
24   Peter Force, *American Archive: A Documentary History of the English Colonies in North America*, series 4, vol. 1, hereafter (Washington, DC: M. St. Clair Clarke and Peter Force, 1848), p. 749.
25   *Essex Gazette*, August 23–30, quoted in Breen, *American Insurgents*, p. 89.
26   Description of "outrages" found in Force, *American Archives*, vol. 1, pp. 1260–1263, quoted in Philip McFarland, *The Brave Bostonians* (New York: HarperCollins, 1998), p. 84.
27   John Andrews to William Barrell, August 10, 1774, *Letters of John Andrews*, p. 26.
28   Abigail Adams to John Adams, August 19, 1774, Adams Papers, MHS.
29   Ibid.
30   Ibid.
31   Abigail Adams to John Adams, August 19, 1774, Adams Papers, MHS.
32   John Adams to Abigail Adams, August 28, 1774, Adams Papers, MHS.

Chapter 22: Grand Object of Their View

1   Josiah Quincy Jr. to Abigail Phillips Quincy, November 24, 1774, *Memoir of the Life of Josiah Quincy*, p. 205.
2   Dr. Charles Chauncy to Dr. Thomas Amory, September 13, 1774, Quincy, *Memoir of the Life of Josiah Quincy*, p. 159; James Lovell to Josiah Quincy Jr., November 25, 1774, ibid., p. 180.
3   Josiah Quincy Jr. to John Dickinson, August 20, 1774, Quincy Family Papers, MHS.

4   Reverend Charles Chauncy to Samuel Adams, August 26, 1774, Quincy Family Papers, MHS.

5   Josiah Quincy Jr. to John Dickinson, August 20, 1774, *Memoir of the Life of Josiah Quincy*, p. 150.

6   *Boston Gazette*, May 16, 1774, MHS; See Benton John Lossing, *Our Country: A Household History of the United States for All Readers*, vol. 2 (New York: James A. Bailey, 1895), p. 707.

7   Josiah Quincy Jr. to John Dickinson, August 20, 1774, Quincy Family Papers, MHS.

8   Thomas Gage, Correspondence, in Force, *American Archives*, vol. 1, p. 374.

9   Josiah Quincy Sr. to Josiah Quincy Jr., October 4, 1774, *Memoir of the Life of Josiah Quincy*, p. 160.

10 Josiah Quincy, quoted in *American History Told by Contemporaries*, vol. 2 (New York: Macmillan, 1910), p. 400.

11 Josiah Quincy Jr. to John Dickinson, August 20, 1774, Quincy Family Papers, MHS.

12 John Adams to Josiah Quincy Jr., September 18, 1774, Adams Papers, MHS.

13 Robert Treat Paine Diary, September 6, 1774, Robert Treat Paine Papers, MHS.

14 John Adams to Abigail Adams, September 18, 1774, Adams Papers, MHS.

15 John Adams to Abigail Adams, September 8, 1774, Adams Papers, MHS.

16 Abigail Adams to John Adams, September 2, 1774, Adams Papers, MHS.

17 Ibid.

18 Philbrick, *Bunker Hill*, p. 78, citing *Letters of John Andrews*, pp. 355–374.

19 John Adams to Abigail Adams, October 7, 1774, Adams Papers, MHS.

20 Abigail Adams to John Adams, ibid.

21 Ibid.

22 Abigail Adams to John Adams, October 16, 1774, and September 2, 1774, Adams Papers, MHS.

23 John Adams to Abigail Adams, September 8, 1774, Adams Papers, MHS.

24 Diary of John Adams, vol. 2, September 7, 1774, Adams Papers, MHS.

25 John Adams to Abigail Adams, September 8, 1774, Adams Papers, MHS.

26 John Adams to Abigail Adams, September 18, 1774, Adams Papers, MHS.

27 Ibid., September 14, 1774, Adams Papers, MHS.

28 John Adams to Abigail Adams, September 18, 1774, Adams Papers, MHS.

Chapter 23: In the Cause of Liberty

1   Adams, *The Works of John Adams*, vol. 2, p. 325.

2   Edmund Quincy IV to Katy Quincy, September 1774, Quincy Family Papers, MHS.

3   Ibid.

4   Samuel Quincy to Hannah Hill Quincy, June 21, 1780, Quincy Family Papers, MHS.

5   Abigail Adams to John Adams, September 16, 1774, Adams Papers, MHS.

6   Richard Frothingham, *Life and Times of Joseph Warren* (Boston: Little, Brown, 1865), p. 529, citing *Essex Gazette*, September 20, 1774.

7   Diary of John Adams, vol. 2, September 17, 1774, Adams Papers, MHS.

8   Allan, *John Hancock: Patriot*, p. 165.

9   *New England Historical and Genealogical Register*, vol. 21 (Boston: 1867), p. 60.

10 Allan, *John Hancock: Patriot*, p. 168, citing *The British in Boston: Being the Diary of John Barker*, edited by E. E. Dana (Cambridge, MA: Harvard University Press, 1924), pp. 25–26.

11 Diary of John Adams, vol. 2, September 8, 1774, Adams Papers, MHS.

12 Ibid., October 24, 1774; October 10, 1774, Adams Papers, MHS.

13 Ibid., October 24, 1774, Adams Papers, MHS.

14 John Quincy Adams to John Adams, October 13, 1774, Adams Papers, MHS.

15 John Adams, "The Bill of Rights; A List of Grievances, October 14, 1774," Adams Papers, MHS.

16 Abigail Adams to John Adams, September 22, 1774, Adams Papers, MHS.

17 Diary of John Adams, vol. 2, October 20, 1774, Adams Papers, MHS.

18 John Dickinson, *The Political Writings of John Dickinson, Esq.*, vol. 2 (Wilmington: Bonsal and Niles, 1801), pp. 51–52.

Chapter 24: On This Island, This England

1 "In Provincial Congress, Cambridge, October 22, 1774," (Boston: Printed by Edes and Gill, 1774), Collections of MHS.
2 Abigail Adams to John Adams, July 25, 1775, Adams Papers, MHS.
3 Edmund Quincy IV to Katy Quincy, December 21, 1774, Quincy Family Papers, MHS.
4 *A Report of the Record Commissioners of the City of Boston: 1893, Selectmen's Minutes, 1769–1775*, vol. 23 (Boston: Rockwell and Churchill, 1893), p. 238.
5 James Lovell to Josiah Quincy Jr., November 1774, Quincy Family Papers, MHS.
6 Ibid., p. 244.
7 Josiah Quincy Jr. to Abigail Phillips Quincy, November 5, 1774, Quincy Family Papers, MHS.
8 Ibid.
9 Josiah Quincy Jr., "The London Journal, 1774–1775," November 9–11, 1774, Quincy Family Papers, MHS.
10 Ibid., November 12–15, 1774.
11 Ibid., November 27, 1774.
12 Ferling, *Independence*, p. 9.
13 Josiah Quincy Jr., "The London Journal," November 19, 1774, Quincy Family Papers, MHS.
14 Ibid., November 18, 1774.
15 Ibid., November 20, 1774; Josiah Quincy Jr. to Abigail Phillips Quincy, November 24, 1774; Quincy Family Papers, MHS.
16 Josiah Quincy Jr. to Abigail Phillips Quincy, November 24, 1774, Quincy Family Papers, MHS.
17 Josiah Quincy Jr., "The London Journal," November 22, 1774; Quincy Family Papers, MHS.
18 *Observations on the Act of Parliament Commonly Called the Boston Port-Bill*, memoir of Josiah Quincy Jr., p. 247.
19 Thomas Hutchinson, *Diary and Letters*, p. 301.
20 Josiah Quincy Jr. to Abigail Phillips Quincy, December 7, 1774, Quincy Family Papers, MHS.
21 Ibid.
22 Ibid.
23 Josiah Quincy Jr. to Joseph Reed, December 16, 1774, Quincy Family Papers, MHS.
24 Josiah Quincy Jr., "The London Journal," November 18, 1774, Quincy Family Papers, MHS.
25 See David Hackett Fischer, *Albion's Seed: Four British Folkways in America* (New York: Oxford University Press, 1989), p. 823.
26 Josiah Quincy Jr., "The London Journal," November 29, 1774, Quincy Family Papers, MHS.
27 Fischer, *Albion's Seed*, p. 823.
28 Josiah Quincy Jr. to Joseph Reed, December 17, 1774, Quincy Family Papers, MHS.
29 Josiah Quincy Jr. to Abigail Phillips Quincy, November 24, 1774, Quincy Family Papers, MHS.
30 Josiah Quincy Jr. to Abigail Phillips Quincy, 2d letter, December 7, 1774, Quincy Family Papers, MHS.
31 Barry Alan Shain, ed., *The Declaration of Independence in Historical Context* (New Haven: Yale University Press, 2014), p. 283.
32 Josiah Quincy Jr., "The London Journal," November 29, 1774, Quincy Family Papers, MHS.

33 Josiah Quincy Jr. to Abigail Phillips Quincy, December 14, 1774, Quincy Family Papers, MHS.

34 Josiah Quincy Jr. to Joseph Reed, December 17, 1774, Quincy Family Papers, MHS.

35 Horace Walpole to Henry Seymour Conway, December 15, 1774, quoted in Philip McFarland, *The Brave Bostonians*, p. 137.

36 *The Political Writings of John Dickinson*, vol. 2 (Wilmington: Bonsal and Niles, 1801), p. 52.

Chapter 25: Sharpening Quills and Swords

1 *Massachusetts Gazette and the Boston Post-Boy and Advertiser*, December 5, 1774, cited in Walter R. Borneman, *American Spring* (New York: Little, Brown, 2014), p. 62.

2 John Adams, *Novanglus and Massachusettensis: Political Essays* (Boston: Hew & Goss, 1819), p. vi.

3 John Adams to William Tudor, November 16, 1816, Adams Papers, MHS.

4 John Adams as Novanglus, "To the Inhabitants of the Colony of Massachusetts-Bay," March 13, 1775, Adams Papers, MHS.

5 Josiah Quincy Sr. to Josiah Quincy Jr., October 26, 1774, Quincy Family Papers, MHS.

6 Joseph Warren to Josiah Quincy Jr., November 21, 1774, *Memoir of the Life of Josiah Quincy*, p. 179.

7 Josiah Quincy Jr. to Josiah Quincy Sr., January 22, 1775, Quincy Family Papers, MHS.

8 Josiah Quincy Jr. to Abigail Phillips Quincy, December 7, 1774, Quincy Family Papers, MHS; see also James Henry Stark, *The Loyalists and the Other Side of the American Revolution* (Boston: James H. Stark, 1910), p. 367.

9 Josiah Quincy Jr., Notes on Parliamentary Speeches, *Memoir of the Life of Josiah Quincy*, p. 276.

10 Josiah Quincy Jr. to Abigail Phillips Quincy, January 11, 1774, Quincy Family Papers, MHS.

11 Josiah Quincy Jr. to Abigail Phillips Quincy, January 7, 1774, Quincy Family Papers, MHS.

12 Josiah Quincy Jr. to Abigail Phillips Quincy, January 11, 1774, Quincy Family Papers, MHS.

13 Josiah Quincy Jr., "The London Journal," January 23, 1775, Quincy Family Papers, MHS.

14 Abigail Adams to Mercy Otis Warren, February 3, 1775, Adams Papers, MHS.

15 Wednesday, February 15, 1775, Minutes of the Provincial Congress, Robert Treat Paine Papers, vol. 3, MHS.

16 Rowe, *Letters and Diary*, January 21, 1775, p. 289.

17 Abigail Adams to Mercy Otis Warren, January 25, 1775, Adams Papers, MHS.

18 Ibid.

19 Ibid.

20 James Lovell to Josiah Quincy Jr., Fall 1774, Quincy Family Papers, MHS.

21 Benjamin Franklin to James Bowdoin, February 25, 1775, quoted in Edmund Quincy, *Life of Josiah Quincy of Massachusetts* (Boston: Ticknor and Fields, 1867), p. 11.

22 Josiah Quincy Jr., "The London Journal," January 27, 1775; Quincy Family Papers, MHS.

23 Ibid., February 26, 1775.

24 Ibid.

25 Thomas Hutchinson, *Diaries and Letters of His Excellency Thomas Hutchinson*, vol. 1, ed. Peter Orlando Hutchinson (Boston: Houghton Mifflin, 1884), pp. 528–529; cited in Forman, *Dr. Joseph Warren*, p. 228.

26 "An oration delivered March the 6th, 1775: At the request of the inhabitants of the town of Boston, to commemorate the bloody tragedy, of the fifth of March, 1770 / By Dr. Joseph Warren," Collections of the MHS.

27 Ibid.

28 See William Wells, *The Life and Public Service of Samuel Adams* (Boston: Little, Brown, 1865), pp. 309–310.

29 Ibid.

30 Ibid.

31 Ibid.

32 Edmund Quincy to Katy Quincy, April 5, 1775, Quincy Family Papers, MHS.

Chapter 26: Ship in a Storm

1 *Letters of William Lee*, ed. C. Ford Worthington (New York: 1891), p. 138.
2 Josiah Quincy Jr. to Thomas Bromfield, March 17, 1775, Quincy Family Papers, MHS.
3 Ibid.
4 Josiah Quincy Jr., "The London Journal," March 1, 1775, Quincy Family Papers, MHS.
5 John Adams to James Warren, March 15, 1775, Adams Papers, MHS.
6 Ibid.
7 *Massachusetts Spy*, April 6, 1775, quoted in Borneman, *American Spring*, p. 100.
8 Josiah Quincy Sr. to Benjamin Franklin, March 25, 1775, Quincy Family Papers, MHS.
9 Allan, *John Hancock: Patriot*, p. 170.
10 Ibid.
11 *The Journals of Each Provincial Congress of Massachusetts in 1774 and 1775* (Boston: Dutton and Wentworth, 1838), p. 12.
12 John Hancock to Dorothy Quincy, March 25, 1775, Quincy Family Papers, MHS.
13 John Andrews to William Barrell, March 1775, *Proceedings of Massachusetts Historical Society*, vol. 8 (1866), p. 401.
14 Ibid.
15 John Hancock to Edmund Quincy IV, April 7, 1775, Houghton Library, Harvard; quoted in Unger, *John Hancock: Merchant King*, p. 190.
16 Helena Bayard to Dorothy Quincy, April 14, 1775, Quincy Family Papers, MHS.
17 See Borneman, *American Spring*, pp. 115–116.
18 *The Journals of Each Provincial Congress of Massachusetts in 1774 and 1775*, p. 12.
19 Elias Phinney, *History of the Battle at Lexington, on the Morning of the 19th of April, 1775* (Boston: Phelps and Farnham, 1825), p. 16.
20 Ibid., p. 17.

Chapter 27: Lexington and Concord

1 Allan, *John Hancock: Patriot*, p. 181, citing W. H. Sumner, "Reminiscences," *New England Historical and Genealogical Register*, vol. 8 (1854), p. 187.
2 Ibid.
3 Ibid.
4 Allan, *John Hancock: Patriot*, p. 179, citing Deposition of William Munroe, March 7, 1825, in E. Phinney, *History of the Battle of Lexington*, pp. 33–34.
5 Ibid.
6 Allan, *John Hancock: Patriot*, p. 181, citing Elizabeth Clark to Lucy W. Allen, April 19, 1841, in *Lexington Historical Society Proceedings* 4 (1912): p. 91.
7 Frank Warren Coburn, *Battle of April 19, 1775 in Lexington, Concord, Lincoln, Arlington, Cambridge, Somerville, and Charlestown, Massachusetts* (Lexington, MA: F. W. Coburn, 1912), p. 63.
8 Allan, *John Hancock: Patriot*, p. 181, citing Sumner, "Reminiscences," p. 187
9 John E. Rexine, "The 350th Anniversary of the Boston Latin School," *Classical Journal* 82, no. 3 (Feb.–Mar., 1987): p. 238.
10 Edmund Quincy, *Life of Josiah Quincy*, p. 21.
11 Benedict Arnold sold the home after his father's death and now lived in New Haven, where he served as a captain in the Connecticut Colony Militia.
12 Lord Percy to General Harvey, April 20, 1775, quoted in Allen French, *The Day of Concord and Lexington: The Nineteenth of April 1775* (Boston: Little, Brown, 1925), pp. 270–272.
13 Edmund Quincy IV to Edmund Quincy V, May 19, 1775, Quincy Family Papers, MHS.
14 Abigail Adams to Mercy Otis Warren, May 2, 1775, Adams Papers, MHS.
15 *A Narrative, of the Excursion and Ravages of the King's Troops Under the Command of General Gage, on the Nineteenth of April, 1775*, Collections of the MHS.

16 Ibid.

17 Thomas Hutchinson, *Diary and Letters*, vol. 1, p. 466.

18 Ellen C. D. Q. Woodbury, *Dorothy Quincy: Wife of John Hancock* (New York: Neale Publishing, 1905), p. 69.

19 Sumner, "Reminiscences," p. 188.

20 John Hancock to the Gentlemen Committee of Safety, April 24, 1775, quoted in Abram English Brown, *John Hancock: His Book* (Boston: Lee and Shepard, 1898), pp. 196–197.

21 John Adams, *Diary and Autobiography*, vol. 3, p. 314.

22 Ibid.

23 Ibid.

24 Abigail Adams to John Adams, June 16, 1775, Adams Papers, MHS.

25 Josiah Quincy Jr., "The London Journal," At Sea April the 21st 1775, Quincy Family Papers, MHS.

26 Ibid.

27 Ibid.

Chapter 28: Clouds over Boston

1   John Adams to Abigail Adams, April 30, 1775, Adams Papers, MHS.

2   Abigail Adams to John Adams, May 4, 1775, Adams Papers, MHS.

3   Mercy Otis Warren to Hannah Quincy Lincoln, June 3, 1775, quoted in full in E. F. Ellet, "Women of the Revolution: Mrs. Lincoln," *Godey's Lady's Book*, vol. 42, May 1851, p. 293.

4   Ibid.

5   William Lee to Josiah Quincy Jr., April 3, 1775, *Proceedings of the Massachusetts Historical Society*, vol. 50 (Boston: MHS, 1917) p. 493.

6   Edmund Quincy IV to Henry Quincy, May 11, 1775, Quincy Family Papers, MHS.

7   John Hancock to Dorothy Quincy, May 7, 1775, Quincy Family Papers, MHS.

8   John Adams to Abigail Adams, May 8, 1775, Adams Papers, MHS.

9   Ibid.

10 John Hancock to Dorothy Quincy, May 7, 1775, Quincy Family Papers, MHS.

11 John Adams to Abigail Adams, letters dated May 29, June 2, June 10, June 23, 1775, Quincy Family Papers, MHS.

12 John Adams to Abigail Adams, June 10, 1775, Adams Papers, MHS.

13 John Adams to Abigail Adams, July 17, 1775, and May 29, 1775, Adams Papers, MHS.

14 John Adams to Abigail Adams, June 2, 1775, Adams Papers, MHS.

15 John Adams to Abigail Adams, May 29, 1775, Adams Papers, MHS.

16 Thaddeus Burr to Tapping Reeve, May 15, 1775, quoted in Allan, *John Hancock: Patriot*, p. 192.

17 Dorothy Dudley to Esther Livingstone, August 30, 1775, quoted in ibid.

18 Ibid.

19 John Hancock to Dorothy Quincy, June 10, 1775, Quincy Family Papers, MHS.

20 John Hancock to Dorothy Quincy, June 21, 1775, "The historical love letter . . . John Hancock President of Congress to Dorothy Quincy, the second 'Dorothy Q' whom he married two months later"; https://www.loc.gov/item/rbpe.16203400/.

21 Abigail Adams to John Adams, May 24, 1775, Adams Papers, MHS.

22 Ibid.

23 Ibid.

24 Abigail Adams to John Adams, May 7, 1775, Adams Papers, MHS.

25 "Intercepted Letters of the Soldiers in Boston," April 28, 1775, in Force, *American Archives*, vol. 2, pp. 440–441, quoted in Ferling, *Independence*, p. 121.

26 Jonathan Sewall to Thomas Robie, June 7, 1775, quoted in Shipton, *New England Life*, p. 575.

27 Ibid.

28 Rowe, *Letters and Diary*, January 20, 1776, p. 297.

29 Samuel Quincy to Henry Hill, May 13, 1775, Quincy Family Papers, MHS.

30 Ibid.

31 Ibid.

32 Hannah Quincy Lincoln to Samuel Quincy, May 11, 1775, Quincy Family Papers, MHS.

33 Ibid.

34 Ibid.

35 Samuel Quincy to Henry Hill, May 13, 1775, Quincy Family Papers, MHS.

36 Hannah Quincy Lincoln to Samuel Quincy, May 11, 1775, Quincy Family Papers, MHS.

37 Samuel Quincy to Henry Hill, August 18, 1775, Quincy Family Papers, MHS.

38 "Proscription of Thomas Gage, June 12, 1775," quoted in Allan, *John Hancock: Patriot*, p. 193.

39 John Adams, *Diary and Autobiography*, vol. 3, p. 321.

40 See Philbrick, *Bunker Hill*, p. xiii.

41 Abigail Adams to John Adams, June 18–20, 1775, Adams Papers, MHS.

42 Ibid.

43 Letter of General William Howe dated June 22–24, 1775, quoted in Philbrick, *Bunker Hill*, p. 230.

44 John Adams, *Diary and Autobiography*, vol. 3, p. 323.

45 John Hancock to Joseph Warren, June 18, 1775, *Letters of Members of the Continental Congress*, vol. 1, ed. Edmund Cody Burnett (Washington, DC: Carnegie Institution, 1921), p. 134.

46 John Adams to Josiah Quincy Sr., July 29, 1775, Adams Papers, MHS.

47 Josiah Quincy Sr. to Samuel Adams, July 11, 1775, Quincy Family Papers, MHS.

48 Allen French, *The First Year of the American Revolution* (Boston: Houghton Mifflin, 1934), p. 267.

49 Edmund Quincy IV to Dorothy Quincy, July 22, 1775, Quincy Family Papers, MHS.

50 George Washington, *The Papers of George Washington: Revolutionary War Series*, vol. 1, ed. W. W. Abbot, Dorothy Twohig, Philander D. Chase, Edward C. Lengel, Theodore J. Crackel, and David J. Roth (Charlottesville: University of Virginia Press, 1985), "General Orders," July 4, 1775, p. 54.

Chapter 29: The Unhappy Contest

1 Braintree, Deposition of John Spear, May 20, 1775, Quincy Family Papers, MHS.

2 George Washington to Richard Henry Lee, July 10, 1775, quoted in Ron Chernow, *Washington: A Life* (New York: Penguin Books, 2011), p. 195.

3 William Cheever diary, July 7, 1775, MHS.

4 Philbrick, *Bunker Hill*, p. 149.

5 See George Washington to Samuel Washington, July 20, 1775, quoted in Chernow, *Washington: A Life*, p. 196.

6 Francis Drake, *Life and Correspondence of Henry Knox: Major-General in the American Revolutionary Army* (Boston: Samuel G. Drake, 1873), p. 17.

7 Abigail Adams to John Adams, July 31, 1775, Adams Papers, MHS.

8 Ibid.

9 Ibid.

10 John Adams to Abigail Adams, July 7, 1775, Adams Papers, MHS.

11 Ibid.

12 Ibid.

13 John Adams to Abigail Adams, October 1, 1775, Ibid.

14 John Adams, *Diary and Autobiography*, vol. 3, p. 318.

15 Abigail Adams to John Adams, June 22, 1775, Adams Papers, MHS.

16 John Adams, *Diary and Autobiography*, vol. 3. p. 318.

17 John Adams to Abigail Adams, July 24, 1775, Adams Papers, MHS.

18 John Adams to James Warren, July 24, 1775, Adams Papers, MHS.

19 Ibid.

20 "The Declaration of the Causes and Necessity for Taking Up Arms," July 6, 1775, quoted in Ferling, *Independence*, p. 169.

21   Ibid.
22   John Hancock to George Washington, July 10, 1775, quoted in Allan, *John Hancock: Patriot*, p. 196.
23   George Washington to John Hancock, July 21, 1775, quoted in Allan, *John Hancock: Patriot*, p. 197.
24   John Hancock to the Honorable Assembly of the Massachusetts Bay, June 4, 1775, quoted in Lorenzo Sears, *John Hancock* (Boston: Little, Brown, 1913), pp. 195–196.
25   Benjamin Harrison to George Washington, July 21, 1775, quoted in Allan, *John Hancock: Patriot*, p. 201.
26   George Washington to John Hancock, July 21, 1775, Founders Online, National Archives, https://founders.archives.gov/documents/Washington/03-01-02-0085.
27   Ibid.
28   Abigail Adams to John Adams, July 22, 1775, Adams Papers, MHS.
29   George Washington to John Hancock, July 21, 1775, Founders Online, https://founders.archives.gov/documents/Washington/03-01-02-0085.
30   Abigail Adams to John Adams, July 25, 1775, Adams Papers, MHS.
31   Jonathan Sewall to Thomas Robie, July 15, 1775, *Proceedings of the Massachusetts Historical Society*, vol. 30, 1895, 1896, p. 419.
32   Jonathan Sewall to Thomas Robie, August, 1775, quoted in Shipton, *New England Life*, p. 576.
33   Edmund Quincy IV to Dorothy Quincy, August 4, 1775, Quincy Family Papers, MHS.
34   Edmund Quincy IV to John Wendell, September 1775, Quincy Family Papers, MHS.
35   Abigail Adams to John Adams, August 11, 1775, Adams Papers, MHS.
36   Charles Lee to John Adams, October 5, 1775, Adams Papers, MHS.
37   John Hancock to Dorothy Quincy, August 14, 1775, Quincy Family Papers, MHS.
38   Frank S. Child, *An Historic Mansion, Being an Account of the Thaddeus Burr Homestead, Fairfield, Connecticut, 1654–1915* (1915), p. 14.
39   *Pennsylvania Gazette*, September 6, 1775; extract printed in Woodbury, *Dorothy Quincy*, p. 93.
40   Edmund Quincy IV to Dorothy Quincy, July 22, 1775, Quincy Family Papers, MHS.
41   Edmund Quincy IV to Lydia Hancock, September 8, 1775, Quincy Family Papers, MHS.
42   Ibid.

Chapter 30: Complications of Evil and Misfortune

1   Abigail Quincy to Josiah Quincy Sr., September 18, 1775, Quincy Family Papers, MHS.
2   Ibid.
3   Ibid.
4   Josiah Quincy Jr., "The London Journal," December 21, 1774, Quincy Family Papers, MHS.
5   Ibid., January 20, 1775.
6   Ibid., December 14, 1774.
7   Josiah Quincy Sr. to Abigail Phillips Quincy, August 5, 1775, Quincy Family Papers, MHS.
8   Abigail Phillips Quincy to Josiah Quincy Sr., September 18, 1775, Quincy Family Papers, MHS.
9   Thomas Hutchinson to Charles Paxton, February 16, 1776, quoted in Mary Beth Norton, *The British-Americans: The Loyalist Exiles in England, 1774–1789* (Boston: Little, Brown, 1972), pp. 48–49.
10   Samuel Quincy to Hannah Hill Quincy, September 5, 1775, Quincy Family Papers, MHS.
11   Samuel Quincy to Henry Hill, August 18, 1775, Quincy Family Papers, MHS.
12   George M. Wrong, *Canada and the American Revolution: The Disruption of the First British Empire* (New York: Macmillan, 1935), p. 405.
13   Samuel Quincy to Hannah Hill Quincy, September 5, 1775, Quincy Family Papers, MHS.
14   Samuel Quincy to Henry Hill, August 18, 1775, Quincy Family Papers, MHS.
15   John Adams to James Warren, September 19, 1775, Adams Papers, MHS.

16 Sumner, "Reminiscences," p. 189.

17 John Adams to Abigail Adams, November 4, 1775, Adams Papers, MHS.

18 Ira Stoll, *Samuel Adams* (New York: Simon & Schuster, 2008), p. 174.

19 John Adams to Abigail Adams, November 4, 1775, Adams Papers, MHS.

20 Abigail Adams to John Adams, September 8, 1775, Adams Papers, MHS.

21 Abigail Adams to John Adams, addendum dated September 10, 1775, to letter dated September 8, 1775, Adams Papers, MHS.

22 Abigail Adams to John Adams, September 29, 1775, Adams Papers, MHS.

23 Abigail Adams to John Adams, September 8, 1775, Adams Papers, MHS.

24 Abigail Adams to John Adams, September 25, 1775, Adams Papers, MHS.

25 Abigail Adams to John Adams, September 8, 1775, Adams Papers, MHS.

26 Abigail Adams to John Adams, September 25, 1775, Adams Papers, MHS.

27 Abigail Phillips Quincy to Josiah Quincy Sr., September 18, 1775, Quincy Family Papers, MHS.

28 Abigail Adams to John Adams, October 1, 1775, Adams Papers, MHS.

29 Abigail Adams to John Adams, October 21, 1775, Adams Papers, MHS.

30 Abigail Adams to John Adams, October 9, 1775, Adams Papers, MHS.

31 Abigail Adams to John Adams, September 25, 1775, Adams Papers, MHS.

32 Abigail to John Adams, October 9, 1775, Adams Papers, MHS.

33 I have seen the glass etching for myself, preserved in the Josiah Quincy House, maintained by Historic New England.

34 Abigail Adams to John Adams, October 25, 1775, Adams Papers, MHS.

35 Ibid.

36 Ibid.

37 Abigail Adams to John Adams, November 12, 1775, Adams Papers, MHS.

38 George Washington to General Philip Schuyler, October 26, 1775, quoted in Chernow, *Washington: A Life*, pp. 208–209; David McCullough, *1776* (New York: Simon & Schuster, 2005), p. 56.

39 Proclamation for Suppressing Rebellion and Sedition, August 23, 1775, quoted in Ferling, *Independence*, p. 179.

40 The King's Speech to Parliament, October 26, 1775, quoted in Ferling, *Independence*, p. 180.

41 John Adams to Richard Henry Lee, November 15, 1775, Adams Papers, MHS.

42 Abigail Adams to John Adams, November 27, 1775, Adams Papers, MHS.

43 John Adams, *Diary and Autobiography*, vol. 3, p. 350.

44 Abigail Adams to John Adams, November 12, 1775, Adams Papers, MHS.

45 Nathan Miller, *The U.S. Navy: A History*, 3d ed. (Annapolis, MD: Naval Institute Press, 1997), p. 15.

46 Ibid.

47 William Alexander, Lord Stirling to John Hancock, December 17, 1775, Hancock Family Papers, MHS.

48 John Hancock to Philip Schuyler, January 10, 1776, Hancock Family Papers, MHS.

49 George Washington to John Hancock, December 17, 1775, quoted in Philbrick, *Bunker Hill*, p. 349.

50 Philbrick, *Bunker Hill*, p. 255.

51 Allan, *John Hancock: Patriot*, p. 210; Unger, *John Hancock: Merchant King*, pp. 225–226; *American Quarterly Review*, nos. 1–2 (1827): p. 405.

52 Force, *American Archives*, vol. 4, p. 379.

Chapter 31: Surrender of Boston

1 Abigail Phillips Quincy to Josiah Quincy Sr., September 18, 1775, Quincy Family Papers, MHS.

2 Josiah Quincy Jr. as "Hyperion," September 1767, *Memoir of the Life of Josiah Quincy*, p. 11.

3 Ibid.

4 Samuel Quincy to Hannah Hill Quincy, September 5, 1775, Quincy Family Papers, MHS.

5 Samuel Quincy to Hannah Hill Quincy, September 5, 1775; and July 24, 1775, Quincy Family Papers, MHS.

6 Samuel Quincy, "To the Memory of General Montgomery," Quincy-Hill-Phillips-Treadwell Papers, 1699–1969, Brinkler Library, Cambridge Historical Society.

7 Jonathan Sewall to Edward Winslow, January 10, 1776, quoted in Shipton, *New England Life*, pp. 576–577.

8 George Washington to Joseph Reed, January 14, 1776, Founders Online, https://founders.archives.gov/documents/Washington/03-03-02.

9 Ibid.

10 John Adams to Abigail Adams, March 19, 1776, Adams Papers, MHS.

11 Abigail Adams to John Adams, February 21, 1776, Adams Papers, MHS.

12 Thomas Paine, *Common Sense*, p. 57, Collections of the MHS.

13 Ibid., pp. 27–28.

14 Abigail Adams to John Adams, February 21, 1776, Collections of the MHS.

15 Abigail Adams to John Adams, November 27, 1775, Adams Papers, MHS.

16 Edmund Quincy to Dorothy Quincy, February 8, 1776, Quincy Family Papers, MHS.

17 Benjamin Franklin to William Strahan, July 5, 1775 (unsent but publicized), quoted in Walter Isaacson, *Benjamin Franklin: An American Life* (New York: Simon & Schuster, 2003), p. 296.

18 Isaacson, *Benjamin Franklin*, p. 320.

19 Edmund Quincy IV to John Hancock, February 8, 1776, Quincy Family Papers, MHS.

20 George Washington to John Hancock, February 18, 1776, Quincy Family Papers, MHS.

21 Council of War, February 16, 1776, Founders Online, https://founders.archives.gov/documents/Washington/03-03-02-0229.

22 William Gordon to Samuel Wilson, April 6, 1776, *Proceedings of the Massachusetts Historical Society*, ser. 3, vol. 60 (October 1926–June 1927), p. 363.

23 Abigail Adams to John Adams, March 2, 1776 (with additions through March 10), Adams Papers, MHS.

24 Ibid.

25 Ibid.

26 Ibid.

27 Ibid.

28 Ibid.

29 James Lovell would return to America in a prisoner exchange and served as a delegate to the Continental Congress from 1777 to 1782; his father, John, died in Halifax in 1778.

30 Josiah Quincy Sr. to George Washington, March 21, 1776, in Force, *American Archives*, vol. 5, pp. 455–456.

31 Abigail Adams to John Adams, March 16 1776, Adams Papers, MHS.

32 Abigail Adams to John Adams, May 27, 1776, quoting Psalm 118:23, Adams Papers, MHS.

33 John Adams to Abigail Adams, March 29, 1776, Adams Papers, MHS.

34 Edmund Quincy, *Life of Josiah Quincy*, p. 28.

35 Edmund Quincy IV to Dorothy Hancock, March 25, 1776, Quincy Family Papers, MHS.

36 James Warren to John Adams, March 30, 1776, quoted in Nancy Rubin Stuart, *The Muse of the Revolution, The Secret Pen of Mercy Otis Warren and the Founding of a Nation* (Boston: Beacon Press, 2008), p. 107.

37 Mercy Otis Warren, *Mercy Otis Warren: Selected Letters*, ed. Jeffrey H. Richards and Sharon M. Harris (Athens: University of Georgia Press, 2010), p. 74.

38 George Washington to John Hancock, March 19, 1776, in Force, *American Archives*, vol. vi, p. 420.

39 Abigail Adams to John Adams, March 31, 1776, Adams Papers, MHS.

40 John Adams to Abigail Adams, April 14, 1776, Adams Papers, MHS.

41 Abigail Adams to John Adams, March 31, 1776, Adams Papers, MHS.

42 Rowe, *Letters and Diary*, March 11, 1776, p. 302.

43 Abigail Adams to John Adams, April 10, 1776 (added to April 7 letter), Adams Papers, MHS.

44 Josiah Quincy Jr. to Abigail Phillips Quincy, January 7, 1775, Quincy Family Papers, MHS.

Chapter 32: Debating Separation

1 John Adams, *Diary and Autobiography*, vol. 2, p. 231, "Memorandum of Measures to Be Pursued in Congress, February? 1776."

2 John Adams to Joseph Palmer, June 19, 1775, Adams Papers, MHS. Abigail Adams refers to the recipe sent to her by John Adams on March 8, 1775, in her March 31, 1776, letter to him, but his letter to her containing it has disappeared. I've substituted the recipe Adams sent to Palmer in June 1775.

3 Abigail Adams to John Adams, March 31, 1776, Adams Papers, MHS.

4 Ibid.

5 Abigail Adams to John Adams, April 11, 1776, added to her April 7 letter, Adams Papers, MHS. John responded to Abigail's mention of intimacies with "The Conclusion of your Letter makes my Heart throb, more than a Cannonade would," in his April 28, 1776, reply to her.

6 John Adams to Abigail Adams, April 14, 1776, Adams Papers, MHS.

7 Ibid; Abigail Adams to John Adams, May 7, 1776, Adams Papers, MHS.

8 Abigail Adams to John Adams, May 9, 1776, Adams Papers, MHS.

9 Abigail Adams to Mercy Otis Warren, April 27, 1776, Adams Papers, MHS.

10 Abigail Adams to John Adams, May 7, 1776, Adams Papers, MHS.

11 George Washington to Josiah Quincy Sr., March 24, 1776, quoted in *Memoir of the Life of Josiah Quincy*, Appendix, pp. 416–417.

12 George Washington to Josiah Quincy Sr., April 25, 1776, quoted in ibid., p. 417; Benjamin Franklin to Josiah Quincy Senior, April 15, 1776, quoted in ibid., pp. 418–419.

13 John Adams to James Warren, April 22, 1776, Adams Papers, MHS.

14 Diary of John Adams, vol. 3, In Congress, Spring 1776, and Thomas Paine, Adams Papers, MHS.

15 John Adams to James Warren, April 22, 1776, Adams Papers, MHS.

16 John Hancock to the Massachusetts Provincial Assembly, May 16, 1776, quoted in Ferling, *Independence*, p. 267.

17 Burnett, ed., *Letters of Members of Continental Congress*, vol. 1, pp. 473–474.

18 Edmund Quincy IV to Katy Quincy, May 27, 1776, Quincy Family Papers, MHS.

19 John Hancock to George Washington, May 21, 1776, *Correspondence of the American Revolution*, vol. 1, ed. Jared Sparks (Boston: Little, Brown, 1853), p. 205; John Hancock to George Washington, May 16, 1776, in Force, *American Archives*, vol. 6, p. 473.

20 Abigail Adams to John Adams, April 18, 1776, Adams Papers, MHS.

21 Jonas Clarke, "The fate of blood-thirsty oppressors, and God's tender care of his distressed people: a sermon, preached at Lexington, April 19, 1776, to commemorate the murder, bloodshed, and commencement of hostilities, between Great Britain and America, in that town, by a brigade of troops of George III, under the command of Lieutenant-Colonel Smith, on the nineteenth of April, 1775, to which is added a brief narrative of the principal transactions of that day," Collections of MHS.

22 *Boston Gazette*, May 6, 1776, MHS.

23 Abigail Adams to John Adams, March 31, 1776; John Adams to Abigail Adams, April 28, 1776, Adams Papers, MHS.

24 John Adams to James Warren, May 15, 1776, Adams Papers, MHS.

25 John Adams, "Preamble to Resolution on Independent Governments," Papers of John Adams, vol. 4, Adams Papers, MHS.

26 John Adams to Abigail Adams, May 17, 1776, Adams Papers, MHS.

27 Diary of John Adams, vol. 3, Wednesday, May 15, 1776, ibid.

28 "Resolution introduced in the Continental Congress by Richard Henry Lee (Virginia) proposing a Declaration of Independence, June 7, 1776," http://avalon.law.yale.edu/18th _century/lee.asp.

29 Thomas Jefferson, "Notes of Proceedings in the Continental Congress, 7 June–1 August, 1776," Jefferson Papers, Founders Online, National Archives, http://founders.archives.gov /documents/Jefferson/01-01-02-0160.

30 See Donald A. Grinde Jr. and Bruce E. Johansen, *Exemplar of Liberty: Native America and the Evolution of Democracy* (1990) chap. 8, citing *Journals of the Continental Congress*, ed. Worthington Chauncey Ford, vol. 5 (Washington, DC: GPO, 1906), p. 430.

31 Isaacson, *Ben Franklin*, p. 310.

32 John Adams to Abigail Adams, June 16, 1776, Adams Papers, MHS.

33 Adams, *The Works of John Adams*, vol. 2, p. 514.

34 Jefferson, "Notes of Proceedings in the Continental Congress."

35 Ibid.

36 Abigail Adams to John Adams, July 14, 1776, Adams Papers, MHS.

37 Abigail Adams to John Adams, March 31, 1776, Adams Papers, MHS.

Chapter 33: The Signature of Independence

1 See Ferling, *Independence*, p. 324, citing David Hawke, *A Transaction of Free Men: The Birth and Course of the Declaration of Free Men* (New York: Scribner, 1964), p. 177.

2 Jefferson, "Notes of Proceedings in the Continental Congress."

3 Diary of John Adams, vol. 2, September 3, 1774, Adams Papers, MHS.

4 Reverend John Hancock, "A Memorial of God's Goodness. Being the Substance of Two Sermons, Preach'd in the First Church of Christ in Braintree, Sept. 16th. 1739. On Compleating the First Century Since the Gathering of It," Collections of MHS.

5 John Adams to Abigail Adams, July 3, 1776 (first letter), Adams Papers, MHS.

6 John Adams to Abigail Adams, July 3, 1776 (second letter), Adams Papers, MHS.

7 John Adams to Abigail Adams, July 3, 1776 (first letter), Adams Papers, MHS.

8 For a fascinating exploration of the significant impacts that Native American culture, political structure, and traditions had on the institutions, rhetoric, and emblems of the nascent United States, see Donald A. Grinde, Jr. and Bruce E. Johansen, *Exemplar of Liberty: Native America and the Evolution of Democracy* (1990), https://ratical.org/many_worlds /6Nations/EoL/index.html#ToC.

9 Jefferson, "Notes of Proceedings in the Continental Congress."

10 Benjamin Franklin, *The Autobiography of Benjamin Franklin* (Boston: Houghton, Mifflin Company, 1888), p. 233.

11 McCullough, *John Adams*, p. 135.

12 Jefferson, "Notes of Proceedings in the Continental Congress."

13 Adams, *The Works of John Adams*, vol. 2, p. 514.

14 John Adams to Abigail Adams, July 3, 1776 (second letter), Adams Papers, MHS.

15 Josiah Quincy Jr., "The Southern Journal," pp. 91–95, Quincy Family Papers, MHS.

16 Jefferson, "Notes of Proceedings in the Continental Congress."

17 I am persuaded by the arguments set forth in the editorial notes to "Jefferson's Proceedings in the Continental Congress" that although there is much negative evidence as to who signed the Declaration of Independence on July 4, 1776, there is also Thomas Jefferson's positive evidence, in which he clearly states that "in the evening of the last . . . the declaration was . . . signed by every member" of Congress, referring to July 4. The New York delegation would not have been able to sign until July 19, when they received authority from their own assembly. On August 2, 1776, a copy printed on parchment was signed by all the delegates (more or less), and reprinted; it is this copy that is the widely recognized and iconic version of the Declaration of Independence.

18 Jefferson, "Notes and Proceedings in the Continental Congress."

19 Josiah Quincy Jr. as "Hyperion," *Boston Gazette*, October 1767, *Memoir of the Life of Josiah Quincy*, pp. 10–11, 19.

20 Benjamin Rush to John Adams, July 20, 1811, quoted in Ferling, *Independence*, p. 345.

21 James P. Byrd, *Sacred Scripture, Sacred War: The Bible and the American Revolution* (New York: Oxford University Press, 2013), pp. 100–101.

22 Ibid.

23 The Declaration of Independence, as printed in the *Pennsylvania Evening Post*, July, 6, 1776, National Archives. The iconic painting of this event, which hangs in the Rotunda of the United States Capitol Building, was done by John Trumbull, the young man who had written to Sam Quincy in September 1773 proclaiming he wanted only to be in the "party of truth." (See chapter 19, note 27.)

24 Abigail Adams to John Adams, July 13, 1776, Adams Papers, MHS.

25 Abigail Adams to John Adams, July 21, 1776, Adams Papers, MHS.

26 Letter of Daniel Greenleaf, October 1841, printed (?) in *Boston Transcript*, August 2, 1855, J. L. Bell, "Boston 1775," http://boston1775.blogspot.com/2007/07/sheriff-greenleaf-and-col-crafts-read.html.

27 Abigail Adams to John Adams, July 21, 1776, Adams Papers, MHS.

28 Hancock, "A Memorial of God's Goodness."

29 Abigail Adams to John Adams, July 21, 1776, Adams Papers, MHS.

Epilogue: Friends to Mankind

1   John Hancock to David Evans, August 11, 1777, Receipt/Bill, Hancock Family Papers, Baker Library, Harvard Business School.

2   See Bernard A. Weisberger, "Petticoat Government," *American Heritage* 44, no. 6 (October 1993).

3   McCullough, *John Adams*, p. 623.

4   Jonathan Sewall to Judge Joseph Lee, September 21, 1787, quoted in Carol Berkin, *Jonathan Sewall, Odyssey of an American Loyalist* (New York: Columbia University Press, 1974), p. 142.

5   John Adams, *Novanglus and Massachusettensis: Political Essays* (Boston: Hew and Goss, 1819), pp. vi–vii.

6   Josiah Quincy IV, *Figures of the Past*, p. 65.

7   Samuel Quincy to Hannah Hill Quincy, October 28, 1776, Quincy Family Papers, MHS.

8   Benjamin Franklin to Josiah Quincy Sr., September 11, 1783, *Memoir of the Life of Josiah Quincy*, p. 425.

9   Stark, *The Loyalists of Massachusetts*, p. 367.

10 Coquillette and York, *Portrait of a Patriot*, vol. 1, p. 44.

11 Edmund Quincy, *Life of Josiah Quincy of Massachusetts*, p. 22.

12 In 1792, the village of Braintree was renamed Quincy in honor of John Quincy, grandfather of Abigail Adams, but many inhabitants still called it by the old name.

Bibliography

Manuscript Collections

Adams Papers, Massachusetts Historical Society.
Burr Family Papers, Fairfield (CT) Museum and History Center.
General Harvard History Collection, Harvard Archives, Pusey Library, Harvard University.
Hancock Family Papers, Massachusetts Historical Society.
Quincy, Wendell, Holmes, and Upham Family Papers, Massachusetts Historical Society.
Quincy-Hill-Treadwell Papers, Brinkler Library, Cambridge (MA) Historical Society.
Papers of George Washington, University of Virginia.
Papers of Thomas Jefferson, Princeton University.

Selected Books

Abbott, W. W., Dorothy Twohig, Philander D. Chase, Edward G. Lengel, Theodore J. Crackel, and David J. Hoth, eds. *The Papers of George Washington: Revolutionary War Series.* 18 vols. Charlottesville: University of Virginia Press, 1985.
Adams, Charles Francis. *History of Braintree, Massachusetts (1639–1708).* Cambridge, MA: Riverside Press, 1891.
———, ed. *Letters of Mrs. Adams, Wife of John Adams,* vol. 1. Boston: Wilkins, Carter, 1848.
———, ed. *The Works of John Adams.* 10 vols. Boston: Little, Brown, 1856.
Allan, Herbert S. *John Hancock: Patriot in Purple.* New York: Macmillan, 1948.
Andrews, John. *Letters of John Andrews, Esq., 1772–1776,* ed. Winthrop Sargent, Cambridge, MA: John Wilson and Sons, 1866.
Baxter, William T. *House of Hancock.* Cambridge, MA: Harvard University Press, 1945.
Berkin, Carol. *Jonathan Sewall, Odyssey of an American Loyalist.* New York: Columbia University Press, 1974.
———. *Revolutionary Mothers: Women in the Struggle for American Independence.* New York: Knopf, 2005.
Borneman, Walter R. *American Spring.* New York: Little, Brown, 2014.
Bowen, Catherine Drinker. *John Adams and the American Revolution.* Boston: Little, Brown, 1950.
Bradford, William. *History of Plymouth Plantation.* Boston: Massachusetts Historical Society, 1856.
Brandes, Paul Dickerson. *John Hancock's Life and Speeches.* Lanham, MD: Scarecrow Press, 1996.
Breen, T. H. *American Insurgents, American Patriots.* New York: Farrar, Straus & Giroux, 2010.
Brown, Abram English. *John Hancock: His Book.* Boston: Lee and Shepard, 1898.
Brown, Richard Maxwell. *Strain of Violence: Historical Studies of American Violence and Vigilantism.* New York: Oxford University Press, 1975.

Bunker, Nick. *An Empire on the Edge: How Britain Came to Fight America*. New York: Knopf Doubleday, 2014.

Burnett, Edmund Cody, ed. *Letters of Members of the Continental Congress*, vol. 1. Washington, DC: Carnegie Institution, 1921.

Butterfield, L. H., ed. *Diary and Autobiography of John Adams*, vols. 1–3. Cambridge, MA: Belknap Press/Harvard University Press, 1961.

Byrd, James P. *Sacred Scripture, Sacred War: The Bible and the American Revolution*. New York: Oxford University Press, 2013.

Carretta, Vincent. *Phillis Wheatley: Biography of a Genius in Bondage*. Athens, GA: University of Georgia Press, 2011.

Chandler, Peleg W. *American Criminal Trials*, vol. 1. Boston: Timothy H. Carter, 1841.

Chernow, Ron. *Washington: A Life*. New York: Penguin Books, 2011.

Chidsey, Donald Barr. *The Loyalists: The Story of Those Americans Who Fought Against Independence*. New York: Crown, 1973.

Coburn, Frank W. *Battle of April 19, 1775 in Lexington, Concord, Lincoln, Arlington, Cambridge, Somerville, and Charlestown, Massachusetts*. Lexington, MA: F. W. Coburn, 1912.

Coquillette, Daniel R., and Neil Longley York, eds. *Portrait of a Patriot, The Major Political and Legal Works of Josiah Quincy Jr.*, vols 1–3. Charlottesville: University of Virginia Press, 2009.

———. *Josiah Quincy, Jr. Political and Legal Works*, vol. 6. Boston: Colonial Society of Massachusetts, 2014.

Cushing, Harry Alonzo, ed. *The Writings of Samuel Adams, 1770–1773*, vol. 2. New York: Putnam, 1906.

De Windt, Caroline Amelia Smith, ed. *Journal and Correspondence of Miss Adams*. New York: Wiley and Putnam, 1841.

Dickinson, John. *The Political Writings of John Dickinson*, vol. 2. Wilmington: Bonsal and Niles, 1801.

Donne, W. Bodham, ed. *The Correspondence of King George Third with Lord North, from 1768 to 1783*. London: John Murry, Albemarle Street, 1867.

Earle, Alice M., ed. *Diary of Anna Green Winslow, a Boston School Girl of 1771*. Boston: Houghton Mifflin, 1894.

Ellet, E. F. *The Women of the American Revolution*. New York: Baker and Scribner, 1850.

Ferling, John. *Independence: The Struggle to Set America Free*. New York: Bloomsbury Press, 2011.

Fischer, David Hackett. *Albion's Seed: Four British Folkways in America*. New York: Oxford University Press, 1989.

Force, Peter, ed. *American Archives: A Documentary History of the English Colonies in North America*, series 4, vols. 1–6, Washington, DC: M. St. Clair Clarke and Peter Force, 1848.

Forman, Samuel A. *Dr. Joseph Warren: The Boston Tea Party, Bunker Hill, and the Birth of American Liberty*. Gretna, LA: Pelican, 2012.

Fowler, William M. *The Baron of Beacon Hill*. Boston: Houghton Mifflin, 1980.

Franklin, Benjamin. *The Autobiography of Benjamin Franklin*. Boston: Houghton, Mifflin Company, 1888.

French, Allen. *The Day of Concord and Lexington: The Nineteenth of April 1775*. Boston: Little, Brown, 1925.

———. *The First Year of the American Revolution*. Boston: Houghton Mifflin, 1934.

Frothingham, Richard. *Life and Times of Joseph Warren*. Boston: Little, Brown, 1865.

———. *The Rise of the Republic of the United States*. Boston: Little, Brown, 1873.

Grinde, Donald A. Jr., and Bruce E. Johansen. *Exemplar of Liberty: Native America and the Evolution of Democracy*, Los Angeles: UCLA American Indian Studies Center, 1991.

Gross, Robert A. *The Minutemen and Their World*. New York: Hill and Wang, 1976.

Hart, Albert Bushnell, and John Gould Curtis, eds. *American History Told by Contemporaries*, vol. 2, *Building of the Republic*. New York: Macmillan, 1919.

Holton, Woody. *Abigail Adams*. New York: Free Press, 2009.

Howe, M. A. Dewolfe, ed. *The Articulate Sisters*. Cambridge: Harvard University Press, 1946.

Hutchinson, Peter Orlando, ed. *The Diary and Letters of His Excellency Thomas Hutchinson, Esq.* Boston: 1884.

Hutchinson, Thomas. *The History of Massachusetts Bay*, vols. 1 and 2. London: M. Richardson, 1765.

Isaacson, Walter. *Benjamin Franklin: An American Life*. New York: Simon & Schuster, 2003.

Isenberg, Nancy. *Fallen Founder: The Life of Aaron Burr*. New York: Penguin, 2007.

Jacobs, Diane. *Dear Abigail*. New York: Ballantine, 2014.

Ketcham, Ralph. *From Colony to Colony: The Revolution in American Thought, 1750–1820*. New York: Macmillan, 1974.

Kittelstrom, Amy. *The Religion of Democracy: Seven Liberals and the American Moral Tradition*. New York: Penguin, 2015.

Langguth, A. J. *Patriots: The Men Who Started the American Revolution*. New York: Simon & Schuster, 1988.

Lothrop, Samuel Kirkland. *A History of the Church in Brattle Street, Boston, by its Pastor Samuel Kirkland Lothrop*. Boston: Wm. Crosby and H. P. Nichols, 1851.

Maier, Pauline. *From Resistance to Revolution: Colonial Radicals and the Development of American Opposition to Britain, 1775–1776*. New York: Random House, 1972.

McCullough, David. *John Adams*. New York: Simon & Schuster, 2001.

———. *1776*. New York: Simon & Schuster, 2005.

McFarland, Philip. *The Brave Bostonians*. New York: HarperCollins, 1998.

McGaughey, Robert A. *Josiah Quincy, The Last Federalist*. Cambridge: Harvard University Press, 1974.

Meacham, Jon. *Thomas Jefferson: The Art of Power*. New York: Random House, 2012.

Mercantini, Jonathan. *The Stamp Act of 1765: A History in Documents*. Peterborough, ON: Broadview Press, 2017.

Morison, Samuel Eliot. *Builders of the Bay Colony*. Boston: Houghton Mifflin Company, 1930.

———. *Three Centuries of Harvard, 1636–1936*. Cambridge, MA: Harvard University Press, 1946.

Morton, Thomas. *New English Canaan of Thomas Morton*. Boston: Prince Society, 1883.

Nagel, Paul C. *The Adams Women*. New York: Oxford University Press, 1987.

———. *John Quincy Adams: A Public Life, a Private Life*. Cambridge: Harvard University Press, 1997.

Norton, Mary Beth. *The British-Americans: The Loyalist Exiles in England, 1774–1789*. Boston: Little, Brown, 1972.

Pattee, William S. *History of Old Braintree and Quincy*. Quincy, MA: Green and Prescott, 1878.

Philbrick, Nathaniel. *Bunker Hill*. New York: Viking Penguin, 2013.

Phinney, Elias. *History of the Battle at Lexington, on the Morning of the 19th of April, 1775*. Boston: Phelps and Farnham, 1825.

Quincy, Edmund. *Life of Josiah Quincy of Massachusetts*. Boston: Ticknor and Fields, 1867.

Quincy, Eliza S. M. *Memoir of the Life of Eliza Susan Morton Quincy*. Boston, 1861.

Quincy, Josiah III. *Memoir of the Life of Josiah Quincy, Junior, of Massachusetts*, Boston: Press of John Wilson & Son, 1874.

Quincy, Josiah IV. *Figures of the Past from the Leaves of Old Journals*. Boston: Roberts Brothers, 1883.

Rebora, Carrie, and Paul Staiti. *John Singleton Copley in America*. New York: Metropolitan Museum of Art, 1995.

Reid, John Phillip. *In a Rebellious Spirit*. University Park: Pennsylvania State University Press, 1979.

Richard, Jeffrey H., and Sharon M. Harris, eds. *Mercy Otis Warren: Selected Letters*. Athens: University of Georgia Press, 2010.

Rowe, John. *Letters and Diary of John Rowe, Boston Merchant*. Edited by Anne Rowe Cunningham. Boston: W. B. Clarke, 1903.

Russell, David Lee. *The American Revolution in the Southern Colonies*, Jefferson, NC: McFarland, 2000.

Sabine, Lorenzo. *Biographical Sketches of Loyalists of the American Revolution*, vol. 1. Boston: Little, Brown, 1864.

Sears, Lorenzo. *John Hancock: The Picturesque Patriot*. Boston: Little, Brown, 1913.

Shaw, Peter. *American Patriots and the Rituals of Revolution.* Cambridge, MA: Harvard University Press, 1981.

Shields, John C. *Phillis Wheatley and the Romantics.* Knoxville: University of Tennessee Press, 2008.

Shipton, Clifford K. *New England Life in the Eighteenth Century.* Cambridge: Belknap Press/Harvard University, 1963.

———. *Sibley's Harvard Graduates,* vol. 13. Cambridge, MA: Harvard University Press, 1965.

———. *Sibley's Harvard Graduates,* vol. 15. Boston: Massachusetts Historical Society, 1970.

Sibley, John Langdon. *Biographical Sketches of Graduates of Harvard University in Cambridge, Massachusetts,* vol. 3. Cambridge, MA: Charles William Sever, 1885.

Standiford, Les. *Desperate Sons.* New York: HarperCollins, 2012.

Stark, James Henry. *The Loyalists and the Other Side of the American Revolution.* Boston: James H. Stark, 1910.

Stark, Jared, ed. *Correspondence of the American Revolution,* vol. 1. Boston: Little, Brown, 1853.

Stoll, Ira. *Samuel Adams.* New York: Simon & Schuster, 2008.

Stuart, Nancy Rubin. *The Muse of the Revolution: The Secret Pen of Mercy Otis Warren and the Founding of a Nation.* Boston: Beacon Press, 2008.

Triber, Jayne E. *A True Republican: The Life of Paul Revere.* Amherst: University of Massachusetts Press, 1998.

Tyler, John, and Elizabeth Dubrulle, eds. *The Correspondence of Thomas Hutchinson, 1740–1766.* Charlottesville: University of Virginia Press, 2014.

Unger, Harlow Giles. *John Hancock: Merchant King and American Patriot.* New York: John Wiley & Sons, 2000.

Walmsley, Andrew S. *Thomas Hutchinson and the Origins of the American Revolution.* New York: NYU Press, 1999.

Ward, George Atkinson. *Journals and Letters of the Late Samuel Curwen, An American Refugee in England from 1775 to 1874.* New York: C.S. Francis, 1842.

Warren, Mercy Otis. *History of the Rise, Progress, and Termination of the American Revolution.* Boston: Manning and Loring, for E. Larkin, No. 47, Cornhill, 1805.

Wells, Williams. *The Life and Public Service of Samuel Adams.* Boston: Little, Brown, 1865.

Wilson, Daniel Munro. *Where American Independence Began.* Boston: Houghton Mifflin, 1902.

Withey, Lynne. *Dearest Friend: A Life of Abigail Adams.* New York: Simon & Schuster, 1981.

Woodbury, Ellen C.D.Q. *Dorothy Quincy: Wife of John Hancock.* New York: Neale Publishing, 1905.

Wrong, George M. *Canada and the American Revolution: The Disruption of the First British Empire.* New York: Macmillan, 1935.

Zobel, Hiller B. *The Boston Massacre.* New York: Norton, 1970.

Articles and Pamphlets

Bullion, John L. "British Ministers and American Resistance to the Stamp Act, October–December 1765." *William and Mary Quarterly* 49, no. 1 (January 1992).

Gelles, Edith B. "Abigail Adams: Domesticity and the American Revolution." *New England Quarterly* 52, no. 4 (December 1979): 500–521.

Heath, William. "Thomas Morton: From Merry Old England to New England." *Journal of American Studies* 41, no. 1 (April 2007): 135–168.

Shea, Daniel B. "'Our Professed Old Adversary': Thomas Morton and the Naming of New England." *Early American Literature* 23, no. 1 (1988): 52–69.

Sumner, W. H. "Reminiscences." *New England Historical and Genealogical Register* 8 (1854).

Zuckerman, Michael. "Pilgrims in the Wilderness: Community, Modernity, and the Maypole at Merry Mount." *New England Quarterly* 50, no. 2 (June 1977): 255–277.

OF INTEREST

The Latin Legal Maxims, as recorded by Josiah Quincy Jr. in his Law Commonplace Book: www.colonialsociety.org/node/2777.

Index

Note: Women are indexed under their family name with crossreferences from any married name. 's.' means 'son of', 'd.' means 'daughter of', 'b.' means 'born in', 'm.' means 'married to.'